ALSO BY ANNA CLARK

Michigan Literary Luminaries

A Detroit Anthology (editor)

THE POISONED CITY

THE

FLINT'S WATER AND THE

POISONED

AMERICAN URBAN TRAGEDY

CITY

ANNA CLARK

METROPOLITAN BOOKS

HENRY HOLT AND COMPANY   NEW YORK

Metropolitan Books
Henry Holt and Company
Publishers since 1866
175 Fifth Avenue
New York, New York 10010
www.henryholt.com

Metropolitan Books® and m® are registered trademarks of
Macmillan Publishing Group, LLC.

Library of Congress Cataloging-in-Publication Data

Names: Clark, Anna, author.
Title: The poisoned city : Flint's water and the American urban tragedy /
  Anna Clark.
Description: New York : Metropolitan Books, Henry Holt and Company,
  2018. | Includes bibliographical references and index.
Identifiers: LCCN 2018021437 | ISBN 9781250125149 (hardcover)
Subjects: LCSH: Drinking water—Contamination—Health aspects—Michigan—
  Flint. | Drinking water—Lead content—Michigan—Flint. | Health risk
  assessment—Michigan—Flint. | Heavy metals—Toxicity testing—Michigan—
  Flint.
Classification: LCC RA591 .C53 2018 | DDC 363.6/10977437—dc23
LC record available at https://lccn.loc.gov/2018021437

Our books may be purchased in bulk for promotional, educational, or
business use. Please contact your local bookseller or the Macmillan Corporate and
Premium Sales Department at (800) 221-7945, extension 5442, or by e-mail at
MacmillanSpecialMarkets@macmillan.com.

First Edition 2018

Designed by Kelly S. Too

Printed in the United States of America

1 3 5 7 9 10 8 6 4 2

For my parents, Patrick and Patricia Clark, and
for my sister, Elizabeth, and for my brother, Aaron

All water has a perfect memory
and is forever trying to get back to where it was.

—Toni Morrison, "The Site of Memory"

CONTENTS

Prologue   1

PART I: TAUGHT BY THIRST

1. The Well   13
2. Corrosion   31
3. Revelations   43
4. Saturation   62

PART II: DIVINATION

5. Alchemy   79
6. Citizen/Science   101
7. Meditations in an Emergency   122
8. Blood   138

PART III: WATER'S PERFECT MEMORY

9. Switchback   153
10. Legion   166
11. Truth and Reconciliation   182
12. Genesis   195
    Epilogue   210

Notes   217
Selected Bibliography   289
Acknowledgments   292
Index   295

FLINT MICHIGAN

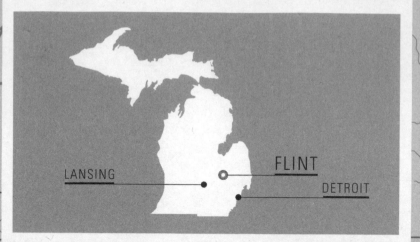

LANSING

FLINT

DETROIT

LANDMARKS

1) Saints of God Church
2) Mission of Hope
3) Antioch Missionary Baptist Church
4) City water plant
5) Berston Field House
6) Joy Tabernacle Church
7) Hurley Medical Center
8) C.S. Mott Foundation
9) University of Michigan–Flint
10) Flint Cultural Center
11) *East Village Magazine*
12) *The Flint Journal*
13) City hall
14) Buckham Alley
15) Chevy Commons
16) Kettering University
17) McLaren Flint
18) General Motors engine plant
19) The Walterses' house

City water plant

Joy Tabernacle Church

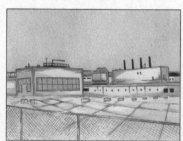

General Motors engine plant

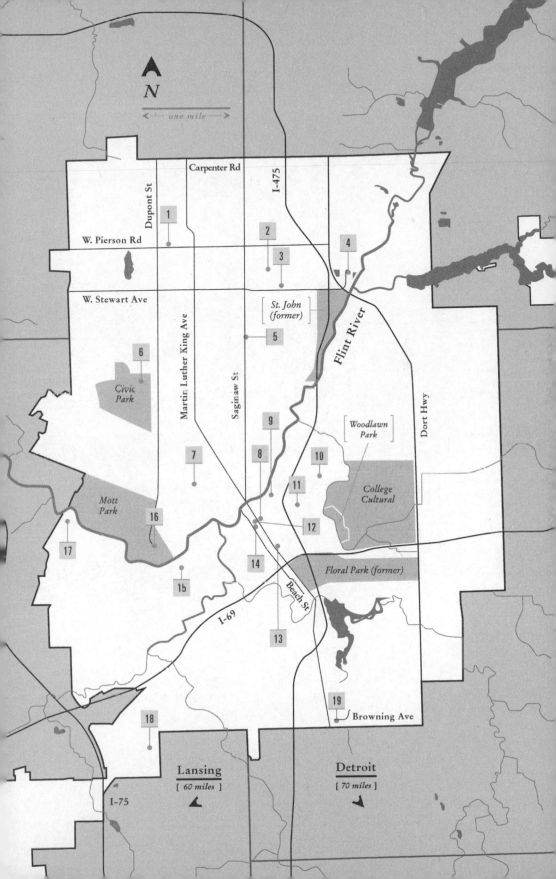

Prologue

I.

On a hot day in the summer of 2014, in the Civic Park neighborhood where Pastor R. Sherman McCathern preached in Flint, Michigan, water rushed out of a couple of fire hydrants. Puddles formed on the dry grass and splashed the skin of the delighted kids who ran through it. But the spray looked strange. "The water was coming out, dark as coffee, for hours," McCathern remembered. The shock of it caught in his throat. "Something is *wrong* here."

Something had been wrong for months. That spring, Flint, under direction from state officials, turned off the drinking water that it had relied upon for nearly fifty years. The city planned to join a new regional system called the Karegnondi Water Authority, and while it waited for the KWA to be built, it began bringing in its water from the Flint River. McCathern didn't pay much attention to the politicking around all this; he had enough to worry about at his busy parish. But after the switch, many of his neighbors grew alarmed at the water that flowed from their kitchen faucets and shower heads. They packed public meetings, wrote questioning letters, and protested at city hall. They filled clear plastic bottles from their taps to show how the water looked brown, or orange, and sometimes had particulates floating in it. Showering seemed to be connected with skin rashes and hair loss. The water smelled foul. A sip of it put the taste of a cold metal coin on your tongue.

But the authorities "said everything was all right and you could drink it, so people did," McCathern said later.[1] Residents were advised to run their faucets for a few minutes before using the water to get a clean flow. As the months went by, the city plant tinkered with treatment and issued a few boil-water advisories. State environmental officials said again and again that there was nothing to worry about. The water was fine.

Whatever their senses told them, whatever the whispers around town, whatever Flint's troubled history with powerful institutions telling them what was best for them, this wasn't actually hard for people like McCathern to believe. Public water systems are one of this country's most heroic accomplishments, a feat so successful that it is almost invisible. By making it a commonplace for clean water to be delivered to homes, businesses, and schools, we have saved untold lives from what today sound like antiquated diseases in a Charles Dickens novel: cholera, dysentery, typhoid fever. Here in Flint, it was instrumental in turning General Motors—founded in 1908 in Vehicle City, as the town was known—into a global economic giant. The advancing underground network of pipes defined the growing city and its metropolitan region, which boasted of being home to one of the strongest middle classes in the country.

McCathern is a tall, bald man with a thin mustache and a scratchy rasp in his baritone voice. At the time of the water switch, he had led the nondenominational Joy Tabernacle Church for about fifteen years. It was founded in the YWCA in downtown Flint, where it held baptisms in the swimming pool. But in 2009, it made a home in Civic Park, when a Presbyterian church closed after eighty-five years and gave its sanctuary over to the young and hopeful congregation.

By then, Civic Park, one of America's oldest subdivisions, was "a desert of deserted historically significant homes," the pastor said. Built between 1917 and 1919 by General Motors and DuPont and Company along curving, tree-lined boulevards, the tidy houses were designed for Flint's autoworkers and their families.[2] But over the years, the neighborhood was blighted by vacancy. Empty two-stories with lurching front porches and crumbling roofs sat alongside crisply painted homes where Flint residents—they sometimes call themselves "Flintoids" or "Flintstones"—still lived their lives. When the sound of gunshots on the street outside interrupted services, McCathern gave a nod to the church musicians, urging them to play louder. Some called Joy Tabernacle a "thug church," he said, but McCathern saw the good. The young men filling his pews built a proud society, if not by getting their names on the honor roll, then by tagging their names with spray paint.[3] In the end, people just want to be seen.

The ghosts of the past went well beyond Civic Park. Between General Motors and the United Auto Workers (which won the right to collectively bargain in Flint's sit-down strike in the 1930s), the city had been a flourishing hub for American innovation.[4] There were more than a hundred different manufacturing establishments in town—ten of them employed at least a thousand people—and they made not only automobiles, but paints, varnishes, tools, dies, cotton textiles, and a wealth of other products.[5] Flint had one of the highest per capita incomes in the nation and, despite being severely segregated, it was a magnet for African American migrants from the South. When Vice President Hubert Humphrey stopped by during the campaign for the 1964 presidential election, he praised Flint for "zooming ahead with unbelievable economic growth and progress." Workers earned wages that "are very good," Humphrey said, "and because of the great labor management program in this community over many years, there has been a constant rise in the standard of living."[6]

Away from the assembly lines and the executive suites, the people of Flint felt that the city shouldn't just be a place to work; it should also be a place to thrive. Charles Stewart Mott, an auto pioneer who became GM's largest single stockholder and a three-term mayor, created a nationally renowned community schools program that provided education, skills-building workshops, and social services. (His influence is still felt through the C. S. Mott Foundation, a philanthropic power broker headquartered in the city.) The Parks Department had a robust Forestry Division that cultivated a beautiful thicket of willow, oak, and elm trees along the avenues.[7] The Michigan School for the Deaf expanded into new buildings that served hundreds of students from around the state. And on a green campus just east of downtown, the city invested in its cultural life by developing the Flint Symphony Orchestra, as well as a state-of-the-art stage and auditorium, schools for both the performing arts and visual arts, a youth theater, a sunny public library, museums of local history and classic cars, the largest planetarium in the state, and the sweeping Flint Institute of Arts, which lined its galleries with everything from Matisse paintings to Lichtenstein silk screens to carved African masks.

But in the latter part of the twentieth century, GM closed most of its plants in the city and eliminated almost all the local auto jobs.[8] Smaller companies followed suit or simply shut down for good. Between 1998 and 2013 alone, nearly 150 of them exited the downtown area.[9] With the shuttered businesses came the shuttered houses and schools. More than half the population, which had reached a high point of nearly two hundred thousand in 1960, disappeared. Some twenty-two thousand left between 2000 and 2010, an 18 percent drop in just ten years, and the fourth-largest population loss in the country, behind only Detroit, New Orleans—which had suffered Hurricane Katrina—and Gary, Indiana. Not long later, Flint's population plunged below a hundred thousand for the first time since 1920.[10] The empty structures they left behind were both disheartening and dangerous, not only because they were prone to break-ins and fires, but also because they literally crumbled onto the sidewalks where people passed by. At the same time, the Flint metro region—that is, the suburbs—grew exponentially. It was a widening circle of wealth with a deteriorating center.[11]

With so much lost, Flint needed help. An emergency plan. A large-scale intervention of some kind. But not only was there no hope of a bailout—of the kind given to the auto industry and Wall Street banks in 2008 and 2009—the State of Michigan exacerbated Flint's woes by dramatically reducing the money that it funneled to its cities. In a practice called revenue sharing, the state redistributes a portion of the money it collects in sales taxes to local governments. That plus property taxes are what cities use to pay for public services. But between 1998 and 2016, Michigan diverted more than $5.5 billion that would ordinarily go to places such as Flint to power streetlights, mow parks, and plow snow. Instead, the state used the money to plug holes in its own budget. This was highly unusual. As Michigan made cuts, forty-five other states managed to increase revenue sharing to their cities by an average of 48 percent, despite a national economic downturn that affected everyone. Among the five states where revenue sharing declined, Michigan slashed more than any other, by far. For Flint, this translated into a loss of about $55 million between 2002 and 2014. That amount would have been more than enough to eliminate the city's deficit, pay off its debt, and still have a surplus.[12] But the money never came, and, at the same time, Flint was thumped with the Great Recession, the mortgage crisis, a major restructuring of the auto industry, and a crippling drop in tax revenue.

If you wanted to kill a city, that is the recipe. And yet Flint was very much alive. In 2014, the year of the switch to a new source of drinking water, it was the seventh-largest city in the state. On weekdays, its population swelled as people commuted into town for work in the county government, the region's major medical centers, four college campuses, and other economic anchors. For all the empty space, teens in shining dresses still posed for prom photos in the middle of Saginaw Street, the bumpy brick road that is Flint's main thoroughfare. Parents still led their children by the hand into the public library for Saturday story time. Older gentlemen lingered at the counter of one of Flint's ubiquitous Coney Island diners, and the waitresses at Grandma's Kitchen on Richfield Road kept the coffee flowing. For about ninety-nine thousand people, Flint was home.

And they did what they could to fill the gaps. When Pastor Sherman

McCathern and his congregation at Joy Tabernacle realized that Civic Park was not on anyone's list of priorities, they launched their own programs to fix up the neighborhood. They covered over the vacant windows and doors "to take the abandonment look away," helping people to imagine what a healthy Civic Park could look like. They paid young men to mow lawns and board up empty homes. People who never dreamed of owning a place of their own moved into some of the left-behind houses. The church created the Urban Renaissance Center to serve as a social ministry for single parents, seniors, ex-offenders, recovering substance abusers, and anyone else who walked in the door. In its vision for Flint, they adopted President Barack Obama's campaign slogan, which itself was an adaptation of an old union worker chant: "Yes, we can!" Inspired by these efforts, local institutions such as the University of Michigan's Flint campus and Habitat for Humanity started to work alongside the church. "The community was at one time totally ignored by everybody," McCathern said. "But because young people stood up, now everybody came on board." You could feel a shift in the momentum. You could see the change. "It was a different Flint that was coming."

But on that sweltering summer day, there was that water pouring out of the fire hydrant, as children sprinted back and forth through its spray. Dark as coffee.

II.

This is the story of how the City of Flint was poisoned by its own water. It was not because of a natural disaster, or simple negligence, or even because some corner-cutting company was blinded by profit. Instead, a disastrous choice to break a crucial environmental law, followed by eighteen months of delay and cover-up by the city, state, and federal governments, put a staggering number of citizens in peril.

Their drinking water, it turned out, was full of lead and other toxins. No amount of lead exposure is safe. There is no known cure for lead poisoning. The threat invaded the most intimate spaces of people's lives: their bodies, their homes, their meals, the baths they gave their children, the formula they fed their babies. Yet it will be years before we can fully assess the effect of lead exposure on a whole generation of children. We must wait for them to grow up and see.

The tainted water also triggered an outbreak of deadly Legionnaires' disease, a severe form of pneumonia caused by waterborne bacteria that can be contracted by inhaling tiny droplets. And, according to one research team, the water switch correlated with a serious drop in fertility for women in Flint and a 58 percent increase in fetal deaths. In an echo of how women once ingested lead to control their reproduction, an estimated 275 fewer children were born than expected during the emergency.[13]

When residents noticed that there was something odd about their water, they asked for help. But they were routinely dismissed. Among the many ravages attributed to the water crisis—the rashes, the hair loss, the ruined plumbing and pipes, the devalued homes, the diminished businesses, the homeowners who left the city once and for all, the children poisoned by lead, the people sickened or killed by Legionnaires' disease—the lost faith in those who were supposed to be working for the common good was among the most devastating. That this happened in the Great Lakes State, which is surrounded by one fifth of all the freshwater on the face of the Earth, makes it all the more haunting.

Fifty years ago, civil unrest tore through American cities—Flint included—and revealed how inequality was built into their very foundations. It cued a national reflection from which the *Kerner Report* emerged, a six-volume investigation into the riots of the 1960s by a bipartisan presidential commission. With passion, the *Kerner Report* urged the country to recommit to its cities and to rebuild them as places of opportunity. "These programs will require unprecedented levels of funding and performance," the authoring commission wrote, "but they neither probe deeper nor demand more than the problems which called them forth. There can be no higher priority for national action and no higher claim on the Nation's conscience."[14] Avoiding the issue, it warned, was itself a choice. And it was one that would send cities on a downward spiral.

That's exactly what happened. After decades of negligence by both public and private actors, the well-being of residents in twenty-first-century Flint sat atop a teetering tower of debt, dysfunctional urban policy, disappearing investment, disintegrating infrastructure, and a compromised democratic process. It didn't take much to tip the city into catastrophe.

Flint was not alone. Thousands of communities across the country are in a similarly precarious situation. From Akron to Albany, South Bend to St. Louis, Baltimore to Buffalo, Flint is just one of a large class of shrinking cities. Once among America's finest communities, they have been hollowed out by generations of public policy that incentivized suburban living. The subsidized freeways, shopping malls, and segregated real estate all contributed to an outmigration of mostly middle- and upper-class people—white folks first, and then, more recently, African Americans and other communities of color. The cities they left are pressured to cut spending at all costs while at the same time maintaining the services and infrastructure designed for a much larger population. It is impossible. There isn't enough money to fix a broken window at city hall, and there certainly isn't enough to upgrade the aging lead-laced water infrastructure.

The Flint water crisis illustrates how the challenges in America's shrinking cities are not a crisis of local leadership—or, at least, not solely that—but a crisis of systems. Paternalism, even if it is well meaning, cannot transcend the political, economic, and social obstacles that relegate places such as Flint to the bottom. The chronic underfunding of American cities imperils the health of citizens. It also stunts their ability to become full participants in a democratic society, and it shatters their trust in the public realm. Communities that are poor and communities of color—and especially those that are both—are hurt worst of all.

If "Watts" came to represent the twentieth-century urban crisis, then "Flint" represents that of the twenty-first. Systemic inequality and disenfranchisement are at the heart of both tragedies. But what happened in Flint reveals a new hydra of dangers in civic life: environmental injustice, the limits of austerity, and urban disinvestment. Neglect, it turns out, is not a passive force in American cities, but an aggressive one.

While there is moral cowardice in the story of Flint, there is also heroism. It's found most especially in the lionhearted residents who chose, again and again, to act rather than be acted upon. They turned themselves into top-notch community organizers and citizen scientists, and they built relationships with a diverse ensemble of professionals—including journalists in Detroit and Ann Arbor, a regulations manager at the Environmental Protection Agency in Chicago, an engineer who was working from her suburban home, a pediatrician at a local hospital, and a team of scientists and civil engineers all the way down in rural Virginia to make themselves visible.

This city did not deserve what happened to it. Neither does any other shrinking city. Half a century after the *Kerner Report* tried to inspire a new approach to urban life, we are at another crossroads between how things were once done and how we can choose to do them in the future. In a way, public drinking water systems are the perfect embodiment of the ideal that we might reach toward. The sprawling pipelines articulate the shape of a community. House by house, they are a tangible affirmation that each person belongs. They tie the city together, and often the metropolitan region as well. If only some have good, clean water and others do not, the system breaks down. It isn't safe. The community gets sick. But when we are all connected to the water, and to each other, it is life-giving—holy, even.

PART I

TAUGHT BY THIRST

The Well

And pines with thirst amidst a sea of waves.

—Homer, *The Odyssey* (eighth century B.C.E.)

I.

Men in jewel-toned ties grinned and held their clear plastic cups high, each filled with water poured from an insulated pot. The shine of their watches and wedding rings winked under the fluorescent lights. Outside the old treatment plant, the April air was gray and cool. The edges of the spider-legged water tower seemed to blur into the morning haze.

"Here's to Flint!" said Mayor Dayne Walling. He was a city native, born to two schoolteachers, and energy hummed through him. He had a tendency to fidget, to gulp his coffee, and to speak with passion on a fast-moving series of topics. A Rhodes scholar with a master's degree in urban studies, he returned to his hometown in 2006, the year he turned thirty-two. Three years later, he became its mayor.

And now, in the spring of 2014, Walling was leading the toast. The dozen or so others gathered that day in a small outbuilding off Dort Highway hoisted their cups higher and chorused in response. "Hear,

hear!" They tilted their heads back, marking the moment when, for the first time in two generations, the people of Flint would drink from their namesake river.[1]

"It tastes like . . . water," remarked city councilman Joshua Freeman. That was surely a good sign.

Darnell Earley, the city's emergency manager, was also at the treatment plant. He was the latest in a string of emergency managers, or EMs, that were first appointed by the State of Michigan in 2011 to lead Flint out of serious financial distress. It was a peculiar position. Earley held the full power of both the mayor's office and the City Council to do what needed to be done to stabilize the community. The idea of emergency management is that an outside official who is not constrained by local politics or the prospect of a reelection bid will be able to better make the difficult decisions necessary to get a struggling city or school district back on solid ground. In Flint, that meant that the authority of Mayor Walling and the council had been suspended for more than two years. Their roles were now symbolic and advisory, or empowered (and paid) only to the extent that Earley allowed.[2]

In a city with plenty of urgent matters competing for attention—poverty, vacancy, schools, crime, jobs—one thing Flint didn't have to worry about was the quality of its water. The Detroit Water and Sewerage Department had supplied Flint with good water for nearly fifty years. The big public utility drew from the freshwater of Lake Huron, a lake so deep and fierce that it once swallowed eight ships in a single storm.[3] The DWSD then treated and pumped Flint's water at a plant near the shoreline and delivered it through a 120-inch pipeline to another pump station. From there, the flow was pushed through a smaller line until it reached the city's kitchen sinks. Flint's own treatment plant, which it had used to treat its river water before joining the DWSD in the 1960s, sat idle. It remained on hand only because the state required a backup water source for emergencies.

While the quality of DWSD water was reliable, its cost was not. Long before the emergency managers came to town, residents had urged their leaders to relieve the burden of pricey water. Monthly rates in Flint were among the most expensive in the country, and yet 42 percent of residents lived below the federal poverty level.[4] And the rates kept rising—a 25 percent increase here, a 45 percent increase there. Many residents just couldn't afford their bills. But at this point it was difficult for the city to do much about it. Its infrastructure was built to serve Flint when it had twice the people it had now; to maintain it, fewer ratepayers had to carry a heavier burden. Efforts to negotiate a better wholesale deal with the DWSD didn't go far, either. The Detroit system charged more for delivering water to higher elevations and across longer distances. While it served communities across eight Michigan counties, Flint was easily the farthest out, at the end of the DWSD's northernmost line. There was just no wriggle room. It seemed to Mayor Walling that the DWSD was taking Flint, its second-largest customer, for granted.[5]

Jeff Wright agreed. He was Genesee County's drain commissioner, holding an elected office that made him responsible for water management issues.[6] Wright was fond of portraying the DWSD, a public utility, as a price-gouging monopoly, and he saw an opportunity to develop an alternative. He called it the Karegnondi Water Authority, using a common moniker for Lake Huron on seventeenth-century maps.[7] This new water authority was just an idea at first, and seen as a negotiating tactic to pressure the DWSD for better rates. But then the not-yet-existent KWA got a permit from the Michigan Department of Environmental Quality to pull 85 million gallons of water per day out of the Great Lakes. The MDEQ reasoned that the big diversion wouldn't be a problem for the ecosystem because it would all balance out: the Detroit system would use less water as its customers moved over to the KWA. Then the new public system incorporated, and it became a real force. Flint and its neighboring communities were invited to help build it from the ground up. At the first meeting of the KWA board, Walling was elected chair.

Unlike the Detroit system, which delivered treated water, the KWA would pump raw water to the communities it served. That meant they would have to treat the water first before selling it on to residents and businesses. For Flint, it would mean rebooting the old treatment plant off Dort Highway and navigating the complexities of water chemistry in-house.

Darnell Earley championed the switch to the KWA as a way for Flint to build self-sufficiency. "The city has had virtually no control over managing its most important resource and service, and that is the water," he argued.[8] What's more, he said, it would save the city a lot of money. The region would gain $200 million a year over twenty-five years, and far more after that, according to the numbers from Ed Kurtz, Earley's predecessor as EM. They implied that Flint would be one of the beneficiaries of that.[9] It wasn't lost on them that the fury over high water rates—and the shutoffs and the arrests of people with illegal water hookups—was escalating. The KWA would create a more cost-efficient water system over the long term, they said, and it would spare residents unpredictable fee hikes.

With Flint under emergency management, the EM was the sole person with the authority to make decisions for the city. So the council was surprised when it was convened for a rare vote in 2013, to decide whether it should join the KWA. At the time, a pending lawsuit threatened to overturn Michigan's emergency manager law, so the champions of the KWA wanted to get Flint's elected leaders on the record as supporting the switch. As an engineering consultant described the strategy in an email, the emergency manager "has given powers back to Mayor and Council to make the decision on KWA as a precaution if the EM court challenge holds up. This will enable the Mayor and Council to approve the KWA agreement and not be challenged in court!"[10]

After a heated hearing, the council voted 7–1 in favor. The one "no" vote was cast by Bryant Nolden, or BB, a middle school teacher who represented the Third Ward in north Flint. "It wasn't that I was really against the KWA," he said later. "It was just the process in which it was done, and having people wanting you to vote on something without having all of the information. And I just wasn't going to be a party to that."[11]

While the council vote had no power behind it, the event was played up to suggest that the city had determined its own future. "I have said from the beginning that this decision must be made by Flint's City Council and Mayor," said Jeff Wright in a press release. He indicated that while the emergency manager supported the switch, the council vote was a condition for Flint to join. "There is a basic tenet that government is best when it has local control."[12]

Michigan's state treasurer approved the change (even though it meant that Detroit's water department would lose a major source of revenue just as that city, which was also under emergency management, was about to declare bankruptcy).[13] Flint's EM then contracted with the KWA to purchase 18 million gallons of water for the city per day, 2 million more than the council had approved in its vote.

But construction on the KWA hadn't even begun yet. The new system wouldn't be able to deliver water for at least a couple more years. Until it was ready, the other Genesee County communities that were moving to the new system simply paid the DWSD for continuous water service. Flint, however, made the unusual decision to enlist a different source of water during this transition period. The city turned to its emergency supply: the Flint River.

To treat the river water, the old Dort Highway plant needed a series of upgrades. Many of these improvements would be required anyway, since the plant would soon have to treat raw water from the KWA.[14] But getting the facility up to speed was difficult, and while cost estimates varied widely, only a fraction of the early figures proposed by the engineering consultants was spent on the project.[15]

The month of the water switch, Michael Glasgow, Flint's utilities administrator, didn't believe the plant was ready.[16] He emailed three people at the MDEQ, the state environmental agency, with a warning. "I have people above me making plans" to distribute the water as soon as possible, Glasgow wrote, but "I do not anticipate giving the OK to begin sending water out anytime soon. If water is distributed from this plant in the next couple of weeks, it will be against my direction. I need time to adequately train additional staff and to update our monitoring plans before I will feel we are ready. I will reiterate this to management above me, but they seem to have their own agenda."[17]

Still, other decision makers gave the treatment plant their vote of confidence.[18] And so, on a dull spring morning, Mayor Walling's toast was the start of a cheerful ceremony. Metal chairs for the guests and media were lined in rows on the yellow tiled floor, facing a podium that stood between the national and state flags. After remarks from several officials, Walling approached a circular gray box that was mounted on the cinder block wall. It controlled the rush of water through Flint.

"This is our moment, so I think we need a countdown," Walling said, looking back at the crowd. He wore a navy blazer, a light blue tie, and an American flag pin on his lapel. His left index finger was poised atop a small black button. "From three?"

The men smiled back at him. "Three! Two! One!" they chanted. Then, a hush. Walling pushed the button, and the system powered down. He pulled his hand away but kept his eye on the controls until the green light darkened and the red light sparked to life, showing that the freshwater supply from Detroit had been closed off. That's when the applause started. "Yeah!" someone hollered madly. After the residual water flowed out of the system, the City of Flint would be relying solely on the river water.

"Water is an absolute vital service that most everyone takes for granted," Walling said the day of the switch. "It's a historic moment for the city of Flint to return to its roots and use our own river as our drinking water supply."[19] That rousing sentiment was echoed in the local paper. An editorial heralded the switch as a way for the city to reclaim its sovereignty, which had been undermined by disinvestment and emergency management. "Switch to Flint River Water Represents a New Era in Flint," ran the *Flint Journal* headline.[20] "Let's raise our drinking water glasses and cheers to a new direction for the next 40 years," the editorialists wrote.

Stephen Busch, a light-haired district supervisor from the MDEQ's drinking water office, was at the ceremony too. A year earlier, when the city was wrestling with its long-term water options, he had expressed worry about what would happen if Flint treated its own river for drinking water—bacterial problems, exposure to dangerous chemicals, additional regulatory requirements.[21]

In other words, the state's environmental agency had thought that the city should *avoid* the Flint River. And now Flint was using the river anyway. For all his earlier concern, though, Busch seemed tranquil at the treatment plant that April morning.[22] Regarding the drinking water, he said, "Individuals shouldn't notice any difference."

II.

In the beginning, the water was a blessing. Native people were nourished for centuries by the river, which flowed for 142 curving miles. It merged into a broader river network that pours northward into Saginaw Bay, the body of water that separates the Michigan mitten from its thumb. The Ojibwa called it *biwânag sibi*, which translates as "Flinty River."[23] It ran gently downslope. Trees grew along the banks, casting shadows in a flickering lace over the glassy surface. People crossed the river at a shallow point shrouded by alder and black ash trees, near a meadow where some Ojibwa grew corn. It was part of a trail that ran between the young cities of Saginaw and Detroit.[24] French traders baptized this point as the *grande traverse*, or the "main crossing." Or Grand Traverse, as it is today rendered in the name of a street and a neighborhood in Flint.[25]

In the early 1800s, this swath of riverside land caught the eye of Jacob Smith, a butcher from Quebec who remade himself into an enterprising fur trader in the territorial woods. Smith was an agile man with a slight frame who would later be depicted by an artist in the costume of an archetypal frontiersman: buckskin, boots, a wide-brimmed hat. He moved to a country that had only just won its independence, settling in Detroit, but he often spent time trading in the Saginaw Valley woods. He spoke a local dialect fluently, and he extended thousands of dollars of credit in trade to the Ojibwa. They called him *Wah-be-seens*, or "young swan."

Fortunes were made in the forests of Michigan Territory. For nearly two hundred years, traders bought and sold beneath the heavy branches. Competition was fierce. In the uneasy peace after the Revolutionary War, the British did not forget the wealth in these woods. Just across the border, in Canada, they held out hope that they might regain the Michigan peninsulas for themselves. When war broke out again in 1812, British troops marched into Detroit, which they reclaimed without firing a shot.[26] The hostilities brought the fur trade to a halt, but meanwhile Smith collected wartime experiences that are the stuff of novels: he was a soldier, spy, prisoner, escape artist, and military captain. Eventually, in 1819, he used sneaky tactics with both Ojibwa leaders and the territorial governor Lewis Cass to get a controversial treaty signed that created Indian reservations and opened up about 4.3 million acres of Michigan Territory for white settlement.[27] It also allotted eleven square miles of land around the *grande traverse*, where Smith wanted to set up a trading post, to his children. Much of that land would become modern-day Flint.

About ninety feet from the river, Smith built a small log cabin and opened for business. All went according to plan: Ojibwa trappers brought him pelts of beaver, muskrat, mink, otter, and raccoon, and Smith in turn sold the pelts to merchants from Detroit and Saginaw.[28] He hired several employees to keep up with the brisk work. As native people were pushed farther out, and eastern settlers felt that the territory might be safe enough to buy land, traders such as Smith developed a habit of exaggerating stories about "ferocious animals"—mosquitoes, especially—and "treacherous Indians" as a way to keep out people whose presence would hurt their supply chain.[29]

But within six years of the treaty Smith was dead. Thus, the man who is conventionally credited as the founder of Flint never lived to see it as a real city. And thanks to years of reports about the land by the river being swampy, sandy, and damn near uninhabitable—not to mention land titling problems, cholera outbreaks, and the fearsome reputation of the Saginaw Ojibwa—there were few other white settlers in the area. The community did not even have its modern name yet. Smith's grave marker declares him only to be "the first white set-tler at the Grand Traverse of Flint River Michigan where he died."[30]

The followers came slowly, but they did come (and no doubt most Ojibwa would have preferred they not come at all). More than a decade after Smith's death, someone set up a sawmill on the river. Families from upstate New York and New England began to move in, one of them taking over Smith's empty cabin.[31] Others built them-selves frame and clapboard houses, and even some brick ones. There were so many people in the community from New York State's Gen-esee Valley that when the settlers finally traced their political bound-aries, they named their county Genesee. Flint, sitting directly in the center, was its seat.

About sixteen years after Smith founded the settlement, Alexis de Tocqueville passed through. He ate meals, found overnight hospital-ity, smacked the bugs that alighted on his skin, and wrote about it all in *Two Weeks in the Wilderness*, something of an addendum to his epic *Democracy in America*. The Flint River, Tocqueville wrote, was "strung out like a crimson thread at the end of the valley."[32]

In later years, the river would not be described in such lovely lan-guage. The waterway would bear so much mistreatment from indus-try and development—chemical dumping, sewage effluent—that locals learned to avoid it.[33] After a series of floods in the early twen-tieth century, massive concrete barricades were built to channel the downtown section of the river. They were meant to make the river-front safer, but they became a fortress line that barred people from the water. Several small dams restricted the river's navigability. Gen-erations of kids were taught to fish in the Flint River, casting lines off the grassy banks in their neighborhoods, but invariably they learned to toss the catfish and carp back into the current. It was too danger-ous to eat anything from the water.

This was an extraordinary fate for a river town that is only about seventy miles away from both Saginaw Bay and the shore of Lake Huron, part of the most remarkable chain of freshwater in the world. But so it was.

III.

Call them inland seas. Carved out at the end of the last glacial period, more than ten thousand years ago, and filled first with the meltwater of retreating sheets of ice, the Great Lakes hold about one fifth of the world's surface freshwater.[34] Spill it across the United States, and it will settle over the forty-eight conterminous states at an even depth of ten feet. At ninety-four thousand square miles, their surface area is about equal to that of the United Kingdom, and their drainage basin covers two hundred thousand square miles, almost the size of France.[35] On a map, that basin stretches across ten degrees of latitude and eighteen degrees of longitude. The water is in constant motion, powered by rolling waves and rip currents, an engine strong enough to modulate the climate. If you stand on the moon, you can pick out their telltale shock of deep blue.

Michigan lies like a handprint in the water. An assertion of the human self in the wild sea: *I am here*. Its two curving peninsulas are shaped by where the waves of four of the five interconnected lakes crash. Michigan's thirty-two hundred miles of coastline, more than for any other state except Alaska, turn from soft-blowing sand dunes into craggy beaches into the brilliantly colored cliffs and turrets of the Pictured Rocks, where Henry Wadsworth Longfellow set his famous poem about Hiawatha: *By the shores of Gitche Gumee / By the shining Big-Sea-Water.* Tens of thousands of tree-riddled islands are scattered over the Great Lakes. One of them is Isle Royale, the only national park that is an island, and reachable only by seaplane or a three-and-a-half-hour ferry ride. Moose roam among fat balsam firs, skinny aspens, mountain ash, and red maple trees. At dusk, loons sing their mournful call.

The seas were first crisscrossed by Mackinaw boats and bark canoes; then square-sailed brigs and three-masted schooners; and then lake freighters and passenger steamers that left a black flag of smoke unfurling behind them. In 1831, Alexis de Tocqueville wrote a letter from a steamboat off the southern shore of Lake Erie. "This lake without sails," he wrote, "this shore which does not yet show any trace of the passage of man, this eternal forest which borders it; all that, I assure you, is not grand in poetry only; it's the most extraordinary spectacle that I have seen in my life."[36]

Standing as totems to how the water can be cruel, more than 120 lighthouses ring the coasts, shimmering like stars in the night.[37] But they are not always enough. Lake Superior especially, the largest freshwater lake in the world, holds the wreckage of hundreds of ships, and those who sailed them, in its thousand-foot depths. Tales of ghost ships have been whispered, sailor to sailor, since at least 1679.[38] The Ojibwa people—they lived not only on the shores of the Flint River but also far across the North Country—told stories about a spiny underwater monster called the *mishipeshu*. It conjured storms over the lakes, putting those who traveled on them in mortal danger. With its thrashing tail, it spun calm water into rapids and whirlpools; it broke the winter ice beneath your feet as if the cold, slick glass were as soft as butter. The monster might be appeased with a pinch of tobacco if you offered it at the start of your journey. It might be. Three or four hundred years ago, an artist traced the lynx-like shape of the *mishipeshu* in red ocher on a white crystalline cliff on Lake Superior's northern shore. You can still see its horned silhouette today in an Ontario provincial park, among thirty-some more ordinary shapes of life in this corner of the world: a heron, an eagle, a beaver, a man on a horse. *Mishipeshu* stands in profile with its head cocked, as if watching those who, in their innocence, push off the rock and into the waves.

Inland in Michigan, you are never more than six miles away from a natural source of water. More than eleven thousand lakes are scattered around the state, many with wooden docks jutting into them from white-sand or stony beaches, beloved by tourists who make summer pilgrimages from cities on the lower latitudes: Lansing, Kalamazoo, Chicago, Milwaukee, Cleveland, Indianapolis, Cincinnati. Around the state, a web of slow, dark rivers and streams, thirty-six thousand miles of them, spider from one lake to another, and then out toward the inland seas.

By the middle decades of the nineteenth century, Flint was still something of a frontier town, but it was flush from the lust for lumber. Michigan white pines were sold as far as San Francisco and Shanghai, and Flint was an excellent hub for them.[39] Trees were cut in the woods, floated in on the Flint River during the spring thaw, sliced into boards in the sawmills, and then shipped around the world. With its growing population, Flint finally got around to incorporating as a city in 1855.

As Flint matured, so did other cities around the country. The Industrial Revolution sparked tremendous urban growth, while westward expansion led to ambitious development in new landscapes. One of the biggest challenges: figuring out how to get water to people. Easy access to water was a necessity for health, sanitation, fire prevention, and economic growth—that much was obvious. But working out how to provide it turned into a big, unruly experiment in shaping cities as places that serve the public good. Each community tried out different techniques, tailoring the design to its unique geography and expertise. Some pulled from surface water, others from groundwater, and still others combined the two. Philadelphia, one of the earliest innovators, got serious about building a water system after an epidemic of yellow fever killed about 10 percent of its population. The city installed miles of iron pipes, and, after a disappointing experiment in moving water with steam power, it upgraded to waterwheels. New York City built an expensive aqueduct from a reservoir in Westchester County in 1842, becoming one of the first in the country to use water from outside its own borders. Today the city draws from three lakes and nineteen reservoirs to move more than 1 billion gallons of water each day, and its crystal-clear quality is among the best in the country.[40] Boston cast around for decades, commissioning reports and holding referenda but failing to take any meaningful action toward building a central waterworks. Frustration intensified during the "underground wars" between neighbors, when one would dig a new well that drained the well of the person next door. In 1838, Bostonians petitioned the City Council: "*Let the thing be done, and done as soon as by any exertion consistent with prudence and* reasonable economy is practicable." Eight years later, the city finally broke ground on an aqueduct that drew water from Long Pond, about seventeen miles west. Thanks to gravity, water easily flowed down to the city.

As for the Great Lakes region, Chicago first had a private water-works that served only a small portion of the city, but it didn't work well. Live fish kept showing up in customers' buckets. The city absorbed the company in 1851 and expanded its draw of freshwater from Lake Michigan. But supply was limited. Unless there was a fire, no public water was available on Sundays. Industry dumped so much waste into the Chicago River—chemicals and carcasses—that it contaminated the water that was pulled from the lakeshore, near where the river emptied. It made people sick. But of all the ideas bandied about as to how to make the water safer, nobody seriously entertained the idea of stopping the pollution. Instead, the city outpaced the disgusting effluent by building a two-mile tunnel through the bed of Lake Michigan to reach clearer waters. It then went further by building a canal that reversed the Chicago River, so that rather than emptying into the lake, the water (and pollution) flowed west, ending up in the Mississippi River and the Gulf of Mexico. Both were outstanding feats of engineering, transformative for the health of the rising city, and, while the river reversal is controversial to this day, the water system became a symbol of Chicago's indefatigable spirit.[41] A few years after the tunnel opened, the Great Chicago Fire ripped through the city. One of the few buildings in its path that survived was the Gothic water tower.

In Detroit, about seventy miles from Flint, early residents dipped buckets in the river that is part of the Great Lakes chain.[42] To stave off fire in the wooden outpost, locals were required by law to keep a cask of water on hand. The fort later developed a delivery system by horse-drawn carriage. But in 1805 stray ash from a pipe ignited a fire that swallowed Detroit's tinderbox structures as if they were nothing more than air.[43] Bucket brigades and the city's single fire engine attacked it, but it was no use. About six hours after the fire started, the only structures still standing were a stone warehouse, a little fort high on a hill, and a maze of blackened chimneys that, separated from their homes, now looked like aged tombstones.

The trauma led to the creation of a more sophisticated water system, one that, many years later, would play a large role in the fate of Flint. After an experiment with public wells failed, a wharf and pump were built near the river "at which all persons who may reside within the city of Detroit, shall be at all times . . . entitled to take and draw water for their use and convenience," according to the authorizing legislation.[44] In exchange, residents paid an annual tax of one dollar. They later paid a flat rate of ten dollars a year (commercial customers paid more) for water that ran through the city's first pipelines: tamarack trees, which were rafted down waterways to Detroit, hollowed out, laid end to end, and joined by sleeves made of lead.[45] Contemporary work crews still sometimes stumble upon wooden lines like these when they dig in the ground, and they find them to be in perfect shape.

As in other cities, the young waterworks in Detroit experimented with different technologies for delivery and treatment, but the company lost money while "being continually assailed with complaints of the inadequateness of the supply and the impurity of the water," according to one history. The early administrators were found to have violated their charter to provide the city with safe water. In exclamatory fashion, an investigative committee recommended that the City Council "appoint some person [to lead a new waterworks] that will spend his time EXCLUSIVELY for the INTERESTS of the city."[46] They did so. But the new leadership had many of the same problems. Supply was so inconsistent that in some parts of Detroit, residents could draw water only at night.

For all the challenges, expectations for the right to quality water were rising. A turning point had come in 1854, when a thick-browed English doctor named John Snow made a huge discovery. The world was convulsing through the deadliest year of another cholera pandemic— the third in less than four decades, killing millions of people. Great Britain alone lost twenty-three thousand people the year that Snow used pioneering public health techniques to show that cholera spread through contaminated water. He was even able to pinpoint the specific water pump on Broad Street that was the source of the outbreak in London. Snow pled with local authorities to disable the pump, and when they did the plague ended. Despite this, it took years before Snow's work won widespread acceptance. It contradicted the prevailing theory that cholera spread through miasma, or "bad air." But Snow was eventually proved correct, as was the emerging germ theory—the notion that many diseases are spread by microscopic germs, often waterborne ones.

What this meant was that disease was best averted when *all* citizens were served by fully equipped waterworks and sewers. Providing service to just the wealthy few, as Chicago first tried, didn't work. Cities sped up their work to deliver quality water to residents, not only by building pipes and pumps, but also by disinfecting it with chlorine and filtering it with sand and gravel. The improvements in health and mortality rates, especially among populations who lived in dense urban centers, were profound.

Making the delivery of clean, treated water a basic civic service took another step forward when, in 1881, twenty-two men from six states gathered in St. Louis, a city that had lost at least 6 percent of its population in a cholera outbreak a few decades earlier, when it had no sewer system.[47] The men formed the American Water Works Association with an aim to professionalize water service, exchanging information that would spare cities from having to repeat the costly mistakes that had hindered others.[48] In a foreboding note for twenty-first-century Flint, one of the discussion topics at the first AWWA conference was about the poisonous effect of lead pipes on drinking water.

Participation in the AWWA was voluntary, however. For all the hustle and innovation that went into connecting people to collective water systems, there were no enforceable national standards for safety. Until well into the twentieth century, the federal government's environmental programs focused on conservation—things such as the forest service, the national parks service, and the Depression-era Civilian Conservation Corps. Pollution and public health weren't really on

Washington's radar. Local and state governments were left to make their own rules.

After more than a hundred attempts over fifty years, Congress passed the first major law addressing water quality in 1948. The Water Pollution Control Act was spurred by growing concern over the 2.5 billion tons of raw sewage that was being dumped into America's waterways every single day.[49] The law's intentions were good—to reduce pollution in interstate waters—but as policy it was weak, too stripped down in its final form to improve the condition of water that, like the carcass-strewn Chicago River, bore the indignities of industry, agriculture, and human sewage.

The biggest advance didn't come until the early 1970s, when the environmental movement triumphed with a number of new laws. Foremost among them were the Clean Water Act and the Clean Air Act. Three years after an errant spark set the chemical-slick Cuyahoga River in Ohio on fire—not for the first time, but never before featured so vividly in *Time* magazine—the Clean Water Act dramatically expanded earlier legislation to limit the toxic waste that was unloaded into America's rivers, streams, and lakes.[50] Passed by Congress over President Richard Nixon's veto, it set the norm so that no industry had an automatic right to pollute the water. At about the same time, the Clean Air Act was greatly strengthened, which made for not only clearer skies but also clearer waters, since airborne pollution eventually settles on the waterways. The new Clean Air Act also affirmed the principle that the environment should be treated as a public trust, and, accordingly, it empowered people to file citizen suits to protect it.[51]

Then there was the Safe Drinking Water Act of 1974. It was designed so that there would be a national baseline for tap water. The old way of allowing states to set their own standards broke down after a number of highly publicized emergencies: cancer-causing chemicals found in the water supplies of New Orleans and Pittsburgh; bacterial contamination detected in rural communities with older systems; lead leaching into the water that passed through pipes in Boston.[52] The Safe Drinking Water Act laid out minimum quality standards and developed assistance programs to help drinking water systems meet them. Significantly, as the people of Flint would come to know well, it depended upon utilities to self-monitor and self-report.[53]

Ultimate responsibility for these new laws belonged to the brand-new U.S. Environmental Protection Agency, which President Nixon created with an executive order in 1970.[54] In the decades since, the spectacular recovery of waterways all over the country, including the Great Lakes and the Cuyahoga, Chicago, and Flint Rivers, has proved its worth.

In Michigan, the sprawling Detroit Water and Sewerage Department became the largest supplier of drinking water. It served about four million citizens, or nearly 40 percent of the state's population.[55] DWSD customers lived not only in Detroit, but also in the suburbs, exurbs, and outlying rural towns. In fact, suburban growth was largely made possible because new towns were able to hook onto the Detroit system, providing them with essential infrastructure before they had the resources to build their own.

Flint's consumption of Detroit water began with a deal made in the spring of 1964. At the time, nearly two hundred thousand residents, and about a thousand people outside the city limits, were connected to the city's own water system, which used the Flint River.[56] It withdrew about 36 million gallons from the river every day, and not just to provide residents with something to drink: about 60 percent of the total was absorbed by Flint's mighty industrial plants, which were then at their roaring peak.

It seemed that Flint's water needs would only grow. Civic leaders worried about whether the river could support the population and industries for decades into the future. Or would its limited capacity stunt development? For years, there were passionate debates about what to do, and it came down to this choice: Flint could either sign on with the Detroit water department, which would build a pipeline to deliver treated water from the seemingly unlimited supply of Lake Huron, or build its own pipeline to Lake Huron and treat the water itself at its city plant.

Outrage over a corruption scandal effectively killed the plan for the city to construct its own pipeline. While Flint was weighing its options, three people with insider knowledge were charged with buying land where a pumping station would be built and then reselling it to the city for a personal profit.[57] As the case was playing out, Flint's City Commission, as the council was then called, voted 7–2 to join Detroit's system. Going forward, the DWSD would provide wholesale water to Flint, which in turn delivered it to local residents and to a number of Genesee County suburbs. Flint also provided water to the GM plants that were increasingly being built in the suburbs.[58] The taxes paid by GM would fund the development of these young communities, which would eventually compete with the core city for residents and business.

A few years after the deal was signed, when Detroit mayor Jerome Cavanagh dedicated the new connection to Flint, he emphasized its public-spirited symbolism. "This marks a further demonstration of a regional problem being solved by a regional government tool," Cavanagh said at the 1967 ceremonial event.

"We have gone beyond the stage where a community can think no further than its own boundaries," the mayor continued. "We must be concerned with our neighboring cities. When the problems become too large then we must gather together in common interest to find a mutually beneficial answer."[59]

Half a century later, that deal was dissolved. The men in jewel-toned ties gathered in Flint to commemorate its end, toasting the virtues of going it alone in the moments before they turned the water off.

Corrosion

All things are poison and nothing is without poison; only the dose makes a thing not a poison.

—Paracelsus (early sixteenth century)

I.

Summer is the time of year when Flint becomes lush. Eagles, osprey, and red-tailed hawks linger in the greenery along the Flint River. Wild raspberries grow in the creekside ravines. Community gardeners bring bushels of heirloom tomatoes, peppers, cucumbers, squash, green beans, and kale to the farmers' market. In 2014, when Flint was emerging from its snowiest and coldest winter on record, the warm sun was especially welcome.[1] Volunteers led weekly bike rides along the Flint River Trail, with the first ride of the season drawing cyclists between the ages of eight and eighty-four.[2] The UAW 598 local of GM workers and retirees held its annual Soberfest family picnic at the Union City Ball Fields, a tradition begun two decades earlier by auto-workers in recovery. Flint Lake Park was brought back to life after years of community cleanups. About one hundred residents celebrated with a picnic under a wooden pavilion, punctuated by the cheers of adults and children as they reeled in catfish from a nearby dock.[3]

wn hummed as well. The historic *Flint Journal* building
ted as a teaching space for Michigan State University. A
.... mile away, musicians with the Flint Symphony Orchestra
experimented with midday performances at the bus terminal. "I don't
have a car, so even though there might be concerts that may play
throughout the area, I don't have the money or the time," one woman
told an interviewer.[4] She skipped her first bus so she could listen
awhile longer.

And the city was getting to know its new drinking water. In late
May, one month after the switch off of the Detroit system, the Michigan Department of Environmental Quality announced the results of
the first tests. The Flint River drinking water had residual chlorine
and bacteria in it, but not so much that it violated the legal standards.
Mike Prysby, an owlish district engineer with the MDEQ, told a
reporter that there were "a couple of complaints logged" about the
quality, but a different taste and smell was to be expected because
river water is naturally harder than the Lake Huron water that Flint
drank for decades.[5] Hard water has minerals in it, accrued from the
earth it flows along, which gives it a distinct taste. Dish soap and
shampoo also take a longer time to lather in hard water than soft
water, which might be unsettling at first, but it was normal. In any
case, the river water was only temporary. The Karegnondi Water
Authority was expected to finish construction on its plant and pipeline in about two years. Flint would be back to Great Lakes water
soon enough.

This did not satisfy Bethany Hazard. The water coming out of the
tap in her west side home seemed murky and foamy. She had survived
cancer twice, forcing her into early retirement, and she lived on a limited income. She paid about $90 a month for her water and sewer
bill, she said, but nonetheless she started buying bottled water. The
new Flint water, she told a *Journal* reporter, was "just weird."

Another Flint resident, Lathan Jefferson, was so troubled that
within weeks of the switch he contacted officials at the Environmental Protection Agency's District 5 office in Chicago, the division that
oversees environmental issues in Michigan. The manager who took

his calls, Jennifer Crooks, described them in an email to her colleagues: "Mr. Jefferson said he and many people have rashes from the new water. He said his doctor says the rash is from the new drinking water, and I told him to have his doctor document this and he can bring it to the attention of the MI DEQ, since lab analyses to date show that the drinking water is meeting all health-based standards."[6]

By June 2, less than five weeks after the switch, the local NBC affiliate station reported that Bethany Hazard wasn't alone. Many residents were "avoiding the tap" and "drinking bottled water instead."

"I don't know how it can be clean if it smells and tastes bad," a bearded middle-aged resident named Senegal Williams told the television reporter.[7] His neighbor, a woman with a low voice who wore her hair in braids and did not give her name, agreed. She used bottled water to drink, cook, and wash. "When I'm showering and bathing, my skin feels different. So the smell from the water and the showering kind of convinced me that the water is just not the same."

Asked to respond, the city said again that the water met all safety requirements and that it was continually monitoring for potential problems. "City officials also say the water is perfectly safe for everybody to drink," the reporter told viewers.

But in fact there was a problem. A serious one. Flint's new water treatment program did not include corrosion control. The staff at the plant had been told by the MDEQ that it wasn't necessary.[8] But this was breaking federal law. In the years to come, the question of whether the authorities omitted this knowingly or through a terrible misunderstanding of the law would be a matter of intense dispute. What's more, the upgrades to the old plant on Dort Highway were not sufficient to deal with the river water, which was more corrosive and difficult to treat than lake water. Together, this was a dangerous combination.

Because America's infrastructure is generally quite old, large systems are required to add corrosion control treatment to the water to keep the pipes from disintegrating. It extends the life of the pipes and, because it prevents metals from fouling the drinking water, it helps protect public health as well. There are a few different methods to do corrosion control. In about half of all American water companies, including the Detroit system, orthophosphates are added to the water at the treatment plant.[9] The orthophosphates—sometimes short-handed as "phosphates"—create a protective coating that helps keep metals from leaching into the water as it flows through the water mains (the large pipes that run under the street, carrying water to a neighborhood) and the service lines (the smaller pipes that branch off the main, connecting to individual dwellings).

Without orthophosphates or any comparable treatment, the pipes are eaten away, especially when they are old and most especially when they are exposed to a corrosive water source such as the Flint River. There are various reasons why water might be corrosive, but in the river's case unusually high chloride levels were part of it.[10] Chlorides exist in most drinking water without causing any trouble.[11] But in large amounts they break down the metals in water mains, service lines, water heaters, household appliances, and plumbing fixtures.[12] Rivers and streams in northern climates such as in Michigan are particularly vulnerable to high chloride levels because they absorb run-off from the road salt (sodium chloride) that has been widely used as a deicer since the 1970s.[13] And the water is shallower in rivers and streams, which makes them more concentrated. High chloride levels also come from agricultural runoff and wastewater. Flint's treatment plant added still more to the mix by using ferric chloride as a coagulant for the water.[14]

Whatever the source, without proper treatment, corrosive water causes pipes to rust, flake, and leak. The brown water that Pastor Sherman McCathern saw gushing from the Civic Park fire hydrants, dark as coffee: that was corroded iron. Flint residents did not yet know the details of all this. But they did know that the water stank. As Reverend Barbara Bettis, who lived in southeastern Flint, said at a council meeting that summer, "It's nasty, and we shouldn't even be drinking it."[15]

To add insult to injury, this weird water was expensive. Residents were charged about $140 per month on their water and sewer bills—$35 more than the town with the second-highest rates in Genesee County and $90 more than the lowest. For just water, not including sewer, their bills were about twice the median cost in the water-rich Midwest.[16] Out of the five hundred largest water systems in America, Flint's rates were the very highest.[17] This made for some peculiar juxtapositions. One man, Nijal Williams, paid almost $65 more per month for his water and sewer service than his neighbors who lived just one hundred yards away but who had an address in Burton, the town on the other side of Flint's southeastern border. Some suburban leaders saw this as an opportunity. In the unincorporated community of Beecher, which also shares a border with Flint, an administrative superintendent put it bluntly to a reporter: "I hope people read this [article about high water rates in Flint] and move to Beecher. . . . We're the cheapest around."

These prices hurt people with limited resources. Nearly 80 percent of working residents in Flint earned $40,000 or less a year. Forty percent of them earned $15,000 or less.[18] The United Nations recommends that water and sewer bills be not more than 3 percent of a household's income. In Flint, the bills were well beyond that.[19]

Expensive water was a direct result of Flint's depletion. The infrastructure, of course, didn't shrink along with the population. Not only were the pipes designed for double Flint's current population—and then some, going by the optimistic projections of the 1960s—but they were built with a wide circumference to sustain all those chuffing GM plants. Now those huge lines needed to be kept up by a community that was much smaller and poorer. It is far more costly to wait until water mains fail before fixing them, but for Flint the money just wasn't there anymore.[20] About half the city's water supply was lost through leaky lines—it's been known to have nearly three hundred main breaks in a single year—which pushed the bills up even more.[21]

Whether a city is well-to-do, struggling, or somewhere in between, there are a thousand reasons for local officials to delay maintaining or replacing the old pipes. It's easy to forget about them, for one thing. The pipes are underground and, unless something goes wrong, largely invisible. Replacing them is very expensive, and money for infrastructure is harder than ever to come by. In 1976, two years after the Safe

Drinking Water Act passed, federal funding provided utilities with $17 billion to keep their infrastructure in good condition. By 2014, that had fallen to $4.3 billion.[22] Also, a full upgrade would take years to complete, extending well beyond any individual's elected term. And water infrastructure is rarely a top priority for residents. When it requires disruptive trench digging and road closures, or higher taxes, it can even anger people. There's also often a lot of disputes about who is responsible for what. Public drinking water systems are generally responsible for the water mains that run under the street, but property owners are held responsible for all or part of the service lines. And for all the trouble that can come out of improving the infrastructure, you don't even get the satisfaction of a proper ribbon cutting.[23]

As a result, water infrastructure all over the United States hasn't been upgraded in decades. In Flint, the average main was more than eighty years old.[24] More than fifteen thousand lead service lines were laid so long ago that nobody really knew where they were. The only way to locate them was to sort through forty-five thousand index cards kept in a big file drawer, deciphering smeared pencil handwriting to read someone's incomplete notes about which pipes were made of what.[25] Flint's distribution system included nearly four thousand fire hydrants, the oldest of which was more than fifty years old, and more than seventy-two hundred valves, which were never replaced unless they outright failed.[26]

Flint's infrastructure was in a death spiral. The water rates were expensive because the pipes were bad because vacancy rates were high because the city had been shrinking for so long. Costly bills tempted residents to move to the suburbs, as the city administrator in Beecher hoped they would. Then there were even fewer people to pay into the system, which meant there was even less money to maintain it, which meant rates went up further. Repeat ad infinitum.

So it was easy to understand the desire to make Flint's drinking water more affordable. The switch off of the Detroit system was pitched as a way to do just that. As per an annual water report delivered to residents, the use of the Flint River "was a temporary move driven largely by economics and the financial state of the city."[27] But then the bills kept rising. In the early summer, just a couple of months after the switch, Emergency Manager Darnell Earley proposed a budget that included a 6.5 percent hike in water and sewer rates for the first year and another 6 percent increase the following year.[28] Flint was no longer paying Detroit's wholesale prices, but it turned out that setting up the infrastructure for a new temporary water system and operating it with fewer ratepayers—the Genesee County suburbs opted to stick with Detroit water—was not an especially economical plan.[29]

Although Earley did not need the approval of the City Council, the mayor, or the community to enact his proposed budget, he decided not to proceed until people had a chance to speak their minds. About a dozen people attended one public meeting, where a resident of the Mott Park neighborhood declared that she is "trying really hard to support the emergency manager," but Flint's budget problems could not be fixed "on the backs of working people." The council president sympathized with this. "The people I feel really sorry for are the senior citizens who are on a fixed income and can't afford to move," he said. "They've become prisoners."[30]

Nonetheless, Earley signed the budget including the price hike. Monthly bills could now reach an average of $149, compared to the average in neighboring Burton of less than $58.[31] "As much as the high rates for providing water and sewer services pose significant financial challenges and community implications," read the adopted budget, "the alternative of not addressing basic maintenance . . . is equally challenging."[32] Earley also carved out money for six new jobs to help with the recently revived treatment plant.

But it was all too much for city councilman Wantwaz Davis of the Fifth Ward. Coming after a series of dramatic rate hikes in recent years, he had no patience for more. He led the second of a series of summer demonstrations that protested the unaffordability of the water, even now, when it was under local control.[33] About a hundred people congregated outside city hall on Saginaw Street, joined by pastors, who offered a predemonstration prayer, and young people, including a teenager who carried a bright green poster: "No More High Water Bills." When Davis had the soapbox, he read from 1 Corinthians off his smartphone and urged protesters to drum up the kind of national attention to social inequities in Flint that Detroit was getting. The big city to the south was swamped with reporters and documentarians when it declared bankruptcy that summer, the largest of its kind in U.S. history. "People cannot afford their water bills," Davis said. "It's surpassed their capacity. The bills are unreasonable, and should be brought down to a level low-income people can afford. You can go without food, but not water." Aaron Dionne, vice president of the Genesee County landlords' association, added that the water rates were "killing our business. Our tenants can't afford [water], so they're finding ways to turn it on illegally. We need some sort of attention. We just need something done. I don't understand how the emergency manager can come in here and kill big business like this."[34]

One person who was acutely aware of the risks of unaffordable water was Laura Sullivan, a professor of mechanical engineering at Kettering University, a cooperative college where about two thousand students attend classes. As the water rates escalated, she and her students experimented with ways to distribute rain barrels to neighborhoods where there had been a lot of shutoffs due to unpaid bills so that people could meet their basic sanitation needs. That in turn could fend off a public health crisis.[35]

The switch to river water worried Sullivan, but she believed the authorities when they said it was safe to drink. At her home in southwestern Flint, the water didn't look or taste bad. Mostly, she figured, people complaining about its quality were just reacting to the morbid stories that had been passed down from one generation to another about pollution in the Flint River. The river was vastly improved nowadays. The community was haunted more by old legends than by bad water, Sullivan believed, and if people understood the thorough treatment process that water goes through, they'd realize that it was fine.

II.

Many of Flint's most gracious houses are in the College Cultural neighborhood. If you walked along its streets in the summer of 2014, you'd see stately Tudors, Colonials, and ornate cottages. Any one of them could have been plucked from a fairy tale. But in the patches of grass out front, you'd also come across the sight of one open fire hydrant after another. "In response to localized complaints of discolored water," a press statement explained, city workers were opening the hydrants, letting the water rush out and pool uselessly on the ground.[36] They did the same thing in other neighborhoods, too, including downtown and eventually Civic Park. The idea was to push the muddiness out of the supply. In the huge water mains that ran beneath the closed manufacturing plants and depopulated streets, water sat stagnant for too long. Without enough residents or big industries to keep the water moving at a quick clip, the contaminants became more concentrated. "Residents in the affected areas may see increased water cloudiness for a short time, but the water will be safe to drink," the city authorities said in a statement to a local news outlet, adding, as usual, the assurance that the "water throughout the City meets all required drinking water standards."[37]

Explanations for the brown-tinged water were vague and contradictory. When asked about the discoloration by the dogged Ron Fonger of the *Flint Journal*, the city spokesperson said he wasn't sure. A couple of weeks later, Mike Prysby of the MDEQ told a reporter in Detroit that the color was the result of workers' "unauthorized drafting of water from fire hydrants in these areas for street sweeping activities."[38] That, plus frequent main breaks, stirred up sediment and rust in the pipes, which caused the discoloration. The unauthorized hydrant use, he said, "will be discontinued."

So some officials said that open hydrants would help solve the discoloration problem: they cleared the water by moving it through the system faster. Others said that open hydrants were contributing to the problem: the surge of water caused iron to flake off the mains. The city's annual water quality report opted for an all-encompassing explanation: the rusty color was due to the "change in source water, water main breaks, and routine maintenance" that caused the cast iron pipes to deteriorate faster than usual.[39] Among the steps taken to fix the problem would be more flushing—open hydrants—and budgeting for the repair of a twenty-four-foot water main in an unspecified "area of concern."

It was all very confusing. But public figures spent the summer counseling residents to have patience as they worked out the kinks. "It's a quality, safe product," said Mayor Dayne Walling. "I think people are wasting their precious money buying bottled water."[40]

Walling was deferring to the expertise of the MDEQ, just as the EPA had done when residents called the federal agency to report problems back in May. The state's top drinking water authorities, Prysby and Stephen Busch among them, insisted that the water was safe, and there seemed to be no reason not to trust them. They were charged with serving the public good, after all. Darnell Earley also stood by the water. "We understand there are going to be complaints," he said, but until the MDEQ declared it to be unsafe, "it will be the water source" for Flint.[41]

And yet before the end of the summer, the city issued three separate boil-water advisories in a span of twenty-two days.[42] These relatively common notices come when there's a system disturbance that could affect water quality, such as a drop in pressure caused by a broken main or maintenance work. Boiling water is a precaution that kills bacteria and other harmful organisms. But in Flint, which was already uneasy about this expensive and strange-tasting water, the advisories did not seem ordinary at all. They felt like an evil spell.

The first notice came on August 16 after fecal coliform bacteria, also known as E. coli, had been detected.[43] It was a surprising discovery. Statewide, the bacteria show up in drinking water about three times a year on average, and sometimes not at all.[44] Its presence suggests that the water is contaminated by human or animal feces, which can make people ill, especially older people, young children, and those with weak immune systems. The advisory covered half a square mile on the city's west side. Everybody with a tap was told to boil water for one minute before drinking, bathing, brushing teeth, washing dishes, cooking, or making ice. Or they could purchase bottled water.

Follow-up tests were negative. But there were positive results for total coliforms, a group of microorganisms that includes *E. coli*, so the advisory was kept in place for four days. Still, the city and state said the first test seemed to be a one-off abnormality—maybe even a sampling error.

"We don't know yet what caused this," said the MDEQ's Mike Prysby in response to questions. "We don't have a smoking pistol."[45]

He still didn't have one when the city issued a second boil-water advisory, on September 5. It covered a different swath of the city, this time encompassing Civic Park and the campus of Kettering University. The advisory forced the manager of a popular restaurant to go to a store each day to buy canned and bottled drinks for his customers. An elementary school that was barely outside the advisory area shut down its water fountains, just to be safe. It depended on the school district and parents to bring bottled water for the children.[46]

Follow-up tests were just like before—a positive test for total coliform bacteria, an extension of the advisory to four days total. It was still in effect when yet another boil-water advisory was issued, on September 6, for part of the city's west side, again covering Civic Park. Total coliform bacteria. Three days.

Three advisories over a period of three weeks, each one reaching farther into Flint.[47] No doubt that it was a sign of system weakness, Darnell Earley acknowledged, but it was not "an actual threat to citizen safety."[48] A *Journal* reporter ran that claim by both Mike Prysby and a water expert at Michigan State University. Both agreed that the advisories were a red flag but did not pose an inherent danger to residents. As a fix, the city announced that it would increase the disinfecting chlorine treatment and flush the system in the advisory areas. Earley also pointed to the $11 million allocated to water and sewer infrastructure in his adopted budget. It was a level of investment that the city had not seen in decades.

But these were solutions for a problem that did not yet have a name. Officials were saying different things about what caused the

E. coli contamination in the first place, just as they had conflicting explanations for the discoloration. Earley said he would open an investigation to find the cause. Prysby speculated that the problem could have originated with the main breaks, or improper chlorine levels, or maybe with a faulty collection of water samples—in that case, it was a process problem that had unduly given the appearance of unsafe water. And Howard Croft, a Flint native who ran the city's Department of Public Works, said on the radio that the contamination was caused by a broken valve on an "ancient water system" and that it would take a long time to replace it.[49]

There was agreement on one thing: the water leaving the treatment plant off Dort Highway met the standards of the Safe Drinking Water Act. People could drink it without worry. That's what city and state officials said, over and over and over, in public statements, news reports, interviews, and at meetings: the water was safe. The deadening drumbeat would last for another year.

Revelations

For you are not powerless. . . . We do not need to become each other in order to work together. But we do need to recognize each other, our differences as well as the sameness of our goals. Not for altruism. For self-preservation—survival.

—Audre Lorde, "Commencement Address: Oberlin College" (1989)

I.

An astonishing difference in water bills across the invisible border between Flint and its suburban neighbors; tap water that was more discolored in some neighborhoods than in others. The disparities in the water traced a pattern of inequality and disinvestment that was decades in the making. The whole city was exposed to toxic water—and so were commuters and other visitors—but the people who had it worst lived in the poorer, more decayed neighborhoods. And they tended to be black. Flint's black majority, about 57 percent of the population, was more than twice the proportion of the metro region. Many were the descendants of the bright-eyed southerners—thousands upon thousands of them—who had packed their cardboard suitcases and boarded northbound trains, steaming across the country, finding their way to Flint after hearing about the promise of opportunity in a bustling industrial town.[1]

It's not just the lofty rhetoric of nostalgia: for many people, Flint really was one of the best places in the country to live and work. By the 1950s, when General Motors held 54 percent of the market share, about seventy-seven thousand people in the Flint area worked for the company. The community celebrated with a song written for GM's golden anniversary:

> The city of Flint salutes you
> for the goal you've reached today
> We are proud to be your neighbor
> and we're glad that you came to stay![2]

The auto companies had it right when they boasted that, as *Time* magazine once had it, "motor prosperity can vibrate into every corner of the land." The industry consumed so much iron, lead, steel, rubber, oil, plate glass, upholstery leather, tin, cotton, mohair, copper, glue, cork, turpentine, silicon, cadmium, and even the "vegetable hair" stuffing it pushed into cushions that the national economy blossomed with robust car production.[3] Flint rose with that wave. The union movement that caught fire in Flint's GM plants empowered workers thousands of miles away to negotiate their wages, hours, and work conditions. And during World War II, GM was the chief supplier of the defense industry. No cars at all were made during the war. Instead, the factories were retooled to build aircraft, trucks, tanks, and other machinery that proved to be essential for fighting the war.

"Vehicle City" was not just what Flint was; it was how it had contributed to the country and to the world. But the identity in which the city took such pride began to break down in the second half of the century—slowly at first, as GM began to build its plants farther afield, and then rapidly, as the auto industry restructured. Mass layoffs and closures decimated the town. Although GM is the largest employer in Flint to this day, its payroll is a tiny fraction of what it once was. This was both an economic cataclysm and a social trauma.

For years, Flint tried hard to rebuild. To transform, just as it had before: from river crossing to trading post to lumber town to a city that moved the world. But this time it wasn't so easy. "There was an expectation that the city could recover on its own from this economic body blow," said Gordon Young, a Civic Park native and the author of *Teardown: A Memoir of a Vanishing City*.[4] Flint and local leaders were supposed to simply pull themselves out of it. But the city was at a particular disadvantage, struggling against a pattern that had been established almost a century earlier, when a series of decisions created a supposedly "separate but equal" metropolitan region.

During the boom years, GM was desperate for workers. In 1919, the year that it produced its millionth car, GM created the Modern Housing Corporation to entice new workers and help them get settled in Flint. It advertised in large eastern cities, appealing to demobilized World War I soldiers. A *New York Times* brief headlined "Detroit Needs Labor" noted that "Flint, where the General Motors Company has made plans for building 1,000 homes for workingmen, is declared to be particularly short of labor, and all classes of workers are wanted at the Chevrolet plant."[5]

GM eventually constructed nearly three thousand homes in the neighborhoods of Civic Park, Chevrolet Park, and Mott Park.[6] They were not sold on the public market, and they were offered to workers on friendly terms: 10 percent down payment, 6 percent interest, and mortgage payments that were about 1 percent of the total cost. But even if they could afford them, black people—who could work only in lower-tier jobs at GM, such as janitors or laborers in the dangerous foundries—were not allowed to buy them.[7] Multifamily dwellings, liquor sales, and outhouses were all banned from GM-developed neighborhoods, and, as if they were an equivalent nuisance, so were people who were not white. This was explicit: the houses could not "be leased to or occupied by any person or persons not wholly of the white or Caucasian race."[8] An ad in the 1920s from the exclusive Realtor of GM homes promised buyers "the maximum of beauty, utility and value," in part because "no shacks, huts or foreign communities will be allowed" in the neighborhood.

Segregation was the standard. Racially restrictive covenants—an agreement, written into deeds, to keep people out based on their race—were strictly enforced both in GM neighborhoods and throughout

Flint.[9] That included, especially, exclusive Woodlawn Park, where auto execs and shareholders (Charles Stewart Mott among them) built graceful mansions of stone and brick. It was spelled out in one deed after another and mandated by the so-called code of ethics from the National Association of Real Estate Boards. Realtors could lose their license for the supposed ethical violation of showing a house to a person of color in a white area.[10] The only option for black people in Flint was to crowd into just two neighborhoods: dense St. John on the near north side, an area that bordered the Flint River, a rail line, and a polluting Buick factory; and Floral Park, south of downtown, an economically diverse area that was first settled in the nineteenth century by former slaves and freedmen.[11]

This apartheid approach to city building wasn't just tolerated by the federal government; it was exacerbated by it. Federally funded public housing, a product of the New Deal, was segregated from the start. And when the government began providing people with long-term, low-interest home loans, the notorious policy of redlining was part of the plan. The mortgage program was a revolutionary practice of providing long-term, low-interest home loans that helped stabilize families, curb foreclosures, and boost the economy at the time it needed it most. But federally backed mortgages were available only in neighborhoods that were deemed safe bets for lending. On the maps provided to assessors, the areas that were cast in red could not receive them. In Flint's first evaluation, St. John and Floral Park were redlined, and all but one of the neighborhoods that bordered them received low grades. The only one that didn't earned its higher grade specifically because it had a racially restrictive covenant.[12] Several white neighborhoods in Flint's outskirts and early suburbs were also redlined, on account of their underdevelopment. They were filled with cheaply built cottages and they didn't have public utilities. However, locals could improve those conditions to get a higher score, and they did so.

But because the presence of black residents was in itself seen as a negative factor, there was nothing, by definition, that neighborhoods that housed them could do to become eligible for secure loans. When evaluators gave a neighborhood a low grade or redlined it outright, they pointed to a population of "Undesirables—aliens and negros."[13] On rating sheets, evaluators ticked off a list of nuisance factors that included odors, noises, fire hazards, and "infiltrations of lower grade population or different racial groups."[14] Policies to ensure private loans through the Federal Housing Administration mimicked this technique of making risk and race synonymous. One manual for FHA assessors gave instructions for them to reject loans for "all blocks in which there are more than 10% Negroes or race other than white" as well as "areas in which there are a considerable number of Italians or Jews in the lower income group." It bluntly stated, "If a neighborhood is to retain stability, it is necessary that properties shall continue to be occupied by the same racial group."

In 1937, the year that the sit-down strike triumphed at Flint's GM plants, nearly every white homeowner in the city had a long-term, low-interest, guaranteed loan.[15] It put them on the path to middle-class stability. At the same time, Flint was the third most segregated city in the nation and the most segregated of all northern cities.[16] This pattern extended beyond the city borders. As the suburbs expanded, many either were explicitly for whites only or they were so de facto because of the restrictions on housing loans and insurance. And so, in metropolitan Flint, the highest-value homes largely served white people. Their children typically inherited the property or it was sold to others who looked like them. Black families also often left their homes to their children or sold it to people of the same race. But their properties were generally located in officially declared "undesirable" neighborhoods, served by infrastructure that was destined to suffer from neglect. Individual white homeowners in Flint might have been racists or they might have been champions of civil rights—it didn't matter, really. The system was set up to create unequal living conditions for people of different races and to pass them down through the generations.

GM's workforce became integrated during World War II. To fulfill its defense contracts, the company needed twenty-five thousand new hires in the Flint area alone, and President Franklin Roosevelt had issued an executive order that prohibited racial and ethnic discrimination by contractors. After the war, the GI Bill provided low-cost mortgages for all veterans, though only a minuscule number of them went to returning soldiers who were not white, in part because very few developments would let them purchase a house in the first place.[17] That included the new postwar suburbs such as Levittown, New York, pristine communities that were built en masse with federal loans that had been issued on the condition that the homes not be sold or resold to black people.[18] In 1948, the movement for equal opportunity got a boost when the U.S. Supreme Court declared that racially restrictive covenants could not be enforced by the government—but private parties could do as they pleased.[19] Even though such covenants couldn't be upheld in court, they could still be inserted into real estate contracts and deeds, and honored in day-to-day practice.

In Flint, all this meant that mortgages for homes outside two designated neighborhoods remained beyond reach for African Americans. Black real estate agents were barred from joining the Flint Board of Realtors, serving as appraisers, or accessing property listings on the industry-standard Multiple Listing Exchange.[20] If a few black families in Flint found a way to move into a white school district—perhaps through a private purchase from an open-minded owner, or the common trick of working with a white ally who acted as a front for the real home buyers—the school board promptly redrew the boundaries to place their child back in the "transitional" school that they came from.[21] There were also the plain old tactics of intimidation. "On the east side of Flint, the blacks who tried to move there had crosses burned on their lawn," remembered Melvin McCree, son of the city's first African American mayor.[22] He grew up in St. John.

Because Flint's African American population exploded during the Great Migration—quintupling between 1940 and 1960—and because African Americans could not buy homes outside St. John and Floral Park, those neighborhoods suffered extreme overcrowding. Even after better-paying postwar jobs brought some families enough money to purchase homes in tonier neighborhoods, they faced one hurdle after another. Of nearly six thousand houses built in Flint in the early

1950s, fewer than one hundred were open to African Americans, all in St. John and Floral Park.[23] And despite the building boom, as late as 1959, fewer than 2 percent of FHA-insured housing loans nation-wide had been made available to people who weren't white.[24] Land-lords exploited this by charging black people exceptionally high rents, often for dilapidated apartments that were not up to safety codes. They got away with it because residents had nowhere else to go.[25]

Segregation wormed its way into the city's business and cultural hubs as well. The luxurious Durant Hotel didn't open its rooms to a black guest until 1954.[26] Downtown businesses refused to hire African Americans, and entertainment venues—movie theaters, skating rinks, concert halls, and bowling alleys—let black patrons visit only during limited hours. Flint's elected officials performed in blackface at min-strel shows, playacting as cartoonish characters for laughs, to raise money for charity. Berston Field House welcomed white children to swim in its pool six days a week, while black children were relegated to city sprinklers across the street. Wednesdays were the only day that black children were allowed in the Berston pool. And every Wednesday evening, after they left, the pool was drained and cleaned before the white children returned the next morning.[27]

Meanwhile, the underdeveloped communities on Flint's outskirts were becoming a lot more appealing. They initially relied on wells and unregulated septic tanks, but this was inconvenient and unpleas-ant, and it taxed the water table and threatened a water shortage.[28] One accidental drought hit the village of Flushing in 1954, obliging it to buy and distribute water from the City of Flint by the truckload for months.[29] But once the suburbs were connected to Flint's water and sewer services, the housing market got a jolt. The lack of adequate infrastructure had kept urban sprawl in check, but now, as the Mich-igan Civil Rights Commission later described it, development followed the pipes. By the end of the 1940s, about four thousand new homes were built in the young burgeoning communities.[30] As they grew in stability and attractiveness, they pulled both population and resources out of the city they circled.

With all their cheap open space, industry, too, was tempted by the

suburbs. Communities competed with one another to offer companies such as GM the sweetest deal for their own particular patch of
land, where they would then build plants and enjoy an influx of new
jobs and tax revenue. The Truman administration encouraged this
with its Cold War–era policy of industrial dispersion, which urged
manufacturers to move out of cities so that they would be less vulnerable to enemy attack.[31] Between 1947 and 1960, GM built eight
new manufacturing plants in Genesee County, all of them outside
Flint, while also shutting down several plants within the city borders.
It did this even though the city bolstered the company—then number
one on the Fortune 500 list of the largest concerns in America—by
charging it a deeply discounted rate for water use.[32] Residential rates
were about one and a half times what the company paid, even though
residents consumed less water overall.[33] By midcentury, when the
automaker absorbed more than half of the water pumped by the city,
it provided only about a third of Flint's total water revenue.[34]

At first, the city supported GM's regional expansion. Flint built
roads to the new suburban plants and, every time GM asked, the City
Commission voted to give them a water and sewer hookup.[35] This
was important because the young suburbs did not yet have the resources
to provide these services themselves. "Never mind that it builds the
plant and pays taxes in the next township, if it's good for GM it will
be good for Flint," as the Michigan Civil Rights Commission described
the thinking of city leaders. "Flint was, at least in their minds, a metropolitan whole that would rise or fall together."[36]

Not everyone was a fan of sponsoring GM's exit from the core
city, however. Andrew R. Highsmith, in his remarkable book *Demolition Means Progress*, describes a union leader who argued that Flint
was allowing GM "to enjoy all of the major services rendered by the
city, including fire and police protection; water and sewage disposal—
everything except the doubtful privilege of paying taxes."[37] By sharing its infrastructure with the suburbs and getting little in return, Flint
was effectively subsidizing its own disinvestment.

Even though these neighboring communities relied on Flint to kick-
start their growth, in time many of them developed their own infra-

structure and public services. They didn't mind paying for it, either. As one report from the era described it, "Not surprisingly, complaints over the quality of the water supply, sewers, and schools were foremost in the minds of suburban dwellers. . . . Most of these unhappy homeowners were desperate to bring the conveniences of urban living to their new neighborhoods—even if that meant higher taxes."[38] By 1956, the number of public water systems in Genesee County jumped to nine, and many more developed their own sewer systems.[39]

Any inconvenience of a move to the suburbs was mitigated by the construction of a massive interstate highway system beginning in the 1950s, which made it easier to commute as needed, and also easier for businesses, which typically thrive in transit hubs, to spread out. Brand-new shopping malls began to provide an alternative to dusty downtown retail. Early suburban residents loved the places they helped build for the quieter streets and cleaner air, for the green lawns and the extra space, and for being a place where everything could be made new. Each tiny town constructed a sense of itself as a unique community, untethered from the core city, with their own traditions, festivals, and proud high school sports teams. It grew stronger with every passing generation.

As the region grew, many people envisioned a metropolitan community that was not a collection of separate, competing enclaves, but a unified whole. In 1957, the plan for New Flint was launched. It was a proposal to merge Flint and twenty-five small inner-ring suburbs into a single municipality. The hope was to reduce redundancies in infrastructure, create economies of scale that would improve public services for all, and minimize shortsighted intraregional competition. New Flint was framed as a win-win strategy. The nascent suburbs would get the revenue, infrastructure, and cultural heft they needed to develop. Flint would get the land and resources it needed to keep humming along as an economic engine.[40]

GM was a champion of New Flint; it would have been happy to see new city limits drawn to include the suburban plants.[41] The city's elected officials, the trade unions, and the C. S. Mott Foundation were all on board, too. But suburbanites largely opposed the plan, not only in words but also in deeds. As the New Flint Resistance Committee, they campaigned against it—"Flint doesn't need us and we don't need Flint"—and one community, which wasn't even included in the plan, was spooked enough to hurriedly incorporate, drawing the border around itself as thick as it could.[42] Most African Americans also opposed New Flint. Their community groups had not been included in the proposal's development, and they were concerned that, just as their voting power in the city was increasing, regionalization would dilute it.

No matter: there never was a vote on New Flint. Even though there were enough petition signatures to put it on the ballot, Genesee County's Board of Supervisors rejected it. Supporters challenged this, but the Michigan Supreme Court upheld the decision. In killing the proposal, not only did the suburban communities fortify their individual boundaries, they also showcased what a powerful force they could be, even when going up against the big city and its most commanding institutions.[43]

Less than a decade after New Flint failed, the Michigan Civil Rights Commission confirmed that "rigid segregation" was endemic in Flint.[44] At its hearings, a clergyman's wife testified that when she and her husband tried to buy a home, they could do so only by arranging to have a white third party buy it first and then resell it to them. Black students were assigned to overcrowded black schools rather than white schools that had more space and were closer to their homes. Five years after the U.S. Supreme Court declared separate public schools unconstitutional in *Brown v. Board of Education*, the complaints of white parents prompted one second-grade teacher to isolate the single black child in her class of twenty-nine by making him sit alone in a small closet.[45]

In 1966, the commission's number one recommendation for Flint was that it pass a fair housing ordinance that banned racial and ethnic discrimination in real estate.[46] All residents should have equal access to decent living conditions. But the issue was postponed from one City Commission meeting to the next. Nothing was changing. Nothing ever seemed to change. Until, that is, the evening of July 24, 1967.

Hundreds of frustrated residents gathered in northern Flint to protest the commission's refusal to vote on the housing ordinance. What
followed was a rebellion that, for American cities in the 1960s, was
both extraordinary and familiar.

II.

In August 1965, the predominantly black Los Angeles neighborhood
of Watts exploded into a six-day riot. Triggered by a clash between
an African American motorist and a white police officer, it involved
arson, beatings, mass arrests, the militarization of city streets, more
than a thousand injuries, and thirty-four deaths. Bayard Rustin, the
civil rights activist, wrote in *Commentary* magazine that Watts
"brought out in the open, as no other aspect of the Negro protest has
done, the despair and hatred that continue to brew in the Northern
ghettoes despite the civil-rights legislation of recent years and the
advent of 'the war on poverty.'" Watts, Rustin wrote, served as a kind
of "manifesto."[47]

If that was so, then people around the country were signing on. In
the year after Watts, chaos broke out in at least eleven more cities. In
1967, the year of the "long, hot summer," there were more than 160
uprisings.[48] One was in Flint, catalyzed by the desperate overcrowding caused by segregation.[49] "Riots were happening in other parts of
the country," recalled Melvin McCree, son of Mayor Floyd McCree.
"Police wanted to put security on my father, but he didn't want it. He
was getting death threats."[50]

On a Monday evening in July, after the fair housing rally in north
Flint died down, a small group turned violent. It was a blur—a tumult of
vandalizing cars, hurling rocks, firebombing storefronts, and looting.
White-owned businesses were targeted, including a meat market, a
drive-in restaurant, and a large furniture store. Law enforcement
from Saginaw, Bay City, and the Genesee County Sheriff's Department
joined the Flint police on twelve-hour patrols.[51] Mayor McCree, only
seven months into the job and invariably described in news reports as

"the Negro mayor," walked alongside the officers. So did the Michigan National Guard. With McCree's support, Governor George Romney temporarily banned liquor sales and the carrying of weapons countywide.[52]

Over at city hall, McCree worked with the county prosecutor and with civil rights activists such as Willie Nolden Jr., father of future city councilman BB Nolden, to arrange a deal. All 102 people arrested the first night would be released on the condition that they persuade others to stop the violence.[53] It was a controversial move, but it worked. Almost all the people who left jail kept their promise, according to the *Detroit Free Press*, returning "to the streets on foot and in cars, using loudspeakers to amplify their calls for peace." The unrest cooled after about two days. No injuries were reported.

Things were much worse in Detroit, where, that same week, the urban crisis of the 1960s crescendoed. A police raid at an illegal after-hours club full of black patrons—Vietnam veterans, a homecoming party—escalated into a street confrontation that morphed into a riot. Thousands of federal troops arrived, intervening in an American city for the first time in a generation.[54] Local reporters rode in a military tank to track the story. Detroit's landscape was permanently changed with the destruction of 2,509 buildings.[55] Forty-three people were killed, mostly African Americans, over five brutal days. As the UPI news service put it, the Detroit battle was "the bloodiest and most costly Negro turmoil in modern U.S. history."[56]

Besides Flint and Detroit, there were insurrections in about eighty different cities that week. New York, Chicago, Toledo, Phoenix, South Bend, Cincinnati, San Francisco, Philadelphia, and Minneapolis were among them. In Michigan alone, violence (in some cases minor and short-lived) also flared up in Kalamazoo, Grand Rapids, Saginaw, Mount Clemens, Muskegon, Benton Harbor, River Rouge, Ecorse, Highland Park, Albion, and Pontiac, where two people were killed, both African American, one who was shot by a state legislator.[57] Typical language described the chaos as being instigated by "young Negro rowdies."[58]

As the fires cooled, President Lyndon B. Johnson took to national television. "My fellow Americans," he said solemnly. "We have endured a week such as no nation should live through: a time of violence and tragedy." The only solution, Johnson declared, "lies in an attack—mounted at every level—upon the conditions that breed despair and violence."[59]

To accomplish this, Johnson created the National Advisory Commission on Civil Disorders, an eleven-member team led by Otto Kerner. It was a purposefully moderate and bipartisan group. Kerner was a former governor of Illinois and an army officer. New York City mayor John Lindsay, a liberal Republican, was the commission's vice chair. Other members included the Atlanta police chief, the head of the NAACP, and Senator Edward W. Brooke, the only African American member of the Senate. The Kerner Commission investigated what turned Watts and Detroit into searing emblems for American cities. After seven months of field studies, hearings, surveys, and research, they released their report on February 29, 1968—and it was a riveting account of how the poisonous belief in separatism was built into American cities.[60] If left to fester, it would ruin them.

> The events of the summer of 1967 are in large part the culmination of 300 years of racial prejudice. Most Americans know little of the origins of the racial schism separating our white and Negro citizens. Few . . . understand that today's problems can be solved only if white Americans comprehend the rigid social, economic and educational barriers that have prevented Negroes from participating in the mainstream of American life.[61]

Cities weren't roiling with unprecedented trauma, the report said; they were following a familiar script. Since slavery days and beyond, murderous violence had plagued settlements where African Americans tried to participate in civil society. In 1866 in Memphis, for example, white mobs led by police officers marched into the African American side of town and shot whomever they could find, including black Union soldiers, women, and children. No one was ever prosecuted. In the aftermath, many residents, both white and black, fled the city.[62]

The Great Migration forced the nation to confront the limits of a separate-but-equal society. In 1910, 91 percent of black people lived in the South, few of them in towns that had more than twenty-five hundred residents. By the time Floyd McCree became mayor of Flint, about one third lived in the country's twelve largest cities.[63] Although their moves north and west were fueled by the search for jobs, African Americans were more than twice as likely as whites to be unemployed, and black men were more than three times as likely to be in low-paying, unskilled, and dangerous jobs—such as the ones in the Buick foundry in Flint, where even the mayor worked.[64] This "policy of separation," as the *Kerner Report* described it, relegated black people to a "permanently inferior economic status" and undercut the myth that if impoverished European immigrants could transcend their ghettos, then so could African Americans.[65]

So much time, effort, and money went into making this divided society. The commission called for an equivalent investment into unmaking it. That included more investment in education, jobs, housing, and social services. "The vital needs of the Nation must be met; hard choices must be made, and, if necessary, new taxes enacted," they wrote.[66] They also asked us to push back against the trend of metropolitan sprawl around an emptying center by focusing "the interests of suburban communities on the physical, social, and cultural environment of the central city."[67]

More than 740,000 copies of the *Kerner Report* were sold, making it a bestseller.[68] It even outsold the Warren Commission's report on the assassination of President John F. Kennedy. It made headlines around the country, often provocative ones. "Suburbs Can Fight 'Country Divided'/Riot Report Points to You," read a lead story on March 17, 1968, in the *Roselle Register*, from a Chicago suburb. Civil rights leaders, including Martin Luther King Jr., applauded the report, and it so inspired the leader of the National Conference of Catholic Bishops, he ordered clergy to give sermons on combating racism.

But the report's fate was just as its authors feared: it was shelved.

Conservatives disliked it because they felt it diminished the individual responsibility of rioters and underplayed, as one columnist put it, "an even more bloody-minded black racism" toward whites.[69] Leftists believed that it wasn't revolutionary enough; they had little faith in political solutions.[70] Governors disavowed it. George Romney in Michigan, who had only recently dropped his presidential campaign, opposed the creation of big government programs. Georgia governor Lester Maddox argued that the cause of the riots "isn't racism, it's Communism, I know it is."[71]

And Lyndon Johnson himself kept quiet. His press secretary offered only a bland statement: "The President wants to do everything he can in this field, and the report will be very carefully considered."[72] Later accounts suggested that the president believed the commission had called for an impossible federal investment at a time when the nation was at war in Vietnam, and that it didn't give enough credit to the Great Society reforms of his administration.

In any case, soon after the *Kerner Report*'s release, Johnson announced that he would not run for reelection. Less than a week later, the murder of Martin Luther King Jr. instigated no small amount of civil disorder in about a hundred cities. A few months later, Robert Kennedy was killed after winning the California Democratic primary. The Vietnam War churned on with sickening brutality, and in Chicago police officers attacked demonstrators at the Democratic National Convention. Against this turmoil, the *Kerner Report* faded into the noise. And when Richard Nixon won the presidency in November, it cued a new era of law-and-order politics. As political historian Julian E. Zelizer wrote, urban policy was replaced by "the war on crime and the war on drugs."[73]

III.

The unrest in Flint had quieted by July 27, the same day that President Johnson's speech was broadcast on national television. The City Commission soon agreed to vote on a fair housing ordinance, one that included penalties for violators and a process to investigate complaints.[74]

On the day of the vote, Mayor Floyd McCree spoke to his fellow members of the commission and pled for justice. His father had fought in World War I, he said. He and his brothers fought in World War II. Other McCree family members fought in the Korean and Vietnam Wars. "Yet today," he said, "those persons we fought to preserve democracy [for] can come to Flint and buy a house wherever they wish. But members of the Negro race cannot do so, simply because of the color of their skin. I hope this city commission has the guts to pass this ordinance."[75]

Three commissioners voted for it, five against. Housing discrimination was still legal.

With tears in his eyes, McCree resigned in protest. "Last November this city commission saw fit to make me mayor and that was fine all over the country, very wonderful. I thought here at last we have a local government willing to accept people on the basis of their ability and not because of race. And I have lived with this and I have preached this to my community. Tonight, however, I've changed my mind. I'm not going to sit up here any longer and live an equal opportunity lie."[76]

At least sixteen other city workers backed him up, saying that if McCree was leaving, they were too. Soon after the vote, McCree was admitted to the hospital for a stomach ulcer and exhaustion. His cousin Woody Etherly Jr. visited him. During their talk, Etherly came up with a big idea—a sleep-in on the lawn of city hall. Before long, young people had set up camp and said that they would not leave until the commission reconsidered the ordinance. "Amazingly, all the networks came," Etherly said.[77] "And we came in with our little sleeping bags and stuff. We went down to city hall and began to spread our sleeping bags and the city cut on the [lawn sprinklers] and were up on the roof with their guns looking down on us."

Flint's housing demonstration made national news. More supporters showed up. Over ten days, about two hundred people took part in the sleep-in, and nearly five thousand people supported them and the mayor with a unity rally, including Governor George Romney.

Someone made eggs and pancakes for the demonstrators to eat at breakfast.

The ground shifted. The commission agreed to take up housing once again. McCree returned to the mayor's office and began working on a new policy. In October, he was victorious when a fair housing ordinance, albeit a watered-down one, narrowly passed.[78]

But even then the fight wasn't over. Within minutes of the vote, opponents took up a petition to repeal it. The Committee to Repeal Forced Housing Legislation included at least fifty Ku Klux Klan members and was led by a member of the John Birch Society. With nearly six thousand signatures, the bid to overturn fair housing got on the ballot. The new ordinance was suspended until the vote. An interracial group worked to defend it, including McCree, who took a leave of absence from his job at the Buick foundry to campaign.

At the time, the housing question was tormenting cities all over the country. When Mayor Henry Maier of Milwaukee testified to the Kerner Commission, he spoke plainly: "There is a system of apartheid confining the poor and the Negro to the city." Maier warned that core cities could not "long endure within a segregated metropolis."[79]

On February 20, 1968, more than forty thousand Flint residents voted on whether to repeal the policy of allowing people to live where they chose, no matter the color of their skin. By a hairsbreadth margin—just thirty votes—repeal was denied. Fair housing won.

"I'm overwhelmed by the decision but the people of Flint should take the credit," said McCree, after the final vote tally came through.[80]

This was a big deal. Flint was first in the nation to support fair housing by popular vote. Similar votes failed in Seattle, Berkeley, Toledo, Akron, and Tacoma, and the U.S. Congress had been dragging its feet on a federal fair housing law for ages.[81] It seemed to be going nowhere until after Martin Luther King Jr.'s death; as cities exploded in anger and sorrow, the legislation was fast-tracked. The fires had scarcely ceased in the nation's capital when the Fair Housing Act finally passed.

For Flint, though, the fair housing victory was bittersweet. The city's population had already begun to slip. Along with school desegregation, the new housing laws accelerated the exodus as mostly white people left the city. Two years after the adoption of the ordinance, the Census marked Flint's first ever drop in population. It happened in other cities, too. In the years following the groundbreaking civil rights laws and U.S. Supreme Court decisions, residential segregation in America effectively increased as people found novel ways of dividing themselves up. In the early seventies, a federal civil rights commission concluded that "the zeal with which Federal officials carried out policies of discrimination" decades earlier "has not been matched by a similar enthusiasm" in carrying out fair housing policies.[82]

Most people who left Flint could cite rational reasons for doing so: they simply wanted to make the best investment for themselves and their families. And, indeed, they were often rewarded with better housing values and, increasingly, better schools and public services. There was also more green space and less congestion. The suburbs were set up to succeed. After explicitly racist housing policies became illegal, many of them retained their relative homogeneity with new exclusionary policies: bans on multifamily housing, minimum square footage requirements, and refusal to accept affordable housing vouchers. Proposed developments that would make a community more integrated were sometimes shot down on the grounds that they would overtax the water and sewer systems.[83] George Romney, the governor who became an ally of Mayor McCree, went on to lead the Department of Housing and Urban Development in Washington. He described urban sprawl as a "high-income white noose" around black cities, and proposed withholding federal money for redevelopment projects, including sewer and water, in exclusionary suburbs.[84] He acted on it, too, with some success. A Boston suburb, for example, agreed to proceed with a housing development so that HUD would release funds for a water project. But Romney's strategy was controversial— he needed a police escort to exit a public forum in a Detroit suburb— and Richard Nixon's administration eventually brought his efforts to a halt.

White people who stayed in Flint were essentially punished. The worth of their homes tumbled. Even those who may have morally resisted what was happening in their city would have a hard time staying when their children's inheritance seemed threatened.[85] The other side of the coin was that when a black family purchased a home, its worth dropped the moment they signed their papers. Black families therefore could not build financial stability that secured their retirements and legacies for their children in the same way that white families generally could. And, in this self-fulfilling spiral, their houses generated less money in property taxes, which meant fewer resources to invest in schools and infrastructure. African American neighborhoods were "objectively" worth less, setting up the cold, contextless accounting that led state and city officials to select St. John as the community to demolish when it built freeways in the 1960s, and Floral Park to displace with a highway interchange.[86] It was just economics.

Saturation

Thousands have lived without love; not one without water.

—W. H. Auden, "First Things First" (1957)

I.

The General Motors engine plant sprawled over 1.2 million square feet, a long, white, windowless expanse of modern industry on West Bristol Road in Flint. It was filled with about eight hundred workers, most of them making hourly wages, who built engines for the Chevrolet Cruze and the Chevrolet Volt.[1] They needed about seventy-five thousand gallons of water a day to do the job. But in the summer of 2014, workers noticed that rust was forming on engine crankshafts and blocks. Suspecting that Flint's new water supply was causing the problem, GM experimented with a costly reverse osmosis technique to purify it. The company also tried diluting it with water from Detroit that it brought in on semi-trucks. But nothing worked.

In October, a little more than a month after three boil-water advisories swept Flint, GM announced a water switch of its own. It made a deal to buy Lake Huron water from the neighboring suburb of Flint Township. This was one of the communities that had also joined the

Karegnondi Water Authority but still used water from the Detroit Water and Sewerage Department until the new system was ready.

For all the diminishment of GM in the city where it was born, it was still Flint's largest employer and one of its biggest taxpayers.[2] The engine plant's switch would cost Flint about $400,000 in water revenue per year. But GM promised that it would return to the city system once the KWA was in operation. Two other GM facilities in Flint, an assembly plant and a stamping plant, both of which used less water, remained on the city system.

The city needed to give permission for the deal to go through, and under the authority of emergency manager Darnell Earley that was done without much hassle. But some council members worried that the change would incite a panic. They wondered whether the company's move would prompt other businesses to leave the system. Seventh Ward councilwoman Monica Galloway said she had the uncomfortable feeling that by remaining on river water that was unsuitable for GM, "we are like guinea pigs. It's like a research project" of the kind that would normally be done "on rats."

The headlines—"General Motors Shutting off Flint River Water at Engine Plant over Corrosion Worries"—did indeed trigger alarm.[3] The day she heard the news, Jan Burgess, a legally blind homeowner in her early sixties, complained to the EPA through its website.[4] "People in Flint have had to resort to buying bottled water or having purification systems installed in their homes," Burgess wrote. Some had private wells dug. "The water is not safe to drink, cook, or wash dishes with, or even give to pets. We worry every time we shower. The City of Flint is still very economically depressed and most citizens cannot afford to do anything other than use the river water."

The anxiety reverberated all the way to the state capital, Lansing, where Governor Rick Snyder was weeks away from winning reelection to a second term. His chief legal counsel, Michael Gadola, wrote in an email: "To anyone who grew up in Flint as I did, the notion that I would be getting my drinking water from the Flint River is downright scary. Too bad the [emergency manager] didn't ask me what I thought, though I'm sure he heard it from plenty of others. My Mom is a City resident. Nice to know she's drinking water with elevated chlorine levels and fecal coliform. . . . They should try to get back on the Detroit system as a stopgap ASAP before this thing gets too far out of control."[5]

But that didn't happen. Darnell Earley argued that it would be too expensive and that any problems at the plant were fixable. He had no expertise in water treatment, of course; he was relying on people such as Mike Prysby, the district engineer for the Michigan Department for Environmental Quality. Like a ringmaster improvising as the set goes up in flames, Prysby assured everyone that there was no need for worry. While rust was spreading like a stain on GM's machinery, probably due to high chloride levels in the water, Prysby said the chlorides were well within public safety regulations. He reported measurements that showed the chlorides at less than a quarter of the amount that would be legally unacceptable.[6] So Prysby urged everyone to avoid "branding Flint's water as 'corrosive' from a public health standpoint, simply because it did not meet a manufacturing facility's limit for production."

Over at Kettering University, a GM representative happened to visit the campus. Mechanical engineering professor Laura Sullivan seized the opportunity to ask about the company's water switch. She was informed that the corrosion had appeared because the plant recycled its water four or five times. "After we've used it," she remembered being told, "we run it back through a few times. And it really is only a problem on the last run through because it's gotten concentrated." Concentrated, that is, because with every use, some of the water is lost as steam. This made sense to Sullivan. She reported back to her friends and colleagues who were wondering if it was safe to drink from the tap. "They're running [the water] through their machines four times," she advised them. "I mean, obviously that's not the same as what you're drinking. I really think it's fine."[7]

Whatever the reason for the rust, GM workers were unsettled. They didn't just use the water for manufacturing. They had used it to brew coffee and wash their hands, take showers, and sip something cool when they were thirsty. Even after the plant went back to Detroit water, many workers lived in the city, or they had family and friends who did. When they visited a downtown restaurant, their glasses were filled with tap water and crackling ice. At school, their children sipped from the drinking fountains. Over at the UAW, members were beginning to ask, "If it's too corrosive for an engine, what's it doing to the inside of a person?"[8]

II.

On a January evening in 2015, cold enough to make your eyes water, hundreds of people packed into the fellowship hall of Antioch Missionary Baptist Church, a large brown building less than a mile from the Flint River. It was standing room only. Some folks kept their winter jackets and their stocking caps on. Mayor Dayne Walling was there, as well as public works director Howard Croft, state representative Sheldon Neeley, and members of the City Council. They settled in to hear the stories of their constituents, some of whom shook with anger or wept. Only hours before the meeting, there had been another protest downtown, one of several in the past week. Winter weather seemed to deter no one from outdoor demonstrations. People needed to be seen.

The situation was getting murkier. The MDEQ had just informed the city that its water violated the federal limit for total trihalomethanes, or TTHMs. This is a group of four colorless, odorless chemical compounds that are a by-product of the chlorine disinfection process. (This was also what the governor's legal counsel was referring to months earlier when he mentioned "elevated chlorine levels" in his exasperated email message.) When ingested over many years, TTHMs can increase the risk of cancer and cause liver, kidney, and nervous system problems. It was a violation of the Safe Drinking Water Act, and so, as required by law, a notice was mailed to Flint residents on January 2.[9] They were told that steps were being taken to fix the problem, including the installation of a TTHM monitor and a charcoal filter at the treatment plant. "This is not an emergency," the notice repeated several times. If it had been, the city would've been required to notify residents within twenty-four hours. At the same time, though, the elderly and people with compromised immune systems were advised to talk to their doctor about drinking the water.

This satisfied no one. Coming after GM said the water wasn't good enough for making engines, it was especially upsetting. Business at local restaurants was down—people seemed nervous about eating food cooked with city water. The manager of a popular Mexican restaurant said that he'd lost about a quarter of his clientele. Customers yelled at waiters or left handfuls of change as tips because they didn't like paying extra for bottled water when the tap water was compromised. Hospitals stocked up on bottled water to treat specialized equipment that, like the GM machinery, had not fared well. The executive chef for Flint's public schools had long since started buying gallons of water in bulk for the food served to students.[10] People traded hair-raising stories. Corodon Maynard, a twenty-year-old who lived on Flint's east side, said that a few hours after he drank two glasses of water, he was retching over a toilet. "I was throwing up like bleach water. It came up through my nose burning," he told a reporter.[11] Cancer survivor Bethany Hazard spotted brown rust circles around her drains and an inexplicable oily film in her bathwater. Her cats were sick. Her houseplant was on its deathbed. Residents pushed bottles of ugly water into officials' faces. "Look!" they said. "Look!"

There were whispers of a lawsuit. One woman started the Flint Water Class Action Group on Facebook, which quickly attracted more than thirteen hundred members and would grow well beyond that. Activists in the Democracy Defense League, which had been formed to oppose emergency management, announced their own investigation. The league had already begun holding bottled water drives, but now it planned to host neighborhood workshops about how residents could challenge "plummeting water quality, soaring water rates," and "alleged water theft," which referred to the arrest and prosecution of people who set up illicit connections after their water service had been turned off for unpaid bills.

Under the dull fluorescent lights at Antioch Missionary Baptist, more disturbing stories were added to the record. Qiana Dawson said that her children, ages four and two, were breaking out in rashes and her doctor's bills were way up. LeeAnne Walters, a sharp-eyed woman with long, dark hair, worried about similar skin problems on one of her sons, a three-year-old with a compromised immune system.[12] Councilman Eric Mays, who called the meeting, framed the problem bluntly. "The water is bad," he said, "and if you buy a bad product, you return it for a refund. While researchers try to figure out the Flint water, we should turn the Detroit water back on," Mays said. The room exploded in applause.

This was possible. The day before the meeting, Sue McCormick, director of the DWSD, wrote to Mayor Walling and Darnell Earley, offering them a deal. We "take very seriously the matter of drinking water quality," she wrote with an overabundance of sedate professionalism, "and we are as concerned as you must be by the continued quality issues faced by the city and the concerns expressed by your citizens."[13] She presented the city with "a solution for reliable, safe, high quality water on an expeditious timeline." If Flint signed a long-term contract, the DWSD would waive the reconnection fee, estimated at $4 million. Flint could return to the terms of its old contract, though it would be revised to reflect the 4 percent price increase that had gone into effect for wholesale customers the previous summer. The DWSD, McCormick wrote, was "ready, willing, and able" to resume services to Flint immediately "if you so desire."

But going back to Detroit water was too costly, Earley insisted at the church meeting, even if the reconnection fee was waived, and especially if it required a lengthy contract. The DWSD's rates could rise again as soon as July, and Flint would be right back where it was before, fighting a hopeless battle against expensive water over which it had essentially no local control. Besides, the terms of Flint's contract with the KWA were unusually punishing. Not only would the millions of dollars spent on upgrades for the treatment plant be for naught, but if Flint left the KWA, it would still be on the hook for 30 percent of its costs—about $85 million of a $300 million project. That translated into seven-figure annual bond payments. If Flint missed a single one, the KWA could seize the city's treatment plant, plus 25 percent of its state revenue-sharing money. It could also get its share of the money by forcing Flint to levy a tax. Basically, Flint was paying for the KWA either way, so it was best to stick with it.

While the city "can ill-afford to switch course," Earley said, he promised to hire a consultant to correct the troublesome water treatment.[14] That would end up being Veolia, an enormous multinational company that prides itself as being "the world's leading provider of environmental solutions."[15] Mayor Walling, too, said that he preferred investing in the city's "own system at the treatment plant and on fixing older pipes throughout Flint," rather than going back to the DWSD and "paying their premium." Still, as Walling wrote on social media and in a letter to Governor Rick Snyder, Flint needed more water testing; lowered bills; elimination of reconnection fees for those who had been cut off; and millions in state or federal funds to improve the aging infrastructure. He also wanted assistance for people whose doctors advised them to stop drinking the city water.[16] At the same time, the Flint River was cleaner now than it had been in years. The state environmental experts were certain that it was safe. He and his family continued to drink city water.

A week after the gathering at the church, there was another meeting about the water, this time in the domed auditorium of city hall. A panel of experts spoke to a crowd of about 150, some of whom had tucked bottles of discolored water in their bags and coat pockets.[17] "Is there a risk in the short-term?" the MDEQ's Stephen Busch asked attendees.[18] "That depends on you . . . it's an individual thing. You can make a judgment after talking to your doctor." At the same time, Busch said that the water was both good to drink and improving. In other words, the water isn't a risk to your health—unless it is. Furious people shouted back. Others walked out in frustration. One woman reportedly tugged down part of her pants to show the authorities the red rash on her buttocks.[19] Before answering all the questions submitted in writing, Howard Croft, the public works director, brought the unruly meeting to an end.

The city trumpeted an offer to provide free water tests to anyone who requested one. Croft called it one-on-one civil service. The city would learn what was going on in individual homes, which was important because the complaints did not sync with the current results. And residents could learn about the different factors that affect water quality. But by now, the tension in Flint had reached such a feverish pitch that famed activist Erin Brockovich was weighing in on Facebook. Flint was one of "hundreds" of cities and towns whose community water systems are failing, she wrote. "Bottom line, they have made many bad choices . . . yet [there] are real solutions." In the meantime, it was a fog of "EXCUSES . . . EXCUSES . . . EXCUSES."[20]

In mid-January, not long before the meeting in the city hall dome, Jerry Ambrose became Flint's new emergency manager, effectively filling in the tail end of Earley's term after Earley accepted a job as the EM of Detroit's public schools.[21] Ambrose had been serving as finance director, so he was quite familiar with the water struggles. He picked up where his predecessor left off. Ambrose agreed that there were insurmountable barriers to reconnecting with Detroit, including the fact that the city no longer had a direct line to the Detroit system. Earley had sold a critical nine-mile section of transmission pipe to Genesee County the previous year for $3.9 million.[22] The county used it for its own drinking water.[23]

Ambrose believed that the city handled the TTHM crisis as well as could be expected. Flint had surpassed the legal limit for carcinogenic TTHMs in May, August, and November of the previous year, but it didn't alert residents until January because it was legally required to announce only a high annual average. The first notice was sent nine months after the initial violation. Ambrose defended the delay at a public meeting. In a neat suit and tie, speaking into a microphone, he gestured before a restless crowd. "When we knew, we started immediately to address the problem," he said.[24]

"Without telling the public!" said Claire McClinton. The distinctive voice of the leader of the Democracy Defense League rose above the chorus of rumblings.

Ambrose's face hardened. "We're telling you now."

In the midst of this standoff, the State of Michigan made a quiet but revealing change: installing new water coolers in its Flint offices and supplying them with cases of bottled water. State employees were spared from drinking Flint's tap water. "While the City of Flint states that corrective actions are not necessary," a notice to the staff of one state department said, we are "in the process of providing a water cooler on each occupied floor, positioned near the water fountain, so you can choose which water to drink. The coolers will . . . be provided as long as the public water does not meet treatment requirements."[25] So, while one state department told residents that the water was safe to drink, another doubted it enough that it, like General Motors, preferred to pay for a new supply.

In early February, Governor Snyder announced a $2 million grant to hire a consultant to find leaky water lines and to replace Flint's wastewater incinerator. The old facility, which cleaned the city's wastewater before discharging it into the river, no longer met environmental standards. The money came from a program for financially distressed communities, and Flint's award was the maximum sum allowed.[26] But Dayne Walling thought Flint needed at least $50 million over the next six years to fix the plant and the pipes. The grant, he said, was "a down payment" on the state's responsibility to provide safe, clean water to an emergency-managed city. Flint needed more. As Sheldon Neeley, its state representative, wrote in a letter to the governor, people "are on the verge of civil unrest."[27]

III.

BB Nolden gave up. The ex–city councilman and now Genesee County commissioner bought his water from the grocery store. It took about eight gallons a week for all the cooking, cleaning, teeth brushing, and drinking. He still needed to shower in the city water, so he began using a large amount of lotion to soothe his dry, irritated skin. "It's extremely trying," Nolden said later.[28] "It's time inhibitive. . . . I used the bottle water for everything."

Not everyone in Flint was having the same experience. Some saw an orange or brown tinge in their water when they filled their sinks, but in other homes, including the one where Laura Sullivan lived in southwestern Flint, among historic mansions from the city's twentieth-century heyday, the taps ran perfectly clear. Some had water with a distinct chlorinated odor or the smell of rotten eggs; others did not. From the city's perspective, tests showed that the water was safe when it left the plant. Its supervising agency, the MDEQ, agreed. Discoloration happened when the water sat too long in the oversized pipes that crisscrossed a landscape with long stretches of vacancy. The city tried to help where it could by flushing the hydrants, but there was only so much it could do to keep the water moving when the infrastructure was built for twice the population. In the meantime, discoloration and odors, in and of themselves, did not mean that the water was bad.[29] And as for all the horror stories—rashes, hair loss, nausea, and worse—they were just anecdotes. Distressing, to be sure, but no one had proved beyond a doubt that it was the water causing their problems. It could have been anything. Maybe even just bad luck.

This was partly right. The contamination was indeed worse when the water sat stagnant for too long. But the contradictory reports were not random: they more or less followed the pattern of inequality that dated back to Flint's development as a segregated city. People who lived on streets that were pockmarked with the most unoccupied homes and empty storefronts—that is, the poorest of them—generally had worse water. People who lived in denser areas were less likely to see, taste, or smell the same problems.

But there was some good news. Early tests in 2015 showed that the TTHMs in the water had dropped to an acceptable level.[30] "Possible causes and corrective measures" had been identified, a city notice claimed, although it didn't offer an explanation for what had caused the problem in the first place.[31] The suspect seemed to be over-chlorination. Since the treatment plant didn't have an activated carbon filter, and river water had so much organic matter, chlorine had been used excessively to disinfect the water. The city said that getting a filter was now a priority.[32]

For people working for Flint's revitalization, there were plenty of other demands on their attention. BB Nolden asked Mayor Walling for the keys to the old Berston Field House in north Flint, which had fallen into neglect. After years of doing what he could by opening the doors "just to give the kids something to do," multiyear grant support came through. As volunteer director, Nolden led Berston's revival, programming it with everything from ballet to boxing—and doing it much more inclusively than the old days, when its segregated pool was notorious. Meanwhile, the city planning commission adopted a five-year framework to deal with decrepit properties. "Beyond Blight" was developed with help from more than two dozen community groups as a data-driven strategy to eliminate blight in every neighborhood. That included about 22,000 houses, commercial buildings, and vacant lots—more than one third of all the properties in Flint.[33] Of those, about 5,500 needed to be demolished, mostly houses; another 5,000 were to be boarded; and 850 houses were to be rehabilitated. That, plus better property code enforcement and maintenance, would vastly improve the quality of life. The plan would cost more than $100 million to implement. Until it was funded, volunteers would sign up to plant clover on vacant lots and mow the lawns of thousands of empty properties. It was a start.

Elsewhere, Chevy in the Hole, a former GM manufacturing complex that had become a ruin, got new life. Once the setting for the sit-down strike in the 1930s, it would be transformed into a park along the Flint River with wetlands, woodlands, walking paths, and native plants. It would get a new public-spirited name: Chevy Commons. In preparation for the redevelopment, led by the county land bank and funded by a federal grant, thousands of trees were planted to remove contaminants from the soil. And over at the historic ice rink on Lapeer Road, once the home of the popular minor-league Flint Generals, the Ontario Hockey League announced the name of a new team that it was bringing to the city. After a contest that drew four thousand submissions, the league picked the Firebirds as the team mascot. "Flint is a community that has been built and sustained on the fierce resilience of its residents, and we see the Firebird as a symbol of that resilience," the team president said in a press release. "Flint has pulled through a difficult journey, and is now standing on the verge of great potential and promise."[34]

Yet, all along, the water complaints kept coming. On February 4, LeeAnne Walters showed the City Council a video of the rashes on her young son's skin. And over at the Chicago office of the EPA, Jennifer Crooks was getting an earful. "Let me tell you, this Flint situation is a nasty issue," she wrote in an email. "I've had people call me 4 letter words over the phone, yell at me and call me a crook. I'm developing a thick skin."[35] Two days later, she called the complaints "ticking time bombs."

In March, the City Council voted to "do all things necessary to reconnect to the Detroit Water and Sewerage Department."[36] But emergency manager Jerry Ambrose was the only one with the power to act, and he disagreed, calling the vote "incomprehensible": a switch back would cost more than $12 million a year. Touching on the long-simmering anger over high rates, he claimed that "water from Detroit is no safer than water from Flint. Users also pay some of the highest rates in the state because of the decreased numbers of users and the age of the system." What's more, Ambrose told yet another crowd at yet another meeting, the DWSD had forced the city to switch to the Flint River. "It was Detroit that sent us a letter that said, 'We're canceling your contract. Go find your water someplace else.' All right?"[37] He was referring to a pro forma letter the DWSD had sent when Flint signed the KWA contract. But he failed to mention that Detroit had made repeated offers to restore service, which had been rejected, and that many Genesee County communities, also without an active contract, were still using Detroit water until the KWA was ready.

Ambrose was a month away from leaving office. Governor Snyder would soon announce that the financial disaster in Flint was over and that the city would return to the leadership of its elected mayor and council. Flint would still have to report to a state receivership board, though, for an indefinite length of time, and it was customary for EMs to bar their decisions from being overturned for at least a year after their term finished. However, Flint still had a deficit of about

$7 million. Ambrose and the Michigan treasurer resolved it with a last-minute emergency loan. The loan came with a provision that blocked the city from switching its water supply or lowering rates without state approval. A return to Detroit water was impossible.[38]

When it came to safe drinking water, then, people had to fend for themselves. It was a far cry from the spirit of collectivity that once built the infrastructure of American cities. It was more like the early days when citizens were expected to dig their own wells, even if they drained their neighbor's well as they did so.

This is what an atomized approach to urban life looked like. A GM plant trying to treat water on its own, and then trucking it in from elsewhere, before finally giving up and contracting with another municipality for its water supply. The State of Michigan distributing water coolers to its offices in Flint, even as its environmental department told residents that the water was fine. Parents left to make judgment calls about whether there was a connection between the river water and the health ailments that befell their families.

Residents did their best to look out for each other. A Head Start program spent some of its limited money to buy bottled water for small children. Volunteer groups held water giveaways around town. Flint Strong, a group that promotes the city, distributed two hundred cases in just thirty minutes. Local churches, charities, and a United Auto Workers chapter delivered shrink-wrapped cases of water out of their offices, where residents lined up in snowy, single-digit weather to receive them.[39] One day in January, Absopure Water Corporation sent a semi-truck to downtown Flint. With the help of Flint Strong and a local Realtors association, it handed out about two thousand free cases of water. A resident who was in the queue, a fifty-three-year-old man, told a reporter that he was there because the water in his home smelled like bleach and upset his stomach. "I love Flint, but they're treating us like dirt," he said.[40]

The town's biggest institutions were also on their own, trying to figure out how to care for their communities. After the TTHM notice, the University of Michigan–Flint, Kettering University, and Mott Community College hired consultants to test their water.[41] "Our large student body ranges from teenagers to seniors and includes those with disabilities and other health issues," a Mott spokesperson explained to the *Flint Journal*. "While we still believe that city water is safe for the vast majority, it is essential that everyone make an informed decision as to how they should respond."

One of UM–Flint's earliest tests showed a new problem. It wasn't bacteria, or discoloration, or odor, and it wasn't TTHMs. This time it was lead.

On Friday, February 6, 2015, the university delivered news of "an elevated lead concentration." Most of the campus water tested as safe, but high lead was found in two fountains in two separate buildings. The university's email offered an assurance based on a testing loophole, one that is so often abused nationwide it is often misunderstood as a best practice. As the email described it, "after water was flushed/purged through the fixtures," lead was either undetectable in the samples or they were below the legal threshold for drinking water, "with only one exception." It was unclear if the water was flushed immediately before collecting a sample—allowing the water to flow for a while before filling a container—or if it was flushed the night before, but either way, it's a tactic that artificially lowers the lead levels. It makes the water seem safer than it is.

UM–Flint updated its water fixtures and added filters at the two points with high lead.[42] It posted signs that read, "Do Not Use/Water Sampling in Progress" in other places and continued to conduct tests.

But on campus and across the city, all these efforts were stopgap solutions. They were certainly no use to people such as LeeAnne Walters. Her children were getting sicker by the day, and she had had enough.

PART II

DIVINATION

Alchemy

The obligation to endure gives us the right to know.

—Jean Rostand, as quoted by
Rachel Carson, *Silent Spring* (1962)

I.

LeeAnne Walters couldn't figure out where the rashes were coming from. Her whole family had them, but on different parts of their bodies. Her husband, a naval reservist named Dennis, had rashes on the sides of his stomach and inner thighs. Kaylie, her oldest, had them between her fingers and toes and under her breasts. JD, her fourteen-year-old son, had them on his chin, the backs of his legs, and under his arms. They were on LeeAnne's chin as well, and on her upper chest, and also behind her knees. And the three-year-old twins, Gavin and Garrett, were streaked with red on their hands, feet, and buttocks. While some of the rashes were scaly, itchy, and burning, others were raised bumps. Either way, they seemed to be getting worse. There were various diagnoses from the pediatrician—scabies, perhaps, or contact dermatitis, or maybe eczema. But when the family celebrated Kaylie's high school graduation in August 2014 with a pool party at their home on Browning Avenue, everybody who emerged from the water had angry red blotches on their skin.[1]

The hair loss started in the fall. Kaylie lost clumps of her long brown hair. The hairdresser whom LeeAnne had been seeing for years noticed thin patches and asked if she was sick. LeeAnne's eyelashes fell out. They never quite grew back right, so, feeling self-conscious, she began to wear fake ones.[2] Meanwhile, the twins complained of aches and pains. The two little ones had developed in tandem their whole lives, but now Gavin, who had a compromised immune system, slowed down. He stopped gaining weight and sometimes seemed unable to pronounce words that his mother was sure he knew.[3] Then, around Thanksgiving, JD complained of abdominal pain so severe that he struggled to walk. He missed school and ended up in the hospital. JD's father lived on the west side of the state, near the Lake Michigan shore, and JD was supposed to visit him over the Christmas break, but since he'd been so sick, there was a lot of discussion about whether or not this was a good idea. "We just didn't understand what was happening," LeeAnne remembered.[4] JD did end up going to see his father. As it happened, when he went out of town, his symptoms vanished.

LeeAnne didn't see connections among all these strange ailments until just after Christmas, when brown water spurted out of her tap. Not long after that, the TTHM notice arrived in her mailbox. And their whole-house water filter, which typically needed a new cartridge every six months, now filled so rapidly with particulates, it first needed a change every two to three weeks, and then every six to fourteen days. LeeAnne wanted to be a good mom—she encouraged her kids to drink water rather than juice or soda—but the tap now seemed like a threat. The family sought relief from their refrigerator filter, but then they stopped drinking water from their house altogether. LeeAnne also instituted a five-minute shower rule.[5]

In January 2015, she, Dennis, and Kaylie all went to the meeting at the city hall dome, bringing along plastic bottles of discolored water collected just one day earlier at their kitchen sink, each marked with the date and time. At the end of the rowdy gathering, as people were filing out of the room, LeeAnne and Kaylie worked their way to the front and showed the brown water to emergency manager Jerry Ambrose, holding the bottles by their fingertips, as if the contents were something gruesome.

That's not your water, she remembers Ambrose telling her. He didn't take the samples or inspect them closely. Nor did Mike Prysby of the Michigan Department of Environmental Quality, whom Lee-Anne remembers standing in the small knot of people around them, shaking his head. She didn't take kindly to the suggestion that she was a liar, and she and Ambrose got into a heated conversation. After the meeting, nobody followed up about the water at her house. It wasn't until February, after LeeAnne got a doctor's note about her son's compromised immune system, and how badly he seemed to be reacting to the water, that she was bumped to the top of a waiting list for the city to come to carry out a test.

Michael Glasgow, Flint's utilities administrator, came over on the morning of Wednesday, February 11. He inspected the plumbing in the kitchen, basement, and bathroom. He observed the sediment accumulating in the toilet, and, after removing the house filter, he collected samples of the water. About a week later, he delivered the results to LeeAnne. The iron levels were so high, they exceeded the limits of the testing instruments. It was the iron that had turned her water dark. And it prompted Glasgow to recommend a second test, this time for lead and copper. LeeAnne methodically followed the written instructions, which said that before she collected a sample, her water needed to sit stagnant for six to eight hours and be pre-flushed.

Not long after she submitted this new sample to the city, she got a frantic voice-mail message. Sounding very upset, Glasgow told her not to let anyone drink the water at her house, and specifically not to use it to make juice for her children. LeeAnne called back immediately after hearing the message, but it was after business hours; she couldn't get ahold of anyone at the Water Department. But the next morning, she was at his office. Glasgow walked her through the two-page lab report, marked with the logo of the MDEQ. Drinking water is expected to meet the standards of the national Lead and Copper Rule, which sets the federal action level at 15 parts of lead per billion parts of water (15 ppb). The lead levels in LeeAnne's water were about seven times higher than that—104 ppb. Glasgow told her that he "had never seen a number that high for lead."

What LeeAnne did next would change the course of the Flint water crisis. Going above the MDEQ to the EPA's District 5 office in Chicago, she reached a soft-spoken regulations manager in its drinking water division named Miguel Del Toral. He connected her with Marc Edwards, a civil and environmental engineering professor at Virginia Tech. Edwards had received a MacArthur "genius" grant in 2007 for his work on drinking water safety and deteriorating infrastructure. The citation highlighted his involvement in exposing a lead-in-water crisis in Washington, D.C., though Edwards remained aggrieved that his efforts had not won reparations for those who had absorbed toxic lead for years, not even an apology.

The alliance of these three would make a citizen scientist out of LeeAnne Walters and a detective out of Miguel Del Toral. For Marc Edwards, it was an opportunity to grasp at some kind of redemption.

II.

The old alchemists believed lead could be spun into gold. It was one of the base metals that men fiddled with for generations in fire-lit rooms, using the techniques of chemistry to transmute the elements of the earth. Back then, there was scarcely a difference between wizardry and science. Sir Isaac Newton, the force behind modern physics and calculus, was an alchemist, though he practiced it illegally and under fanciful pseudonyms, such as Jehovah Sanctus Unus, or Jehovah the Holy One.[6] For about three decades, he copied recipes in his notebook for the mythical philosopher's stone that was believed to be the key to curing ill health and transmuting metals. He riddled his language to keep the recipes secret by, for example, giving earthly elements the names of the gods. Iron became Mars, gold became Sol, and lead became Saturn, the ringed planet then believed to be at the farthest edge of the solar system. But for all the experimentation, lead persistently stayed lead.

Alchemists weren't the only ones who wished lead to be something it was not. A natural element found in the earth's crust, the bluish-gray metal isn't hard to extract from rocks. It often comes alongside lustrous silver, which was being mined anyway, so it was natural to look for ways to use it. Lead is soft enough to scratch with a fingernail, but it's dense and stable. It's malleable, durable, abundant, and far less vulnerable to oxidation than iron.[7] Lead pipes are flexible enough to bend through an underground landscape of tree roots and cellars, but sturdy enough to last a long time—two qualities that made lead popular in drinking water systems. Mixed with paint, lead gives a boost to the color, helping it to shine and stick. As part of a gasoline formula, it makes the engine run smoothly. But unlike some metals, such as copper and zinc, lead has zero health benefits. Indeed, it is toxic to humans, even to the point of death.

Because we found almost infinite uses for lead, we are exposed to it in an astonishing number of ways. Lead particles can be inhaled or ingested. People breathe in leaded dust, for example, in buildings where the paint is deteriorating or where disruptive repairs or rehab work is being done. It also comes through the drinking water that streams through lead pipes and plumbing fixtures, and it flakes off pretty ceramic dishes that are glazed with lead. People draw lead into their lungs when they inhale the exhaust of leaded gasoline, or while working in jobs where lead is handled, such as recycling, smelting, mining, or making stained glass and lead-acid batteries. Lead has been widely used for ammunition and fishing tackle.[8] Through certain lipsticks, eyeliners, and dyes, lead is painted onto our skin and hair.[9] Infants consume it by drinking baby formula made with contaminated water, or by sucking pacifiers coated with a thin fur of lead dust. A child might lick fingers or toys dirtied with leaded soil, or suck a sweet-tasting paint chip that peeled off a wall.

Children are most vulnerable to lead poisoning because their developing bodies absorb up to five times more lead than an adult from the same amount of exposure. Undernourished children who do not receive enough mineral nutrients absorb even more than that. Once in the bloodstream, lead disrupts the normal operation of a child's cells, particularly the way that they produce energy and communicate to the nervous system.[10] Lead accumulates in the teeth, bones, and soft tissues—the same places that collect calcium—which means that small, sustained exposures can build up to a severe amount of lead in the body.[11] This can cause brain swelling, fatigue, anemia, vomiting, abdominal pain, irritability, aggressive and antisocial behavior, slowed growth, hearing problems, learning disabilities, diminished IQ, reduced attention spans, kidney failure, seizures, coma, and, in extreme cases, death.[12] The Institute for Health Metrics and Evaluation, an independent research center at the University of Washington, estimates that about 494,550 deaths worldwide in 2015 can be attributed to lead exposure, mostly in low- and middle-income countries. It also estimated a loss of more than 9 million life years due to the long-term impact of lead.[13]

Adults are at risk from exposure, too. Lead can cause anemia, hypertension, joint and muscle pain, memory difficulties, headaches, mood disorders, kidney damage, low sperm counts, abnormal sperm, miscarriages, and stillbirths. During pregnancy, lead that has accumulated in a woman's bones is released, just like calcium. The calcium helps form the bones of the fetus, but lead can limit its development and cause premature birth.[14]

None of this is news. Written accounts of lead poisoning were first found on papyrus scrolls from Egypt, which go so far as to describe how the toxicity was sometimes exploited as a murder weapon. In the second century B.C.E., the Greek physician Dioscorides made the connection between lead exposure and its sickening results. "Lead makes the mind give way," he wrote.[15] Pliny the Elder described how lead poisoning was an occupational hazard of shipbuilding; a disproportionate number of workers suffered from the material that surrounded them. In the sixteenth century, the Swiss physician and alchemist Paracelsus investigated "the miner's disease," which was his name for an illness that was widespread among workers who inhaled metallic vapors—mercury and lead.[16] Bernardino Ramazzini, an Italian doctor in the early 1700s, described potters and tinsmiths who worked with the metal as becoming "paralytic, splenetic, lethargic, cachectic, and toothless, so that one rarely sees a potter whose face is not cadaverous and has the color of lead."[17] Artists who used lead paint—that includes Michelangelo, Francisco Goya, and Vincent van Gogh—were also vulnerable. White lead, otherwise known as lead carbonate, is a pure white color that mixes well with oil and brushes easily on a canvas.[18] Ramazzini noticed that of the many painters he knew, "almost all I found unhealthy. . . . If we search for the cause of the cachectic and colorless appearance of the painters, as well as the melancholy feelings that they are so often the victims of, we should look no further than the harmful nature of the pigments."[19] In a 1786 letter, Benjamin Franklin described the laborers in a London print shop as experiencing something he called "the dangles." Their wrists and feet drooped strangely.[20] An old worker advised Franklin, who was employed there, to stop drying cold cases of lead type by the fire, because "I might lose the Use of my Hands by it, as two of our Companions had nearly done."[21]

Fifty years after that, a researcher published a clinical description of lead poisoning in plumbers and white lead manufacturers, dubbing it "plumbism." (In fact, the words "plumbing" and "plumber" come from *plumbum*; the Latin name for lead is why it's represented as "Pb" on the periodic table.) Between 1875 and 1900, there were about 30,000 cases of reported lead poisoning in Utah alone, or about 1,200 per year in a territory that had not yet cracked 278,000 in total population.[22] In the early 1900s, women swallowed lead pills to induce abortions.[23]

But a sort of ideological alchemy set in. Despite being one of the world's best-known neurotoxins, lead was embraced by fast-developing nations. It was seen as nothing less than the key to their prosperity. Lead was built into the infrastructure of American cities such as Flint, lurking not only in the pipes that carried water, but also in the paint used in houses, businesses, hospitals, jails, train stations, and schools. It became part of the solder and brass fixtures in indoor plumbing, and it powered the automobiles that sped down the high-ways of a sprawling metro region. And yet no amount of lead expo-sure is safe. While its effects can be mitigated with good nutrition and health care, there is no known cure.

III.

Charles Kettering was a poor farm boy from Ohio who grew up to become one of the twentieth century's most imaginative inventors. A lanky, bespectacled man with dark, imploring eyes and protruding ears, he notched an even side part in his thinning hair for as long as he had hair enough to part. Kettering moved to Flint to become the head of research at General Motors, and then served as the company's vice president from 1920 to 1947. It was an exciting time to be at the company. By the end of the twenties, GM had introduced color and the annual model update to cars, and it had bested Ford as the nation's top automaker.[24] In keeping with the company's rise, Flint's population grew by more than 70 percent. Its percentage of African American residents doubled.[25]

"Ket," as his friends called him, invented the electric ignition in automobiles, which ended the unhappy era of starting cars with hand cranks. Among the 186 patents in his name, there is also the incuba-tor for premature infants, the electric cash register, the Freon refriger-ant that became standard in refrigerators and air conditioners, and the enamels and lacquers that were the first color paints on mass-produced automobiles. He also helped to found the famed Memorial Sloan Kettering Cancer Center in New York City. The cooperative university in Flint once known as the General Motors Institute is today called Kettering University, named in his honor. So is the town of Kettering, Ohio, a suburb of Dayton that grew dramatically in the postwar years when Daytonians fled the city for newer communities.

Kettering also helped develop leaded gasoline. It's made with something called tetraethyl lead, or TEL, and it successfully stopped the obnoxious engine knock that caused trouble for automobiles.

Vehicles ran better and at higher speeds. The fuel also burned more efficiently, which conserved petroleum. After many "noxious experiments which filled the laboratories with vile odors," as *Time* described it, the first gallon was sold at a Dayton service station in 1923. It was a technological triumph, but through car exhaust, it also put a known toxin into the air. Lead particulates settled into soil, onto waterways, and into lungs. Fumes were especially thick in cities that, like Flint, were both densely built and increasingly reengineered to favor automobiles through widened streets, ample parking lots, and a general dismantling and defunding of public transit systems. Only a year earlier, the League of Nations had recommended the banishment of white-lead paint for indoor use because of health concerns.[26]

Kettering wanted to avoid using the word "lead" in the commercial market, so the fuel was sold under the brand name Ethyl, eventually through a company that was developed as a partnership of the Dayton lab, DuPont, and Standard Oil.[27] But skeptics still slowed the march of progress. In response to queries from the surgeon general about the impact of TEL on public health, a DuPont executive said that while "no actual experimental data has been taken," the makers felt confident that it was safe. To support their case, the industrialists funded a study that would be conducted by the Bureau of Mines, the federal agency for scientific research at the time. The industrialists demanded—and the bureau largely accepted—extreme control over the results. The contract gave the makers of TEL not only the right to view and comment on the bureau's analysis, but also the right of final approval.[28] As the historians David Rosner and Gerald Markowitz have pointed out, the people who profited from leaded gasoline therefore had "veto power over the research of the United States government."[29]

And a lot was riding on this research. Lead was already injuring workers, just as it had injured Paracelsus's miners, Ramazzini's artists, and Benjamin Franklin's print shop colleagues. Five men died while making TEL at a Standard Oil plant in New Jersey in 1924. An additional thirty-five men who were exposed to the "odd gas," as the *New York Times* described it, experienced severe neurological symptoms that looked an awful lot like lead poisoning.[30] While the company's executives blamed the workers for, variously, working too hard, not being careful enough, or being physically unfit, the bleak fact was that exposure to TEL left forty of the plant's forty-nine workers either insane or dead.[31]

When journalists began to follow the thread on TEL, they found that at least two workers had died at GM's Dayton plant, along with another sixty who "became seriously ill with frightening symptoms of mania."[32] Four men had died at a DuPont plant in New Jersey, and more than three hundred others were poisoned.[33] Workers called the plant "the house of the Butterflies" because so many of them were hallucinating. They batted at the ghostly butterflies that fluttered before them but caught only fistfuls of air.

The distressing reports did little to inspire faith in TEL as a good way to power automobiles. New York City, Philadelphia, and other cities banned the sale of leaded gasoline outright, despite early findings from the Bureau of Mines that declared it to be safe—a conclusion roundly mocked by scientists and labor activists, not least because of the questionable independence of the research.[34] An internal memo at GM indicated that the company felt the rising public outrage to be "a deadly threat" to "the survival of the industry."[35]

The automaker would have the chance to defend itself when the surgeon general convened a national conference to discuss the future of leaded gasoline—or if it should have any future at all. It was May 1925, and while Ethyl Corporation had voluntarily suspended TEL production, it was prepared to fight for it.[36] The fortunes of the nation's most dominant industries were at stake. What exact amount of risk is acceptable for innovations that build the economy, the culture, and the great cities of America? Was the burden on TEL advocates to prove it harmless or on skeptics to prove it hazardous? How do you even measure the toxicity of lead without purposefully exposing human beings to its potential dangers? And what role do government and private industry have in keeping poisonous materials out of the environment in the first place?[37] Maybe they should stop bigfooting around people's lives, measuring out one persnickety rule after another as if they were spoonfuls of medicine. Maybe risk—and even some unquestionable losses of life and health—was the necessary cost of freedom and growth.

To attack these thorny questions, Charles Kettering brought in a formidable weapon: a thirty-year-old medical school graduate named Robert Kehoe. While on GM's dime, and alongside other titans of American business, Kehoe spent the next forty years delaying and defeating legislation that would put limits on environmental pollution in the United States. He was the architect of a monumental doubt strategy about lead that would later be mirrored by both the tobacco industry in the face of cancer concerns and fossil fuel companies in the face of climate change.

At the surgeon general's conference, Kettering opened by telling the story of TEL as a victory against clunky engines.[38] He and Kehoe both emphasized its potential to conserve fuel. Leaded gasoline was essential for civilization's progress, they argued. Any new development came with some new hazards—like automobiles themselves!—and this was no different. TEL was "an apparent gift of God," according to one of the Ethyl representatives at the table. And all those news reports of ghastly deaths and illnesses were inflated by the fact that workers did not follow instructions for the proper management of the material. As evidence, the industrialists cited ample research, all of which had been conducted on behalf of their own companies. GM vowed to tighten discipline. The minute a laborer showed signs of delirium, he'd be laid off. If he spilled TEL on himself, he'd be fired. That should scare workers into being more careful.

The skeptics made their case as well, but they were at a disadvantage. Epidemiological research—the kind that studies patterns of disease in groups of people—was in its infancy.[39] Early public health pioneers were still figuring out how to show, irrefutably, why certain illnesses spread. It is one thing to observe that people who live near a toxic chemical dump are twice as likely to get cancer, for example. It is quite another to prove that one specific person's cancer was caused by those specific chemicals, as opposed to any other variable or sheer chance. And with lead poisoning in particular, which develops slowly with cumulative exposure, it is difficult to present conclusive proof that lead itself, even in small amounts, is the problem.[40]

Kehoe and his peers exploited this research gap. They pointed out that not everyone exposed to lead got sick, and that the symptoms of lead poisoning look an awful lot like other diseases.[41] Those who were worried about lead's noxiousness might be spreading hysteria when it could all just be a misdiagnosis. They also shifted blame whenever possible. Kehoe, Kettering, and others insisted not only that laborers who got sick were at fault, but that if a child was poisoned it was probably because its parents were neglectful.

TEL was soon back on the market again, and thriving. And at the surgeon general's conference, Kehoe had established himself as the go-to national expert on lead. He used not only rhetoric to minimize the seriousness of exposure, but also his own industry-funded research. Kettering opened a lab for him at the University of Cincinnati's medical campus.[42] Any further occupational disasters for those working with TEL would be muted by the dominant narrative that came out of that lab. After conducting a number of tests on young male volunteers who ate leaded salts and sat in rooms filled with leaded exhaust, for example, Kehoe concluded that humans could absorb a certain amount of lead, and that most of what they ingested or inhaled was eliminated naturally.[43]

Decades later, a pioneering scientist named Clair Patterson would target Kehoe's research and show that a so-called normal amount of lead in the body wasn't natural, or harmless. It was simply common.[44] It would take a long time for that idea to gain widespread acceptance, not least because its implications were inconvenient. American society had been built around the idea that lead could be alchemized for everyday use.

By 1970, almost 90 percent of all gasoline sold had TEL in it.[45] Its production in the United States used more than 100,000 metric tons of lead every year.[46] Only four states and ten cities prohibited the indoor use of lead paint, and the number of Americans with lead poisoning was as high as 250,000. Patterson published a paper that showed how the amount of lead in the atmosphere of the Northern Hemisphere had risen 400 percent from the start of the Industrial Revolution in 1750 to 1930. It had grown an additional 350 percent between 1930 and 1965, with the use of leaded gasoline.

Lead was also widely used in the pipes and plumbing for drinking water systems. Some cities, such as Chicago, made it mandatory. It built 385,000 lead service lines into its foundation, more than any other city.[47] That means that they were 100 percent pure lead; unlike gasoline or paint, they were undiluted by other materials. Early on, people doubted whether it was wise to use lead in water systems—the Massachusetts State Board of Health urged localities to avoid lead pipes in 1890—but there were no regulations against them. In this pre–Clean Water Act era, even many professionals who were staunch foes of using lead in the built environment did not advocate for legislative involvement in its abatement. Meanwhile, the Lead Industries Association conducted a massive, multipronged campaign to promote the use of lead pipes. For decades, the LIA lobbied with "plumbers' organizations, local water authorities, architects and federal officials," according to researcher Richard Rabin, and it published "numerous articles and books that extolled the advantages of lead over other materials."[48]

It was a similar story for lead paint, which would become a plague for generations to come. The connection between lead paint and childhood poisoning was first made in 1904. Over the next couple of decades, twelve countries on four continents banned the interior use of such paint.[49] But the lead industry worked to defeat a regulatory movement in the United States. The figure of the Dutch Boy painter carrying a pail of white lead was designed to appeal to children. "Lead helps guard your health," went the tagline in an ad in *National Geographic* from the National Lead Company.[50] But by the mid-1940s even Robert Kehoe acknowledged that "serious mental retardation" was evident "in children that have recovered from lead poisoning," though he had a much narrower definition of lead poisoning than today's standard, and he nonetheless continued to offer his assistance to the LIA.[51] He and other proponents of lead also still argued that the threat wasn't as much the material itself as the circumstances of people who were exposed to it.

"The major source of trouble is the flaking of lead paint in the ancient slum dwelling of our older cities, [and] the problem of lead poisoning in children will be with us for as long as there are slums," the LIA director declared at an annual meeting in 1957, at about the time that city leaders in Flint were planning the big celebration for General Motors' fiftieth anniversary. The director parroted the point in a letter to Kehoe: "Childhood lead poisoning is essentially a problem of slum dwellings and relatively ignorant parents." The implication was that if you did not live in a slum, you were safe.[52] It's an idea that still has traction today, but it's wrong—lead pipes and paint are widespread; the legacy of leaded fuel is scattered everywhere; and to this day it's difficult to purchase new plumbing fixtures that contain zero lead. However, the argument underscores the fact that certain places—and certain people—bear the worst of cumulative exposure. Old cities have a greater number of homes and buildings with lead paint, and when they are left vacant or when residents can't afford to maintain them, then that paint is more likely to flake. The lead in the soil is typically more concentrated, too, because of the dense development of the city in the leaded gasoline years. And people who live in places with deteriorating infrastructure are more likely to have lead in their drinking water. Small amounts of exposure from all these different sources build up in the bones.[53]

The same year the LIA director was talking about slums, Dr. Herb Needleman was treating a three-year-old girl at the Children's Hospital in Philadelphia. She had more than 60 micrograms per deciliter (μg/L) of lead in her blood, an extraordinary amount. Later research would find neurobehavioral damage in children with less than 5 μg/L. But even by the loose standards of the time, the girl was plainly poisoned. She was on the brink of falling into a coma when Needleman began chelation, a chemical process to extract the lead. Within a few days, the little girl began to brighten and become responsive. Needleman, full of pride and relief, gave the girl's mother the good news, but he advised her not to return to the same house. He believed that the girl was exposed to lead paint—perhaps it was falling off the walls and ceiling onto her toys, or it flaked off the exterior of the house where she played in the yard. Whatever it was, no amount of cleaning could eliminate it completely. It was best for the girl's health for the family to move elsewhere. But the young mother said, "Where can I go? The houses I can afford are all the same." She wrapped up her child and returned home.

The doctor couldn't write a prescription for this kind of ailment. He couldn't administer chelation to the whole neighborhood. It was a revelation for Needleman, who would become one of the earliest and most effective anti-lead advocates. "It wasn't enough to make a diagnosis and prescribe a medication," he said later. "I'd treated her for lead poisoning, but that was not the disease—the disease was much bigger. The real causes of lead poisoning were in the lives of the people. Her disease was where she lived and why she was allowed to live there."[54]

IV.

When LeeAnne Walters reached Miguel Del Toral at the EPA, she told him about Flint, about her family's health problems, and about her house with the brown water. While the city tinkered with treatment at the plant and scheduled further tests at her house, Del Toral's office contacted the MDEQ to discuss what was going on.

LeeAnne had complained of black sediment, noted the EPA's Jennifer Crooks in an email thread that included the MDEQ's Stephen Busch and Mike Prysby. When the discolored water settled, it left behind oily particulates, which seemed to be accumulating in her toilet tank and plumbing. And then there were the water tests conducted by Flint's utilities administrator. "WOW!!!," Crooks wrote. "Did he find LEAD! **104 ppb.** . . . Big worries here."[55] Del Toral believed the black sediment contained an extremely high concentration of lead. Crooks speculated about whether the river water was leaching contaminants out of the pipes. "Miguel is wondering if Flint is feeding phosphates," she wrote. "Flint must have Optimal Corrosion Control Treatment—is it phosphates?"[56]

Stephen Busch replied the next day with a false claim: yes, of course Flint had corrosion control. He avoided specifying what kind of treatment it was. And in a voice-mail message, the MDEQ told Del Toral and Crooks that the lead problem at the Walters house was caused by indoor plumbing. The implication was that the contamination affected only a single house, not a whole city, and that the responsibility to fix it fell to the homeowner.

But this made no sense. The plumbing at LeeAnne Walters's home had been installed in 2011, just after the family bought the house, and it was nearly all made of plastic. Built in 1922, when General Motors was developing segregated neighborhoods in the city, the house on Browning Avenue was in a redlined working-class area. It was now part of a broader south Flint community that battled vacancy, though active neighborhood associations had brought stability to some pockets. Most residents were African American.[57]

When LeeAnne and her husband moved in, their empty house had no plumbing at all. Probably the metal had been scrapped and sold by needy young men. The Walterses did a full renovation, adding the whole-house filter and new plastic plumbing, which couldn't possibly be the source of the lead in the water.

A third test from LeeAnne's kitchen tap didn't pick up high levels of lead, but a fourth showed levels at 397 ppb. Del Toral decided to check things out for himself. He traveled to Flint and visited the Walters home, where he confirmed that, except for a few minor pieces, all the interior plumbing—pipes, valves, and connectors—was made of plastic and certified for drinking water use. Her faucets also met lead-free requirements. By the time he headed back to Chicago, Del Toral was armed with photographs, some of the iron filters from the home filter system, and an acute sense that something wasn't adding up.

The water problem at LeeAnne's house was so bad that, in about the middle of March, the city decided to replace the unusually long service line that connected it to the water main, at no cost to the family. Howard Croft, the public works director, came to her house with a city councilman to discuss it. They wanted her to sign an agreement that would hold the city harmless for any ill effects of the old line, but LeeAnne refused. The replacement proceeded anyway, though slowly. There was other construction work happening outside her house—the kind that can disturb the pipes and cause an uptick in the amount of lead falling into the drinking water. And it wasn't easy to find where, exactly, the service line was. The city came out numerous times to look.

LeeAnne Walters's concern about the link between the water and her family's health wasn't hypothetical. Her twin boys had been tested for lead before the April 2014 water switch, and the results were considered low. After the water tests at her house, she had them checked again. Gavin's lead levels had soared to 6.5 micrograms per deciliter, more than three times what it had been before. No amount of lead is healthy or natural, but exceeding 5 µg/L put Gavin's level in the top percentile for children nationwide. He had been poisoned. As decades of research and observational experience have shown, this can result in permanent neurological and physiological damage. In hopes of determining the source of the lead exposure, his doctor took an X-ray of the boy's stomach to see if perhaps he'd swallowed paint chips, but they found nothing. Perversely, given the iron content of their water, Gavin was also diagnosed as anemic. He was prescribed iron supplements.[58]

In April, not long after the family got the results of Gavin's medical tests, another sample from the house measured the lead at an astonishing 707 ppb. It was so bad that the city shut off the water altogether. The six family members now relied on four garden hoses that were hooked together and connected to their neighbors' spigot. The winding white snake slipped over their driveway and through a chain-link fence. It was for bare-bones use only—they were told they could shower in it—though in the temperamental early spring, water pressure issues and freezing temperatures sometimes stopped their supply. Then they had to go out into the cold and switch out the hoses.

V.

Thanks to the Clean Air Act in 1970, the new EPA became responsible for regulating lead.[59] It first focused on cars. Over the next decade, as part of a complete phaseout, the first low-lead and unleaded gasoline became available in the United States. The EPA also backed catalytic converters for newly made automobiles—any model that had one could use only unleaded fuel. But a total ban on leaded fuel didn't go into effect until 1996, more than seventy years after the surgeon general had convened a meeting to discuss its risks.[60]

A nationwide ban on lead paint in housing went into effect in 1978. The use of new lead pipes was eliminated with an amendment to the Safe Drinking Water Act in 1986.[61] Five years later, the Lead and Copper Rule (LCR) set the first national limits for lead and copper in municipal drinking water. The rule's threshold—15 parts per billion—is fairly arbitrary and not based on any standard of health.[62] As a technical benchmark, it struck a tricky balance: the goal for lead in water was zero, but no action was required until tests showed 15 ppb or more in a certain percentage of homes.[63]

The new policies restricting lead in paint, water, and gasoline were a coup for public health. But they didn't reckon with the lead that was already around us. Before its phaseout, leaded gasoline accounted for about 90 percent of airborne lead. It settled on lawns, waterways, and even the icecaps, and it didn't just vanish with the signing of a law. About 3 million tons of lead was painted onto walls, toys, and furniture between 1910 and 1977.[64] To this day, any house built before the ban that hasn't been remediated likely has lead paint in it. For any structure built before 1986, there's a decent chance that lead pipes connect it to the water main. There is also probably lead solder and brass in the indoor plumbing. Newer structures aren't immune, either. In the original law, lead-free pipes were defined as containing no more than 8 percent lead. It wasn't until 2014 that Congress reset the limit to 0.25 percent for pipes and plumbing fixtures, and slightly less for solder.[65] Many anti-lead advocates insist that it should be zero.

There are no reliable numbers on how many lead service lines are in use in the United States. The best estimates range between 3.3 million and 10 million, but either way, it's clear that millions of people drink water out of them every day. And unlike paint or gasoline, water is essential for every living being. Along with regular screenings, the Lead and Copper Rule attempts to manage the risk by requiring water systems serving more than fifty thousand people to use corrosion control, which helps reduce the amount of metals that leach into the water. Besides protecting public health, it's also cost effective. Every dollar spent on corrosion control saves ten by extending the life of the pipes and lessening maintenance costs.

Corrosion control is essential, but it's not a permanent or fail-proof solution. Treatment can fail when lead lines are disrupted by street work, plumbing repairs, or changes to the water chemistry. Washington, D.C., is one place that implemented corrosion control but still found itself with a major crisis. In 2000, the city switched disinfectants. It began treating water with chloramine instead of chlorine, which authorities believed would improve the quality by reducing the amount of by-products in the water. (It was also much less expensive.)[66] But the new disinfectant was a disaster for the pipes and plumbing fixtures. Chloramine quickened the corrosion, causing an infusion of lead into the water. Instead of informing the public, the authorities buried the news. Residents were unknowingly exposed to water with significantly higher lead levels for at least *three years*.[67]

Thanks to the organizing of a broad coalition of community members and reporting by the *Washington Post*, the lead contamination became public news in 2004. That same year, the Centers for Disease Control and Prevention published a report that claimed no one had been harmed by the high lead levels. The study was influential enough to be used by communities around the country to justify why they, too, failed to act urgently when lead showed up in their water. Why would they if no less an authority than the CDC, the nation's leading institute of public health, said that lead in drinking water didn't hurt anyone?

The allowance of *some* lead under the LCR was the EPA's way of acknowledging that without adequate funding to rebuild America's massive lead-based infrastructure, not to mention all the plumbing fixtures in individual homes, there was simply no way to eliminate it completely from drinking water. Only a colossal investment, thoughtfully executed, would make zero tolerance possible. The EPA estimated that it would cost up to $80 billion to replace all of the nation's lead service lines, while the American Water Works Association calculated it at about $30 billion—or $1 trillion, if we repaired and expanded our old water mains, too.[68]

This never became a priority. Not yet, at least. In the meanwhile, some communities tried to address the lead problem on their own, mostly focusing on paint. But in places such as Flint, where was the money for upgrades supposed to come from? Federal and state funding for such programs declined, and the resources that did make it to local communities were rarely spent on preventive solutions. It was no coincidence that eight of the ten cities with the highest rates of childhood lead poisoning, as determined by the CDC in 2003, were shrinking cities: Cleveland, Philadelphia, Buffalo, Providence, Milwaukee, St. Louis, Detroit, and Baltimore. (The others were Chicago and New York City.)[69]

To make matters worse, poor people—who tended to be concentrated in older cities—also had less access to health care to help manage the harm done by cumulative exposure. The cycle of deprivation affected African American communities most of all. Between 1999 and 2004, black children across the country were 1.6 times more likely to test positive for lead than white children, and nearly three times more likely to have very high blood-lead levels.

No one—not taxpayers, not school districts, not the state, and not the federal government—wanted to pay to fix an expensive infrastructure problem. Therefore, many preferred not to know if the children in their communities were drinking lead in their water. There was no onus to act if there was no proof. It was a twenty-first-century adaptation of the strategy of doubt and denial pioneered by Charles Kettering, Robert Kehoe, and their fellow industrialists.

Despite the particular vulnerability of children, there was no federal mandate for schools and child-care centers to test for lead in their water. Forty-four states did not require it either. Part of the problem was that if testing were mandatory, what would happen when lead was found, as it was in about half the public schools in Newark in 2016?[70] Do you install all-new pipes, fountains, and faucets, and, if so, who should pay for it? Do you shut off the school's water and ask the community to donate bottled water? When Camden, New Jersey, found high levels of lead in the water at its schools—New Jersey is one of six states that do require testing—the fountains were turned off. The district went on to spend about $100,000 a year to supply the schools with water coolers.[71]

The *Washington Post* investigation that helped uncover the D.C. lead story also revealed how testing was manipulated all over the nation, in both poor and wealthy cities: Boston, Seattle, New York City, Portland, Oregon, and, as it would turn out, in Flint, Michigan.[72] The Lead and Copper Rule relies on utilities to self-monitor their water, and it quickly became common for them to exploit the loopholes in the LCR by, for example, pre-flushing the taps before collecting a sample, drawing water at a slow flow rather than a fast one, and disproportionately testing in places where officials believe there are no lead pipes. All these tactics make the amounts of metals in the water appear to be lower than they really are, helping the utility to get a passing grade under the law. Call it modern-day wizardry. However, even with this rule skirting, about 18 million Americans got their water from sources that had lead violations in the previous twelve months, according to a 2016 report from National Resources Defense Council.[73]

Lead persistently stays lead. Just as it accumulates in the bones of people, it accumulates in the infrastructural bones of cities such as Chicago, Washington, D.C., and Flint. Today, about half a million children have a dangerous amount of lead in their blood.[74] But lead poisoning has never catalyzed a movement the way that polio, for example, did. "In the 1950s, fewer than sixty thousand new cases of polio per year created a near panic among American parents and a national mobilization of vaccination campaigns that virtually wiped out the disease within a decade," write Gerald Markowitz and David Rosner in their book *Lead Wars*. "At no point in the past hundred years has there been a similar national mobilization over lead despite its ubiquity and the havoc it can wreak."[75] Perhaps it is because both the contaminant and the health effects are invisible.[76]

Only a few major cities have replaced all their aging lead-laced service lines. Those that have—such as Madison, Wisconsin, and, just fifty miles west of Flint, the state capital of Lansing—have created a promising blueprint for how communities can act before an emergency happens. But, for now, they have few peers.

Citizen/Science

The people in the city of Flint are resilient, and we've created our own paths to resolve this problem.

—Claire McClinton (2016)

I.

Though he is barely more than fifty years old, somewhere deep in Marc Edwards there burns the fury of an Old Testament prophet. He is a tall, lanky man—he runs most every day—with brown hair, silver wire-rimmed glasses, and an enviable amount of get-it-done energy. But he carries himself heavily. His temper has become infamous in his field, erupting at the perceived moral failings, hypocrisies, and errors of others.

Edwards grew up on the shores of Lake Erie in western New York when it, the shallowest of the Great Lakes, was a symbol for the emerging environmental movement.[1] After decades of bearing the detritus of industry, agricultural pollution, and human sewage, huge swaths of the 9,910-square-mile lake were declared "dead." When Edwards was five years old, the slick of oils and chemicals on the Cuyahoga River, which empties into Lake Erie, caught fire.[2] Dr. Seuss, in his 1971 children's book *The Lorax*, imagined a toxic place where "fish walk on their fins and get woefully weary in search of some water that isn't so smeary. I hear things are just as bad up in Lake Erie."

From his tiny town, where children attended a K–12 school housed in a single building, Edwards remembered the foul smell of the lake and the ominous absence of fish. But, as he would tell the story later in life, he also remembered environmental engineers who worked feverishly to clean up the lake, part of a youthful movement that led to reforms that limited water pollution. The Clean Water Act, the Clean Air Act, and the creation of the Environmental Protection Agency were among the biggest triumphs, debuting not long after the nation celebrated the first Earth Day. Lake Erie had a remarkable recovery. Because it is far less deep than the other Great Lakes, it is still a harbinger for environmental woe, but there was enough improvement to inspire two Ohio State University graduate students to write Theodor Geisel, otherwise known as Dr. Seuss, in 1985. They invited him to Cleveland to see the renewal for himself and asked him to remove the dig from his book. The author declined the trip, but said, "I do agree with you that my 1971 statement in the *Lorax* about the condition of Lake Erie needs a bit of revision. I should no longer be saying bad things about a body of water that is now, due to great civic and scientific effort, the happy home of smiling fish." He made good on his promise to take the line out of future editions.[3]

When the time came for Marc Edwards to choose a major at the state university in Buffalo, he opted for biophysics. Always a contrarian, he did so, he claimed, "mainly to spite" his sister after she told him it "was the toughest major in the school" and that he "wouldn't be able to hack it." It certainly was difficult, almost blindingly so. But Edwards made it through, while working on weekends with intellectually disabled adults to help pay tuition. As he neared graduation, he began to think about what to do next. Should he become a veterinarian? Maybe a medical doctor? He even considered becoming a dolphin trainer, until a dolphin broke his ribs.

As he mulled it over, one of the most significant environmental catastrophes of the twentieth century was playing out just twenty miles from Buffalo. It steered Edwards toward his life's work.

In the summer of 1978, in Niagara Falls, New York, residents of a neighborhood called Love Canal were making national news by protesting the toxic dump they lived on. Love Canal was designed as a model community near the shores of the Niagara River, which links Lake Erie with Lake Ontario. Love Canal's memorable name came about when an entrepreneur named William T. Love designed a clay-lined canal that was supposed to branch off the river, bypassing Niagara Falls. But the project was never completed. Instead, the area became a dump site in the 1940s and 1950s for about twenty-one thousand tons of chemicals contained in fifty-five-gallon drums, some of which were already corroding when workers put them in the ground. After covering the mess with dirt, the Hooker Chemical Company sold the site to the Niagara Falls Board of Education. The price: one dollar and a signed waiver that excused the company from all liability. The board knew that the site contained dangerous chemicals, including aniline derivatives and benzene, but Niagara Falls was growing fast, and it was in desperate need of affordable land for a new elementary school—which was built right on top of the dump. Soon the school was surrounded by hundreds of new family homes. None of the homeowners were told about the toxins seeping through the ground beneath them.[4]

Twenty-some years later, vigorous reporting by a *Niagara Gazette* reporter shed light on what was already obvious to Love Canal residents. Miscarriages, birth defects, epilepsy, asthma, migraines, and cancer were alarmingly common in the neighborhood. So were dying back-yard plants, bad odors, and even, after steady rain, the sight of old drums of toxic waste poking through the earth. One resident, Lois Gibbs, emerged as a particularly powerful leader after her son, a kindergart-ner, developed epilepsy and a low white blood cell count. Gibbs mapped the health problems; led demonstrations; and, along with her neigh-bors, called for an evacuation of the entire development. New York State finally intervened after studies by the Environmental Protection Agency and the state's Health Department confirmed that there were toxic vapors in the Love Canal houses. The elementary school closed. Families were evacuated from 239 homes, which were demolished over the next several decades. About thirty more families in the area adjacent to Love Canal were also temporarily relocated.[5] In time, a second school was closed, and President Jimmy Carter declared a federal disaster in Love Canal. It was the first time that a man-made emergency had been designated as such. In 1980, as a result of the community's frontline activism, the Love Canal evacuation zone was expanded to include up to nine hundred more homes.[6] Nowadays, the area has been "landscaped into banality," according to historian Richard S. Newman—a green field, studded with shrubs that block the monitoring wells, surrounded by weedy old driveways and a chain-link fence.[7]

The Love Canal movement pushed the nation to reflect on how it should reconcile its industrial past with public health and environmental wisdom. Even *Jane Fonda's Workout Book*, America's number-one bestseller for more than six months in 1981, discussed the crisis at length in a chapter called "The Body Besieged." (Fonda toured Love Canal with Lois Gibbs in 1979, and she also funded a speaking tour for Gibbs.[8]) In Washington, the Carter administration developed what became known as the Superfund program to pay for the careful and comprehensive cleanup of toxic waste. It required the EPA to find the parties responsible for hazardous waste and force them to clean up their mess. Failing that, the agency could use Superfund money to clean up a site and then refer polluters to the U.S. Department of Justice to recover costs (and then some). Significantly, polluters were liable even if their dumping had been legal at the time.[9] By 1983, the first National Priorities List named 406 hazardous waste sites around the country—Michigan had 41, the second most listings— and it eventually added about 1,200 more. The dross of industry had so saturated the environment that by 1996 the EPA was pouring more than $1 billion a year into the Superfund—about 20 percent of its budget.[10]

Marc Edwards had found his field. The engineers working to solve the Love Canal disaster were heroes, and he very much wanted to be seen as a hero, too. He eventually found his academic home at Virginia Polytechnic Institute and State University, commonly known as Virginia

Tech. A land-grant college in rural Blacksburg, it was founded on the principle of solving real-world problems. Its motto is *Ut Prosim*, which translates as "That I may serve."

The lead crisis in Washington, D.C., broke open in January 2004. One morning, residents woke up to an alarming headline in the *Washington Post*: "Water in D.C. Exceeds EPA Lead Limit."[11] There had been elevated lead in the water for years—residents had discovered it, pooled their tests results together to create a database, mapped it, and tipped off the *Post*—but this was the start of the explosive public revelations. Edwards had been part of the group looking into the issue. He worked on the case as a subcontractor for the EPA, and, shortly before the story became front-page news, D.C.'s water utility offered him a consulting contract. But by that point, Edwards had become so disgusted by its handling of the water problems that he refused it—he felt as if he would be working for the wrong side.[12] Edwards continued on as a volunteer.[13]

His expertise on lead infrastructure and drinking water turned out to be an asset to residents who were pushing for answers. Once the Centers for Disease Control and Prevention issued its now-infamous report—the one that claimed that no one was harmed by the water, even in homes that had more than 300 parts per billion of lead— Edwards became fixated on refuting it, especially as the report began to be used around the country to justify relaxed standards for drinking water.[14] Officials at both the EPA and the CDC disputed his allegations by saying that he was only an engineer, not a public health expert.[15]

For the galvanized community, the resolution to the D.C. water crisis was slow, iterative, and never wholly satisfying. After the *Post* began reporting on it, the city's Health Department launched a massive, albeit piecemeal, campaign to protect people from unsafe water. By 2006, the lead levels had lowered significantly, thanks to adjusted treatment. (Pre-flushing was still used, though, which prompted many to question the test results.)[16] There was another uptick when the city began doing partial-line pipe replacements.[17] Replacing only part of a service line disrupts the section that remains in the ground. That can cause a spike in lead levels that lasts for months.

Edwards doubled down on researching the catastrophe. Along with other community organizers, he filed endless public records requests over many years to see if the rise in lead levels had, in fact, harmed children.[18] It cost his family tens of thousands of dollars in fees, he said, and by his own estimation he gave the crisis about thirty volunteer hours a week. He was met with obstinacy at nearly every step—the CDC and other agencies refused to provide him with information about the community's blood-lead levels during the years when there was especially high lead in the water. When Edwards sent requests under the Freedom of Information Act for the raw data of the CDC report, he got nothing back, for years. Then the agency sent him a single spreadsheet with a list of anonymized subjects who had been tested—but it didn't make much sense, because it included people who were tested *after* the study was published, and only thirteen people who were not drinking bottled or filtered water.

In early 2008, Edwards was finally able to evaluate information from the Children's National Medical Center. In a peer-reviewed paper published in the journal *Environmental Science & Technology* in January 2009, he and his coauthors shredded the conclusions of the CDC's report. The data proved, as he later described it, "what we'd known actually for two thousand years. Which is, if little kids drink high lead in drinking water, they get lead poisoned. They get hurt." Hundreds of children—maybe even thousands of them—had been lead-poisoned after being exposed to D.C.'s water during the years of contamination. In the most high-risk area, the number of children with elevated blood-lead levels had more than doubled.[19]

In 2010, a bipartisan congressional investigation into the D.C. lead-in-water crisis confirmed what Edwards and the frontline community organizers had been arguing for years. Its unequivocal report was titled "A Public Health Tragedy: How Flawed CDC Data and Faulty Assumptions Endangered Children's Health in the Nation's Capital." In 2004, it alleged, while worried residents were demanding answers, the CDC had rushed the report to publication, knowingly using incomplete data to tamp down the public outcry.[20] As its senior author wrote in an email to her boss at the time, "Today has been the first day in over a month that there wasn't a story on lead in water in the Washington Post and also the first that I haven't been interviewed by at least one news outlet. I guess that means it worked!"[21]

One of the problems with the rushed report is that it did not mention that many of the residents it observed had long since stopped drinking tap water, so it was dubious to claim that they were evidence of the water's harmlessness. A large group of children who drank water with very high lead levels were left out of the cross-sectional study. Partial-line replacements were recommended as remedy for the crisis, even though the process is likely to increase the lead content of the water. The congressional report skewered the CDC for not notifying the public about how "most of the conclusions" of its study were totally negated, even by much of the agency's own research.[22]

The investigation gave a jolt to the coalition that had been campaigning for safe water.[23] Yanna Lambrinidou, a leading organizer who helped bring the new research to the attention of Congress, told a *Post* reporter that the shameful 2004 report "gave the perpetrators of D.C.'s lead crisis a 'get out of jail free' card," allowing them to escape accountability for their actions for too long.[24] Ultimately, the CDC backpedaled, but it never admitted to conscious wrongdoing. It was all a miscommunication. "Looking backward six years," said the deputy director of the CDC's national center for environmental health, "it's clear that this report could have been written a little better."[25]

Edwards couldn't let it go at that. He wanted the agency to admit that it had purposefully minimized the risk of lead in the water, perhaps because the CDC was worried about distracting attention from its long-running campaign against lead paint.[26] Regardless, the crisis in the nation's capital had real-world consequences. Two thirds of more than six thousand tested homes showed lead levels that exceeded the federal limit. Hundreds of children had elevated lead in their blood, which was associated with the water. About $100 million were spent on partial-line replacements until it came to public notice that children living in homes that received one were even more likely to test for high lead levels.[27] And in 2014 Edwards published a study that showed a correlation between the lead-contaminated water and a spike in fetal deaths and reduced birth rates.[28] There were about twenty to thirty more fetal deaths in the city for each year of the crisis. That was a jump of about 37 percent, even as the comparable numbers in nearby Baltimore were on a long decline. The rate of fetal deaths declined in 2004, when the lead problems became public and people began to take precautions, but they ticked up again during the years when pipes were partially replaced.

The whole episode took a toll on Edwards. Even with the validation that came from his MacArthur grant and the congressional investigation, he was shaken by how difficult the fight had been. There seemed to be enemies everywhere. People in power were working harder to protect themselves and their institutions than to do what was right, he felt, which seemed to him to be an utter betrayal of public trust. "Overall, this was a time of just incredible hopelessness for me," he said. He was in his forties, but "so naïve" that never in his wildest dreams could he have predicted that the "scientists and engineers paid to protect us, the environmental policemen," would become "environmental criminals" who hurt innocent people. "It just didn't make any sense to me at all."[29]

Believing that ethics was a crucial part of educating the next generation of scientists and engineers, Edwards teamed up with medical anthropologist Yanna Lambrinidou, the parent who was an influential organizer during D.C.'s lead crisis. They began teaching a pathbreaking graduate course at Virginia Tech called "Engineering Ethics and the Public." It was designed to prepare students, still at the sunny beginning of their careers, to act when—not if—they are faced with a moral dilemma. Uniquely, it emphasized the voices of marginalized communities that were affected by the decisions made by engineers. One of the signature assignments was to role-play the press conference that took place after the *Post* story broke, featuring representatives from the EPA, the CDC, the D.C. water authority, and other agencies. Armed with the same information those agencies had at the time of the actual conference, students found that they went so far in defending the office they represented, they sometimes invented information on the fly to counter questions they couldn't answer.[30]

For all that Edwards, Lambrinidou, and many others had done to expose the D.C. crisis, nothing really changed afterward. No one was formally held accountable, not in a courtroom or anywhere else. Nobody was fired or demoted. There was no remediation, reform, or even any real apology. Even after the CDC finally backed away from the 2004 report, it admitted to being guilty only of bad writing. Meanwhile, water infrastructure across America was underfunded and in terrible condition, and nobody seemed to care. And the loopholes in the Lead and Copper Rule were still there to be exploited when utilities tested their water, in D.C. and in cities all over the country. People were unknowingly put at risk every day.

Edwards burned with a sense of betrayal. What it comes down to, he said, is "what are you loyal to in this world? Are you loyal to your friends, to your employer, or are you going to be loyal to the truth and humankind?" Every scientist and engineer must decide, not once, but throughout their careers.

Which is all to say that Marc Edwards could not have been more ready for LeeAnne Walters's call from Flint, Michigan.

II.

From the switch to the Flint River to her son's lead poisoning, LeeAnne Walters brought Edwards up to speed on the water crisis. Edwards knew that the only way to find out what exactly was going on in the water at her home was to test it. Although tests done by the city and the MDEQ had already shown excessive lead, Edwards was all too familiar with how the analysis could be manipulated. It was worth doing the tests again and making sure they were analyzed the proper way.

So in April 2015, following instruction from Edwards, LeeAnne collected thirty samples from her home. The water had been shut off at this point, so it had to be temporarily turned back on, and in this unusual case, since it had been sitting stagnant for weeks, it was necessary to flush the taps at low flow for twenty-five minutes the night before. Over the phone, Edwards talked LeeAnne through the whole process: she didn't let the water run first, and she collected samples at a variety of flow rates—not the slow trickle that's often used to lessen the likelihood of lead flaking from the pipes. The bottles were sealed and passed on to the EPA's Miguel Del Toral, who, while traveling, personally dropped them off more than five hundred miles away, at Edwards's lab in Dunham Hall at Virginia Tech.[31]

Within a week, the results were in. The sample with the lowest lead level tested at 300 parts per billion; the highest was more than 13,000 ppb; and the average was 2,000 ppb. The EPA classifies water with 5,000 ppb as toxic waste. Even the low test far exceeded the federal action level. As Edwards relayed to both LeeAnne Walters and Miguel Del Toral, it was the worst lead-in-water contamination that he had seen in more than twenty-five years.

The EPA had been told that Flint's water was treated with corrosion control, and Del Toral had passed that assurance on to LeeAnne. But the only possible explanation for the state of her water was that it wasn't. LeeAnne tracked down public documents that suggested as much, and after making more inquiries Del Toral confirmed their suspicions.[32] Pat Cook, a drinking water official with the MDEQ, told him that Flint hadn't had corrosion control since "the disconnection from Detroit." As Del Toral wrote in an email, this "is very concerning given the amount of lead service lines in the city."[33]

In the meantime, the city began to install a new copper service line to LeeAnne's house. Del Toral seized the opportunity to examine the old line, confirming that it was made of lead. Downstream, he also retrieved a sample of galvanized iron pipe that had become coated with lead. Lead corrosion had flowed through it and stuck to the sides; if rust crumbled into the water, the lead would come with it.[34]

It was increasingly obvious that the MDEQ's pat voice mail attributing the Walterses' problem to indoor plumbing was wrong. The surge of lead had to be coming from outside—and that lead service line was the likely culprit. Since similar lines threaded through all of Flint, and since the contamination in the water at this house had hit hazardous waste levels, any rational person would wonder about the safety of the entire city's water. Perhaps most damning of all for the MDEQ's initial assessment were the results of tests done in May, after the new copper line was installed. The samples showed a dramatic improvement in the water. (The water heater still had high lead though, likely because it was still housing particulates from the old line.)

Elsewhere in Flint, tests were suggestive but spotty. A city test showed high lead at a house a few doors down from the Walters family. A mile away, another test found levels that were almost twice that. But at least two of LeeAnne's neighbors did not have high lead (which is why the family had been advised to rely on the garden-hose connection).[35]

Altogether, though, there was enough evidence for Del Toral to feel that it was time to issue an alert. He synthesized the saga in an eight-page report titled "High Lead Levels in Flint, Michigan." It was confirmation of the contamination in the Browning Avenue household and an indictment of the overall management of the water the city had been drinking for more than a year. The report also documented Flint's problems with *E. coli* and TTHMs.[36] Setting aside the MDEQ's contradictory claims about corrosion control, Del Toral bluntly stated that after the switch from Detroit, Flint did not continue to treat the water in a way that would mitigate the lead and copper levels. It was both against the law and a threat to public safety.

Additionally, Del Toral's report explained that the city's water tests were unreliable. "The practice of pre-flushing . . . has been shown to result in the minimization of lead levels in the drinking water," he wrote. "Although this practice is not specifically prohibited by the LCR, it negates the intent of the rule to collect compliance samples under 'worst case' conditions, which is necessary for statistical validity given the small number of samples collected." Del Toral noted that the MDEQ supported the practice of pre-flushing. But Flint was now flirting with a public health emergency. He urged the EPA to intervene by reviewing the suspect sampling and the lack of corrosion control.

The report was addressed to Tom Poy, head of the groundwater and drinking water branch of the EPA in Chicago. Seven others were copied on it, including four MDEQ officials: Liane Shekter-Smith, head of the drinking water division; Pat Cook, the community drinking water specialist; and the ever-present Stephen Busch and Mike Prsyby. Two EPA water experts were also listed as recipients, as was Virginia Tech's Marc Edwards. When Poy followed up by asking why Del Toral was so certain that the lead problem was widespread, given the narrow set of tests, he was told that it was basic chemistry. "We don't need to drop a bowling ball off every building in every town to know that it will fall to the ground in all of these places," Del Toral wrote in an email. The only reason there wasn't more data beyond LeeAnne Walters's house was because "the City of Flint is flushing away the evidence before measuring for it."[37]

Then he got even more pointed: "I understand that this is not a comfortable situation, but the State is complicit in this and the public has a right to know what they are doing because it is their children that are being harmed. At a MINIMUM, the City should be warning residents about the high lead, not hiding it telling them that there is no lead in the water. To me that borders on criminal neglect."

When an employee writes a report like this, the EPA has a protocol. Its conclusion needs to be checked and rechecked before the agency signs off and releases a final version. Del Toral's dispatch was thus considered an interim draft. But he couldn't shake his worry about a looming disaster. Time was precious. If his analysis was correct, the corrosion of Flint's pipes was worsening every day, causing more lead to saturate the water and more exposure to a dangerous neurotoxin.

That's why he had sent copies to the people at the MDEQ who were directly involved with Flint's water. And when LeeAnne Walters asked for a copy, he gave her one, too. She in turn shared the report with a journalist she trusted. The Flint water crisis, a local worry for more than a year, was about to move into the spotlight.

III.

Curt Guyette is tall and lean, with hooded eyes and gray-threaded brown hair that he'd tied back in a low ponytail for years but later cut short. He has a resounding laugh and an easy manner that belies the ferocity of his approach to mission-driven journalism—a mixture of skepticism of people in power, disdain for hypocrisy, and kinship with underdogs.[38]

Guyette's was a familiar byline at the *Metro Times*, a Detroit alt-weekly that was distributed in Flint. For eighteen years, he turned out features about emergency management ("It's Good to Be the King"), medical marijuana ("Cutting Through the Smoke"), and industrial pollution ("The Big Stink"). His pieces tended to be long, sardonic, and wonky, backed up with original reporting, punctured by colorful quotes, and displaying an unvarnished leftist point of view. Sometimes he wrote chatty interviews with people he simply found interesting: comedians, artists, kiteboarders, superfans of the Detroit Tigers. He once hiked the entire U-shaped span of Detroit's Outer Drive, all forty-four miles of it, and produced a two-part series about his adventures. "I wonder what its bizarre and beautiful existence means to Detroit, if anything," he wrote about the road. "I wonder what seeing it all by foot will mean to me."

But his tenure at the alt-weekly came to an abrupt end when new ownership fired him in 2013 for revealing the contents of a company press release to another journalist a few minutes before the news was posted online. Soon after, Guyette signed on as an investigative reporter with the Michigan chapter of the American Civil Liberties Union, the only branch in the country to have a journalist on staff.[39] Guyette was the test case in a pilot program supported by a Ford Foundation grant, and he had a mandate to cover shifts in democratic governance under emergency management. He began work at an opportune moment: Detroit was just a few months into its municipal bankruptcy, and Flint was preparing to switch its water supply, both tremendous changes that were steered by emergency managers.

Guyette's stories had fairly wide latitude to stake out his beat. His articles were published on the ACLU's Michigan website, and occasionally in other local outlets, including the *Michigan Citizen* and, ironically, the *Metro Times,* which had yet another new owner and appeared to regret the loss of one of its best-known bylines. In winking self-acknowledgment, it named Guyette the "Best Journalist Who Worked at *Metro Times*" in one of its "Best of Detroit" issues.

Guyette's reporting about emergency management led him to Flint and, inevitably, to the water wars. He was by no means the only reporter covering the story. Even in a region with a news infrastructure that had been devastated by layoffs, buyouts, and closures, beat reporters and local television stations followed the day-by-day developments. Even the *New York Times* had caught wind of the trouble. It published a feature that focused on Melissa Mays, a music promoter in her thirties who had become a prominent presence at water protests and public meetings.[40] Like LeeAnne Walters, she said that she and her family had struggled with skin rashes and other ailments since the water switch. Her hair was falling out in clumps and lightening from brown to a brassy shade. After the boil-water advisories, the Mays family—Melissa, her husband, their three sons, and their pet cat and fish—used only bottled water. It cost them hundreds of dollars a month.

The article was featured on the home page of the *Times* website. But for all the media coverage, the story of the water crisis was stuck. Journalistically, it kept repeating itself. First came a disturbing news item about Flint's water. Then came assurances from experts who said that it was fine and that treatment would improve. This in turn was followed by resident testimonials, demonstrations, and independent investigations that disputed the official claims. Then the cycle started all over again. It kept coming back to the fact that Flint residents were saying one thing about the water, and city and state authorities were saying another. It didn't help that Michigan had some of the worst transparency laws in the country. Residents and reporters might have been able to help break the information stalemate by filing open records requests for internal details about Flint's water switch, but they were limited by the fact that Michigan is one of only two states where both the governor's office and the legislature were exempt from the Freedom of Information Act.

Over at the ACLU, Guyette got together with Kate Levy, a local documentarian, to make a short film called *Hard to Swallow: Toxic Water under a Toxic System in Flint*. It was a six-minute recap of the water troubles that focused on the role of emergency managers. Resident activists were at the center of the story, including retired autoworker Claire McClinton, from the Democracy Defense League. "We knew that this emergency manager law was undemocratic," McClinton said in the film. "We knew it was unprecedented. But we never dreamed that we would be faced with not being able to use our municipal water." The film also included Melissa Mays, who said that she and her neighbors had heard for years about the pollution in the Flint River. When there was talk of using it as the community's new source of drinking water, "we all thought it was a joke," she said. And the Reverend Alfred Harris of the Concerned Pastors for Social Action testified that over at his Saints of God Church on West Pierson Road, they no longer conducted baptisms. "If we baptize, we go outside of the city of Flint."

Emergency manager Darnell Earley made an appearance as he argued his case at a town meeting. "The work that has gone into preparing the City of Flint to eliminate its dependence" on the Detroit Water and Sewerage Department, "that's a major step, a *huge* step in the right direction, because that now gives you the opportunity to . . . better control the costs." But residents were exasperated when water bills continued to get more expensive. Melissa Mays expressed alarm at how this would affect residents who couldn't afford to pay them. "There's no relief for your bills, you're going to get shut off, and then everybody knows: you lose your water for ninety days, they cap your sewer, condemn your home, take your children."

LeeAnne Walters spoke to the filmmakers as well. From her stoop, the stay-at-home mother precisely explained the problem: the change to a more corrosive water source, without adequate treatment, caused the protective coating in the city's pipes to break down. This led to her son's diagnosis. She showed his medical report on camera: "The LEAD level is abnormally high."

Hard to Swallow was released on YouTube and the Michigan ACLU's website on June 25, one day after Miguel Del Toral had delivered his report. It proved to be a fortunate coincidence. The film strengthened Walters's confidence in Guyette. And so she gave him a copy of Del Toral's briefing.[41] For the first time, a reporter was armed with hard data about the lead toxicity of Flint's water, data that contradicted the MDEQ's numbers.

With Del Toral's analysis in hand, Guyette contacted city and state officials to get their side of the story. But his affiliation with the ACLU, an advocacy organization, prompted skepticism about how seriously to take him. An email between city employees discussing his interview request described Guyette's role in *Hard to Swallow*, saying that it "somewhat discredits his objectivity."

Another email from an MDEQ public information officer to Brad Wurfel, the communications director, had the same concern. "I got a weird call from a 'reporter' at the ACLU asking about Flint drinking water," she wrote, adding that she felt almost positive that "it's the same guy who used to work at Metro Times." Guyette told her that he had a source at the EPA who said that "we use a 'flawed methodology' to collect our samples," which led to lead levels being seriously underestimated. "Apparently the EPA and Virginia Tech sampled a house using a different methodology and found 13,000 ppb of lead."[42]

Guyette followed up the next afternoon. "ACLU guy is back today," the information officer wrote as she forwarded his email to Wurfel. But Guyette was not the only one being snubbed. Mayor Dayne Walling also inquired about the report after hearing from Guyette, and he asked the EPA's Chicago office if he could get a copy of it. Susan Hedman, the head of the office, didn't send it to him. Instead, she told him that the report was a "preliminary draft" that "should not have been released outside the agency" until after it had been "revised and fully vetted by EPA management." That would take months.[43]

The MDEQ never did get back to Guyette, not even to say "no comment." Despite the lack of cooperation, Guyette wrote a long story that ran on the ACLU's website on Thursday, July 9. It linked to a full copy of the report and included an interview with Del Toral, whom he described as a "whistleblower," although he wasn't that, since he hadn't reached out to a journalist himself or otherwise released his report to a public audience. And he had been purposefully transparent about his investigation all along, copying his EPA superiors at every step. Guyette's article was packaged with a short video titled *Corrosive Impact: Leaded Water and One Flint Family's Leaded Nightmare*.

In the leafy college town of Ann Arbor, at the headquarters of Michigan Radio, someone was watching.

It wasn't long ago that Michigan Radio, the state's leading public radio service, primarily broadcast classical music.[44] In 2007, there were about five people on staff who gathered news. By the time Del Toral wrote his report, there were more than twice that, including reporters, digital producers, and on-air hosts. This upward swing was rare in journalism, but the station's annual operating budget had also grown, in part due to rising listener support. Its programming reached about 450,000 listeners each week via transmitters in Ann Arbor, Grand Rapids, and Flint.

Michigan Radio had filed dispatches about Flint's water—the switch from Detroit, the affordability crisis, the boil-water advisories and TTHMs, even features about, for example, an art installation that one resident made from plastic water bottles.[45] The station was well situated to take the story further. But when reporters and producers read the report that Guyette published, they had a hard time believing it. "There was a disagreement in the newsroom," the news director, Vincent Duffy, recalled. "Some wanted to get it out right away, and others in the newsroom were saying, 'These numbers can't be right. This can't actually be happening that the lead levels are this high in a municipal water system.' Turned out that actually was the case."

On July 9, the same day the ACLU story ran, Michigan Radio's

Lindsey Smith reached out to the MDEQ. Brad Wurfel alerted a number of officials, including Stephen Busch, about her inquiry.

"Steve, I just got a call from [Michigan] Public Radio about an EPA notice to Flint about elevated lead levels in the water," Wurfel wrote. "Apparently, you were cc'd on EPA's note. Can you give me a call ASAP."

"This is what Curt Guyette had been calling about, by the way," wrote the public information officer a minute later. "Apparently it's going to be a thing now."

There was apparently some confusion about Del Toral's report—not everybody at the MDEQ had seen it or realized that it had already been sent to four agency officials. The public radio reporter ended up emailing Wurfel a link to the ACLU site, which he in turn forwarded to his colleagues: "Miguel apparently asserts that the DEQ and EPA are at odds on proper protocol. Which seems weird. Let's discuss!"

Stephen Busch replied to the thread. "Obviously we are not going to comment on an interim draft report," he wrote.

But Brad Wurfel did do an interview with Lindsey Smith, discussing Flint's water issues in a more general way. The segment was broadcast on Michigan Radio on Monday, July 13. It opened with a comment from Wurfel that would become infamous: "Let me start here—anyone who is concerned about lead in the drinking water in Flint can relax."[46]

In light of the state's tests of nearly 170 homes in Flint, Wurfel said, the numbers at LeeAnne Walters's home were outliers. "It does not look like there is any broad problem with the water supply freeing up lead as it goes to homes," he said. He also told the statewide audience that anyone living in a house that was more than thirty years old should get their water tested, no matter what city they lived in.

But just as Wurfel was reassuring Michigan Radio listeners about the water, other people at his agency were noticing that the latest numbers were worrisome. Those 170-some tests cited by Wurfel were from the routine twice-a-year checks that are required by the Lead and Copper Rule. One hundred tests had been done in Flint at the end of 2014. The next batch was due by June 30, 2015. As the deadline neared, Adam Rosenthal, an MDEQ water expert, had emailed Mike Prysby and Stephen Busch: "We hope you have 61 more lead/copper samples collected and sent to the lab" and that they "will be below the AL [action level] for lead. As of now, with 39 results, Flint's . . . over the AL for lead." If the result held, it would trigger a series of requirements, including public notification and active steps to reduce the lead.

After a lot of last-minute scrambling, the MDEQ allowed the city to drop the number of samples from one hundred to sixty on the grounds that Flint's population had slipped to fewer than one hundred thousand people.[47] The city turned in a total of seventy-one. As usual, collectors had been instructed to pre-flush the water. They also side-stepped the EPA guideline to focus on high-risk locations—that is, homes that are likely to be serviced by lead lines, where contamination would be expected to be more severe. Flint couldn't easily find those homes even if it wanted to, since the records on the location of lead pipes were kept on decaying maps and spotty index cards.[48] But after Rosenthal sent his warning, nearly one quarter of the final tests were done at a stretch of road where a major part of the water main had been replaced some years earlier. When mains are updated, lead pipes, if they are there, are often removed, too.[49] In Flint, these samples recorded very little lead.[50] Finally, the rules require that homes tested in the first batch in 2014 be retested in the second round to make it easier to spot changes in the water quality. Yet only thirteen homes were retested—and all of these had scored low lead levels the first time around.[51]

Despite all that, Flint still exceeded the federal limit on lead, according to a report dated July 28. Even by the state's own numbers, Wurfel's claims on Michigan Radio didn't hold up. The water wasn't safe after all. The state would have to work with the city on a major notification campaign, advising residents on how to protect themselves.

But then the MDEQ did a curious thing. It supervised a revision of the results, with two of the seventy-one samples—both with extremely high lead—dropped from the calculation. One of them came from

LeeAnne Walters's home. Scrapping those tests brought the city's lead level down to 11 ppb. That's high, but within acceptable limits. When these revised results were made official, Michael Glasgow, Flint's utilities administrator, added a handwritten note, "Two samples were removed from list for not meeting sample criteria."[52]

LeeAnne Walters had been giving these public reports her close attention, and she noticed that her sample was excised. She wanted to know why. The MDEQ explained that she had a filter, which altered the water's quality and invalidated the sample. (In fact, Walters had been told to remove the filter before the test, and she had done so.) The second sample was disqualified because it didn't come from a single-family residence. Being stringent about the Lead and Copper Rule only when it lowered the lead count, while exploiting loopholes at every other turn, made the water seem perfectly compliant with the law.

As Flint endured an unseasonably hot summer, and media attention became sharper, Mayor Dayne Walling went on local television to calm the rising panic. He said that he and his family still drank the city water, and he encouraged others to do the same.[53] He took a sip of it from a mug, live and on air, calmly telling the news anchor, "It's your standard tap water."

Meanwhile, the EPA's Chicago office was fielding complaints about Del Toral's report. Aggrieved staffers in the MDEQ protested that they had "obtained a copy from an outside [ACLU] website." At least one of those complaints came from someone who had in fact been copied directly. The EPA's repeated defense was that Del Toral's report was the product of his own research; it hadn't been reviewed or approved by the EPA. By releasing it outside the agency, he essentially acted outside his authority. The EPA did urge the MDEQ to tell Flint to get going with a corrosion control program (the state agency still disputed its necessity), but it had a generous timeline to implement it. So long, in fact, that Flint probably wouldn't complete the program before it switched to lake water from the KWA.

By now, Miguel Del Toral was nowhere to be seen. He wasn't

doing interviews, he wasn't included on email threads about Flint, and he didn't appear to join any interagency conference calls. When LeeAnne Walters went to Lansing with a group of organizers, she was told by the MDEQ that the report was flawed and that "Miguel had been handled." There, it seemed, his work in Flint would end.[54]

"When I heard that, I grew quite concerned," Marc Edwards recalled. "It wasn't just smoke here, there was fire."[55]

Meditations in an Emergency

Destroy yourself, if you don't know!/It is easy to be beautiful; it is difficult to appear so.

—Frank O'Hara, "Meditations in an Emergency" (1957)

I.

What do you do when a city is in a crisis? How do you fix a decades-old, slow-burn emergency? By the time of Flint's water switch, the city's problems were so deep-rooted and familiar that just about anyone in the state could have rattled them off (and so could people well beyond Michigan, thanks to storytellers such as native son Michael Moore). For local leaders like BB Nolden, the water issues seemed like one more thing on a long list of worries. *Everything* was urgent; in a strange way that made nothing urgent. This might explain the sluggish response of people who could have looked closer, sooner, at Flint's water: public servants, journalists, environmental organizations, academics, medical professionals. But the water crisis was not just one more thing. Not only was the risk mortal, it was shaped from the start by the unusual political context of the city. Under emergency management, Flint didn't have the power to make decisions for itself.

The story went back to 2011, Election Day, a downright balmy November afternoon. It reached 63 degrees in Flint at one point. Not bad at all for door knocking in the neighborhoods. Mayor Dayne Walling was running for his first full term in office, after having won a special midterm election two years earlier, and he was taking nothing for granted. He drove his dark silver 2006 Chevy Impala—GM-made, naturally—through town, going house by house and encouraging people to vote before the polls closed. Later, as was his tradition, he would end Election Day at his own polling location.

But plans changed when Walling's cell phone rang. It was minutes before three in the afternoon. He had just parked the Impala outside Neithercut Elementary School on the city's southwest side, and as he lumbered out of the car with the phone pressed against his ear, he found himself talking to Andy Dillon, Michigan's state treasurer. It was a brief conversation. Dillon informed Walling that in two hours, just in time for the evening newscasts, the governor would announce that Flint was a fiscal disaster. The state was appointing an emergency manager to take charge. This was the ninth time that a Michigan city had come under emergency management.[1] Flint now accounted for two of those nine times.

"I was just completely stunned that an emergency manager was being appointed without any substantial consultation with me about next steps," Walling remembered. That the announcement came on Election Day "immediately led me to believe that a strange political calculus was behind that."[2]

With about $25.7 million in accumulated deficits, Flint was designated by a unanimous state panel as being in a "local government financial emergency."[3] The questionable handling of Flint's water and sewer funds got a special mention; in years past, money had been transferred out of them to fill cash shortages in the city's general operations. To replace the depleted funds, water and sewer rates spiked under Mayor Walling. Three of the panel's members had Flint connections: a former state senator who represented the area; a local businessman; and a onetime city administrator: Darnell Earley. Given the emergency designation, which Walling did not dispute, the panel had a choice of options to recommend. One was to reach a consent agreement for the state and city to tackle the difficulties cooperatively. Walling had expected this and was ready with a few proposals for such an agreement. But the panel claimed that local officials had not moved "with a degree of urgency and vigor commensurate with the seriousness of the existing financial emergency."[4] And so, five hours before the polls closed on the day that Flint reelected Dayne Walling with 56 percent of the vote, he learned that he was campaigning for an empty post, one that had been scrubbed of substance.

Walling's shock that afternoon muted his memory of all that was said, which he regrets. But as far as he could recall, Andy Dillon gave him a phone number, saying he should use it if he needed to reach the Michigan State Police. "I couldn't figure out if he thought there was a personal protection issue, or if people would start rioting," Walling said.[5] "Here I had, out of love for my city and motivation to tackle these difficult issues, moved home with my young family . . . and taken on personal and campaign debt, had finally won an election. . . . I probably knew more about government than a lot of state officials combined. I'm out busting my ass, walking the streets of Flint, asking people to support me to be mayor, and the governor's going to sit back in his office, and . . . dial in an emergency manager who's going to show up and become the mayor and the council. It was just so fundamentally wrong."

Emergency management is supposed to be an extreme measure to meet extreme need. Eighteen states have a mechanism for the state to oversee local matters in distressed cities.[6] In the 1970s, a state financial control board maneuvered New York City through its near-bankruptcy. New Jersey was the first to put a school district under its oversight (Jersey City, 1989), and it since did the same for the cities of Camden, Paterson, Trenton, Harrison, Asbury Park, Atlantic City, and Newark.[7] Pennsylvania intervened in dozens of its struggling cities; Pittsburgh's finances were under state control for about fourteen years, beginning in 2004.[8] Congress created a mechanism for the fiscal oversight of Washington, D.C., and the person appointed to the job, Anthony Williams, was so successful and popular, he ended up being elected mayor in 1999. (Dayne Walling worked in Williams's administration.)

Connecticut created its bipartisan Municipal Accountability Review Board in 2017, whereby cities such as Hartford could apply for different levels of state involvement, which came with an infusion of funding to meet basic needs.[9]

In Michigan, the legislature first created a statute in 1988 to assign an "emergency financial manager" in Hamtramck, a small, diverse, independent town within Detroit's borders. Two years later, the statute was expanded so that emergency managers could be deployed to any seriously troubled municipality or public school district. The policy was designed for cities and schools to escape bankruptcy, which destroys credit ratings, while tapping some of its advantages, such as the ability to restructure debt.[10] The measure was used sparingly—only three cities were placed under emergency management over its first decade or so. But in 2002, it came to Flint for the first time. The governor appointed Ed Kurtz, a local resident and the president of Baker College, as the first emergency manager. (He'd show up again in the same role about a decade later.) Kurtz vowed to take no salary. The city then had 125,000 people, 8.3 percent unemployment, a deficit growing close to $30 million, and the dubious distinction of being the largest community in the state to get an intervention. Michigan's treasurer at the time explained to the *New York Times* that Flint needed an emergency manager because it had failed to deal with the reality of its declining tax base. "Why do you have to have the state come in and tell you that you have a problem?" he told the reporter. "If we don't act now, when do we act?"[11]

Kurtz's authority was intermittent at first, as the City Council challenged the takeover in court. But by the end of the first year, he had implemented new code enforcement measures for buildings and homes, cut the pay for the mayor and council members, and eliminated the health, dental, and vision benefits for most city officials.[12] (Two years later, he reinstated some of the pay.) Flint's retirement board, facing Kurtz's threat to replace its members, approved proposals to reduce contributions to the pension system. Kurtz temporarily shuttered recreation centers, closed the ombudsman's office, and worked with the largest union to agree to a 4 percent pay cut. He also approved more than $1 million for sewer and road improvements and raised water bills by 11 percent. After almost two years, Kurtz recommended ending the emergency. But by then "there wasn't much left," Jim Ananich said. A schoolteacher and the son of a city ombudsman, the future state senator was elected to Flint's council just after Kurtz left. "We're rebuilding. The finances were in better shape, but there was nothing there."

In the spring of 2011, Michigan broadened its emergency management system. Public Act 4, signed by Governor Rick Snyder, became one of the most expansive laws of its kind. It gave the governor's office the ability to appoint an emergency manager who, for the first time, could reject, modify, or terminate contracts and union agreements—steps that are typically possible only if a city is in Chapter 9 bankruptcy.[13] It also lowered the threshold for what would warrant state intervention in the first place. And local governments were expected to pay the salaries of their state-appointed managers.

Even in its new guise, Michigan's emergency manager law remained focused on finances. "That's the problem." The goal is "to balance the books, and if you can try to get something else done, I guess you can try that. But that's not what you go there for. And then the state's idea is to get out as soon as possible," said Michael Stampfler, a former emergency manager for the City of Pontiac.[14] It was a short-term strategy for long-term problems. Emergency managers might make real improvements by cutting costs, but they are not necessarily ones that endure. Perhaps the strongest evidence of the mismatch between the problems and the solution is the fact that, despite being approved by the state as the best leader for the job, and with extraordinary powers to act, EMs tend to cycle in and out of the same communities.

Against the argument that this mechanism interrupts the democratic process, supporters of emergency management point out that residents are as much citizens of the state as they are of their city. The governor is an elected leader with jurisdiction over the distressed community. And anyway, emergency management can't be an encroachment on local sovereignty when the state created that sovereignty in the first place. If the state empowered its cities, then it has the authority to disempower them, or even unincorporate them.[15] Also, there is always an effort to choose an EM with local connections, such as Ed Kurtz and Darnell Earley. And—facts are facts—oftentimes EMs have interrupted cycles of corruption in local leadership, including a bribery scandal in the suburb of Ecorse. By the time emergency manager Joyce Parker ended her tenure there, Ecorse had eliminated $14.6 million in debt and had its first positive general fund balance in six years.[16] Parker then became the emergency manager for Allen Park, another inner-ring suburb. It was struggling with debt following a bad movie studio deal that eventually led to fraud charges against a former mayor and city administrator. In a settlement with the U.S. Securities and Exchange Commission, they were barred from any future municipal bond deals, and the mayor faced a $10,000 civil penalty. Parker, meanwhile, exited her role as EM after two years, leaving Allen Park with a projected fund balance of $3.6 million.

And besides, these cities *are* in an emergency. It must be named as such. The state would be remiss to let them unravel without even trying to intervene. Emergency management could be described as a late-coming corrective to the state's apathy over decades of urban distress. Through the EM system, the state is finally admitting that there is a problem in its cities, and it has both the responsibility and the power to do something about it.

However, emergency management in Michigan, and the disenfranchisement that followed, had unmistakable racial overtones. The communities affected were nearly always majority black, including Flint. By 2017, 52 percent of Michigan's black residents and 16 percent of Latinos had lived in cities governed by unelected authorities. Only 2 percent of white people had the same experience, although there were many other impoverished communities in Michigan that were majority white.[17] To put it another way, if you lived in Michigan, there was a 10 percent chance that you lived under emergency management at some point between 2009 and 2016. If you were black, that possibility jumped to 50 percent.[18] The statistics reflected the urban decay resulting from institutionalized segregation, just as the Kerner Commission had foretold half a century earlier.

Under the Voting Rights Act, communities of color that have historically been disenfranchised are supposed to be protected from "a broad array of dilution schemes" that could minimize the power of their votes.[19] Among those schemes, the law explicitly includes the tactic of turning elected posts into appointed ones. But Michigan circumvented that by instituting an appointed post that superseded the elected position.[20] The upshot: white and black voters had different experiences of democracy. It didn't really matter whether that was the intention of the law's architects; the results were the same. The appearance of different rules of law for different groups of people bred disillusionment and distrust that extended far beyond the term of any single emergency manager, even if he or she was exceptionally talented and well meaning. Yet another echo of the Kerner Commission's findings in the 1960s.[21]

It was too much. Activists were determined to repeal Public Act 4. They gathered enough signatures to get it on the ballot, and in November 2012 voters rejected the expanded emergency management law.[22] The count was close, but certain: seventy-five of Michigan's eighty-three counties voted to take Public Act 4 off the books.

But the reprieve was brief. Six weeks later, a lame-duck legislature passed a nearly identical version of Public Act 4 and Snyder signed it. The simulacrum, Public Act 436, had some tweaks that gave local officials a somewhat bigger role. It newly required that the state, rather than municipalities or school districts, had to pay the salaries of emergency managers. But the scope of their powers remained the same. Significantly, the new law came with funds attached, which made it impossible to eliminate through another statewide referendum.

The rush to reinstitutionalize the expanded powers of emergency managers was probably tied to Michigan's plans for its largest city, Detroit. Three months after Public Act 436 was signed, a lawyer from Washington, D.C., was chosen as Detroit's emergency manager. A University of Michigan graduate who had helped Chrysler navigate its brush with insolvency, Kevyn Orr, steered the Motor City through an impossibly complex municipal bankruptcy.

Detroit's bankruptcy was resolved with an $816 million "grand bargain," an unlikely deal that involved philanthropic and corporate donations to spare the Detroit Institute of Arts from being pillaged by creditors and to soften pension cuts (which still suffered harsh losses).[23] More than $7 billion in Detroit's unsecured debt was wiped out, making it possible for the city to reinvest in public services. But Detroit was an unusual case. Rather than recruiting the most talented leader possible to serve as emergency manager, more common is for modestly accomplished administrators—they need only five years of business or government experience—to be shuffled from one distressed city and school district to another.[24]

And state oversight can go on, it seems, indefinitely. Officially, a city council can vote the EM out of office after eighteen months with a two-thirds majority.[25] But the state gets around that term limit (imposed by its own law) with a neat trick—the emergency manager resigns before the term expires. A new one is appointed and the clock starts over. Thus Detroit's public schools were under the control of the state for eight years, and the city of Flint for three and a half years. When the last emergency manager departed Flint in April 2015, the city's $19.1 million deficit had been eliminated (thanks in part to a last-minute $7 million state loan). But the city had endured debilitating cuts and was in the midst of a life-threatening water crisis. In his exit letter, Jerry Ambrose didn't address the water quality, but he acknowledged that the aging infrastructure and sky-high rates were "another factor impeding the City's ability to attract and retain businesses and residents. There needs to be a concerted effort to reduce rates by as much as 50%, but that cannot even be contemplated without the commitment of financial assistance from the state and federal governments." Though Flint was a founding member of the KWA, "it will not be sufficient to lower water costs."[26] Also, the Office of the Ombudsman, formed decades earlier as a watchdog against mismanagement and corruption in local government, had been eliminated by emergency managers. In a parting order, Ambrose, specifically forbid the city from funding it again, or revising any changes made by an EM until it had been out of receivership for at least a year. (It wouldn't be until April 2018 that the governor announced Flint's exit from that form of state oversight.)

What unfolded in Flint revealed not only the limits of austerity, but also the fatal flaw in Michigan's experiment with expansive emergency management: there is no transparency or accountability when things go wrong.

II.

Flint might have suffered a democracy deficit, but its people found other ways of showing up for their community. The city's culture of organizing had been passed down through the generations. The United Auto Workers began their historic sit-down strike in Flint. Frustrated with stunted wages, dangerous conditions, and the company's efforts to intimidate them from forming a union, workers occupied two auto plants on December 30, 1936. Refusing to leave or work, they staged concerts and lectures, while supporters delivered food and picketed outside. The strike spread to a third plant in February. With workers staying inside, it was impossible for the company to hire replacements and get the lines moving again. GM tried turning off the heat to freeze the strikers out, but they remained, burning burlap to stay warm. It took forty-four days, but GM eventually announced a $25 million wage increase and recognition of the union's right to organize—a first for America's auto industry.[27] It changed lives. Unpaid overtime was banned, wages were fairer, and dangerous environmental conditions were improved, including poor ventilation in the paint department. A few decades later, citizens banded together against segregation and racial discrimination in real estate with the sleep-in on the lawn of city hall, a rally that drew thousands, and a first-of-its-kind fair housing vote. And in the twenty-first century, when emergency management came to Flint, residents founded groups such as the Democracy Defense League to challenge it.

So it was no surprise that when they knew the water switch had gone poorly, the people of Flint got organized. Besides protests, petitions, and public meetings, they kept meticulous notes, collected samples, hosted makeshift water distribution sites, created social media pages to share information, and sought public documents. The volunteer staff of *East Village Magazine*, one of the oldest community media outlets in the country, tracked the story in each monthly issue. Residents also enlisted environmental justice experts from around the country for their insight on the crisis. At wateryoufightingfor.com, a website set up by Melissa Mays and her collaborators, they shared research and advice from the leader of the Love Canal movement.[28]

In the spring of 2015, a number of groups banded together as the Coalition for Clean Water to better coordinate their activism. They met in the basement of the Reverend Alfred Harris's Saints of God Church. When LeeAnne Walters and other families learned the disturbing results of their lead tests, the coalition made sure to reach four thousand homes, distributing information about the dangers of contamination. And in March, after emergency manager Jerry Ambrose overruled the City Council's vote to get Flint off the river water as soon as possible, the coalition sought an injunction to force the city to act (an effort that died in the courtroom). The activists also repeatedly made the hour-long drive to Lansing to make their case to the governor's aides and the MDEQ. They invited Governor Snyder to visit Flint—the invitation was declined. In July, the Flint community partnered with activists in Detroit who were facing escalating water shutoffs in their own city. Together they led the Detroit to Flint Water Justice Journey, a seventy-mile march that told the intersecting stories of each city. In short, the organizers did everything they could think of to make their plight—their city—visible.

Despite the activism, the journalism, and the independent monitoring, the state didn't budge from its position. The MDEQ kept pointing to its test results of 169 water samples, which, it claimed, were proof that there was nothing to worry about. On its side, the community had the samples from LeeAnne Walters's home that had been analyzed by Virginia Tech, plus a smattering from other residents who had requested free tests from the city. The community argued that Flint wasn't just facing a lead problem; there had been a pattern of contamination, including *E. coli* and TTHM violations. And they had Miguel Del Toral's damning memo, too. But the state said the earlier contamination issues had been resolved, Del Toral's boss had backed away from his memo, and Flint would be back on Lake Huron water soon enough. The plan, it seemed, was to run out the clock.

The only thing to do was to double down and collect more and better data. Curt Guyette, who saw that the rising media interest hadn't done much to change the state's response, had access to grant money at the ACLU that could be used to pay for expert research. He broached an idea to Marc Edwards at Virginia Tech. What about doing an independent test of the water in Flint? Like the analysis done at LeeAnne Walters's house, but this time spanning the whole city? Edwards liked the idea. It would work, though, only if there were enough volunteers to conduct this massive experiment in a short time. And it would need to be done with the strictest rigor so that the test could withstand all scrutiny—to make it "bulletproof," as Guyette said: "we knew they would come after us."[29] It would take fifty samples for a scientifically valid test. One hundred samples would be better. Each test cost about $70.

Guyette contacted the Coalition for Clean Water. Could its people collect a hundred water samples from all across Flint—and quickly? No problem. As Guyette remembers it, an energized Rev. Harris said that he and his fellow pastors could do it themselves.[30] Guyette then turned to the ACLU: the grant money would need to run to $7,000, at least. But Edwards landed on another option—an emergency stipend from the National Science Foundation. These are usually given in the wake of extreme disasters, such as tsunamis, hurricanes, oil spills, and earthquakes, but Edwards's research team argued for a rapid response to a looming public health catastrophe in Flint. As they wrote in their application, what was happening in the city was "occurring at some level in many other financially stressed U.S. urban centers with decaying drinking water infrastructure."[31] An independent citywide test could "help inform the current policy debate regarding strategies for dealing with cities that have gone bankrupt, as well as the discussion of access to safe and affordable drinking water as a basic human right."[32] Guyette liked this idea better: unlike the ACLU, the foundation was "not an activist organization," he said. "They're pure science."[33] It would be harder for critics to dismiss the citizen-led study as biased.

To staff his side of the team, Edwards recruited a raft of undergraduates, grad students, and postdoc research assistants for a meeting, using free pizza as bait. Many of them had taken the engineering ethics class taught by Yanna Lambrinidou and himself, and the students could see the link between what had happened in Washington, D.C., and what was happening in Flint. About thirty students formed what became the Flint Water Study group.

By August, their test was well under way. The students at Virginia Tech distributed three hundred sampling kits to the organizers in Flint, conducted tests at businesses and homes while visiting the city, and planned tests in Detroit to compare the different water systems.

The sampling kits sent to the coalition were packaged in brown cardboard boxes, each containing three plastic bottles of different sizes, and a set of instructions. All the items in each box were marked with an identifying number to keep them organized.

Grad student William Rhoads hosted an instructional video on YouTube that showed the coalition how to collect samples.[34] After filling the largest bottle with one full liter, they needed to pause for precisely forty-five seconds before filling the second bottle. Another two-minute break, and then they needed to fill the last and smallest bottle. This test could be done only after the taps had been turned off for at least six hours—that's a requirement from the Lead and Copper Rule, though, unlike the instruction LeeAnne Walters received, there was no cap on how long the water had been stagnant.[35] (The longer it's stagnant, the more likely that lead will show up.) There was also no pre-flushing in the Virginia Tech tests, compared to the official rules that said that the tap should run for "at least 5 minutes" before sampling.[36] All three bottles had to be filled from the cold tap at high flow (which is when lead is most likely to flake into the water), with the tap remaining open as the collectors filled each sample. By collecting multiple samples from the same tap, there could be more confidence in the results, since lead release can be erratic. These bottles also had wide mouths, like mayonnaise jars, while the city tests used narrow mouths, which meant the bottle was probably filled at a low flow to keep the water from splattering and was thus less likely to pull lead out of the plumbing. The Lead and Copper Rule doesn't specify what bottles to use. Small-mouth bottles were another opportunity to minimize the lead levels.

Each bottle had to be capped, sealed in a plastic bag, and returned to the cardboard box with the information sheet that identified the source of the water. At that point, the coalition implemented a system to make the samples as tamperproof as possible to answer critics who would surely accuse them of skewing the test results (by deliberately adding lead to the water, for example). When they were later scrutinized, the system proved its worth.[37] Before each cardboard box was sealed, residents would initial near the seam of the flaps. The package was then taped in front of them so that the initials were under the tape.[38] If somebody tried to open the package after it was sealed, the inked initials would peel off. After this, the box went to a collection point in Flint and from there to Blacksburg, Virginia.

The undertaking was a formidable one, involving a simple but exacting process that needed to be replicated again and again. Samples were needed from across the breadth of the city to give a comprehensive picture of Flint's water. Residents had to be able to trust the organizers who knocked on their doors. This is where Flint's genius for community organizing shined. Volunteers first learned the process and then passed on their training to their neighbors. They broke down the city by zip codes as they coordinated deliveries and pickups. "You know, scientifically, we couldn't have done it any better ourselves," Edwards said. "They implemented training procedures that I think the city and EPA should be using around the country."[39]

Guyette joined the coalition organizers as they knocked on doors. "I was really walking a line in my own role as a journalist and activist," he recalled. "I'm not just observing the story. I'm participating in it. In my mind, I'm just trying to get to the truth." And he was not canvassing the streets just to get a story that nailed the authorities. If the testing found that the water was genuinely safe to drink, "we'd do a story on that and put people's minds at ease," he said, because at that point, "there was so much worry and confusion, it'd still be of value."[40]

None of this happened in secret. Edwards notified the MDEQ and the Flint treatment plant about the study.[41] The citizen scientists and Virginia Tech students were perfectly visible as they roved the streets. Guyette posted ongoing reports online, as did the local news outlets. Edwards and other team members published updates on FlintWaterStudy.org, a new blog that was similar to a watchdog site kept by D.C. organizers in the aftermath of that city's lead crisis.[42]

They also posted simple but dramatic experiments on the blog. To illustrate the Flint River's corrosiveness, for example, the team collected Flint water in two clean glass containers. A piece of iron was placed in one of them, and the team measured the levels of chlorine disinfectant in the water as time went on. In the container that held only water, chlorine levels stayed fairly steady. But in the one with the piece of iron, the chlorine nearly vanished after twelve hours. The problem was that the water's level of chlorides—the same compound that the GM engine plant blamed for corroding its machinery—was so high that it made the iron break down. The free-floating iron then swallowed up the chlorine disinfectant, probably to a level that was below the minimum required for drinking water. And the longer the test ran, the less chlorine there was. That suggested that people in Flint who lived in high vacancy areas, where water ran through the pipes more slowly, were more likely to drink water that was dangerous.

In a little over two weeks, the coalition distributed all 300 of the lead-sampling kits to Flint residents and collected back 277—an astonishing rate of return, and substantially more than the city's own collection over the past year.[43] The grant application had assumed it would get only 100 kits returned, or one third of the total. But that didn't account for the coalition's determination. "I bet you'd crawl over broken glass just to get one more kit," Guyette told LeeAnne Walters.[44] He was joking, but she responded with the utmost seriousness: "Yes."

III.

Analysis of the kits showed that the poison was spread across the entire city. The study confirmed what should have been obvious: when corrosive water moves through lead pipes and plumbing, and it isn't treated with corrosion control, a lot of lead ends up in the water. That's especially true if the pipes are old, leaky, oversized, and cross long stretches of vacant land.

In Flint, using the usual federal formula, the water samples had 26.79 parts per billion of lead in them, well over the federal action level and nearly three times the safety standard of the World Health Organization (10 ppb). All ages, all income levels, and all ethnicities were affected by contaminated water, but not evenly. While lead pipes were installed all over the metropolitan region—they had been standard issue for decades—some neighborhoods had worse water than others. The highest tested sample came in at 1051 ppb, and in a couple of hard-hit zip codes, one in five homes had high lead. In keeping with the pattern of inequality built into the region, it could be presumed that commuters were also exposed to the toxic water, but far less than the people living in the city.

The samples and the distribution system were also tested for chlorine. Sure enough, there was very little chlorine in Flint's water, even though it had been added as a disinfectant at the treatment plant. Just as the Virginia Tech experiment had shown, the iron that turned the water brown also consumed the chlorine.[45]

This is how the Coalition for Clean Water and the Flint Water Study group showed that the series of problems with Flint's water were connected. Since the switch from Detroit, rapidly corroding iron negated the chlorine treatment. Without the disinfectant, the water was vulnerable to bacteria growth. The first of the E. coli bacteria violations had come a few months after the switch. To combat it, more chlorine was added to the water. But this likely contributed to the spike in TTHMs, the disinfectant by-product that forms in reaction to organic matter. (Organic matter is also more plentiful in the river water, especially when it's not properly filtered.) As the corrosion worsened, lead leached into the water right along with the iron.[46] The excess iron also turned out to be a perfect nutrient for the growth of other types of bacteria—deadly and, for the time being, undetected.

Nobody should be drinking this water. The Flint Water Study team in Blacksburg wrote to each home with the results of their sample. They also called the residents one by one. One of the graduate students, Siddhartha Roy, found that no one was particularly surprised to hear about high levels of lead. But the calls were still agonizing. Roy managed to get through only six before he had to stop. "I was done," he said. "I was too depressed."[47]

Blood

I just needed time to think, to figure out what was happening.
—Lois Gibbs, *Love Canal: My Story* (1982)

I.

Before a trio of flagpoles on the lawn outside Flint's city hall, the same place that had been the site of innumerable water protests over the past year, an unusual ensemble of people—activists, scientists, professors, students, preachers—stood before a small army from the media. It was Tuesday, September 15, 2015, and this group was ready to formally present the findings from the citywide water test. The numbers were scary. But they had more than a few ideas for what to do about them.

"Thank you all for coming. Today is a huge, huge day for the water fight in Flint," said Melissa Mays, her silver jewelry shining in the sun.[1] The confirmation of lead in the water was "a strong punch," exposing what had been done to Flint's citizens and what had been covered up. The activists clamored for redress: the city should immediately return to the cleanest, freshest water possible—Lake Huron water from Detroit; the MDEQ should distribute free lead-certified

water filters to every house; Flint needed to warn every resident connected to a lead service line about the risk and replace all those lines at
no cost. Marc Edwards said that his team estimated the amount of
lead in the water of about five thousand Flint homes exceeded standards set by the World Health Organization. Someone in the audience gasped.

The biggest response of the afternoon—applause and cheers and
emphatic nods—came when Curt Guyette called for a full, independent investigation into how the city conducted its own water tests.
And LeeAnne Walters said that there had to be a complete philosoph-
ical turnaround in environmental oversight. "Basically, the bottom
line is, stop trying to come up with ways to try and hide the lead,"
she said. "You should be *looking* for the high lead. That is your job
as the DEQ. When you find it, you tell us. . . . Do your job, the way
the EPA intended for you to do it."

At the Saints of God Church later that day, the wooden pews were
packed with a diverse swath of Flint residents. They wore orange
baseball caps and straw hats, blue-collared shirts and white T-shirts,
turquoise jackets and tank tops. But their faces were universally grim
as they took in the details of the test results. Most of the lead was
found in the central belt of the city. Many samples exceeded 100 ppb,
and as a whole Flint's water measured at an astonishing 27 ppb. That
was almost twice the federal action level, and what's more, it presented an extreme picture of what calculated disinvestment looks
like in the modern day. Flint's neighborhoods were no longer graded
one by one by federal assessors, with African American communities
(and those who lived too close to them) redlined. Now that black
people made up the majority of Flint, and close to half the population
was impoverished, the city as a *whole* was effectively redlined. The
test numbers showed excessive lead in every zip code——some more
than others, certainly, but all experiencing the disturbing consequences of being a shrinking city. Flint wasn't being demolished for a
new highway as St. John and Floral Park had been. It was being
demolished by neglect.

"Don't drink the water," the coalition said again—it couldn't be emphasized enough. If the water must be used, it should be flushed first at a high flow (for exactly the same lead-clearing reason that makes this a suspect tactic for sampling in water tests). Infants who drank formula made with Flint's tap water were at especially great risk. The Flint Water Study group set up a crowdfunding campaign to get lead-certified filters to residents. They were hoping for $25,000; so far, they'd raised $520.[2]

People like Sonya Lee were beginning to wonder what the water crisis might have cost them. It wasn't just the itchy rash on her arm, which she treated with Vaseline. And it wasn't just that when she washed with the water that came out of the faucet "there is like a slimy film that comes on my hair. Of course, me being African American, that is not good."[3] What hurt most was that her two beloved German shepherds, Kizzy and Soldier, had gotten sick. "We never gave them bottled water. It was always from the faucet." One day, Sonya's son Kendrick told her, "'Momma, Soldier's not gonna last long.' And I said, 'Ken, don't say that!' And he said, 'Well, I just want you to know because his head is shaking like he's got Parkinson's.' And I just, I was just, kinda devastated." Kizzy died on a Saturday night. Within a month, Soldier died as well. "I believe with the lead and whatever the contamination was, that affected them," Sonya said. (She said that her home tested at 68 ppb of lead.) "Who would've thought that we were poisoning them ourselves, with the water?"

II.

For more than a year, the concerns of the people in Flint hadn't been taken seriously. Now, with Miguel Del Toral's memo and the Virginia Tech study, they had another level of authority backing them up. But even that wasn't enough to turn the state around—at least, not publicly.

This group "specializes in looking for high lead problems," Brad Wurfel, the MDEQ spokesperson, told Ron Fonger of the *Flint Journal*.[4] "They pull that rabbit out of that hat everywhere they go."

Members of the Virginia Tech team were outsiders who had "just arrived in town and quickly proven the theory they set out to prove . . . while the state appreciates academic participation in this discussion, offering broad, dire public health advice based on some quick testing could be seen as fanning political flames irresponsibly. Residents of Flint concerned about the health of their community don't need more of that."

Wurfel held fast to the old claim that the lead levels in LeeAnne Walters's house had nothing to do with the source water or city pipes. To the Michigan governor's office, which was fielding questions from a U.S. senator, Wurfel said that Walters had had an "EPA lead specialist come to her home and do tests, then released an unvetted draft of his report (that EPA apologized to us profusely for) to the resident, who shared it with the ACLU, who promptly used it to continue raising hell with the locals."[5] Folks in Flint were upset, Wurfel added, "because they pay a ton for water and many of them don't trust the water they're getting," and they were confused "because various groups have worked hard at keeping them confused and upset. We get it. The state is trying like mad [to] get the word out that we're working on every aspect of the health [and] safety of local water that we can manage, and the system needs a lot of work," but, he said, "it's been rough sledding with a steady parade of community groups keeping everyone hopped-up and misinformed."[6]

Still, behind the scenes, the state seemed to be hedging its bets. The governor's office quietly tapped an unnamed donor to purchase fifteen hundred faucet filters. The Concerned Pastors for Social Action distributed them on September 1; the filters were gone in three hours.[7] But the news wasn't made public until weeks later—the governor's staff had asked the organization not to talk about it. While the state stood by the safety of Flint's water, a spokesperson for the governor's office later explained, the filters were a way to relieve the discoloration and odor problems, and the state was respecting the wishes of the donor by not making a big deal out of the gift. But the Reverend Alfred Harris was quizzical. "If the water was okay, why would the governor work with someone to provide the filters?" he told a reporter. "I think the state working with the private donor is an admission the people needed some help."[8]

Meanwhile, in the Michigan Department of Health and Human Services, there was discussion about how its representatives ought to talk about the water problems in public. One person in the department emailed a colleague: "It may be a good time to float the draft [plan] out to the others because if we're going to take action it needs to be soon before the Virginia Tech University folks scandalize us all."[9]

III.

It was supposed to be a social dinner, just among friends. Elin Betanzo and Mona Hanna-Attisha had gone to high school together in a Detroit suburb. As teenagers, they both joined the environmental club and protested a polluting trash incinerator. They went to different colleges, but both designed their own majors in environmental science and health. Years later, Betanzo played the piano at Hanna-Attisha's wedding. And in August 2015, when a mutual friend from school was passing through town, Hanna-Attisha invited them all to dinner at the West Bloomfield home she shared with her husband and two young daughters.[10]

As it so often does, the kitchen conversation turned toward work. Betanzo was a hydraulic engineer who specialized in drinking water. She had worked for nearly ten years at the EPA's Office of Ground Water and Drinking Water in Washington, D.C., overlapping almost exactly with D.C.'s. lead crisis and its ignoble aftermath. After a stint at a water utility, Betanzo moved back to southeastern Michigan. She had children now, her parents were aging, and so she found a job with a D.C. think tank that allowed her to telecommute. Her job these days involved a lot of tedious research, she told her friends at the dinner party, and it felt like she never left the house.

"At least you don't have to commute," Hanna-Attisha said, as Betanzo remembered it. "I have to drive an hour to Flint every day."

Betanzo sat up straight. As a water expert who had been horrified by the lead crisis in D.C., she'd kept her eye on Flint. At the time, local headlines were tracking the water test by citizen scientists, but only preliminary results had been released. It was all eerily familiar. Betanzo remembered the community activism in D.C., and she knew about Marc Edwards, not only from her time at the EPA but as a graduate of Virginia Tech. She had no doubt that if he was on the case, there was a real problem. But in D.C., Betanzo had also learned that it was not enough to prove your case scientifically. It didn't matter if you broke environmental law, apparently. Nobody would do anything about it unless you could show that people were getting hurt.

"You're in Flint? A hospital in Flint?" Betanzo exclaimed. Hanna-Attisha must have thought her crazy; her friend well knew that she'd been working as a pediatrician at Hurley Medical Center for years. "Do you have access to all the medical records in your hospital?"

"Yeah. That's my job!"

"Oh, my God," Betanzo said. And she proceeded to tell her friend that there was something she had to do.

In D.C., it took years for independent researchers and community organizers to get medical data about how the lead-saturated water had affected people. That's why there had been a raft of new investigations and coverage years after the water was first contaminated and after the *Washington Post* first broke the story. At the dinner party, Betanzo realized that her old friend Mona had that crucial information at her fingertips. She directed Hurley's pediatric residency program and she taught in Michigan State University's College of Human Medicine, which was headquartered in Flint. For children on Medicaid, blood-lead levels are supposed to be checked during a child's routine medical screening, so records must have been on file documenting the lead absorption of thousands of Flint children. There were also blood-lead records for Genesee County children, which could be compared with Flint's. Somebody just needed to put the pieces together to see whether leaded water was causing health disparities between children who lived inside the city and those who lived outside of it. If Flint's drinking water was causing harm, the health records would tell the story.

Betanzo caught Hanna-Attisha up on what had happened in D.C., what was at stake in Flint, and why these data were such an important piece of the story. She sent her all the important documents, including the infamous CDC report denying the harm done by high lead levels in D.C., the story of the CDC backpedaling that claim, and Miguel Del Toral's memo about Flint. The pediatrician was all in.

But that didn't mean it was easy. Hanna-Attisha turned to the Genesee County Health Department and asked for its blood-lead data. The records came in individual patient files, one PDF for each child, which made it difficult to analyze for broad trends. She also asked the state for its data—data that Brad Wurfel cited on Michigan Radio to tamp down the fears about lead, saying that there hadn't been a spike in Flint children's blood-lead levels. Meanwhile, Hanna-Attisha and her research assistant worked late in the evenings to sort through Hurley's 1,746 test results for Flint children and 1,640 records for children elsewhere in Genesee County.[11] She and Betanzo went back and forth with the data as well, looking at the numbers in different ways.

Betanzo also realized that the think tank she worked for had congressional contacts. She arranged to talk to an environmental staff member who worked for Representative Dan Kildee, the district's leader in Washington, to tell him what was going on. Residents had been barraging the congressman's office with calls about the water, the staffer told her, but no one knew what to tell them. Betanzo helped fill in the blanks and connected Hanna-Attisha with Kildee's office. She also put her in touch with Virginia Tech's Marc Edwards. The three of them met for the first time on the day of the September press conference at city hall. While the Coalition for Clean Water and the Flint Water Study group kept pushing back against the voices undermining their credibility, a new force was about to enter the politically charged atmosphere.

On Thursday, September 24, about sixty people crowded into a drab room at Hurley Medical Center. Hanna-Attisha, wearing a white lab coat and brown-rimmed glasses, stepped to the front of the room, though not before texting Betanzo: *I think I'm going to throw up.*

The wooden podium was weighed down by a glut of computer screens and microphones, an imposing arrangement that seemed like it might swallow the petite doctor whole. She began to speak.

Since the water switch in April 2014, there was not only more lead coming out of Flint's taps, but also much more lead in the blood of Flint's children. In just eighteen months, the percentage of children under age five with high blood-lead levels had jumped from 2.1 percent to 4 percent—it had almost doubled. When she looked at two zip codes that had registered especially high lead in their water, she saw that there was even greater harm, with the proportion of children with high blood-lead levels rising to 6.3 percent. Both were mostly poor areas with large African American populations, 67 percent and 46 percent, respectively. Altogether, as many as twenty-seven thousand children were vulnerable to persistent lead exposure. "This research is concerning. These results are concerning," Hanna-Attisha said. "And when our national guiding institutions tell us primary prevention is the most important thing, and that lead poisoning is potentially irreversible, then we have to say something."[12]

Melissa Mays was in the room. She had more knowledge about Flint's water than nearly anyone. But still, when she heard the numbers, the measurable harm that the water was causing to children like her own, she pressed her palm to her mouth and froze.

As a pediatrician, Hanna-Attisha advised the community to breast-feed rather than use formula. If formula had to be used, avoid tap water. Pregnant mothers should also avoid tap water. In addition, she called for a public education campaign about how using flushed water and cold water could help minimize lead exposure. (Lead dissolves more easily in hot water than in cold water.) "And," she added, we should "advocate for a connection to a Lake Huron water source."

Like those who came before her, Hanna-Attisha understood that there was zero room for error. She checked her data "a zillion times," knowing it would come under scrutiny.[13] And it did. A spokesperson for Governor Rick Snyder alleged that she had "spliced and diced" the data.[14] Brad Wurfel called her claims "unfortunate." He repeated his defense of the earlier water tests and accused Hanna-Attisha of spreading "near hysteria." Wurfel's communications counterpart at the MDHHS said that the doctor's data were "not in line" with its own, and that a surge in blood-lead levels was "seasonal and not related to the water supply."[15] It's true that lead levels usually rise in the summer—people drink more water, for one thing—but this didn't fully explain her findings.[16]

The portrayal of Hanna-Attisha as reckless ran counter to all evidence. The thirty-eight-year-old pediatrician, born in England to Christian Iraqi parents who had fled Saddam Hussein's regime, had lived a life of considered purpose. As an undergraduate at the University of Michigan, she helped organize a campuswide environmental theme semester. She had been recognized even then as "very competent and talented."[17] Hanna-Attisha first came to know Flint from a professor who was a native of the city and had created the university's environmental justice program. While in medical school, Hanna-Attisha did her clinical rotations in Flint. She began working at Hurley in 2011, the same year the city was assigned the first of its consecutive emergency managers. She trained emerging doctors and treated some of Flint's poorest families. She decorated her office with children's artwork: a watercolor giraffe, tissue-paper butterflies, a shiny pink-lettered sign that read "This is my fight song," a lyric written by one of her young cancer patients.[18]

After the press conference, Hanna-Attisha still felt sick. Her numbers had been checked and rechecked and checked again, but the swift counterclaims by state authorities made her anxious. However, there were others who took her study seriously. Genesee County's health officer asked the MDHHS for evidence to support its claim that the state's analysis was more accurate and more comprehensive than the Hurley study. And the City of Flint issued a lead advisory urging residents to use water only from the cold tap for drinking, cooking, and making baby formula. The notice cited concerns from the medical community—Hanna-Attisha, apparently—but it still claimed that the water was in full compliance with federal drinking water laws.

Significantly, the afternoon after the Hurley press conference, emails exchanged at the EPA in Chicago discussed using money from its Drinking Water State Revolving Fund to purchase home filters for Flint residents. But there was fretting about Flint's financial practices. Buying filters would "not send a good message to all the cities that properly manage their water and sewer fees," as it could set a precedent that the EPA wasn't prepared to defend, according to an internal briefing. "Many other older communities have similar problems with lead in pipes. Using the set-aside funds for this purpose" could prompt them to ask for aid, too. One EPA official said, "I don't know if Flint is the kind of community we want to go out on a limb for."[19]

The *Detroit Free Press* helped break the stalemate. It got access to the data the state used to dispute Hanna-Attisha's claims about rising blood-lead levels, analyzed it, and, in a stunning report, it showed that the MDHHS was misinterpreting its own findings.[20] The state's *own* numbers showed that Flint's blood-lead levels had worsened since the spring of 2014. The MDHHS study looked at children under sixteen (a larger sample size, since Hanna-Attisha had limited her study to younger children) and found that the percentage of children with high lead levels had grown from 2.37 percent before the water switch to 3.21 percent afterward. That's an increase of almost a third in eighteen months, and it counted only the number of children with five or more micrograms of lead per deciliter of blood, the amount most likely to cause damage. The uptick was especially significant because lead poisoning in children in the city and across Michigan had been dropping for years.

Dr. Eden Wells, the state's chief medical executive, began communicating with Hanna-Attisha. Her staff compared the two studies, and the agency's epidemiologists revisited their research. At 7:30 a.m. on Thursday, October 1, exactly one week after the Hurley press conference, Wells found a yellow Post-it note stuck on her office keyboard. It was an alert: her staff had come to agree with the pediatrician. Wells headed down the hallway to let the department's director, Nick Lyon, know that they were about to make an extraordinary reversal. At a news conference that same day, they said, yes, the pediatrician working in Flint was right after all. This was the state's first serious accession to what residents had been saying all along: the water was poisonous.

That day, the Genesee County commissioners declared a public health emergency, citing Hanna-Attisha's study, the *Free Press* report, and Governor Snyder's cautious concession that "it appears that [water] lead levels could be higher or have increased" and that there were "probably things that weren't fully understood when the switch was made."[21] Flint city hall went further, flatly telling residents to stop drinking the water. But community groups were way ahead of them. Volunteers were already delivering bottled water to schools that had turned off their water fountains, and over at the Mission of Hope homeless shelter, Reverend Bobby Jackson was running a water distribution site while working to raise the $1,700 that the shelter owed in unpaid water bills.[22] Even the Genesee County sheriff had begun providing the inmates housed in a Flint jail with bottled water and with food that required no water to cook.[23] "We're just in a heck of a bind," the sheriff said.

Hanna-Attisha's head spun. She was fielding congratulatory messages one moment and the next she was asked to detail the awful harm of lead poisoning in children.[24] She felt both exhausted and vindicated, she told a reporter. "At times I want to cry and then I'm so happy."

The afternoon following the reversal, Governor Rick Snyder, Mayor Dayne Walling, MDEQ director Dan Wyant, and a number of other officials stood before a throng of reporters to bear the most blunt of their questions and to reveal their ten-point plan to fix the crisis. Some of it seemed promising, such as a $1 million commitment to purchase filters; and some of it, such as free water testing for Flint residents, wasn't even new. There would also be no widespread notification campaign. The public notice requirements of the Lead and Copper Rule were never triggered because, technically, the MDEQ had never issued any lead-in-water violations to the city.

Hanna-Attisha listened to all this from the back of the small room. Brad Wurfel was there, too. The pediatrician leaned over and whispered to him. "You called me irresponsible."

He told her he was sorry.

"I had the opportunity to apologize," Wurfel later said, and "I was grateful for the opportunity to do it. I will be the first to say, I came on a little strong on this because I believed the numbers we had in the moment."[25] It was a candid admission. Outside the news conference, as Hanna-Attisha and Wurfel conferred, and as the mayor spoke, having only recently regained the authority of his elected office, about thirty residents were gathered. Holding up hand-lettered signs, they called for clean, safe, affordable water. Some wore homemade biohazard suits. One sign read "Not Your Lab Rats!" Together they chanted, "Flint lives matter!"[26] They hadn't been allowed in the room.

PART III

WATER'S PERFECT MEMORY

Switchback

America is a thousand Flints.

—Carl Crow, *The City of Flint Grows Up:*
The Success Story of an American Community (1945)

I.

There was no toast. No congratulatory countdown. No cheers. But on October 8, 2015, almost eighteen months after the celebratory switch to the river water, Governor Rick Snyder announced that Flint would finally be reconnected to the Detroit system. The news came the same day that the Flint River Fest was scheduled to kick off—kayak giveaways, a fireworks show—but the festivities had been postponed due to the "current drinking water crisis." Snyder salted his announcement with a distinct desire to move on. "Again, this isn't about blaming anyone," he said.[1] "Right now, I want to stay focused in on the solutions and taking actions to solve problems."

It was a remarkable turnaround. But by now everyone knew the water was bad. The crisis was undeniable, what with the empty Brita filter boxes piled up at the makeshift distribution centers and people waiting in long lines to receive a free filter, some with toddlers in tow.

They took videos on their phones as Home Depot employees demonstrated how to attach the filters to their faucets.

On the south side of the city, LeeAnne Walters was coming to terms with the fact that her home, once a place of shelter for her family, was now known as ground zero.[2] "The citizens in Flint are relying on each other" for relief from the water crisis, she said, "because we have no choice." And there were her kids. Gavin, the four-year-old twin with outrageous levels of lead in his blood, had gained just a few pounds in the past year. He still struggled with anemia. He had developed problems with his speech.[3] LeeAnne had worked so hard to expose the toxicity in her house on Browning Avenue. Now she wondered whether she could remain there.

The inequity between communities, long latent, had been made excruciatingly vivid to people who lived outside Flint. For so long, the state had dragged its feet, dismissing the city as if it were too dysfunctional and impoverished for locals to be seen as an authority, even in the matters of their own lives. As Marc Edwards put it, Flint residents had been paying among the highest water rates in the world for "water that was not suitable for anything but flushing toilets," and they had been "told to like it."[4] The state had reversed course only after immense public pressure, a broadening media spotlight, and two independent water analyses left it with no other option.

"I'm happy that the city is finally doing what they should have done a long time ago," LeeAnne told a reporter, sounding weary.[5] "They should have taken it seriously back months ago when we tried to tell them, but they chose to ignore it." As Snyder made his dramatic announcement, he was surrounded by the state's heavy hitters—the mayor, the director of the MDEQ, the president of the C. S. Mott Foundation. Still absent were the community organizers and scientists who had exposed the water troubles.

So the governor's turnaround was greeted with some bitterness. The $12 million bill for the reconnection to the DWSD would be divided among three parties. Snyder asked the state legislature for $6 million—he got it—and $4 million came from the Mott Foundation. The city was expected to pay $2 million. The matter of the essential length of pipe that had been sold to Genesee County was resolved: Flint would pay the drain commission one dollar per month to use it.[6] In less than a year, Flint was expected to cut off the connection to Detroit a second time and begin treating lake water from the Karegnondi Water Authority.

Completed within a week, the switchback was heralded by a *Detroit Free Press* editorial calling the Flint water crisis "An Obscene Failure of Government."[7] The paper, which had twice endorsed Rick Snyder in his gubernatorial campaigns, noted that he had appeared chastened at his public announcement. "He should," the editorialists wrote. "In Flint, he failed."

The consequences of that failure would play out for decades to come. While the lifelong effects of lead poisoning can be mitigated, they can't be cured. No switch could turn that back. It had affected children in their homes, but that wasn't all: three Flint elementary schools had excessive lead levels, too, with one of them testing at 101 parts per billion shortly before the return to Detroit water.[8] There still hadn't been a satisfactory explanation for the rashes or hair loss or a number of other health problems that people thought might be connected to the water. It began to sink in that, no, even after the switchback, the water still wasn't safe. Bottled water and filters were still essential. Another three weeks would have to pass before the remaining river water would be cleared from the pipes, and it would take months, at a minimum, to rebuild the pipes' protective coating, even with the extra corrosion control that Flint planned to add to the properly treated Detroit water.[9] People were cautioned that there would probably be lingering issues with taste, odor, and color. Flint's infrastructure was in a worse state than it had been eighteen months earlier. The corrosive river water had also ruined hot water tanks and plumbing fixtures all around town, forcing people to pay for expensive repairs.[10] And most of all, public trust in the city, already shaky, was gone. It was difficult to imagine residents having confidence in their tap water when thousands of lead pipes still sat in the earth like so many ticking time bombs—and when the institutions that were responsible for fixing the problems were the very same ones that had caused them in the first place.

While a quick reconnection was a public health necessity, researchers at both Virginia Tech and Wayne State University in Detroit worried that there hadn't been enough sampling of the river water—it was important to know exactly what the city had been drinking since the spring of 2014. Up until the last minute before the switch, a number of people were scrambling to sample as much as they could, particularly in large buildings, including hospitals.[11] They were looking for the kinds of bacteria that would thrive in the conditions of Flint's water. Lead was not the only toxin keeping the scientists awake at night. They were right to be worried.

II.

Much as Governor Snyder wished to face forward, there was a reckoning to be done. How had an entire city been poisoned by its own water? The first efforts toward accountability came on the heels of the switchback, and they were modest: Howard Croft, Flint's public works director and a lifelong resident, quit his job, saying that his resignation was necessary for the department to regain public trust.[12] One person at the MDEQ (Liane Shekter-Smith, the top drinking water official) was reassigned.[13] Her boss, Dan Wyant, said he was "convinced our program staff believed they were doing right," but they had made a mistake in Flint by failing to follow federal rules for developing a corrosion treatment program.

"All who brought this issue to the department deserve credit," Wyant said, giving nods to the EPA and Virginia Tech, though not to the community leaders.[14] Around the same time, though, he mysteriously claimed that Flint water had corrosion control all along. The water was treated with lime, he said, and although that proved to be insufficient, it was done with the best of intentions. (According to Marc Edwards, lime actually makes corrosion worse.)[15] With its mixed messages, the MDEQ was doing little to build back the trust it had broken.

The EPA's national headquarters in Washington, D.C., interceded by distributing a memo about Michigan's mishandling of Flint's water, stating unequivocally that large drinking water systems must use corrosion control at all times. But it also said that this kind of citywide contamination "rarely arises," and noted—in an implicit acknowledgment of the gaps in its own regulations—that the Lead and Copper Rule "does not specifically discuss such circumstances."[16] And the EPA in Chicago released its final report about lead-saturated water in Flint, more than four months after Miguel Del Toral submitted his draft version. The memo accompanying the report blithely stated that "most of the recommendations" Del Toral had set out several months earlier were now being implemented.[17] That is, the report declared itself redundant.

It would take a bipartisan, independent investigative task force to start the real work of accountability. About a week after the switchback to Detroit water, Governor Snyder announced that five experts in public health, water management, and the environment would come together to scrutinize what had gone wrong. They were asked to produce "an unbiased report" that included recommendations to "ensure all residents have access to safe, clean water."[18] There were reasons not to invest too much hope in the task force: it had no subpoena power and, like the Kerner Commission in the 1960s, it could not make binding recommendations. And, because it reported to the governor, whose office was exempt from transparency laws, none of its internal work would be open for public review. As it turned out, though, the panel took its job very seriously.

Between Christmas and New Year's Eve, after three months of interviews, the study of countless documents, and several trips to Flint to meet with residents, health providers, water management experts, and public officials, the governor's task force released its preliminary report. It was unsparing. Most of the blame went to the MDEQ for one failure after another, including a culture of "minimalist technical compliance" that took a bare-bones approach to water regulation and public safety; the agency's explicit instruction to Flint officials to not use corrosion control; and its response of "aggressive dismissal, belittlement, and attempts to discredit" those who were concerned about the water. "In fact," the evaluators wrote, "the MDEQ seems to have been more determined to discredit the work of others—who ultimately proved to be right—than to pursue its own oversight responsibility."[19]

Given the MDEQ's central role in the crisis, department emails and documents had already come to light through Freedom of Information Act requests by the media and the Flint Water Study team at Virginia Tech. The exposure confirmed the department's persistent mistreatment of both Flint's water and those who had worried about its safety. District supervisor Stephen Busch's false claim to the EPA that the water was treated with corrosion control drew attention, as did the fact that he had hedged on an offer of expert help from the EPA.[20] Michael Glasgow's early warnings about the treatment plant's readiness were also made public, along with details about the MDEQ's response to complaints and unsatisfactory test results, which the department had treated as if it simply had a public relations problem.[21]

Many people were traveling the week of the report's release, or absorbed in their holiday traditions, or simply trying to stay warm through the darkest days of the year. But the report, preliminary though it was, shook people up. The day it came out, Dan Wyant, who had served in the administrations of three different governors, resigned.[22] So did Brad Wurfel, the communications director. On his way out, Wurfel told reporters that he felt the MDEQ's communications team had a difficult task in dealing with very technical information that changed over time and that "the human element" of their work "got lost in the press account."[23] The two men were the first at the environmental agency to lose their jobs.

Another big change had come to Flint. In November, soon after the reconnection to Detroit water, the city held its first election in four years free of the oversight of an emergency manager. Mayor Dayne Walling campaigned hard for a full-length term of genuine mayoral responsibility. He called for the state to invest tens of millions of dollars into Flint's infrastructure, especially for the replacement of the lead service lines. "Governor Snyder and the emergency managers caused this problem, plain and simple," he said, "and we're making sure they fix it."[24]

But in the end, Walling couldn't shake the image of him toasting the original switch at the plant off Dort Highway—"Here's to Flint!"—and drinking the water on television while swearing that it was safe. People felt betrayed. As one person told a reporter, "I was steady drinking it. My mother and them said, 'Don't drink it,' but I saw the mayor drinking it so I thought it was OK if he was. But then all of a sudden, last summer, I got a bunch of red bumps."[25] Walling lost by about eighteen hundred votes. The city chose Karen Weaver as its new mayor, a psychologist by training who was backed by Flint's influential church leaders.[26] She was also the first woman elected to run the city. One of her earliest acts was to declare a state of emergency. It was the trigger for a chain of events to bring not only state aid to Flint but federal assistance, too. "Do we meet the criteria?" Weaver said at a council meeting in December. "I don't know. I'm going to ask and let them tell us no."[27]

III.

An entire city had been exposed to toxic water for eighteen months and the State of Michigan had even acknowledged it, yet national media had only intermittently taken notice.[28] That was about to change, thanks in large part to Michigan Radio. The public radio station, which had made an impact with its coverage of Miguel Del Toral's memo, continued to doggedly report on each development in Flint— the denials, the data, the reversals, the switchback. But the story was complex, and when it was delivered in one piecemeal dispatch after another, listeners weren't able to put the whole event together.[29] Statewide, many people were only just awakening to the news that something was up in Flint, and the back story couldn't easily be summarized in each news brief.

Now that the governor had confirmed the worst, the station created an hour-long documentary. "Not Safe to Drink" focused on LeeAnne

Walters's story, and it made good use of what reporter Lindsey Smith called "the intimacy of the audio narrative" while losing none of the technical background. LeeAnne showed Smith her family's "water stash"—40 gallons that they replenished once a week for drinking, cooking, and bathing the twins, filling the tub with one heated pot of store-bought water at a time. It was so time-consuming and expensive, especially on top of the water bills that they still had to pay, that the family did baths only once a week for the boys. Otherwise, they relied on baby wipes. The older kids showered at their grandmother's house outside of town, and LeeAnne's husband could shower at work. "How does this happen in the United States?" LeeAnne asked. "I mean, you hear about it in third world countries, but how does this happen, specifically in a state that is surrounded by the Great Lakes?"[30]

The documentary aired in the middle of December. Thanks to the station's partnership with the California-based Center for Investigative Reporting, which produces the radio show and podcast *Reveal,* it was broadcast around the country. This was one of the first complete narratives of the Flint crisis to reach national audiences. And then MSNBC's *Rachel Maddow Show* began covering the city and its water, drawing from the work of local reporters.[31] The rising national attention brought home the painful truth of the disaster. Jan Worth-Nelson, a poet and the editor of *East Village Magazine,* watched Maddow's show from her home in the College Cultural neighborhood. She and her husband, Ted, lived in a gorgeous wood-paneled house on Maxine Street that she had made into a sanctuary; in a loving gesture, they rang a bell in their backyard every evening at the exact moment the sun set. It was one of Flint's denser neighborhoods—her water had never turned brown—and when she saw young families moving into the area, she felt hopeful. "This is not a dying neighborhood," she said. "There are kids here."[32] So that midwinter night, when Jan heard Maddow ask, "Is Flint, Michigan, still habitable?" she caught her breath. "I felt like everything was falling apart," she remembered. "My nerves faltered and I wondered how I—how any of us—have managed to be here all this time."[33]

IV.

A ready explanation for what had happened in Flint quickly took on the appearance of fact: a flawed and hasty decision motivated by careless and petty cost-cutting to meet a budget. But this was not quite the case. Flint's move to join the new Karegnondi Water Authority— which is what precipitated its temporary switch to river water—was a long-considered plan, years in the making.[34] It was also a strange one, since it involved building an entirely new drinking water system in a state that already had more than any other.

The MDEQ was charged with monitoring all those utilities, but after years of budget cuts and instability its capacity was limited. The MDEQ had lost almost one quarter of its salaried employees—1,224 people.[35] The drinking water office and the lab that tested water samples were both strapped, according to an exhaustive federal audit in 2010, even as they were expected to navigate a growing number of regulatory requirements.[36] The water office lost 8.7 percent of its budget over the course of a decade, the *Detroit Free Press* reported, while the lab lost 43 percent of its full-time staff.

Nonetheless, the MDEQ had "one of the largest, if not *the* largest, number of community water systems to regulate," Snyder's investigative task force noted. The KWA would add yet one more to the mix. And while it was touted as a solution to the exorbitant cost of water, the KWA in fact did nothing to address the core structural problems behind the problem of affordability in a shrinking city such as Flint.

"In a state and in a region where we had excess water capacity, why did we think we needed more?" said Chris Kolb of the Michigan Environmental Council, one of the co-chairs of the governor's task force.[37] Why indeed. It's fairly unusual nowadays for a public water system to be built from scratch. That's especially true if the water source hasn't run out or become toxic. But Jeff Wright, Genesee County's drain commissioner, the leading proponent and eventual CEO of the KWA, lobbied fiercely, on the grounds of savings, independence, and stability. The arguments were persuasive: Detroit charged a premium for supplying water over a long distance, plus there were annual rate increases, and it didn't allow Flint a seat on its board. The KWA would provide water from Lake Huron (the same source as Detroit's system), it promised a cooperative model, and it would charge communities a fixed, flat rate. Michael Glasgow, who ran Flint's treatment plant, saw another advantage: "I viewed the plant as a city asset that should be put to good use," he said.[38]

The KWA did not just promote itself as a salvation, however; it was exceptionally involved in steering the politics and financing of the deal. Given the scale of the damage that followed, it prompted a second look at the KWA's dealings with Flint.

It is worth recalling that when the fledgling KWA applied for a permit in 2009, Michigan was in the depths of the Great Recession, exacerbated by Detroit's troubles and the auto industry's near-collapse. So it was especially odd to argue for creating a new water system that duplicated a service that customers already had—and to claim that this was a cost-effective plan. Environmental groups, both regional and national, wrote a joint letter opposing the KWA permit. "We don't need to drive another wedge between Detroit and the rest of the region," wrote Nick Schroeck, a professor at Wayne State University's Environmental Law Clinic. "We should seek to improve upon the efficiency and conservation measures of the water delivery system that we already have rather than spending vast sums of public dollars on projects that are completely unnecessary."[39]

But the KWA nonetheless got the permit (it was at that point largely seen as a weapon to wield in negotiations with the Detroit water authority), and by the time the full cost was assessed, it was a $300 million project with considerable financing needs. Sealing a contract with Flint would go a long way to meet them.

The KWA—still just existing on paper at this point—helped devise the strategy to get the disempowered Flint council to vote on the water switch so that the city's participation would survive emergency management and any legal challenge to that management. Even though the council vote was celebrated as an exercise in sovereignty (which it was not), the emergency manager went on to ignore the council's stipulations and commited Flint to a greater quantity of water, at a higher cost, than the vote permitted.[40] Construction on the KWA began one month after Flint's contract was signed. The city's share: about $85 million, with annual payments of some $7 million.

The KWA got what it needed to move forward. But how was the distressed city going to pay for its part?[41] Flint was so broke that when it was offered loans in 2012 to improve its water infrastructure, it had to turn them down, even though half the debt would be forgiven. "When your pockets are empty, further debt is irresponsible," said the emergency manager at the time. And in January 2013, an MDEQ report had detailed necessary repairs at Flint's treatment plant but noted that the repairs could not "proceed due to the city's current bond debt." The efforts to sign Flint on to the new water authority were especially surprising, given that the state treasury, which approved the contract, was also responsible for the city's financial well-being through the emergency management program—a system that's supposed to make tough decisions, such as reducing debts and redundancies.

Flint had hit the maximum debt allowed by law. So the state arranged a work-around: Flint's share of the money for the construction of the KWA was given a special pass so that it did not count against the debt limit. The work-around was through something called an administrative consent order, or ACO. This is a tool that the state uses to force local governments to fix an urgent environmental problem, even if they must issue bonds that exceed their debt limit to do so. Even among state workers, the ACO raised eyebrows. In December 2013, an MDEQ employee received a call from an attorney "seeking what I'd characterize as a 'sweetheart' ACO intended to ease the city's ability to access bond funding for their possible new water intake from Lake Huron," as she described it in an email.[42] The attorney and "Treasury officials have already been communicating with Steve [Busch of the MDEQ] about an Order of some sort in light of Flint's financial situation."

KWA's bond attorneys exerted pressure on the negotiations. In an email delivered to Earley and future EM Jerry Ambrose about a month before Flint's 2014 water switch, one attorney said that "we cannot continue with the transaction without the ACO." If the delay continued, "the KWA will have expended its initial resources and be forced to stop construction and the project will be delayed for at least one construction cycle."[43] Ambrose asked the Treasury for help, and an employee was instructed to "get a call into the Director," presumably of the MDEQ, "to push this through."

The ACO was finalized two days later. It was written in a way to account for minor work on wastewater lagoons at the Flint treatment plant's lime sludge facility—so to appear to address an urgent environmental problem—but it also covered the entirety of the KWA bond debt. To make sure that it would be legally intact, Stephen Busch and Flint's environmental attorney conferred on the wording: "Steve, I checked with the City's bond counsel, here is the Language that we MUST include in the consent order so that the City can move forward on this."[44]

So the tool that was meant to fix an environmental emergency in this case included language that required Flint to "undertake the KWA public improvement project." In this way, the KWA could count on a broke city to pay for almost a third of its construction. And it did this through the Treasury, which was the steward of Flint's financial health. But the KWA actually *added* to Flint's debt, and it bent state law to do so. Rather than borrowing to invest in schools or public safety, Flint ended up paying for a pipeline that literally paralleled one that already existed.

In December 2014, *The Bond Buyer* honored this cleverness by giving the KWA its Midwest "Deal of the Year" award in a ceremony at New York's Waldorf-Astoria Hotel. The honor was misdirected. As Peter Hammer, a law professor at Wayne State University, described it, the ACO "effectively obligated the City to use the Flint River as the interim source of drinking water during KWA construction. This legal commitment was strategically driven by the need to manipulate rules governing the bond market, not considerations of public safety."[45]

Also, as it turned out, the issues with the wastewater lagoon that the order was supposedly addressing were already being remediated when the ACO was finalized. Much later, as the scope of the water crisis was becoming clear, nobody from the MDEQ would respond to inquiries from a *Detroit Free Press* reporter about the ACO. Jeff Wright claimed that he didn't know much about it at all. The ACO, he said, was "worked out between the state and Flint."[46]

The Flint Water Advisory Task Force noted that the KWA deal cast a shadow over all that happened next: "The influence that KWA and Genesee County Drain Commissioner Jeff Wright exercised was undeniable. They got exactly what they wanted from Flint City Officials, Emergency Managers and State Officials at DEQ and Treasury. The more difficult question to answer is the source of that influence." The governor's task force speculated about how the KWA would end up with hundreds of millions of dollars in contracts "to control and hand out. . . . Whether KWA's influence is just an extreme and tragic illustration of politics as usual or whether there is something more at work is still unanswered."[47]

And then there were the punishing terms of the contract between the KWA and the city. If Flint should miss a single one of its annual bond payments, the KWA could seize the city's treatment plant, plus 25 percent of its state revenue-sharing money, and it could also force the city to levy a tax to get its share of the money. Meanwhile, just as local authority was returned to Flint, the water problem had become a full-blown crisis. And the first $7 million payment would be due in about a year.

Legion

No witchcraft, no enemy action had silenced the rebirth of new life in this stricken world. The people had done it themselves.

—Rachel Carson, *Silent Spring* (1962)

I.

The wheel turned. Flint entered a new year. Nights came early and stayed late. People switched on their lamps and stayed home in the warmth. But the usual wintertime hush was broken by a wave of chattering journalists and volunteers arriving in town. It was more and more common to come across a reporter clutching a voice recorder in her mitten or a photographer pointing his camera at an empty house or the steely river. Although Flint had been restored to a better water source, it still wasn't safe to drink straight from the tap. As the national spotlight fixed on this fact, the response to the disaster accelerated.

On January 5, 2016, nearly three months after Flint reconnected to Detroit's water system, Governor Rick Snyder followed Mayor Weaver and declared a state of emergency. He had been criticized for not acting sooner, but his office defended the delay: he couldn't make a declaration until both the city and the county had done the same. (Genesee County's emergency declaration had come one day earlier.[1])

But the fine points of procedure were no match for the rage that lit up Flint. Nor did the declaration satisfy its furious sympathizers across the state and nation. On the cold evening that Snyder stepped before the House chamber in Lansing to deliver his annual State of the State speech—nearly all of it addressed to the people of Flint—hundreds of protesters banged on the locked doors of the ornate capitol building, shaking its wood panels. They chanted. They tugged futilely at the door handles. They pressed their posters with big block lettering to the windows—"Flint Lives Matter!" "Snyder Has to Go Now!" "Clean Lead-Free Water!"—while blue-uniformed police officers stared back at them through the glass. Their masses poured down the steps of the capitol and out on the lawn, a knot of people in fleece scarves and knit hats, brightened by the reflecting snow, holding the sides of numberless signs: "Arrest Gov. Snyder!" "Justice for Flint!"[2]

Still, the declaration allowed the state to act: soldiers and airmen from the Michigan National Guard arrived in Flint, tramping in their laced-up boots and camouflage uniforms. Instead of cradling rifles, as in decades past, when the cities were afire, they carried cases of bottled water.[3] In a robust outreach, they went door-to-door to some thirty-three thousand homes, delivering free water, filters, and water-testing kits to residents. They also staffed new water distribution sites—first at Flint's five fire stations and eventually at nine locations, one in each city ward.[4] Unlike the earlier stations, these sites would be open indefinitely. Places such as the Masonic Temple in downtown Flint offered free blood tests.[5] A mobile health clinic rolled through town. Governor Snyder also asked President Barack Obama to designate Flint as both a federal emergency and a federal disaster, which would bring still more resources to the city to manage the crisis, including grants and low-cost loans to pay for home repairs and business losses, and recovery coordination from the Federal Emergency Management Agency.

It was a necessary relief effort, but it was, of course, no substitute for the safety and convenience of tap water. Some people stopped using their sinks completely, but others forgot to switch out the unsafe water when they cooked or percolated their morning coffee or made ice cubes. Some believed the water could be purified by boiling it on the stove, though with lead that didn't help. A woman who filled her humidifiers from her tap believed that she developed lung cancer from the tainted water.[6] Ryan Garza of the *Detroit Free Press*, a photojournalist who lived in Flint, said that he had a testing kit on his counter but was afraid to use it. "What can I do if the lead levels are high?" he asked. He still had to rely on the tap water to shower and wash dishes.[7] Outside stores and in parking lots, he watched as mothers awkwardly handled gallon jugs of water to mix their baby formula. Elsewhere, Yvonne Lewis, a longtime leader in community health nonprofits, kept a Crock-Pot in her bathroom so that she could heat bottled water for bathing.[8]

The appearance of military uniforms at the door felt threatening to the city's estimated one thousand undocumented immigrants, mostly from Mexico and Central America, even if the visit brought free water. Increasing immigration raids over the past year had intimidated many of them from accepting the offer of an urgently needed resource. Some had been turned away from the distribution sites because they had no photo identification (undocumented immigrants in Michigan are banned from obtaining a driver's license). And very little information about the water crisis appeared in translation. On the east side, one thirty-four-year-old woman, a mother of four children, had been bothered by the rashes on her baby daughter's back and legs for some time. But she didn't understand English and so knew nothing about the trouble with the water until immigrant friends told her, nearly two years after the switch.[9] Another mother didn't learn about the lead contamination until she saw a report on Univision, the Spanish-language broadcast network.

An outcry led the state to clarify that proof of citizenship was not necessary to receive water, and to lift the photo ID requirement. Bilingual speakers were made available on the state's 211 help line, and cards with basic water information were created in English, Arabic, and Spanish. The Genesee County Hispanic/Latino Collaborative and two churches that served the Spanish-speaking community helped to fill the trust gap by going door-to-door in neighborhoods with sizable Hispanic populations, and Flint's Arab American Heritage Council translated information about water and lead for the city's small Arab American community.[10]

It was telling that despite the emergency relief effort, people continued to provide water for each other independently. The Flint-based landlord for the Michigan School for the Deaf worked around the clock one weekend to replace sixty-two faucets in the dormitory and install new filtered fountains.[11] Joy Tabernacle Church developed a holistic water distribution site of its own in Civic Park and found ways to reach people in all corners of the community. After reports surfaced that two brothers in their late fifties were trekking two miles a day over icy ground to pick up water from a distribution center, pushing shaky shopping carts back and forth, two Flint women crowdfunded $17,845 from 443 people over six days. They delivered four hundred bottles of water to the brothers' door, then worked with a company from Detroit to distribute water to other parts of the city where the need was greatest.[12]

Pastor Sherman McCathern of Joy Tabernacle understood why this was necessary. "It's hard to believe anybody," he said. "It's hard to trust anybody right now."[13] Especially the state institutions that people felt had betrayed them, despite their fix-it promises. And it went even beyond the water. General anger that had simmered for decades now, at long last, had a focal point. The wound was uncommonly clear. The whole world could see it.

Then, on January 13, the same day that the National Guard arrived, Governor Snyder delivered more distressing news. On top of bacterial contamination, TTHM violations, and lead-poisoned water, Flint had suffered an outbreak of Legionnaires' disease. It had been plaguing the city for nearly two years, and it had killed people.

II.

In July 1976, mania for America's Bicentennial was at its peak. Few places were cloaked in more red, white, and blue patriotism than Philadelphia, the old capital where the nation's founders had signed the

Declaration of Independence. More than a decade of planning went into the city's festivities, including $1 billion worth of concerts, street theater, picnics, fireworks, and a hundred-year time capsule placed at the corner of Second and Chestnut. On the Fourth of July, President Gerald Ford was the guest of honor at a five-hour parade with forty thousand marchers. Queen Elizabeth II and Prince Philip presented the city with a Bicentennial Bell that was forged in the same foundry as the Liberty Bell. A fifty-thousand-pound Sara Lee birthday cake was served at Memorial Hall.[14]

Philly was the natural place for the Pennsylvania chapter of the American Legion to host its annual convention. The veterans' organization held it at the Bellevue-Stratford Hotel, a local landmark in Center City.[15] Built with French Renaissance flair, it had more than a thousand guest rooms, a ballroom, and lighting fixtures designed by Thomas Edison himself. The hotel's reputation for luxury made it a hub for the power set. Fifteen presidents had slept in its rooms, beginning with Theodore Roosevelt. And over a hot July weekend, it housed about six hundred Legionnaires.[16] About ten thousand people attended the conference altogether: the Legionnaires, of course, many wearing navy dress caps adorned with patches and pins, as well as their families, friends, and staff.

Afterward, as the crowd returned home, many felt ill. Malaise. Headache. Diarrhea. Coughs. Chest pain. Lung congestion. Fevers reaching as high as 107.4 degrees.[17] One physician called state health officials to report a Legionnaire who had symptoms that might be typhoid fever, the kind of waterborne disease that Philly had sought to vanquish nearly two centuries earlier with its pioneering public water system. Scarcely a month after the close of the convention, news outlets from around the country were variously reporting that between six and fourteen of the Legionnaires were dead. Others were hospitalized.[18] There was no registration list, so it was difficult to track down all the attendees to see how they were faring, but in the end, using the best count available, it appeared that thirty-four people who attended the convention were killed by the same mysterious illness.[19] Another 221 became sick.

The nameless disease that struck war veterans dead, right in the heart of the American Bicentennial, captured national attention. Early reports suggested that they had been struck by a wave of swine flu, but that was just speculation. No one really knew what happened. Frightened friends of at least one Legionnaire skipped his funeral because they worried they might catch whatever it was he had.[20] Health experts offered public assurances, but they were nervous, too. The Pennsylvania health secretary worried that the state might be faced with "an unprecedented condition in modern medicine, one for which we had no really effective antibiotics, drugs, or therapy."[21] He considered imposing quarantines and seizing control of hospitals.

That didn't happen. But the federal Centers for Disease Control and Prevention did deploy twenty epidemiologists to Philadelphia, the largest team it had ever sent for a medical investigation.[22] They worked with the state to review medical records and autopsy reports and conduct interviews. The "disease detectives" were featured in a *Time* magazine cover story, "Tracing the Philly Killer."[23] Or, as *Newsweek* put it in bellowing black-and-white the same week, "Mystery of the Killer Fever." The publicity caused occupancy at the Bellevue-Stratford to plummet to 4 percent before the hotel temporarily closed.

Testing eliminated seventeen metals as the cause of the outbreak. Poison gases were considered, including nickel carbonyl, but that was ruled out when investigators realized that their autopsy tools were skewing the results. Swine flu, typhoid fever, plague, and ornithosis, a bird-carried virus, were all ruled out.[24] Six months passed. It began to look like the mystery might never be solved, and the team of medical sleuths was roundly criticized. There was even a congressional investigation, believed to be the first inquiry by Congress into the cause of a disease. But a breakthrough finally came in January 1977, when a CDC lab scientist traced the outbreak to a previously unknown bacterium that was named for the victims who made it infamous, *Legionella pneumophilia*. It exists naturally in freshwater systems and doesn't typically cause problems. But when it grows—it favors warm water with low levels of disinfectant—it becomes dangerous.[25]

Legionella is inhaled through the microscopic drops of water that make up mists and vapors. It can also enter the lungs if people choke on contaminated water or if it's used during invasive medical procedures.[26] The bacterium loves shower heads, medical respiratory devices, and hot tubs, but it's especially menacing when it proliferates in the distribution lines of large buildings; that's when it puts a lot of people at risk, all at once, for Legionnaires' disease, a virulent inflammation and infection of the lungs. It cannot be transmitted from person to person. It is purely a disease of the environment—and a preventable one.

At the Philadelphia convention, it turned out, the bacteria had bloomed in the hot, damp, cooling towers of the Bellevue-Stratford. It moved through the hotel's air-conditioning system and then into the lungs of the veterans. Once contracted, Legionnaires' disease need not be fatal. Hospitals today treat about eight thousand to eighteen thousand cases each year (the CDC believes that many more are misdiagnosed as something else), and about 90 percent of them are treatable with antibiotics.[27] One of the great lessons of the Philly outbreak, though, was the importance of consistent, accurate, and transparent communication about the disease, even if it's still under investigation. Forty years later, in Flint, that lesson would go unheeded.

III.

On Independence Day in 2014, Tim Monahan, a carpenter in his midfifties, watched the fireworks light up the sky from his front yard in Flint. But he didn't feel well. Even just a couple of hours of helping his neighbor work on her shed had made him feel weak, and now, though it was 90 degrees outside, he was shivering under a thick blanket. His fever hit 104.6 degrees the next afternoon, and he was soon admitted to Hurley Medical Center. After a few days of examination, doctors diagnosed him with Legionellosis, otherwise known as Legionnaires' disease. Monahan lost twenty pounds, and he had to stay in the hospital for nine days, where he lay on a cooling mat with ice packs pressed against him to ease the heat from his body. But with the help of antibiotics he recovered.

Monahan had contracted one of more than ninety cases of Legionnaires' disease that were recorded in Genesee County in 2014 and 2015.[28] That was more than forty cases a year, compared to the tally in previous years that ranged between six and thirteen cases.[29] The disease came in two waves—some consider it two separate outbreaks—but altogether, twelve people died. The surge was one of the worst-ever national epidemics, and it did not escape the notice of the health care community. But a coordinated response was not to be. What followed was an extraordinary tale of buck passing and turf guarding by an alphabet of agencies: Michigan's environmental and health departments, Flint's public works department, and the Genesee County Health Department. Other institutions also played a part in the story—the CDC, the EPA, the governor's office, a local hospital. But for all the heat in this bureaucratic tug-of-war, it never seemed to work out in favor of the people of Flint.

By October 2014, about the time that LeeAnne Walters's family began to struggle with hair loss, the outbreak was in full swing. Jim Henry, the environmental health director at the Genesee County Health Department, wondered if there might be a connection to Flint's new water source.[30] He tried to involve the city's public works department and the MDHHS in an investigation, but he didn't feel that they were responding with sufficient speed. Henry waited for months for the city to answer his questions about its water treatment before resorting to filing a formal public records request. Someone at the MDHHS recommended that Henry's agency map the cases of Legionnaires' disease to see if they matched with the city's water service area, but the state health department didn't get actively involved in trying to find the source of the outbreak.

The weeks ticked by. By March 2015, Henry was worried that the outbreak would return as the weather became warmer, and he still hadn't received the FOIA materials he requested from the city months earlier. In an urgent email to a number of people working for the city and the MDEQ, including Mike Prysby, emergency manager Jerry Ambrose, and Mayor Dayne Walling, Henry said that the outbreak was a "significant and urgent public health issue." Authorities needed to act fast. "The city's lack of cooperation continues to prevent my office from performing our responsibilities." The spreading disease, he added, "closely corresponds with the time frame of the switch to the Flint River water. The majority of the cases reside or have an association with the city. . . . This is rather glaring information and it needs to be looked into now."

Henry's warning reached Harvey Hollins in the governor's office, who worked on urban affairs. Hollins checked in with the MDEQ; if Henry's concerns were well founded, he would let the governor know. Brad Wurfel's response was to put the responsibility for investigation back on the county and to say that making a connection to the water source was "beyond irresponsible," since the county hadn't provided "any conclusive evidence of where the outbreak is sourced, and it also flies in the face of the very thing a drinking water system is designed to do."[31] At about this time, the EPA also began corresponding with the MDEQ about the uptick in Legionnaires' disease, but it didn't take the thread very far. Stephen Busch said that there was no confirmation of *Legionella* in the water supply, though he cited no data, and he also told Jim Henry it was unlikely that *Legionella* was in Flint's water treatment plant, though perhaps there was a connection to the main breaks. Either way, the MDEQ didn't believe this was its turf; that was Henry's job. It referred him back to MDHHS.[32]

But he didn't get much help from that corner, either, although the agency did begin interviewing people diagnosed with the disease—not fast enough, according to Henry.[33] So in an unusual move, his county's health department leaped over the chain of command and went straight to the CDC, asking if the federal agency would assist by collecting and testing respiratory cultures to track down the cause of the disease. The CDC agreed, and looking at the details of the outbreak—about forty-five cases at this point, and five deaths—one researcher observed that it was "very large, one of the largest we know of in the past decade."[34]

Just as Henry was intensifying his investigation, though, the MDHHS brought its involvement to an end. In its May 2015 report, the agency said it was impossible for epidemiologists to determine whether the *Legionella* crisis was caused by the water switch. In any case, it declared confidently, "the outbreak is over." This was followed by a scolding for Genesee County for approaching the CDC directly. "Their involvement really should be at the request of the State, rather than the local health department," the county was told. The state had "not seen any information that would rise to the level of warranting" help from the federal agency.[35]

From the county's health department to the MDHHS to the MDEQ to the governor's office, and back again, with an altogether disappointing response to a fatal outbreak of a rare disease, Jim Henry was led to conclude that state agencies "restricted our actions to the point of interference and inhibition."[36]

That summer, his fears were confirmed: the outbreak indeed returned. But people in Flint still received no notice about it. There was no alert for those who were especially vulnerable to Legionnaires' disease, such as elderly people, or those who had compromised immune systems. Even medical providers were in the dark.[37] In comparison, in an outbreak of Legionnaires' disease in the Bronx that same summer—the largest in New York City history, in which twelve people died—health officials issued a public warning within weeks of the disease's appearance.[38] They provided frequent updates and, after collecting samples and conducting tests, they traced the cause to a hotel cooling tower.

For Flint, there was no news that the outbreak was even happening until twenty months after it began, at Governor Snyder's press conference in January 2016. The information "was just recently presented to me," he said, "and I thought it was important to share." There was no need for people to take additional precautions to protect themselves, and, despite the admonishment sent to Henry, he said that the state had been working with the CDC and the EPA to manage the outbreak since June 2015.[39] The numbers Snyder gave were a bit different from the final tally of cases, but it was clear that the disease "adds to the disaster we are all facing," he said. Nobody could say for sure what had caused the problem.

Most of the sick were men in their sixties, though patients ranged between twenty-six and ninety-four years old.[40] A common thread: McLaren hospital in Flint. Forty-six people who became ill had been patients at McLaren, including ten of the twelve who died.[41] The hospital hadn't been oblivious. After noticing the uptick, it had its water system tested and hired a national expert on Legionnaires' disease as a consultant.

Was the outbreak connected to Flint's water switch? It would take years to establish the link, and, even then, there was plenty for skeptics to wonder about. Medical providers had collected very few sputum cultures from patients, too few to show a pattern definitively tying the disease to the water.[42] And the MDHHS had reported that while about 36 percent of people who had the disease were likely exposed to water sourced from the Flint River, another 30 percent had no known exposure to it in the two weeks before they fell ill.[43]

There was, however, some glaring circumstantial evidence, not least because the outbreak began shortly after the water switch and largely ceased after the city reverted to Detroit's supply.[44] The CDC, using the few sputum samples that were available, looked for a biological link between cases of the disease and *Legionella* bacteria detected at McLaren hospital, and in February 2016 it found two matches.[45] Also, the Virginia Tech team hypothesized early on that the conditions in Flint could breed Legionnaires' disease.[46] Marc Edwards and four of his Virginia Tech colleagues published a study in *Environmental Science & Technology* that posited a probable connection to the corrosiveness of the city's tap water.[47] Miguel Del Toral and another water expert from the EPA made a similar case: as the protective lining in Flint's pipes broke down, depleting the chlorine, *Legionella* would flourish. Del Toral also speculated that the corrosion might have released *Legionella* that had been contained in the lining, aggravated by the flushed fire hydrants.[48]

Almost four years after the disease broke out, big news about its cause finally came from a multi-university investigation led by Wayne

State University. Shawn McElmurry, an environmental engineer at Wayne State, had begun looking into it at the request of the governor's office. In two peer-reviewed studies, McElmurry and his team showed that the risk of the disease grew by more than sixfold across the city's water distribution system after the switch to the Flint River, and that about 80 percent of cases could be connected to the water supply.[49] (The MDHHS, which had initially funded the research, strongly disputed the results.[50] So did Marc Edwards, actually, who challenged McElmurry's credentials.[51]) Chlorine was a big factor: the less disinfectant in a resident's tap water, the more likely they were to get sick. That tied back to the problem of iron corrosion in the pipes. Also, McElmurry said under oath that he believed there to have been "undiagnosed cases of Legionnaires' disease" that might have just been "diagnosed as pneumonia."[52] That resonated with Melissa Mays, the Flint community organizer. Her youngest son had pneumonia back in the summer of 2014. Had it really been Legionnaires' disease? Was the risk worse than she'd known? "Fear is not knowing," she said.[53]

While McLaren hospital wasn't the sole source of the disease, it had been an incubator of it. And it knew more than it had let on. When Snyder dropped his bombshell of an announcement about the outbreak, it caught the attention of Connie Taylor, a sixty-two-year-old woman from Flint. She had been treated at McLaren in 2014, so she thought that it would be a good idea to request her medical records. Taylor had been admitted for stomach problems, but she felt so much chest pain and exhaustion after being released she returned to the hospital. Doctors diagnosed her with pneumonia and moved her to the intensive care unit. They told her daughters that Taylor, a widow, might not survive. But she made it. Her kidneys, however, did not. Taylor was soon on dialysis treatment three days a week, which would continue for the rest of her life, unless she received a kidney transplant. Nobody at McLaren had breathed a word to her about Legionnaires' disease. But more than a year later, in the roar of new revelations about Flint's water, Taylor had her records in hand. She had tested positive for *Legionella*.[54]

IV.

Both Mayor Karen Weaver and Governor Snyder wanted a federal disaster declaration for Flint, to go along with the emergency support—that would open the door to aid money for infrastructure. But the state's request was denied and would continue to be denied over its appeals. The reason: federal disaster designations are earmarked for natural emergencies, such as hurricanes, mudslides, and earthquakes. Flint's disaster was man-made. An exception had been made for Love Canal almost forty years earlier, but there would not be one for Flint. This narrow definition of what counts as a disaster was something the *Kerner Report* had addressed in the urban crisis of the sixties, recommending an amendment to the Federal Disaster Act to permit federal "assistance to cities during major civil disorders, and provide long-term economic assistance afterwards."[55]

Still, other kinds of assistance flooded the city. As the story broke around a scandalized world, it was almost impossible to keep up with the interventions, the rhetoric, the politics, the scores of volunteers and donations and reporters pouring into town. For the first time in a long time, everyone was paying attention to Flint. In the mad rush, it was not easy to sort out the city's allies from its exploiters; people who came humbly to help versus those who came to use Flint, and its limelight, for their own profit—selling water gadgets to fearful residents, for example, or promoting themselves and their pet projects.

The city got a star turn when the Whiting auditorium in the Cultural Center hosted #JusticeForFlint, a benefit featuring African American filmmakers and performers—among them, Stevie Wonder, Ryan Coogler, Hannibal Burress, Janelle Monae—scheduled on the same night as the Academy Awards. Some two thousand people showed up, mostly locals who received free tickets. With help from the livestream, it raised more than $150,000. Superstar Beyoncé also opened a relief fund for Flint, a move that generated $82,234 for the United Way of Genesee County. Aretha Franklin offered hotel rooms and food vouchers to displaced residents. The owner of the Detroit Pistons, a Flint native, pledged $10 million. General Motors and the United Auto Workers gave $3 million for health and education services.

Flint even became fodder for presidential candidates. Shortly before Michigan held its 2016 Democratic primary, candidates Hillary Clinton and Bernie Sanders held one of their national debates in Flint. The Republican presidential candidates faced questions about the water crisis when they debated in Detroit that same week. Several presidential prospects visited the city during their campaigns, including Donald Trump. Clinton also worked with Mayor Weaver to develop a summer jobs program that employed a hundred local teenagers.[56]

An abundance of federal agencies also stepped in to give Flint special assistance. There was a massive expansion of Medicaid coverage for people under twenty-one or pregnant or both (a total of fifteen thousand) who were exposed to the water, and they did not necessarily have to live in the city. Another thirty thousand received a greater range of services through Medicaid. A free Disaster Distress helpline connected callers with trained counselors. New programs were designed to make fresh food affordable and accessible, since good nutrition can mitigate some of the effects of lead exposure. The *Detroit Free Press* published recipes to combat lead's toxic effects and tips on cutting water use in the kitchen. "Cook with frozen vegetables, which don't need washing," it advised. And, "Substitute milk in place of water when it makes sense. Think pancakes and oatmeal."[57]

Under this bright spotlight, in a cascade of belated responsiveness, the state and federal governments ramped up their efforts to investigate the disaster. Michigan's attorney general announced that he was opening a criminal investigation into what had happened in Flint. Because of his inherent conflict of interest—the attorney general's office is constitutionally required to represent the state—a Detroit-area litigator was appointed as a special prosecutor. Also, the Michigan Civil Rights Commission said that it would carry out its own investigation to see if what transpired had violated residents' civil rights. Over in Washington, D.C., Congress proclaimed that it too would hold hearings. And the inspector general of the EPA began to look into how the Region 5 office in Chicago had handled the crisis. Chicago director Susan Hedman resigned but later protested the accusations that she had downplayed Miguel Del Toral's interim report. What's more, she said, while "this tragedy happened on my watch, I did not make the catastrophic decision to provide drinking water without corrosion control treatment; I did not vote to cut funding for water infrastructure or for EPA. And I did not design the imperfect statutory framework that we rely on to keep our drinking water safe."[58]

To help make sense of what had befallen their town, the University of Michigan–Flint created a free one-credit class on the water crisis, open to all. The class, held one block away from the river, featured a mix of experts, from community organizers such as Melissa Mays and Yvonne Lewis to doctors, sociologists, journalists, and public servants. Over a thousand people took part, and many more followed along through videos uploaded onto YouTube. "This will be a class with no assignments," declared Suzanne Selig, the director of the college's Public Health Department, on the first day. "Your attendance will be enough. We want to learn from you."[59]

For all the incoming goodwill, business owners and boosters who had stuck by Flint now worried that the work they'd put into the city would crumble. There had been genuine progress in recent years.[60] UM–Flint had built its first-ever dorm downtown, and it earmarked a former hotel on the riverfront as a second residence hall, designed to attract international students. The farmers' market had doubled its space for indoor vendors: in its first year at a new location, foot traffic doubled. Flint's first brewery opened in a repurposed fire station. More than $1 million in philanthropic grants came through to combat crime in north Flint. In a hard-fought transformation, a slice of land outside the Torch Bar called Buckham Alley, between Beach and Saginaw streets, had become a lively public space strung with bright yellow lights, hosting a popular annual music festival. Kathleen Gazall, an architect and Flint native who lived in a rehabbed loft on Saginaw, had helped bring Buckham Alley to life. She felt that people who had once avoided the city had begun to rediscover it, spending their evenings out on dinner, drinks, a show at one of the theaters or museums in the Cultural Center. Now Gazall and her fellow Flint champions worried that anyone thinking of the city would associate it only with fear, poison, and victimhood, erasing Flint's spirit. To stanch the slide, businesses—restaurants especially—put up hopeful signage to assure passersby: "SAFE WATER HERE." The university, of course, had spent a small fortune testing its own water, purchasing its own filtration systems, and repairing or replacing corroded water heaters and plumbing fixtures.

People also began reckoning with the effect on the value of their homes and their ability to move. Flint was already a tough market for sellers. In 2015, the median house sold for $28,000. That included both large historic homes, beautifully maintained mansions where auto executives had once lived lavishly, and places that needed a lot of rehab work.[61] Of the homes that were occupied, about 50 percent rented for less than $700 a month. The team behind Imagine Flint— the new citywide master plan that included the "Beyond Blight" framework—continued its effort to revive neighborhoods, water crisis be damned.[62] But there were losses as well, including an exodus of people for whom the water crisis was just too much.

That included the Walters family. LeeAnne's husband returned to active duty in the navy, in large part so that the family could get out of Flint.[63] He received a post about seven hundred miles away, in Virginia. They packed up the ground zero house on Browning Avenue, the one with the pretty maple trees out front and the new copper pipe that delivered water that still wasn't trustworthy. Well before the new year, by the time that Flint became an undisputed national catastrophe, they were gone.

Truth and Reconciliation

Shams and delusions are esteemed for soundest truths, while reality is fabulous.

—Henry David Thoreau, *Walden; or Life in the Woods* (1854)

I.

When Governor Rick Snyder gave his State of the State speech in the winter of 2016, it was an unusual event, and not only because of the protesters pressing against the locked doors of the House, their voices reverberating through the chamber during the moment of silence to remember "those who have fallen in protection of our communities." Instead of focusing on his administration's successes, the standard template of the congratulatory annual speech, the governor devoted nearly the entire hour to what would be remembered as its greatest failure.

"Tonight, I will address the crisis in Flint," Snyder said from the podium, his hands clasped before him.[1] "Your families face a crisis, a crisis which you did not create and could not have prevented." He said he was sorry and went on: "Government failed you—federal, state, and local leaders—by breaking the trust you placed in us. I am sorry most of all that I let you down. You deserve better. You deserve accountability; you deserve to know the buck stops here with me.

Most of all you deserve the truth and I have a responsibility to tell the truth, the truth about what we have done and what we will do to overcome this challenge."

Promises were made: Snyder would ask the legislature to allot $28 million in aid to meet Flint's immediate needs, with $22 million from Michigan's general fund and the balance from federal sources. (This passed in a unanimous vote in both chambers.) He requested "an infrastructure integrity study for pipes and connections" and acknowledged that Flint was hardly the only place where the bones of the city were falling apart. The American Society for Civil Engineers had given the state's overall infrastructure a D in its report from 2013 (compared to the nationwide average of D+).[2]

As Michigan's leader, and given the role of state agencies and appointees in causing the crisis, Snyder inevitably had to absorb the bulk of people's anger, not only in Flint but also across the state and nation. Protesters amassed outside his Ann Arbor condominium, circling the block in 12-degree weather and chalking fierce messages on the sidewalk. They put his picture on "Wanted!" signs that they pasted on lampposts, and they heckled him in restaurants. ("Make him drink the water!" went one chant.[3]) A rising drumbeat called for his resignation and even his arrest. Other opinionators suspected that there were people far closer to the crisis who bore the bulk of the responsibility, protected from the scrutiny Snyder faced only because they served in less prominent positions.

And yet not even the sympathizers seriously disputed that the executive branch had a lot to answer for—and it went way back. When was the last time the governor's office had any bright ideas for substantive urban policy? After decades of disinvestment, it had wielded the sledgehammer of emergency management as if it were its only tool. Both Republicans and Democrats had failed the cities. A letter in the *Detroit Free Press* coolly observed that the people of Michigan had "voted for a business person" when they elected Snyder.[4] And they got what they wanted: "someone who is from a culture of what's best for the bottom line and what's best for the investors. As governor, his bottom line has been the state budget and his investors are his donors and fellow Republican legislators." He "missed his duty to the people. I don't question his genuine remorse and anger . . . but he is certainly responsible for the decision his emergency managers made on . . . his behalf. Governing a state as well as governing a nation is *not* like running a business. He and the people of Flint have found out the hard way."

The Flint water crisis was easily the most complex and debilitating of Snyder's career, and when he spoke about it, especially in the presence of Flint residents, he seemed haunted and a little terrified. His apologies were late-coming but now repeated often. "These people I work for and care for got hurt," Snyder told a Detroit columnist.[5] "And the key catalysts were people who work for me and I'm responsible for them. You can't feel good about that." He struggled with the reality that he was on the hook for trusting the state's health and environmental experts. "It's very frustrating. The people did give wrong information. It wasn't just one person. It just makes you mad." He mused out loud about how maybe he should have called in the National Guard sooner.[6]

As a step toward making amends, Snyder pledged that his office would post his 2014 and 2015 emails related to Flint on a Michigan .gov website.[7] This was a concession to months of pressure from citizens and journalists who were unsatisfied with how Michigan's unusual exemption for the legislature and the governor's office from public records requests made it nearly impossible to grasp the complexities of the water crisis. Secrecy ran deep. The state had no independent entity to monitor the use of open access laws to make sure they were fair and effective. People requesting public documents were often asked to pay a hefty price for them. And while the law requires a response time of five to fifteen business days for FOIA requests, in practice, a one- to three-month wait was not uncommon. In 2015, Michigan was ranked dead last in the State Integrity Report Card from the Center for Public Integrity, with particularly low marks for public access to information.[8] Also, in the first five years of his tenure, Snyder signed bills that did more to conceal the actions of state government than to reveal them, including one that shielded the identity of Michigan's biggest political donors.

On top of that, the usual public watchdogs—local journalists—struggled to do their jobs in the face of steep cuts. There were fewer feet on the street after significant buyouts and layoffs at the *Detroit Free Press* and the *Detroit News*, the state's largest news outlets, and only a handful of reporters at the *Flint Journal*. In January 2016, just as the water crisis was making international headlines, the *Journal* was hit with yet more cuts.[9] Lindsey Smith, Michigan Radio's lead reporter on the water story, was based on the opposite side of the state. Steve Carmody, another go-to reporter for Flint coverage, was often on the road for other stories. *East Village Magazine*, Flint's monthly community news journal, depended upon volunteers.

Nearly three hundred pages of emails were put online after Snyder's speech, and thousands more were added in the months that followed. They helped fill in the gaps to the story, and making them available was an important step in rebuilding faith in government. But as an opt-in form of transparency it felt incomplete. The governor did not compel others to release their emails, and there was no independent way to ensure that what was posted included all of the relevant communications. And it was striking that Snyder did not initially include messages from 2013, the year when the KWA's contract was signed. Openness was still an at-will gesture for which Michigan residents and newspaper editorial boards had to plead. It wasn't until March, after a subpoena, that the governor's office released emails going back to 2011.

What the governor's office knew and when it knew it were questions that would be disputed for years to come. But the emails were revealing, showcasing a pattern of information mismanagement and misplaced priorities. Snyder had said that he was first briefed "on the potential scope and magnitude of the crisis" only in late September (days after Dr. Mona Hanna-Attisha announced her findings on high lead levels). Going by the digital trail, the governor's office was indeed told at different times that Flint was in compliance with the Lead and Copper Rule, that a problem existing in one house had been corrected, that the elevated blood-lead levels followed normal seasonal trends, and that there was nothing widespread to address. But the office had also received news that was worrisome enough for close aides to recommend intervention—as two did in the fall of 2014, in the wake of boil-water advisories and the not yet public TTHM contamination, when they asked about reconnecting Flint with Detroit.[10]

In fact, the executive branch was certainly looped into the concerns about Flint's water in July 2015 (just after Miguel Del Toral delivered his report). Dennis Muchmore, the governor's chief of staff, feared that the state was being too dismissive of Flint residents. His message circulated through the health department, which then looked at its lead data, only to conclude a few days later that there was nothing to worry about.[11] In September, Muchmore emailed Snyder and his staff: the MDEQ and MDHHS, he noted, "feel that some in Flint are taking the very sensitive issue of children's exposure to lead and trying to turn it into a political football, claiming the departments are underestimating the impacts on the populations and are particularly trying to shift responsibility to the state," which had "put an incredible amount of time and effort" into the issue. Muchmore alerted the governor that Flint's congressman, Dan Kildee, wanted a call with him. "That's tricky," he wrote, ". . . if you don't talk with him it will just fan the narrative that the state is ducking responsibility. I can't figure out why the state is responsible except that [the state treasurer] did make the ultimate decision so we're not able to avoid the subject. The real responsibility rests with the County, city, and KWA."[12]

Another report surfacing in the news showed that Veolia, the consulting firm hired to advise the city on its water troubles, had recommended investing $50,000 in corrosion control in early 2015. The company, though, had made this suggestion only in response to aesthetic concerns about brown water. It made no mention of lead.[13] Asked why there was nothing in its report about the dangers of not having corrosion control, Veolia said its brief was to focus on taste, color, and odor issues, and on disinfection by-products. Lead contamination was "not part of our scope of work."[14]

Against all the backtracking and finger-pointing, praise rained down on Curt Guyette and Michigan Radio for their early coverage of Flint. Guyette was named Journalist of the Year by the Michigan

Press Association, an extremely unusual honor for someone working not at a traditional news organization but at the ACLU. He and his collaborators also made a lengthier film—*Here's to Flint*, a forty-five-minute documentary that was broadcast nationally via *Democracy Now!*. Michigan Radio's online traffic more than tripled from the average in early 2016 and its "Not Safe to Drink" report would soon win some of the industry's most prestigious awards.[15] The accolades made the station's Steve Carmody uneasy. He was proud of what the news service had done, but he also thought about what might have been different. "It just gnaws on me," Carmody said, "that when people were saying they can't drink this water in May or June of 2014, I was taking, 'Don't worry, it's safe' as an answer from state officials." He should have seen the crisis earlier, he felt. "It just sticks in my craw. . . . That will bother me for the rest of my career."

In retrospect, Michigan Radio, like other news outlets, might have pushed harder, earlier, against official claims that the water was fine. When "there was so much mystery locally" about the water, writers for Flint's *East Village Magazine* did their best to report the facts, said Nic Custer, the managing editor. But, he added, "I realize how some of the stuff I put down, that was given to me by people at the city or state level, were just plain *lies*. It just wasn't reality." His voice rose in frustration. "We sat here and argued. I said our water's poisoned, they said no it's not, you're fine."[16]

In fifteen years or so, Carmody expects to retire from journalism. "I know on my very last day, I'm going to do a story about Flint water. Not because it's my last day, and I feel like I have to, or because it's an anniversary, but because it's still going to be hurting people in this community."

II.

In Love Canal, the chemical company that created the toxic dump and the city that built homes on top of it suffered embarrassment and bad press. But liability was another matter. After about fifteen years of legal wrangling, a federal court found that the company was responsible for cleanup costs—it reached a large settlement with New York State—but it was cleared of wrongdoing and not held liable for punitive damages. That is, it wasn't responsible for the human harm the chemicals caused.[17] In the groundwater contamination case in Southern California, made famous in the film *Erin Brockovich*, the company responsible for the cancer-causing pollution settled the lawsuit without admitting fault. In Toms River, New Jersey, a company that made chemical dyes poisoned the community's drinking water for decades, and it did everything it could to hide its actions. That case, too, ended in settlement with no admission of wrongdoing. Likewise with a notorious case of water contamination in Woburn, Massachusetts, in the 1980s that was featured in the book *A Civil Action*. A number of class action suits have been filed against industries profiting from leaded gasoline, paint, and other lead-based products. The suits charged that the industries, which had manufactured a campaign of doubt about the toxic consequences of lead, knew, or should have known, that their products hurt people. Most of these failed in court.

When it comes to the environment and public health, accountability is a slippery thing to pin down. That's especially true if the contaminants are invisible and their ill effects take years to reveal themselves. Identifying the forces responsible for causing harm becomes even harder when the violation is viewed through the prism of environmental justice, which looks at the links between place, pollution, and power. The EPA created its Office for Environmental Justice in 1992, one year after the passage of the Lead and Copper Rule. Its goal is to ensure that all people are equally protected by environmental laws, and that no groups of people "bear a disproportionate share of the negative environmental consequences"—pollution and toxic hazards—caused by government, industry, or business.[18] Environmental justice hinges on two simple democratic concepts: people are entitled to have a meaningful voice in decisions that affect the health of where they live; and, while majorities may rule, minority groups have the same inalienable rights, which cannot be taken away by others.

Just as it was once difficult to prove that the symptoms of lead poisoning were the direct result of lead exposure, so it is hard to prove environmental injustice. In law, so much depends on showing intention, or motive, to cause harm. But in environmental crimes—a school built on top of hazardous chemicals, a water system turned toxic—it is unlikely that anyone *purposefully* tried to poison children or deliberately contaminated the drinking water. The people weren't targeted one way or another. And no single decision can be blamed for the harm. Much like the structural forces over several decades that left Flint half-empty, evil intent is not necessary for evil consequences.[19]

If you asked people in Flint what a just outcome would look like, accountability in a court of law would be one essential piece of it. That's how democracy is supposed to work, after all. In late 2015 and 2016, a host of lawsuits were filed relating to the poisoned water: lead, *Legionella*, damaged plumbing, lost property values, expensive bills paid for water that was not fit to drink. Jan Burgess, the legally blind woman who sent an early complaint to the EPA, became the lead plaintiff in a suit against the federal agency. Melissa Mays was a lead plaintiff in several class action suits. LeeAnne Walters, now living in Virginia, filed an individual suit on behalf of her four children, who still had health issues.

As with other historic environmental cases, these were expected to take years to resolve, unfolding even as the plaintiffs kept an eye on their children, wondering how, or if, they had been hurt. The Flint cases also involved unique challenges because they were aimed at public agencies and public servants (and the engineering consultants who worked on their behalf), rather than a private company. In Michigan, high-ranking officials have legal immunity for decisions made in the course of doing their jobs. (Lower-ranking officials may still be charged with "gross negligence."[20]) Immunity did not, however, protect the state from charges of violating residents' constitutional rights. Some cases argued that the crisis had betrayed the plaintiffs' "fundamental liberty interest to bodily integrity" or that it was racially discriminatory. However the charges were framed, though, the cases faced an uphill battle. The law, as it stands now, just isn't well equipped to respond to something like this.

But there was one early victory, and it was big. Almost three years after the ill-fated water switch, a federal judge approved a historic settlement in the class action lawsuit filed by Melissa Mays, the Concerned Pastors for Social Action, the Natural Resources Defense Council, and the ACLU of Michigan (where Curt Guyette was still at it). As part of the deal, the state agreed to pay $87 million for the city to locate eighteen thousand lead and galvanized steel water lines and replace them with copper by 2020, at no cost to homeowners. All households with an active water account were covered, including those with overdue bills, but not vacant homes. The state was also obliged to put an additional $10 million in reserve for potential cost overruns and emergencies, and to pay $895,000 to cover the plaintiffs' legal costs.

The deal outlined a strategy for the state's relief efforts. Support from Washington waned when Flint's federal emergency declaration expired, after an extension, in August 2016. The state kept the water distribution sites open but, per the settlement, it could begin closing them as demand tapered off. (Five closed in 2017, and, to the grave dismay of Flint residents, the program shut down entirely, with very little warning, in April 2018.[21]) It would, however, expand the program for installing and maintaining water filters for residents. That included Spanish-language advertising. People would still be able to call the city's 211 phone line for free water deliveries within twenty-four hours, though that service could be canceled pending the results of future water tests. The Medicaid expansion for Flint residents would be extended through March 2021.

The settlement was cause for great celebration. "Flint proved that even while poisoned . . . we are not just victims. We are fighters," said Mays after it was approved. "While this does not fix everything, it's a good start."[22] The *New York Times* editorial board cheered them on: "Michigan Is Forced to Do Right By Flint, Finally."[23]

Advocates for Flint's children got another big win in April 2018 when, in a partial settlement for a separate class action case, the state agreed to spend $4.1 million to create a school-based screening pro-gram for tens of thousands of children who were exposed to the water. Directed by Dr. Mona Hanna-Attisha, it would help determine the health and special education needs of the children, and it would also provide training for school staff to better identify children who may be harmed by lead.[24] But all this was hardly the end of the state's dealings in court. Michigan continued to defend itself against charges of individual suffering and unequal protection. One point of conten-tion: whether or not emergency managers should be considered state officials. The state said they should not.

If justice for Flint meant charges against those whose decisions created and prolonged the crisis, there was some hope. The criminal and civil investigations initiated by the Michigan attorney general began with an abundance of resources: the team had up to eighteen lawyers, twelve investigators, and a host of supporting staff. By October 2016, it had spent $2.3 million of the $4.9 million that was initially allocated to it by the Michigan legislature; as the cases pro-ceeded, though, its means dwindled. And it had an odd bifurcated role. Led by a special prosecutor, the investigation had been prom-ised independence. But Attorney General Bill Schuette was obliged to represent the state's interests, and he did so by fighting for the state in all those other lawsuits. Millions of state dollars also paid the defense bills for just about everyone involved with Flint's water at the environmental and health departments, and the city, as well as the former emergency managers. Michigan was essentially funding both the prosecution and the defense of the Flint water cases.[25] Schuette was also widely expected to run for state governor in 2018, succeeding the term-limited Snyder, which led many to wonder if the investigation wasn't just so much political peacocking. So it was dizzying to see Schuette stand up at press conferences and use sharp language to announce the first three indictments.

The sensational news came in April 2016. Stephen Busch and Mike Prysby of the MDEQ faced charges of misconduct, neglect of duty, tampering with evidence, and violations of the Michigan Safe Drink-ing Water Act. They were also accused of impeding an investigation into the Legionnaires' outbreak, which later brought involuntary man-slaughter charges. "We allege and we will prove that Mr. Busch and Mr. Prysby altered test results which endangered the health of citizens and families of Flint," Schuette declared. Busch in particular had falsely claimed to the EPA that the Flint plant had optimized corrosion control, and both men were charged with ordering Michael Glasgow, the utilities administrator, to alter the 2015 report on lead in the city's water to misleadingly lower the levels. When the indictments were announced, both men were suspended from their jobs. The third person charged was Glasgow himself. The man who had flagged the modified test results and had worried about the treatment plant's capabilities from the very beginning swiftly reached a plea deal with investigators. He said that the MDEQ officials explicitly told him to change the report.[26]

More indictments came in July: six state employees were hit with criminal charges, three at the MDHHS and three at the MDEQ. Among other charges, the prosecutors included the acts of burying an epidemiologist's report that showed a spike in blood-lead levels in Flint's children after the city's water switch, deleting emails about the report, and ignoring its findings. They were charged variously with misconduct in office, conspiring to commit misconduct in office, and willful neglect of duty. The MDEQ's Liane Shekter-Smith was also later charged with involuntary manslaughter. After her initial reassignment—to handle open records requests, of all things—the drinking water chief had been suspended and then terminated months earlier. She remained the only person who was fired because of the Flint water crisis.

By the end of 2016, the criminal investigation had reached another tier of responsibility. Emergency managers Darnell Earley and Jerry Ambrose were variously indicted for false pretenses, obstructing an investigation, and involuntary manslaughter.[27] "All too prevalent in this Flint water investigation is a priority on balance sheets and finances rather than the health and safety of the citizens of Flint," Attorney General Bill Schuette said.[28] The cases focused on the strategy to fund the Karegnondi Water Authority: the administrative consent order, or ACO. Schuette called it a "sham," though it did not escape notice that one of his own assistants had signed off on the deal.[29] Earley, who defended himself shortly after the switchback to Lake Huron water in a column he penned for the *Detroit News*, had stepped down from his post as emergency manager for the Detroit school district many months earlier, when the Flint crisis was exploding in national news. In his op-ed, Earley argued that the switch to the KWA was initiated by local leaders who "were in no way coerced" by the state or the EM, and that his job was to "oversee the implementation of the previously accepted and approved plans. . . . It did not fall to me to question, second guess or invalidate the actions taken prior to my appointment." Investigators didn't see it that way, however. In addition, Howard Croft, the former public works director, was accused of aiding and abetting Earley and Ambrose, and working to require the use of water treated at a plant that was unfit for service. Later, an involuntary manslaughter charge was added to his case, too.[31]

The investigative team wasn't done yet. In June 2017, it raised eyebrows by charging two of the state's most senior health officials. Nick Lyon, the director of MDHHS and a member of the governor's cabinet, was accused of involuntary manslaughter and misconduct in office for "taking steps to suppress information illustrating obvious and apparent harms," allegedly allowing a public health crisis to continue. Dr. Eden Wells, the agency's top medical executive, was accused of misconduct, obstruction of justice, providing false testimony, and threatening to withhold funding from a Flint group investigating the Legionnaires' outbreak.[32] Later, she too faced an involuntary manslaughter charge. Snyder defended them both, saying they had been "instrumental in Flint's recovery." They had his "full faith and confidence." Though others had been suspended without pay after they were charged, these two would remain on the payroll, managing programs that dealt with the Flint health crisis.[33] An MDHHS brochure floating around Flint—"Health Coverage for People Impacted by Flint Water"—was stamped with Rick Snyder's and Nick Lyon's names, though they were both short on credibility in the city.

Though they failed to attract as much attention as the dramatic criminal charges, two civil lawsuits were filed against the consultants who advised the city on the water switch, Lockwood, Andrews & Newnam (LAN) and the Veolia consulting firm, alleging professional misbehavior that worsened and prolonged the crisis.[34] The attorney general's team sought "to recover monetary damages . . . in the hundreds of millions of dollars" from the companies and to put that money into a special fund managed by the Flint community for its own needs.[35]

And yet there was still move to come. In March 2018, as preliminary examinations were underway for those facing charges, the lead prosecutor said that a "spin-off" criminal investigation was already in process. He told a legislative committee that "we believe there was a significant financial fraud that drove this." It was too simple to suggest that Flint's water switch was motivated solely by the desire to save money. Rather, the investigator emphasized, "I believe greed drove this." And while he didn't specify who was being targeted for possible charges, he added that prosecutors were "moving at lightning speed."[36]

Altogether, the avalanche of lawsuits came with a staggering array of hearings, paperwork, testimonies, and legal fees. It was chaotic, time-consuming, and expensive. For those hoping to see the governor accept direct responsibility—if anyone had had the authority to demand a serious intervention in Flint, it was him—the proceedings were unsatisfying.[37] But the legal battles were an opportunity to carve out a place for environmental justice in the law where it had not fully existed before—to acknowledge that Flint, the *grande traverse* of the river, was as deserving of truth and reconciliation as any other place. It was, maybe, a start.

Genesis

We should be allowed to destroy only what we ourselves can re-create. We cannot re-create this world. We cannot re-create "wilderness." We cannot even, truly, re-create ourselves. Only our behavior can we re-create, or create anew.

—Alice Walker, "Everything Is a Human Being,"
Living by the Word (1989)

I.

The Flint River shone, as bright as if it were its own source of light. Trees tilted toward their own reflections, their leaves thick with shades of green that can be found only in late August. Just off the riverbank, a few miles outside of downtown Flint, about thirty people gathered. Kathleen Gazall was one of them, the architect and city booster. So was Congressman Dan Kildee and Steve Carmody, the Michigan Radio reporter. It was an eclectic group brought together by the Flint River Watershed Coalition for one of its summer paddles.[1] That afternoon in 2016, the group rubbed sunscreen into their skin, tugged down the brims of their hats, climbed into plastic kayaks, and, for the next few hours, rowed through the water toward Vietnam Veterans Park. The river was calm and wide, curving around woodlands and meadows, under bridges, and through city neighborhoods. For a while, the white spider-legged water tower at the treatment plant stood before them, straight ahead, like a steeple, or a setting sun.

The problem is not the river. That was the message of the water-shed coalition. The drinking water wasn't dangerous because the river itself was poisonous, as so many assumed, remembering the long shadow of the polluting past. The waterway was in fact becoming healthier all the time, with the advent of environmental laws, the decline of industry, and the day-to-day work of river recovery groups. In the years leading up to the water crisis, nearly four hundred species of birds, reptiles, and fish (some even safe to eat) had been spotted in the Flint River and its tributaries. Even bald eagles had returned.[2] The river's mouth was in the Shiawassee National Wildlife Refuge, a haven for tens of thousands of migratory birds. From there it joined a chain of waterways that flowed out toward the Saginaw Bay and on to the Great Lakes.[3]

The coalition had supported the temporary switch to the river "as an opportunity for education about a fabulous resource," said Rebecca Fedewa, the red-headed director.[4] "'Look, now you're drinking it!'" Had the move been handled well, "it could have been tremendous." But it wasn't. It had brought devastation. One consequence among many was that it perpetuated myths about the river. Fedewa's heart sank when she saw phrases like "the toxic Flint River" show up in news articles and even in the presidential debate held in Flint.[5] She and other volunteers used every tool they had, from an enormous amount of data to social media (#itsnottheriver) to break through the noise. The results were mixed.

The small nonprofit, which relied on volunteers for river cleanup and water monitoring, had big ambitions. Its activities covered all seven counties that touch the river. Its chapters worked on cultivating the Flint River Trail, the downtown river corridor, and the watery stretch that runs through Lapeer County. Through summer paddles and floats, the group sought to end people's alienation from the river. To the coalition, it was an overlooked wonder in an area that was hungry for beauty. And there was something else: all the communities in the 1,400-square-mile watershed—the city, the suburbs, the outlying rural towns and farms—had a common stake in the river's health. It was an opening for a divided region to come together, for people to see themselves as connected through the ecological fact of the land they lived upon. If they took better care of their river, perhaps they would take better care of each other, too.

With the crisis, the watershed coalition feared that its support would plummet and the community's estrangement from the river would only deepen. So it was shocking when the opposite happened. Attendance at the coalition's 2016 annual meeting broke the all-time record.[6] Between thirty and forty people came to each canoeing and kayaking event that year, double the usual number. The cataclysm had made people curious about the river. They wanted to see for themselves.

II.

It took more than two years of squabbling and legal battles, but at the end of 2017 Flint decided to stick with the Detroit water department, forgoing the Karegnondi Water Authority entirely.[7] The city was still responsible for the $7 million annual payment for the KWA bonds, but in exchange for signing a thirty-year contract, the Detroit utility—now restructured as the Great Lakes Water Authority, or GLWA—agreed to credit that sum to Flint's account. The Detroit system would receive the rights to nearly all of what would have been Flint's share of raw water from the KWA. The deal, approved by Flint's council, included funds for relieving high water bills and a promise by the governor to put a city representative on the GLWA board. Governor Snyder also tried to persuade the General Motors engine plant on West Bristol Road to return to Flint's water supply, delivering a letter requesting as much in January 2018. But a GM representative said there were no plans to make the change.[8] Other Genesee County communities that had contracted with the KWA began their water switch in November 2017, with the help of an all-new $72 million treatment facility. KWA got its financing in the end, with or without Flint. "Our treatment goal is to match the water quality of the [Detroit] system," said one of the engineers.

There was still long, hard work to be done rebuilding Flint's water infrastructure, including the full replacement of thousands of lead service lines. With insufficient funding, this started as an excruciatingly dragged-out process, including pilot projects, pricey contractor bids, and best guesses about where the pipes were actually located.[9] For those on the ground, it was maddening. "We need a clear, concise plan of action to replace the pipes so we don't have to live out of a bottle of water when we're surrounded by the Great Lakes of Michigan," declared Yvonne Lewis, one of the community leaders.

So the legal settlement that would replace Flint's service lines was a breakthrough. It was supplemented by an additional $100 million that came through from the federal government, which included a law change that allowed Michigan to forgive the $20 million that Flint owed in water loans, dating back to 1999. This meant that the city would be able to undertake the wholesale replacement of its pipes, both lead and galvanized steel. It was an almost unprecedented public works project. To date, Madison, Wisconsin, and Lansing, Michigan, were believed to be the only major cities that had fully removed their aging lead-based service lines.

But cities around the country now felt unable to take their pipes for granted. Flint's story was a wake-up call. A 2016 investigation by the National Resources Defense Council found that fifty-three hundred water systems were in violation of federal lead rules.[10]

Rural America was vulnerable, too, especially because small utilities, serving a few thousand people or fewer, are given a pass on lead regulations. (They don't have to treat the water to prevent contamination until lead is discovered, and even then, they're rarely compelled to remove it.[11]) Flint helped others to realize the stakes of their public water systems, inspiring communities to examine them with an urgency that had not been seen since the grand old days when they were built. For these modern-day alchemists, though, the trick isn't to turn lead into gold; it's to make it disappear.

Over in Lansing, city hall was inundated by calls from people who wanted to know how it had worked this magic. Lansing's story showed how it could be done. The city, which draws its water from the Saginaw Aquifer, four hundred feet below the surface, had carried out a full pipe replacement program. The overhaul was not prompted by a public health emergency or court order, and it was so efficient and cost-effective residents barely noticed it. "When we show up at homes to replace the lead service lines, people think there's a problem with the water," said Steve Serkaian of Lansing's Board of Water and Light.[12] The notion that there was no problem—that the work was preemptive infrastructure improvement—was so unusual that it came as a surprise.

The project began when Virg Bernero, then a Michigan state senator, learned about the lead-in-water crisis in Washington, D.C., in 2004. He and his staff began asking questions of the city's Board of Water and Light and state agencies. They also contacted Marc Edwards at Virginia Tech. While Lansing had an effective anticorrosion program, and the city's lead tests appeared fine, "we didn't have confidence in the results," Bernero said. By then, he'd learned enough about the loopholes in the Lead and Copper Rule. Given that no amount of lead exposure is safe, his team wanted to err on the side of caution.

Bernero formed a safe drinking water task force that included professors from Michigan State and other experts who "did not have a vested interest in the system such as it was." Together, they put the system under the microscope. They met with a great deal of defensiveness at first, but in 2004 the BWL's commissioners accepted the task force's recommendation to replace all the lead service lines. It got to work on a methodical ten-year, $42 million plan to replace every one of Lansing's fourteen thousand pipes. (Bernero had the opportunity to oversee it; he was elected mayor in 2006.) The plan went slightly over schedule—the city was hit by the recession and state revenue-sharing cuts, just as Flint was—but by the end of 2016 they were done.

The money for the project came the old-fashioned way—Lansing "just raised the rates," Bernero explained, referring to water bills. One unusual advantage: unlike Flint's system, the 130-year-old BWL is a wholly owned city subsidiary, which simplified its ability to build the cost of new infrastructure into its rates.[13] Also, while Lansing has a lot in common with Flint—it's another GM legacy town, one that built Oldsmobiles, and it has roughly the same size population—it was not nearly as challenged by vacancy. It had powerful anchor institutions that sustained it over the years, as the home of the state government and with Michigan State's campus based just two miles away in East Lansing.

Also, because BWL owns the entire water system, it could replace all parts of the infrastructure without involving homeowners. In other communities, the customer may own some portion of the line leading to their property; if a utility wants to replace it, some of the cost is put on the customer's tab.[14] Many anti-lead advocates claim that utilities should be responsible for the whole replacement: the home-owner didn't put the lead line in the ground, and in fact it was often legally required to have it there. Homeowners have no meaningful control over the part that is considered their property.

Lansing's other trick was to design a graceful method for execution that cut the cost and time of pipe replacement in half. After two years of digging trenches, and with the prospect of disrupting untold square miles of streets, sidewalks, and yards, Lansing decided to rethink the way its workers were laying the new lines. Experimentation yielded an innovative technique. All workers had to do was cut two squares in the ground at either end of the line. One exposed the water main and service connection at the curb, and the other exposed the service box. Then, using a special tool invented by engineers in the city's own machine shop, it took just one elegant motion to thread the old lead pipe out and the new copper pipe in.

"We submit notifications [to residents] to explain what's happening," Serkaian said, "because we need permission to enter their basement and disconnect the lead service line to the meter, and hook the meter up to the new copper line. There's a minor inconvenience for an hour or so in not having water service." Occasionally, the city also had to issue traffic advisories; vehicles were diverted when crews were working on major streets. But that was it.

Lansing also minimized disruption by mapping out its pipe replacement to follow the construction of another infrastructure improvement: updating its sewage system to better deal with flooding. The sheer scale of the pipe project also had accelerated efficiency built into it. Work crews had done it so many times, they only became faster and more adept. "They've learned how to overcome any and all obstacles," Serkaian said.

It was a promising picture of how to make cities work better. And it cut against the broader pattern. When the 21st Century Infrastructure Commission that Governor Snyder had called for released its report, it laid out how Michigan's spending on infrastructure is near the bottom nationally. Between 2002 and 2013, it saw the third-largest decline in that allocation as a portion of its GDP.[15] This happened even though infrastructure spending brings an almost immediate economic boost. Every dollar that goes into water and sewer projects returns $2.03 in revenue.[16] And the benefits for the environment and public health are obvious: for example, the opportunity to stop the 5.7 billion gallons of untreated sewage that had flowed into Michigan waterways since 2008.

Nationwide, states and municipalities have slashed infrastructure spending by about 55 percent since 2003, while federal spending has dropped by almost 19 percent. Infrastructure investment plummeted from a high of 3 percent of the nation's GDP in the late 1960s to less than 2 percent in 2014.[17] It happened at a time that roughly correlates with the abandonment of America's core cities in favor of sprawling metropolitan regions. Shaken by the Flint water crisis, Congress passed a federal aid package that President Obama signed in the last weeks of his administration that included $20 million in loans for water infrastructure improvements around the country.

Mayor Bernero is sympathetic to competing priorities in local government. But that's exactly why he felt cities should find out where they stand with their water systems. "We've got pipes in the ground in many cities that are close to one hundred years old, aging, underground and easy to ignore," he said. They have to be replaced eventually anyway—lead ones all the more so—and while it might seem that "no news is good news" when it comes to pipes, any slight change in water chemistry can pose a devastating threat, as it did in Flint and Washington, D.C.

Lansing was fortunate to be able to pay for its new pipes through a simple rate increase. Madison, Wisconsin, used a different model, although it was also served by having a city-owned and -operated system. Within eleven years, it replaced eight thousand lead water lines in a pioneering $19.4 million effort. The city offered $1,000 rebates to homeowners who replaced their own pipes, with the cost averaging $1,300. (Apartment owners paid more.) The reimbursement money came from revenue the Madison water utility received from providing space on its water towers for cellular antennas. The idea of using public money to help pay for replacing private pipes was controversial, especially when some doubted the risk of the lead service lines. But, especially in the wake of the Flint water crisis, the city has received national acclaim.

"Infrastructure issues were never a partisan thing," Bernero said. "We built this country with the greatest infrastructure in world, which resulted in the most productive society, the most incredible middle class in modern history. Now our infrastructure is beginning to go by the wayside, and there's this Tea Party mentality that makes people afraid to raise taxes for anything.

"People will suffer," he said, "and of course, the poor suffer the most. Let's face it, the rich can insulate themselves from travesty . . . [they] can afford bottled water. They can move out to suburbs or wherever. The rich have always found ways to insulate themselves. Though ultimately, when we have a complete and utter infrastructure failure . . . no one is safe."

America's lead service lines took decades to install, and even a wholly committed effort to root them out will in turn take years. It's critical to do so, advocates say, but at the same time, we cannot wait for that to happen. There are other steps we can take now to address lead in drinking water. Among them: taking a closer look at what counts as "lead free" plumbing fixtures; addressing high water bills (since shutoffs cause stagnation, which can worsen contamination); and closing the loopholes in the federal Lead and Copper Rule.

If utilities sampled water in a way that truly set out to find the worst-case levels, between 54 and 70 percent of those with lead lines in their systems would uncover severe contamination, affecting up to 96 million people. That's according to a study by the American Water Works Association, and it echoes the sampling that was flagged in, for example, New York City schools.[18] Yanna Lambrinidou, the medical anthropologist, has continued her advocacy against lead in drinking water, and through public information requests, she's found other ways that water authorities undermine the spirit of the Lead and Copper Rule. Philadelphia's water department, for example, instructed samplers to "run only the cold water for two minutes" before taking a sample, since lead dissolves more easily in hot water. This was similar to stipulations given to people, for example, in Rhode Island and Michigan.[19]

The EPA, perhaps in an effort to repair its beleaguered reputation, urged state governors, environmental agencies, public health commissioners, and tribal councils to reckon seriously with the Lead and Copper Rule, to warn people about the risks of lead pipes, and to seek ways to go beyond minimum requirements to make water safe.[20] Its own reevaluation of the LCR—scheduled for 2017, but delayed—could be an opportunity to address the gaps that are routinely exploited. These include pre-flushing and using small-mouthed bottles, but also the absence of any requirements for testing at schools and the lack of a federal limit on the amount of lead allowed in tap water in any *individual* home. The LCR formula requires action only when there is excessive lead found in *many* homes.[21]

One way or another, the point is to do something—not perpetuate the kick-the-can strategy of past decades. In Michigan, in Snyder's last year of office, he called for a program to replace every lead line in the state. He also wanted the state to implement lead rules for drinking water that were tougher than the federal regulations, which were, after all, a baseline; states can choose to go further. Maybe, instead of being a national disgrace, the Great Lakes State could become a national model.

III.

Civic Park was looking forward to its one hundredth anniversary. From rise to decline to resurgence: that's the journey that Pastor Sherman McCathern hoped to see captured in a centennial mural that the church's Urban Renaissance Center commissioned from an artist.[22] In the early months of 2018, the artist, Cardine Humes, who had moved to the area from the South, was hard at work. Bundled in a parka, he painted on an outside wall of the Dort Meats Company on Dupont Street, bringing color and shadow to ordinary neighborhood scenes, making them as grand as anything: a school, a lawn, a pine tree, children at play. In the center, community leaders are pictured, planning for a better future.

If there's any message to take from Flint, not only the water crisis, but its full history, it's that nobody has a monopoly on wisdom. Lived experience is as important as technical training. One of the ideals of environmental justice—that people should have a meaningful voice in the decisions that affect them—isn't intended just as a respectful courtesy; it also leads to better decisions. The people of Flint had no say at all in what came out of their showers and kitchen sinks, certainly not with four consecutive state-appointed emergency managers in place when critical changes were made to the city's water supply. Residents used every democratic means available to them—meetings, protests, grassroots organizing, citizen science—to spotlight the deteriorating quality of their water. Not only did their concerns go unheard but there was no accountability for poor decisions made under the EMs' tenures, at least not until states of emergency had been declared at every level of government.

The Michigan Civil Rights Commission, which investigated the Flint water crisis, ultimately recommended that the state's EM law be replaced or restructured. It specifically said that EMs should have regional authority, rather than city authority, because many of the most serious problems plaguing cities are not contained by their own borders. Cities are connected to their neighbors, and always have been. For the same reason, the commission suggested that a form of regional government, or at least regional cooperation, be implemented that would require core cities and suburbs to work together collaboratively to solve the problems to which they are both party. In a separate investigation, a joint select committee of the Michigan Legislature suggested that the single emergency manager be replaced with a three-person team, including a local ombudsman, and making EMs liable "for certain harms they cause." Some Flint leaders wanted to see the oversight system completely abolished.[23]

What of the other principle of environmental justice—that specific minority groups not be disproportionately burdened by environmental harm? The people making the ill-fated decisions in Flint were not necessarily racists and did not mean to treat the city differently because most of its residents are black, according to the civil rights commission. But, it said in its report, "the disparate response" to the crisis—the delays and dismissals—was "the result of systemic racism that was built into the foundation and growth of Flint, its industry, and the suburban area surrounding it."[24] Decades of segregation created a cascading series of problems that prove the error in the "separate but equal" doctrine espoused by a flawed U.S. Supreme Court decision more than a century earlier.[25] Current civil rights law is not adequate to address the problems in the state, the commission argued. It's designed for individual complaints, with proof that someone acted in an overtly racist way. That does not appear to be the story of the Flint water crisis. One decision after another, one policy after another: they were colorblind. Nobody explicitly argued that Flint should settle for water with high lead levels because it is mostly an African American city or because so many residents are poor. And yet.

"If this was in a white area, in a rich area, there would have been something done," said Yolanda Figueroa, a Flint resident, at one of the civil rights hearings. "I mean, let's get real here. We know the truth."[26]

Half a century after the civil rights era, segregation persists so much that core cities serve as proxies for communities of color. Disinvesting in cities means disinvesting in them. The legacy of housing discrimination deprived Flint of its political clout—not only by losing

half its population, but by losing the power to elect its own empowered city representatives. The commission itself acknowledged that it
had failed to take the residents' concerns about the water seriously.
Way back in January 2015, in the midst of the TTHM crisis, its staff
was among those who had received coolers and bottled water from
the state for its Flint office.[27] The report said that most of the commission had some vague "awareness of what was happening." The
lack of serious attention spoke "to the level of importance we ascribed
to 'those' people in Flint at the time, not that they didn't exist."

People in Flint were frustrated by the unlikelihood of the state dismissing their complaints had they lived in wealthier and whiter communities. African American leaders in Flint pointed out that the
water crisis didn't seem to register until "our white sisters"—people
such as LeeAnne Walters and Melissa Mays, who were also married
and mothers—became the face of it. Putting them forward in media
accounts was a strategic choice, they said. But not only people in Flint.
"I mean, everybody on the street was asking that question, and by asking the same question, everybody had the same answer. The answer was
'no, it probably wouldn't have,'" said Ken Sikemma, co-chair of the task
force that Governor Snyder commissioned to investigate the crisis.[28]

That erasure didn't really end, even when the Flint disaster was
widely known. There was an addiction to hero narratives, as Yanna
Lambrinidou has described it. As the news story began to shift uneas-
ily into history, the narrative tended to single out one or two figures—
especially Marc Edwards and Mona Hanna-Attisha—while minimizing
the role played by community organizers well before they came along.
The hero narrative replicated a dangerous dynamic of "saviors" and
"saved" that disempowered the community all over again, and what's
more, it was simply false; it didn't sync with what actually happened.
As writer Derrick Z. Jackson observed, in later years, when there
were major environmental or social justice awards to give, many with
large cash prizes, they typically went to non-black figures: Walters,
Edwards, Hanna-Attisha.[29] Of course, the trio indeed made major contributions to bringing the dangers of Flint's water to light, and they

deserved recognition for it. But those who organized the early protests, the pastors and local businesses that ran bottled water drives, the local politicians who spoke out—they were missed by late-coming national media and then overlooked again by the awards circuit. These anonymous black residents of Flint "have not been recognized as possessing the agency of non-black figures involved in the crisis," Jackson wrote. "They figured into the national narrative almost exclusively as helpless or hapless victims. . . . America still too often requires a non-black hero or victim before it can turn proper attention to an issue that primarily affects African Americans."

Environmental disasters don't solely affect people of color—just look at Love Canal or Toms River, New Jersey, both middle-class white areas, or the extraordinary lead-in-water crisis in the nation's capital city. But the higher probability of them is in the DNA of segregation. That's the logical outcome of concentrated vulnerability. Not long after the Love Canal movement, a North Carolina community protested chemical dumping in a landfill near a residential neighborhood where mostly poor African Americans lived. Polychlorinated biphenyls, or PCBs, were contaminating the soil. The protests won the support of the NAACP and led to two national studies that described how hazardous waste facilities were consistently located in places where people of color tended to live. This fact is so persistent that race is the very best predictor of the presence of pollutants, even when controlled for other factors such as income and property values.[30]

In an echo of the racialized practices of the mainstream housing industry, the land where it is most cost-effective for a company to build its hazardous facility usually happens to be near where black and brown people live. Their very presence is part of what, historically, makes the land cheap. The downward cycle continues as the industrial polluter devalues nearby homes even more, undermining residents' stability and the area's tax revenue. While the polluter partly makes up for that devaluation by paying its own share of taxes, the dynamic still results in one of the trademarks of environmental injustice: the polluter's contributions create equal benefits for all the region's residents—taxes, jobs, economic stimulus—but only one group of people bears nearly all the harms and risks, often without their knowledge or consent.

In Flint, about 37 percent of the residents are white. But as researcher Laura Pulido points out, "they suffer a fate similar to their Black neighbors insofar as the entire city is racialized as Black."[31] (To say nothing of other communities in Flint, particularly the sizable Hispanic population.) That's an echo of the days of redlining and racially restrictive covenants, when a neighborhood could be black or it could be white, but never both.

The more that cities are divided by race and class, the more that environmental racism becomes likely. And this isn't just a local metropolitan trend anymore; regional inequality skews it even further. In 2017, the Lincoln Institute for Land Policy examined shrinking legacy cities in the Midwest and Northeast—cities such as Flint, Akron, Syracuse, Muncie, Camden, Scranton, and Albany. Of the twenty-four locations it looked at, twenty were home to at least one Fortune 500 company between 1960 and 2015. Many were home to five or more. Today, only twelve are. Thousands of jobs—between 2 and nearly 40 percent—were erased in nearly all the cities in that time. Flint had the largest drop. (It was home to 62,700 jobs in 2002 and only 39,200 in 2014.) Some of these jobs moved to the suburbs, which grew over the same time period. However, as wealth and economic opportunity have concentrated in a tiny handful of major American cities, even these suburban metropolitan areas are losing ground. And when inner-ring suburbs start looking like core cities—whether because of pollution or crime or unemployment or the presence of people of color—exurbs are built farther and farther away.

To avoid association with hollowed-out cities that have become largely black and poor, some suburban communities have changed their names, zip codes, and school districts. School secessions go back to 1954 in the South; it was a supposedly race-neutral way to redraw the lines of segregation after the U.S. Supreme Court's *Brown v. Board of Education* ruling.[32] Today, a "local control" movement has led to a wave of communities splintering off into new majority-white school districts. In Boston in 2012, the Hyde Park neighborhood won its battle to change its zip code so that it would no longer have the same postal number as neighboring Mattapan.[33] In 2017, Flint Township, the same suburb that allowed the GM engine plant to hook on to its water, made moves to change its name to Carman Hills and get new zip codes. "You gotta take every step to secure your business and that got me thinking separating ourselves from Flint started to make sense," a dive shop owner in Flint Township told a local news station.[34]

Despite trying to make ever-finer distinctions between "here" and "there," the dividing lines are not always neat. Andrew R. Highsmith, in his history *Demolition Means Progress,* observes that the "ascendance of the suburbs during the twentieth century was without question one of the most consequential developments in American history." But while it fostered "easy stereotypes of suburban plenty," there were also "schoolchildren attending study halls in gymnasiums, taking shop classes in converted coal sheds, and learning to read in tents"—images that defied assumptions about suburbia.[35] That's true in the modern era, too. With the rise of exurbs and regional inequality, and with larger numbers of racial minorities and immigrants moving to the suburbs—more than half of African Americans nationwide live in suburbs now (most immigrants, too)—the distinctions have blurred.[36] Nobody has a single story. People in every kind of community, from city to suburb to countryside, experience a particular mix of privileges and disadvantages through which they navigate their lives.

At the same time, the pattern is plain and must be named. The structural underpinnings of environmental racism, replicated again and again, are what the Michigan Civil Rights Commission was trying to get at when it asserted that "it is not enough to say the result is unintended." We must recognize that "being colorblind is not the solution, it is the problem."

Epilogue

Living here is tossed body overboard,
Sacrificing,
It is being Jonah and knowing the whale's belly,
Flourishing in the dark.

We've trained our eyes to still embrace light.
Remember light.

We are that light.

—Raise It Up! Youth Poets, "Flint" (2016)

I.

In the spring of 2018, Joy Tabernacle was still at home in the blond-brick church at the corner of Chevrolet Avenue and Dayton Street in Civic Park. A historic plaque honored the Presbyterian congregation that first filled its pews, and the words "God is Love" were etched above the entryway. Though it was still a neighborhood anchor, Joy Tabernacle was not only a community church but more of a campus. Once-vacant homes nearby had been transformed into sacred spaces of a different kind. One had become the Civic Park Health and Wellness House, serving people's medical, dental, and vision needs. That was done with the help of the University of Michigan-Flint, which now held four classes a week at the church's social ministry, the Urban Renaissance Center, in subjects like social work and English linguistics. The makeshift college classroom had seats reserved for neighborhood residents. Another house was slated to become an agriculture center, where people could learn to garden and farm on vacant land, and then preserve food through canning. Renovations were carried out through an apprenticeship program led by one of Joy Tabernacle's ministers, which trained five young men in construction work. Pastor Sherman McCathern and his collaborators called this widening community Ubuntu Village, using a Southern African term for "I am, because you are."[1]

In the same segregated neighborhood that General Motors had built for white workers and their families, people were constructing a new inclusive model for urban life, where residents weren't just workers in a factory or problems to be solved: they were part of a community that had need for their whole selves. "When you look around," McCathern said, "people can't see it like you can, but there's a lot of improvements." There were the refurbished houses, and the partnership with the university; there was grant support from both the C. S. Mott Foundation and the Ruth Mott Foundation (Ruth was Charles Stewart's wife); there were the plans for Civic Park's centennial and for the forty recent graduates of the church's work readiness program. (Congressman Dan Kildee had been the ceremony's keynote speaker.) There was also the rehab work on Joy Tabernacle's sanctuary.[2] For years, the congregation had been meeting in the fellowship hall because of serious repairs needed in the sanctuary, where part of the ceiling had collapsed. Essential work had been postponed as an insurance dispute dragged on, and then, with Flint's water crisis, the church became a leading emergency resource, which caused further delays.[3] But, McCathern thought, it was finally time to turn back to the renovations. On a cool evening in March, just days after returning from a service trip in Uganda, he was hard at work, drafting a campaign to raise $150,000 "to get back upstairs."

It had been four years since the significance of the dark water spraying from a hydrant had dawned on him. But it felt like a never-ending revelation. McCathern had begun to struggle with short-term memory loss. He'd pat around for his car keys, look up, look down, and finally arrange for someone to pick him up before going outside and seeing that his car was already running, the keys in the ignition where he'd left them. His greatest sadness was that he'd forget if he prayed or not. He'd be getting up off his knees in the morning and it would strike him like a cold shock: *did* he actually pray just then, or no? He wasn't sure. He worried that he was cheating God. And so he'd bend down again, his knees creaking, and he'd pray once more.

McCathern attributed the memory loss to aging. But speaking at a large meeting one day, he asked if others in the room had similar problems; he was surprised when about 250 or 300 people raised their hands. So could memory loss be related to the water in Flint, along with everything else? What about the people he knew who had amputations because of some kind of bacteria-related illness—was that the water, too? And how about the young men in his church who he'd rushed to the hospital with an accelerated heart rate? Was *that* the water's fault? Who knew? Anything seemed possible.

"It takes so long for an American citizen to realize this, but we've been poisoned for real," McCathern said. "I watched it among my own congregation, Sunday after Sunday. I began to realize this is real. It was not play, it was not in your mind, you're not making something up."

The national attention did lead to some positive changes in Flint. New infrastructure was being laid throughout the city. People had better access to health care, thanks to expanded Medicaid and other services. These were longtime needs in the community, and they could help heal wounds that went far beyond even lead and *Legionella*. Also, in the years following the peak of the crisis, there was a cascade of ambitious investment in Flint. An auto supply manufacturer broke ground on the first such facility to come to the city in about thirty years: the colossal Buick City complex was being converted into a factory for Lear Corp., which was set to make car seats for General Motors. It would create up to six hundred new jobs. Downtown, the historic Capitol Theatre, vacant for two decades, reopened after a $37 million renovation brought its glittering marquee back to life. The Flint Institute of Arts went through an enormous expansion, adding a wing for contemporary crafts and creating a multipurpose maker space where visitors could watch glass and ceramic artists at work.

There were other encouraging developments, quieter but no less welcome. Two online news sites launched, Flintside and Flint Beat, providing broader coverage of the city's rich stories. A state grant that was part of the water recovery response brought a youth basketball league back to the city after a fifteen-year absence. The first Flint Literary Festival debuted with the theme of 'Flight,' featuring Christopher Paul Curtis, a city native and a Newbery Medal–winning author who often wrote about his hometown. And a children's education center opened on Gladwin Street, in a brand-new facility built on the site of a former elementary school. With space for more than two hundred Flint children, it was designed to work with those who had been most exposed to lead-laced water.[4]

Above all, McCathern was awed by his neighbors, not only in Civic Park but throughout the city. "Most people in poverty are very resilient and adaptable," he said. "They know how to adapt to situations. They know how to go without this and without that." That spirit was a powerful resource for survival.[5] It gave him hope, even as he worried that this much-tested resilience could slip into a kind of fatalism, where people would settle for less than they deserved as human beings of worth and dignity. He feared that a quick, anxious wash with bottled water might start to seem normal, or that people would ignore health warnings, or just drink water straight from the faucet with an attitude of "I'm going to die some kind of way anyway."

The extraordinary pain of the water crisis: it seemed incalculable. And it had happened in a city already traumatized by poverty and the exit of Flint's life-sustaining companies. The compounding harm would affect this generation, and the next, and the one after that, and its roots stretched back over decades, too, when black Americans from the South were exploited in the city where they came for a better life. "Flint was a social experiment from Day One," McCathern said.

"In all honesty, I don't know how you can righten that," he added. "I'm a preacher and, you see, I'm at a loss for words."

II.

This isn't just Flint's fight. We built all our cities out of lead. We were sure we could make this metal work for us. History revealed a pattern of poisoning, but we were certain that we could contain it, control it. Progress came when we acknowledged how terribly harmful lead is and instituted anti-lead laws that reduced our exposure to one of the world's best-known neurotoxins. But the next great challenge—a tremendously difficult one—is reckoning with the lead that is still in our environment. Individual solutions, from purchasing bottled water and investing in private purification devices, isn't enough. As the nineteenth-century water wars revealed, a community is not safe and certainly will not thrive if only some have access to clean water and others do not. Infrastructure, the ties that literally bind us, one to another, requires our consistent care and attention.[6] At a certain point, "doing more with less" no longer functions as a mandate. Sometimes less is just less. Public health historians Gerald Markowitz and David Rosner put it this way: "If the history of lead poisoning has taught us anything, it is that the worlds we as a society construct, or at least allow to be built in our name, to a large extent determine how we live and how we die."[7]

Lead is one toxic legacy in America's cities. Another is segregation, secession, redlining, and rebranding: this is the art and craft of exclusion. We built it into the bones of our cities as surely as we laid lead pipes. The cure is inclusion. Flint's story is a clear call for committing anew to our democratic faith in the common wealth. As the water crisis demonstrates, it is simply not good enough for government officials to say, "Trust us."[8] For all the inefficiencies and messiness that comes with democracy, the benefits—transparency, accountability, checks and balances, and the equitable participation of all people—are worth it.

Accordingly, federal and state authorities need to recalibrate their responsibility to local governments, casting a close eye on everything from revenue sharing to environmental regulation. At every level, there should be strong open records laws, so that citizens can plainly see the cause and effect of their leaders' decision making and its impact on their neighborhoods. New transparency models are necessary for communities in which private foundations and public-private partnerships are increasingly taking responsibility for public services, as is the case in Flint and other shrinking cities. The wisdom of lived experience must be a valued and necessary part of policy making.

While positive action is imperative, it needs to come with great intention and care, mindful of the boundless mistakes of the past. Pain cannot be papered over with public-relations spin or erased by shiny new programs or buildings, any more than our lead problems were solved when we stopped laying lead pipes but did nothing to extract the ones that were already in the ground.[9] Just and sustainable change requires reckoning with the past even while cultivating a transformational future.

Agencies charged with protecting public health and natural resources deserve to be well-funded, pro-active, and oriented solely toward serving the public interest.[10] And environmental law is due for a shake-up. Depending on how they play out, the Flint criminal and civil cases could help provoke one. So could the pending class action lawsuits, which contend that the mismanagement of the water violated the civil rights and constitutional rights of residents. Not only might the legal battles achieve a measure of accountability for what happened in Flint, but they also might inspire new policy that better accounts for contamination and how it works—even when it is invisible and unintentional.

In the meantime, Flint's story isn't over. And it has no single narrator. From the vantage point of Civic Park, where the city's youngest church is upending the old rules, all are welcome.

NOTES

PROLOGUE

1. For the story of Joy Tabernacle and Civic Park: Sherman McCathern, phone interview with the author, January 2016; Gordon Young, *Teardown: Memoir of a Vanishing City* (Berkeley: University of California Press, 2013); Jennifer Kildee, "The Torch Has Passed: Flint's Joy Tabernacle Church Moves into Community Presbyterian Church Building," MLive—*Flint Journal*, October 30, 2009. Some of this material first appeared in an article for the website of the *New Republic* ("Flint Prepares to Be Left Behind Once More," March 3, 2016).

2. Technically, the first 133 houses in Civic Park were built by the city's board of commerce, but it struggled in the wartime economy. DuPont (which was GM's controlling shareholder) took on the development project. Over about nine months, 950 more houses were built. This history is recorded on the Michigan historical marker in Civic Park, erected in 1982 (Registered Site SO543). See also the writing of Civic Park native Gordon Young, especially his Flint Expatriates blog (www.flintexpats.com) and his book *Teardown*.

3. And, McCathern added, those who didn't get a chance to wear their high school colors have strict rules for the colors they wear on the street. Sherman McCathern, phone interview with the author, January 2016.

4. The United Auto Workers (UAW) was chartered in Detroit by the American Federation of Labor (AFL) in 1935. But the UAW first made its mark when the sit-down strike began in Flint the following year. It ran from December 30, 1936, through February 11, 1937, with workers occupying three plants. The strike's victory won recognition of the union by the auto industry.

S. W. Wiitala, K. E. Vanlier, and R. A. Krieger, *Water Resources of the Flint Area Michigan. Geological Survey Water-Supply Paper 1499-E* (Washington, D.C.: U.S. Government Printing Office, 1963), pp. E6–E7.

6. Hubert Humphrey, "Remarks of Senator Hubert H. Humphrey, Flint, Michigan," September 25, 1964. Typescript from the Hubert H. Humphrey papers at the Minnesota Historical Society. It is among a collection of speeches that is available as a pdf: http://www2.mnhs.org/library/findaids/00442/pdfa /00442-01363.pdf.

7. The Parks Department has a marvelous collection of photographs that document the dedicated work of its Forestry Division, as well as its other activities that made Flint's green spaces lively. The author thanks city planner Adam Marshall Moore for allowing me to peruse them.

8. As late as 1978, more than eighty thousand people worked in the Flint-area auto plants. But over the next decade, hit by an oil crisis, industry restructuring, and automation, that fell to twenty-three thousand in 1990; eight thousand in 2006; and, in 2015, about seventy-two hundred at eight facilities. Eric Scorsone and Nicolette Bateson, "Long-Term Crisis and Systemic Failure: Taking the Fiscal Stress of America's Older Cities Seriously. Case Study: City of Flint, Michigan" (Lansing: Michigan State University Extension, 2011); Melissa Burden and Michael Wayland, "GM to Invest $877M in Flint Truck Plant," *Detroit News*, August 4, 2015; and Ryan Felton, "What General Motors Did to Flint," *Jalopnik*, April 28, 2017.

9. They took 20 percent of the downtown jobs with them, too. Stephen Henderson and Kristi Tanner, "Beyond Bad Water in Flint: Held Back by Jobs and Isolation," *Detroit Free Press*, February 20, 2016, pp. 15A–16A. The analysis uses U.S. Census Bureau zip code patterns and Google maps as its sources.

10. It was in 2013 that Flint's population measured at fewer than 100,000 people for the first time since 1920. On weekdays, commuters brought an additional 35,177 people into the city. According to the Michigan Municipal League, about 86 percent of all jobs in Flint were held by commuters, though their numbers were declining. In turn, 17,436 Flint residents commuted outside the city for work. Only 5,829 people both lived and worked in Flint. In addition, there was a healthy population of college students at the University of Michigan–Flint, Kettering University, Mott Community College, and Baker College. The main sources for these numbers: "Flint, Michigan Population: Census 2010 and 2000 Interactive Map, Demographics, Statistics, Quick Facts," Census-Viewer; and Leonidas Murembya and Eric Guthrie, "Demographic and Labor Market Profile: City of Flint," State of Michigan, Department of Technology, Management, and Budget, April 2016.

11. Flint city population pattern, according to the U.S. Census: 1960: 196,960; 1970: 193,317; 1980: 159,611; 1990: 140,761; 2000: 124,963; 2010: 102,434. Genesee County population pattern: 1960: 374,313; 1970: 445,589; 1980: 450,449; 1990: 430,459; 2000: 436,143; 2010: 425,790. Of course, the Genesee County numbers are inclusive of Flint. "The suburbs" also includes northern Oakland County, from which many people who work in Flint commute. The

area is about equidistant between Flint and Detroit, so it effectively serves as the suburbs of both cities, and naturally leans more toward the magnetism of the larger of the two. But for perspective, it might be worth looking at Oakland's population trends as well: 1960: 690,259; 1970: 907,871; 1980: 1,011,793; 1990: 1,083,592; 2000: 1,194,156; 2010: 1,202,970. Unlike Genesee, Oakland County hasn't seen even the slightest population decline since 1890.

12. There are two kinds of revenue sharing: constitutional and statutory. The latter dipped more or less in proportion to how much less the state was collecting, but the former went far beyond that. The Michigan Municipal League and Great Lakes Economic Consulting are great resources for what is, as they describe it, "the great revenue sharing heist." "Michigan's Great Disinvestment: How State Policies Have Forced Communities into Fiscal Crisis," Great Lakes Economic Consulting, April 2016; Robert J. Kleine, "Rick Snyder Isn't the Only Michigan Leader Who Abandoned Flint," *Washington Post*, February 1, 2016; and Anthony Minghine, "The Great $6.2 Billion Revenue Sharing Heist," *Voice of Detroit*, March 26, 2014 (reprint from MML's March/April 2014 magazine); Anthony Minghine, interview with the author, Ann Arbor, Mich., May 20, 2016; and Robert Kleine, interview with the author, Lansing, Mich., May 19, 2016.

13. In addition to the 58 percent increase in fetal deaths, the research team looking into the reproductive consequences of the Flint water crisis found a 12 percent drop in fertility for Flint women and lower overall health at birth. David S. Grossman and David J. G. Slusky, "The Effect of an Increase in Lead in the Water System on Fertility and Birth Outcomes: The Case of Flint, Michigan," Working Paper No. 17–25, West Virginia University Department of Economics Working Paper Series, August 7, 2017; George Diepenbrock, "Flint Water Crisis Led to Lower Fertility Rates, Higher Fetal Death Rates, Researchers Find," KU News Service, University of Kansas, September 20, 2017; and referring to the history of lead as a way to control fertility, see "The Birth Control Pill: A History," Planned Parenthood Federation of America, 2015, https://www.plannedparenthood.org /files/1514/3518/7100/Pill_History_FactSheet.pdf. It's worth noting that this fertility study was disputed in a seven-page review done by Michigan State University's Nigel Paneth, who essentially argues that the researchers erred by comparing Flint's birth data to other cities in Michigan—failing to acknowledge how economically dissimilar Flint is from most other communities in the state. (His review appears in full at a link in this online article: Kate Wells, "MSU Researcher Finds Fault in Flint Fertility Study," Michigan Radio, October 3, 2017.) At the time of this writing, the original study was under consideration for publication in a peer-reviewed economics journal, and the research team had communicated with Paneth about his feedback.

14. The National Advisory Commission on Civil Disorders, *The Kerner Report* (1968; repr. Princeton, N.J.: Princeton University Press, May 2016), p. 2. This reissue is edited by Sam Wilentz and features an excellent introduction by Julian E. Zelizer. It is part of a series, the James Madison Library in American Politics. The citation for the original edition is as follows: Otto Kerner et al.,

Report of the National Advisory Commission on Civil Disorders (Washington, D.C.: U.S. Government Printing Office, 1968), reprinted as *Report* (New York: Bantam Books, 1968).

CHAPTER 1: THE WELL

1. Video of this ceremony was captured by the local television station WNEM, a CBS affiliate that broadcasts to the Flint, Saginaw, Midland, and Bay City areas; and by Dominic Adams, "Watch Mayor Dayne Walling, EM Darnell Earley Drink Flint River Water Before Turning Detroit Connection," MLive— *Flint Journal*, April 25, 2014, updated December 28, 2016. See also Dominic Adams, "Closing the Valve on History: Flint Cuts Water Flow from Detroit After Nearly 50 Years, MLive—*Flint Journal*, April 25, 2014, updated January 17, 2015.

2. To clarify the confusing chronology of emergency management as it affected Flint, here is a timeline:

    1990: After a couple of experiments in state oversight over troubled local governments, Michigan passes Public Act 72, which allows the state to appoint an emergency financial manager over distressed schools and cities. The authority of EFMs is generally limited to budget matters. The system was rarely used.

    June 2002–June 2004: Ed Kurtz serves as emergency financial manager to Flint.

    2011: One of the first bills signed into law by Governor Rick Snyder is Public Act 4. It beefs up Michigan's emergency management system and lowers the threshold for which a community can be declared in need of an EM.

    December 2011–August 2012: Michael Brown serves as emergency manager to Flint. It's the first appointment under the new state law.

    August 2012–July 2013: Ed Kurtz serves again as emergency manager in Flint.

    August 2012: Public Act 4, Michigan's expanded emergency management law, is suspended pending a statewide voter referendum. The EM system reverts to the original model.

    November 2012: Michigan voters overturn Public Act 4.

    December 2012: The Michigan legislature passes Public Act 436, and Governor Snyder signs it into law. It is nearly identical to Public Act 4, but it has appropriations attached, which makes it immune from a referendum.

    March 2013: Public Act 436 goes into effect. In the same month, an EM is appointed to Detroit who will lead the city through bankruptcy.

    July 2013–October 2013: Michael Brown serves again as emergency manager to Flint.

    October 2013–January 2015: Darnell Earley serves as emergency manager to Flint.

January 2015–April 2015: Jerry Ambrose, who was the finance director under Earley, serves as emergency manager to Flint. At the end of his tenure, the fiscal disaster in Flint is declared over. The city still has a $7 million deficit, but that's resolved with an emergency loan from the state.

3. That was in the Great Storm of 1913. Additional ships were lost during the same storm in Lake Superior, Lake Erie, and Lake Ontario, and thirty more were "driven ashore, crippled or destroyed." At least 250 people were killed, most of them in Lake Huron. Richard Wagenmaker and Greg Mann, "The 'White Hurricane' Storm of November 1913: A Numerical Model Retrospective," Detroit: National Weather Service.

4. The information on water rates is detailed in a later chapter and its notes. For Flint's poverty level: "QuickFacts: Flint City, Michigan; United States," U.S. Census Bureau, https://www.census.gov/quickfacts/fact/table/flintcitymichigan /PST045216, last accessed March 3, 2018.

5. Dayne Walling, interview with the author, Flint, Mich., June 22, 2017.

6. A curious fact about the office of the drain commissioner is that in Michigan it's an elective position, and the only one in the state that can single-handedly levy taxes and borrow money. Wright's argument about the DWSD and the KWA is made at length in his written testimony before the Michigan Civil Rights Commission: "The Flint Water Crisis, DWSD, and GLWA: Monopoly, Price Gouging, Corruption, and the Poisoning of a City," November 22, 2016, https://www.michigan.gov/documents/mdcr/Wright_Monopoly_Price_Gouging _Corruption_and_the_Poisoning_of_a_City_552247_7.pdf.

7. The word "Karegnondi" is used to label Lake Huron on a 1656 map by French cartographer Nicolas Sanson, created for the king of France. It's not wholly clear where he got this name. The founders of the Karegnondi Water Authority cite it as an early moniker for the lake by the Petun Indians, a tribe in modern-day Ontario that morphed into the Wyandot tribe. But either way, the name began to show up on later maps as well. See also Ron Fonger, "Genesee, Oakland Counties Adopt Historic Name for Water Group," MLive—*Flint Journal*, May 3, 2007.

8. Stephanie Parkinson, "Flint Makes the Switch to Use River for Drinking Water," NBC 25 News, April 17, 2014.

9. "The City of Flint is currently in a year to year contract with the City of Detroit for the purchase of water. A study was conducted that projects that staying with Detroit will cost the region $2.1 billion over the next 25 years. In contrast, if the region builds its own pipeline, the project costs are $1.9 billion over the same period. After the initial 25 year period, the project costs would be less than 25% of the projected water costs from Detroit" (Resolution to Purchase Capacity from Karegnondi Water Authority, EM Submission No. 2013EMO41, adopted March 29, 2013). It's worth noting that there were a number of commissioned reports that came to different conclusions about whether the KWA would be the most cost-efficient option for Flint. State treasurer Andy Dillon requested a report from Tucker, Young, Jackson, Tull, which delivered its preliminary findings on December 21, 2012, and a full report in February 2013.

Tucker, Young said that Flint's best option was to stick with the DWSD, but to purchase less and blend it with water from the Flint River. Even better, the report suggested, Flint could connect to a different portion of the Detroit system—which would relieve it of the expensive burden of maintaining its treatment plant. Upon receiving the preliminary findings, emergency manager Ed Kurtz asked Rowe Engineering to review them. On January 7, 2013, Rowe declared the KWA was best for Flint. Neither Rowe nor Tucker, Young was a purely independent entity. The latter has worked for the DWSD and Rowe was hired by the KWA to work on its pipeline. For good summations of all this: Lindsey Smith, "Reporter's Notebook: Some State Officials Still in Denial or Misinformed over Flint River Decision," Michigan Radio, December 17, 2015; and Paul Egan, "Flint Water Mystery: How Was the Decision Made?," *Detroit Free Press*, November 21, 2015, updated November 22, 2015.

10. The email with the subject line "Updated Status on GCDC/KWA" was sent by John C. O'Malia to Liane Shekter-Smith and Karen Teeples, both of the MDEQ, on January 5, 2012. It had a memorandum attached that was dated January 3, 2012, which included this excerpt.

11. Bryant Nolden, interview with the author, Flint, Mich., June 7, 2016. Nolden and others have said that the council members did not have access to the report from Tucker, Young that was commissioned by the state, which questioned whether the KWA would be Flint's most cost-effective option. Video of the council meeting is available online: "Flint City Council March 25, 2013," Spectacle TV; YouTube Video [3.29.45], March 28, 2013, https://www.youtube.com/watch?v=U3gbZ8hZ_KI.

12. "Jeff Wright Statement on Flint City Council Approving Resolution to Join KWA," press release, Genesee County Drain Commissioner's Office, March 26, 2013.

13. The DWSD would soon escalate its program of shutoffs for residential customers that it believed had unpaid bills (though it didn't do the same for commercial customers with hefty unpaid bills). It faced many of the same infrastructural challenges in Flint—enormous system, declining ratepayers—which led to average monthly bills in Detroit that were nearly twice the U.S. average. Details about this have appeared in earlier articles and op-eds by the author. (For example: "Going Without Water in Detroit," *New York Times*, July 4, 2014; "Living Without Water in Detroit," *Next City*, July 3, 2014.)

14. About some of these upgrades: Dominic Adams, "Flint Spends $4 Million on Water Plant in Last Eight Months," MLive—*Flint Journal*, January 4, 2014; Ron Fonger, "Former Flint EM: 'My Job Did Not Include Ensuring Safe Drinking Water,'" MLive—*Flint Journal*, May 2, 2017; Ron Fonger, "Water Consultant Says Former Flint EM Wouldn't Pay to Fully Soften River Water," MLive—*Flint Journal*, January 11, 2018; Nancy Kaffer, "Why Didn't Flint Treat Its Water? An Answer, at Last," *Detroit Free Press*, March 30, 2016, updated March 31, 2016.

15. At the time of this writing, Lockwood, Andrews & Newnam (LAN), the firm contracted to oversee the switch, faces a civil lawsuit for negligence. In 2011,

LAN estimated that it would take $69 million to upgrade the plant. Rowe estimated more than $61 million. By 2013, both Rowe and LAN had significantly lowered their estimates: $25 million and $33 million to $34 million, respectively. By November 2014, LAN lowered it further: $7 million to $10 million. Ultimately, $8 million was put into the plant. "Schuette Files Civil Suit against Veolia and LAN for Role in Flint Water Poisoning," press release, Department of Attorney General, Michigan.gov, n.d., https://www.michigan.gov/ag/0,4534,7 -359-82916_81983_47203-387198—,00.html; Peter J. Hammer, "The Flint Water Crisis, KWA and Strategic-Structural Racism," written testimony submitted to the Michigan Civil Rights Commission, July 18, 2016; and Peter J. Hammer, "The Flint Water Crisis, KWA and Strategic-Structural Racism: A Reply to Jeff Wright, Genesee County Drain Commissioner and CEO Karegnondi Water Authority," written testimony submitted to the Michigan Civil Rights Commission, December 31, 2016.

16. According to later testimony by a Genesee County water expert, the plant wasn't prepared to treat the water safely at the time of the switch. In April 2014, the chlorine room was still under construction, and some employees had been brought in just a couple weeks earlier from working in solid waste management; they needed three to six months of training before they could work independently. The water official said that he too, along with drain commissioner Jeff Wright and another drain official, urged the city to hold off on the switch. Leonard N. Fleming, "Expert: Flint Plant Not Ready Before Water Switch," *Detroit News*, February 5, 2018.

17. Glasgow delivered the email to Adam Rosenthal, Mike Prysby, and Stephen Busch of the MDEQ on April 17, 2014.

18. One of them was Glasgow's boss, Flint utilities manager Daugherty Johnson, who wrote an email on April 24, 2014, to the MDEQ's Mike Prysby and Stephen Busch and Flint's public works director Howard Croft. He assured the MDEQ that the plant could process Flint River water and that it wouldn't even need Detroit's water system as an emergency backup source.

19. Adams, "Closing the Valve on History."

20. "Editorial: Switch to Flint River Water Represents New Era in Flint," MLive— *Flint Journal*, April 13, 2014, updated October 8, 2015.

21. Busch wrote an email on March 26, 2013, to his MDEQ colleagues, in preparation for a call about Flint's potential switch with Treasurer Andy Dillon. The big problem, he wrote, was that Flint would not get a sufficient water supply from the Detroit system, forcing the city "to meet a significant, if not majority, of its water demands by treating water from the Flint River." That was risky, Busch warned, because the river would "pose an increased microbial risk to public health" and "an increased risk of a disinfection by-product (carcinogen) exposure to public health." It would also "trigger additional regulatory requirements under the Michigan Safe Drinking Water Act." Mike Prysby made a similar point in an internal email on January 23, 2013, about the feasibility of the city relying on the Flint River, when it was still on the table for the city to use it as a permanent water source. "I agree that the city should have concerns of fully utilizing the

Flint River (100%) for the following: the need to soften, the potential for more advanced treatment after next round of crypto monitoring, available capacity in Flint River at 100-year low flow, residuals management (disposal of lime sludge)."

22. Adams, "Closing the Valve on History."

23. According to Kim Crawford, a historian who has thoroughly researched the city's origins, the Ojibwa name *biwânag sibi* is generally pronounced with a "p" sound, and with a vowel syllable between the terms for "Flinty" and "River"— so, phonetically, it's "pe-wan-a-go-see-ba."

24. Kim Crawford, *The Daring Trader: Jacob Smith in the Michigan Territory, 1802–1825* (East Lansing: Michigan State University Press, 2012), chap. 2. Much of the Flint history from this chapter is sourced from this book, as well as from Crawford's generous feedback on an early draft of this chapter.

25. "Grand Traverse" is also the name of a bay in northern Michigan, formed by the Leelanau Peninsula jutting into the northwest part of Lake Michigan. Traverse City sits at its edge, a thriving community popular with tourists and the seat of Grande Traverse County. In the Upper Peninsula, there is also a Traverse River and a small Finnish community known as the Big Traverse Historic District. Michigan does love its crossings.

26. William Hull, "Letter to William Eustis," Fort George: August 26, 1812, vol. 40 (1929): 460–69, https://www.cmich.edu/library/clarke/ResearchResources /Native_American_Material/Excerpts_from_the_Michigan_Pioneer_and _Historical_Collections/Documents/william_pg460-469.pdf.

27. Ibid.; Carl Crow (in *The City of Flint Grows Up: The Success Story of an American Community* [New York: Harper & Brothers, 1945], p. 6) puts it at "about six million acres."

28. Crow, *The City of Flint Grows Up*, pp. 191–92.

29. Crawford notes that there were a lot of factors that shaped the slow early settling of Flint, especially the reputation of the Saginaw band of the Ojibwas and the conflicting claims over the area around the Flint River, which made it difficult to buy land with a clear title in the early 1820s. Those who tried were making a risky investment. And alarming stories from government surveyors gave a negative overall impression of southeastern Michigan, which was exacerbated in the 1830s by the Black Hawk War.

30. Smith's body was moved from where he was first buried to Flint's historic Glenwood Cemetery. Images of his tombstone are, at this writing, available at FindAGrave.com.

31. Crow, *The City of Flint Grows Up*, pp. 10–13.

32. Alexis de Tocqueville, *Democracy in America and Two Essays on America*, trans. Gerald E. Bevan (London: Penguin, 2003), pp. 902–3.

33. S. W. Wiitala, K. E. Vanlier, and R. A. Krieger, *Water Resources of the Flint Area Michigan. Geological Survey Water-Supply Paper 1499-E* (Washington, D.C.: U.S. Government Printing Office, 1963), pp. E13, E24–27.

34. A wonderful resource about the Great Lakes is Dan Egan's *The Death and Life of the Great Lakes* (New York: W. W. Norton, 2017).

35. For these striking comparisons that put the scale of the lakes in perspective:

Jerry Dennis, *The Living Great Lakes: Searching for the Heart of the Inland Seas* (New York: St. Martin's Press, 2003), p. 4; and Peter Fox, "From Montreal to Minnesota, by Inland Sea," *New York Times*, August 19, 2016.

36. Tocqueville was twenty-six years old at the time and bound for Detroit. As quoted in Dennis, *The Living Great Lakes*, p. 5.

37. Eric Spitznagel, "Letter of Recommendation: Michigan," *New York Times Magazine*, April 20, 2017.

38. The author can't resist describing the other strange things in the depths of the Great Lakes. It took 106 years to find the steam locomotive from the Canadian Pacific Railway train that derailed and dropped sixty feet into Lake Superior in 1910. There is a caribou hunting camp at the bottom of Lake Huron; the camp was built nine thousand years ago on land that had not yet been deluged. A cache of rare cars—268 Nash automobiles, never driven—lies under the waves of Lake Michigan, about 450 feet deep, alongside the steamship that had been ferrying them. It sank on Halloween in 1929, two days after the stock market crash. It was one of three Lake Michigan shipwrecks that week, killing eighty people altogether. And near Mackinac Island, a popular tourist destination in Lake Huron that sits between the two peninsulas, there is a submerged one-hundred-foot waterfall that is about ten thousand years old—a wildly unlikely phenomenon. Waterfalls are erosion on fast-forward, after all; they are designed to make themselves disappear. But during the post-glacial rebound, geography shifted rapidly. Mackinac Falls poured over a limestone cliff into a river that ran to the Atlantic Ocean. When Lakes Huron and Michigan hydrologically merged and a major channel was blocked, the lakes became so deep so fast that Mackinac Falls was buried underwater. Despite approaching the size of Niagara Falls, and being one mile off a resort island, nobody realized the ancient submerged waterfall was there until a research vessel stumbled across it in 2007 while testing new sounding equipment.

39. Crow, *The City of Flint Grows Up*, pp. 17–20. By the late nineteenth century, Flint's economy included not only sawmills, but also flour mills and the wagon and carriage factories that would evolve into the auto industry. The city was also home to makers of cigars, bricks, tile, and boxes, as well as printing and publishing houses, and dairies. In greater Genesee County, most of the land, by far, was used for farming. Rhonda Sanders, *Bronze Pillars: An Oral History of African Americans in Flint* (Flint, Mich.: *The Flint Journal* and Alfred P. Sloan Museum, 1995), p. vii.

40. For this chapter's accounts of Philadelphia, Boston, and Chicago, the author relied on Carl Smith's *City Water, City Life: Water and the Infrastructure of Ideas in Urbanizing Philadelphia, Boston, and Chicago* (Chicago: University of Chicago Press, 2013). For New York City's water system: Winnie Hu, "Billion-Dollar Investment in New York's Water," *New York Times*, January 19, 2018.

41. Chicago's almost unbelievably bold move to reverse the flow of the Chicago River meant that, instead of emptying into Lake Michigan, where it drew its drinking water, it turned the dirty current the other way, toward the basin of the Mississippi River and on to the Gulf of Mexico. In a U.S. Supreme Court

case (*Missouri v. Illinois & Sanitary District of Chicago*, 180 U.S. 208 [1901]), the State of Missouri argued that Chicago had no right to send its pollution its way. But it lost, and to this day the river is reverse-engineered. Within the Great Lakes Compact, ratified in 2009 as a protocol for who gets to take water out of the lakes, and for what reasons, Chicago's daily diversion from Lake Michigan is exempt. Dan Egan details some of the modern-day implications of this in *The Death and Life of the Great Lakes* (New York: W. W. Norton, 2017). See also Peter Annin, *The Great Lakes Water Wars* (Washington: Island Press, 2006), and Carl Smith's *City Water, City Life*.

42. That would be the Detroit River. The whole Great Lakes system moves eastward, with Lake Superior and Lake Michigan flowing toward Lake Huron (linked, respectively, by the St. Mary's River and the Straits of Mackinac). Water in Lake Huron then moves through the St. Clair River, Lake St. Clair, and the Detroit River before opening out into Lake Erie. Then there's a steep drop—that's Niagara Falls. After a stint in the Niagara River, the water reaches Lake Ontario. (The alternative route between Lake Erie and Lake Ontario: the Welland Canal, which bypasses the Falls.) From there, it flows through a chain of smaller lakes (Lake St. Lawrence, Lake St. Francis, and Lake St. Louis) before becoming the St. Lawrence River, and, finally, reaching the Atlantic Ocean. An enormous watershed replenishes the Great Lakes water system.

43. As the story goes, the fire started in the stable of a baker named John Harvey, when a worker, or perhaps Harvey himself, let the hot ash from his pipe drop into the dry hay. On this windy day, flames leaped beyond the livery. Detroiters streamed into the river for safety. They pulled their snuffling horses behind them and carried armfuls of possessions. There, with the cool water making their clothing heavy, they watched the inferno devour nearly every one of the city's three hundred buildings. The memory of the fire inspired Detroit's city motto: *Speramus meliora; resurgent cineribus*, or, "We hope for better things; it shall rise from the ashes." The Detroit Historical Society is a good resource on the fire. It's also summarized in Michael Daisy, ed., *Detroit Water and Sewage Department: The First 300 Years* (Detroit: Detroit Water and Sewage Department, n.d.), http://dwsd.org/downloads_n/about_dwsd/history/complete_history.pdf.

44. This was in 1824. It was amended in 1873. Clarence Monroe Burton, William Stocking, and Gordon K. Miller, eds., *The City of Detroit, Michigan, 1701–1922*, vol.1 (Detroit: S. J. Clark, 1922), pp. 371–77; and "History of the Water Works of the City of Detroit" (Detroit: Raynor and Taylor, 1890), p. 3, compiled in Detroit (Mich.) Board of Water Commissioners, *Act of Incorporation. Regulation. History.*

45. Daisy, *Detroit Water and Sewage Department*, p. 4.

46. "History of the Water Works of the City of Detroit," pp. 6–8.

47. Instead of a sewer system, St. Louis, where the American Water Works Association held its inaugural meeting, decided on the cheaper option of moving wastewater through a series of underground limestone caves. This led to at least one incredibly unfortunate flood.

48. "AWWA History," American Water Works Association. In a video on this page

(last accessed March 3, 2018), Jack Hoffbuhr, a former AWWA executive director, describes how lead pipes and drinking water were discussed at the first
conference. He also gives a good overview of John Snow's cholera breakthrough,
https://www.awwa.org/about-us/history.aspx.

49. Gary Grant, *The Water Sensitive City* (West Sussex, U.K.: John Wiley & Sons,
    2016), p. 163; and Gregory L. Poe, *The Evolution of Federal Water Pollution
    Control Policies* (Ithaca, N.Y.: Department of Agricultural, Resource, and
    Managerial Economics, College of Agriculture and Life Sciences, Cornell Uni-
    versity, 1995), p. 4.

50. The infamous fire happened on June 22, 1969, reported variously as having
    been ignited by a stray spark from a passing train or by molten slag from a steel
    mill. *Time* gave it big play a couple of months later, featuring dramatic photos
    of the Cuyahoga River engulfed in flames—photos that were actually taken
    during another fire on the same river in 1952. "Unfortunately, water pollution
    knows no political boundaries," the magazine piece read. It indicted the way
    that rivers were treated as "convenient, free sewers." "America's Sewage System
    and the Price of Optimism," *Time*, August 1, 1969. See also Doron P. Levin,
    "River Not Yet Clean, but It's Fireproof," *New York Times*, June 25, 1989.

51. Another legislative victory of the environmental movement was the Resource
    Conservation and Recovery Act of 1976, where the government for the first
    time attempted to articulate what hazardous waste is and how it should be
    handled. Rather than just addressing end-of-pipeline waste, as earlier laws did,
    it also made the reduction or elimination of waste one of its primary goals.

52. This was described in an article by James L. Agee, the EPA's assistant administra-
    tor for water and hazardous materials, in an article in *EPA Journal* (March 1975,
    vol. 1, no. 3), titled "Protecting America's Drinking Water: Our Responsibilities
    Under the Safe Drinking Water Act." He wrote, "This may seem to be a restate-
    ment of the obvious, but it is a principle all too often violated by the Federal
    government. Paperwork cannot protect health—only action can."

53. A little more on the Safe Drinking Water Act. It is the law that requires the EPA
    to develop and enforce drinking water standards. That includes the ability to
    set Maximum Contaminant Levels, or MCLs, for any substances that might
    be in drinking water that could harm public health. The early limit on lead
    was 50 parts per billion (ppb), and it applied only to water as it entered the
    distribution system, rather than at the tap (after its flow had come in contact
    with lead service lines, lead solder, and indoor plumbing). Eventually, the EPA's
    Lead and Copper Rule of 1991 set a lower limit for lead at the tap: 15 ppb.
    (However, the regulatory formula still allows up to 10 percent of samples in
    any given community to exceed 15 ppb before taking any action about it.) For
    implementation of this and other SDWA regulations, the EPA relies on state
    agencies, Native American tribes, and local water systems for monitoring and
    treatment. In Michigan, that meant the Michigan Department of Environmen-
    tal Quality had primacy—or primary enforcement responsibility—for making
    sure that the state's public water systems met all the safety requirements,
    including lead limits. U.S. Environmental Protection Agency, "Drinking Water

Requirements for States and Public Water Systems: Primacy Enforcement
Responsibility for Public Water Systems." EPA.gov, n.d., https://www.epa.gov
/dwreginfo/primacy-enforcement-responsibility-public-water-systems,last
accessed March 2, 2016; Yanna Lambrinidou, Simoni Triantafyllidou, and
Marc Edwards, "Failing Our Children: Lead in U.S. School Drinking Water,"
New Solutions, vol. 20(1), 2010, pp. 25–47; Yanna Lambrinidou, written communication to the author, February 20, 2018.

54. U.S. Environmental Protection Agency, "Reorganization Plan No. 3 of 1970,"
https://archive.epa.gov/epa/aboutepa/reorganization-plan-no-3-1970.html.

55. According to its archived website, this made the DWSD "the third largest provider of high-quality drinking water and wastewater treatment services in the
United States."

56. Flint's first water system was founded in 1883, a private concern called the
Flint Water Works Company, which delivered raw water from the Flint River
to ratepayers. Twenty years later, the city purchased it for $262,500 and made
it a public utility. In 1911, the plant began filtering water. As the city rapidly
grew, about $12.5 million in capital improvements were put into the system
between 1947 and 1955, which improved storage, treatment, and pumping. The
Dort Highway plant that was rebooted in the twenty-first century was built in
1952. This is outlined in the Flint Water Advisory Task Force Final Report
(March 2016), which in turn cites a brochure called "The Water Supply of
Flint, Michigan," which the city provided to the task force. For more on Flint's
drinking water history, including the information that follows on its water
consumption, see S. W. Wiitala, K. E. Vanlier, and R. A. Krieger, *Water Resources
of the Flint Area, Michigan. Geological Survey Water-Supply Paper 1499-E*
(Washington, D.C.: United States Government Printing Office, 1963).

57. The corruption scandal in the 1960s and Flint's decision-making process about
its future with drinking water were chronicled by the robust newspapers, espe-
cially the *Detroit Free Press* and, published by Freep reporters during a strike,
the *Detroit Daily Press*. Among them: "2 City Officials Ousted at Flint," *Detroit
Free Press*, February 8, 1964, p. 21; "$39 Million Water Bond Sale OK'd,"
Detroit Daily Press, October 7, 1967, sec. B, p. 4; Hal Cohen, "Water Sale to
Stall City's Fluoridation," *Detroit Free Press*, January 25, 1964, sec. A, p. 3;
Harry Golden Jr., "City No Trickster in Fluoride Fight," *Detroit Free Press*,
January 10, 1965, sec. C, p. 3; "Huge Waterway for Michigan Studied," *Detroit
Free Press*, October 10, 1967, sec. A, p. 8; "Indicted in Flint Scandal: Pontiac
City Manager Quits," *Detroit Free Press*, February 12, 1964, sec. A, p. 1; George
Jaksa, "3 Officials in Flint Cleared," *Detroit Free Press*, February 24, 1964,
sec. A, p. 3; George Jaksa, "Flint Votes for Detroit Water Deal," *Detroit Free
Press*, April 23, 1964, sec. A, p. 3; "Lake Huron Water Plant Deal OK'd," *Detroit
Free Press*, July 6, 1962, sec. A, p. 3; Eric Pianin, "Suburb Raises an Uproar over
Water Rate Hike," *Detroit Daily Press*, December 26, 1967, p. 5; "Pipe Job to Start
for Huron Water," *Detroit Free Press*, January 29, 1964, sec. A, p. 1; "Pontiac
Manager Indicted in Fraud," *Detroit Free Press*, July 29, 1965, sec. A, p. 3;
"Two Face Conspiracy Charges," *Detroit Free Press*, November 27, 1964, sec.

A, p. 3; "Water Officials to Confer Here," *Detroit Daily Press*, September 3, 1964, p. 13. For more contemporary sources on this debacle: "The Flint Water Crisis: Systemic Racism Through the Lens of Flint," Report of the Michigan Civil Rights Commission, February 17, 2017, pp. 52–54, https://www.michigan.gov/documents/mdcr/VFlintCrisisRep-F-Edited3-13-17_554317_7.pdf; Ron Fonger, "50 Years Later: Ghosts of Corruption Still Linger Along Old Path of Failed Flint Water Pipeline," MLive—*Flint Journal*, November 12, 2012.

58. Andrew R. Highsmith discusses this in-depth in *Demolition Means Progress: Flint, Michigan, and the Fate of the American Metropolis* (Chicago: University of Chicago Press, 2015), especially in chap. 5.

59. "New Huron Water Line Is Hailed," *Detroit Free Press*, December 15, 1967, p. 3; and "2nd Step of Huron Water Project Near Finish," *Detroit Free Press*, December 12, 1967, p. 2. The Detroit water system grew into one of the largest public utilities in the nation. Its headquarters suggested the sort of majesty with which the city approached water during the nineteenth and twentieth centuries, and the people were invited to be part of it. The water department was situated on a 110-acre riverfront park on the east side. It featured a man-made canal with two islands, two greenhouses, and a 185-foot minaret tower that offered spectacular views of the city to those who braved its winding staircase. There was also a hobby center for woodcrafts, a mooring basin for seaplanes, playgrounds, rowboats, a baseball diamond, groves of chestnut and pear trees, a children's wading pool, and a popular floral clock made of more than seven thousand plants that was powered by paddlewheels. The first branch of the Detroit Public Library opened there, staffed, somewhat awkwardly, by employees of the water department. To this day, a massive Beaux-Arts gateway monument marks the entry onto the campus, built to honor the longtime president of the Board of Water Commissioners who left nearly all of his estate for the maintenance of the grounds. But in 1945 the minaret tower, deemed too expensive to maintain, was demolished. Six years later, the whole park was shut down. Public outcry compelled the city to reopen a bit of it, but the effort was halfhearted and short-lived. Water Works Park has been closed for more than fifty years. The locked gateway is the only sign that it once existed.

CHAPTER 2: CORROSION

1. Blake Thorne, "Even the Trees Had a Bad Time in the Flint-Area This Winter," MLive—*Flint Journal*, May 6, 2014.

2. Nicole Weddington, "Friends of the Flint River Trail Kick Off Weekly Sunday Bike Rides," MLive—*Flint Journal*, May 6, 2014.

3. Adrian Hedden, "Fixing Flint: Revitalizing Flint Lake Park Brings North Side Residents Together," MLive—*Flint Journal*, July 17, 2014.

4. William E. Ketchum III, "Flint Nonprofit Brings Flint Symphony String Performance to MTA Bus Terminal," MLive—*Flint Journal*, July 16, 2014, updated July 17, 2014.

5. Ron Fonger, "State Says Flint River Water Meets All Standards but More Than Twice the Hardness of Lake Water," MLive—*Flint Journal*, May 23, 2014, updated January 17, 2015.

6. Crooks sent the email on May 15, 2014, to three of her colleagues. She notes that Lathan Jefferson spoke with her and with another EPA expert.

7. Ahmad Bajjey, "Flint Residents Avoiding the Tap, Drinking Bottled Water Instead," WEYI-TV NBC25, June 2, 2014, news, video, and article available online, http://nbc25news.com/news/local/flint-residents-avoiding-the-tap-drinking -bottled-water-instead, last accessed March 3, 2018.

8. The final report of the Flint Water Advisory Task Force sums this up: "In advance of the City of Flint's conversion from DWSD water supply to use of Flint River water, MDEQ had multiple communications and meetings with Flint Utilities Department staff and their consultants. A plan of treatment of Flint River water was discussed and covered numerous issues including dosing of chemicals, use of polymers, and unit process performance. When asked by Flint water plant personnel about adding phosphate in the treatment process, as DWSD does for corrosion control, MDEQ said that a corrosion control treatment decision would be made after two 6-month monitoring periods were conducted to see if corrosion control treatment was needed." Flint Water Advisory Task Force, *Final Report*, March 2016, p. 27. Also, on June 17, 2014, Adam Rosenthal of the MDEQ emailed Michael Glasgow, Flint's utilities administrator, and confirmed to him that no monitoring for orthophosphates was needed because no orthophosphates were being added to the water (p. 90).

9. The corrosion control requirements come from the EPA's Lead and Copper Rule, and it applies to all community water systems that serve at least fifty thousand people. As early as the 1950s, when Flint still treated its own river water, it was using "polyphosphate . . . to lessen the corrosion of water pipe when in contact with the cold water" ("The Water Supply of Flint, Michigan," city brochure, p. 11, as quoted in the final report of the Flint Water Advisory Task Force). Corrosion control ceased in Flint after the April 2014 switch. The MDEQ argued that this was appropriate. According to its interpretation of the rules, it could do two six-month evaluations on the river water before deciding whether to use corrosion control at all, and, if so, what kind was best. For more on corrosion treatment technology: John R. Scully, "The Corrosion Crisis in Flint, Michigan: A Call for Improvements in Technology," *Bridge* 46, no. 2 (Summer 2016): 16–29. For the note about half of water systems using orthophosphates: Siddhartha Roy, "Test Update: Flint River Water 19x More Corrosive Than Detroit Water for Lead Solder; Now What?," FlintWaterStudy.org, September 11, 2015.

10. Keith Harrison, "Flint Water, Corrosivity, and Lead," TapTalk, Delaware Health and Public Services, Division of Public Health, Office of Drinking Water, Spring 2016.

11. "Chlorides," Bureau of Water, South Carolina Department of Health and Environmental Control, n.d., https://www.scdhec.gov/HomeAndEnvironment/Docs /Chlorides.pdf.

12. Gwen Pearson, "Road Salt Is Polluting Our Rivers," *Wired*, March 12, 2015.

13. Walter R. Kelly, Samuel V. Panno, and Keith Hackley, "The Sources, Distribution, and Trends of Chloride in the Waters of Illinois," Bulletin B-74, Illinois State Water Survey, Prairie Research Institute. Champaign: University of Illinois–Urbana-Champaign, March 2012, http://www.isws.illinois.edu/pubdoc /B/ISWSB-74.pdf; and Mary Hunt, Elizabeth Herron, and Linda Green, "Chlorides in Fresh Water," College of the Environment and Life Sciences, University of Rhode Island, March 2012, http://cels.uri.edu/docslink/ww/water-quality -factsheets/Chlorides.pdf.

14. "Half of the chlorides came from using ferric chloride instead of ferric sulfate coagulant . . . added during water treatment," Marc Edwards, email message to the author, February 23, 2017.

15. Ron Fonger, "City Adding More Lime to Flint River Water as Resident Complaints Pour In," MLive—*Flint Journal*, June 12, 2014.

16. For the $140 and $35 numbers: Dominic Adams, "Flint Monthly Water and Sewer Bills Highest in Genesee County by $35," MLive—*Flint Journal*, June 1, 2014, updated June 27, 2014; Ann Espinola, "Water Rates Revealed for Small, Medium, Large Utilities," American Water Works Association, *Connections*, March 27, 2017. The latter describes the findings from the AWWA's 2016 Waste and Wastewater Rate Survey. "Median water bills at medium-sized utilities were just $31.09 per month for 7,480 gallons of water, but soared to $46.61 for wastewater services and fees," Espinola writes. "And among the four regions of the United States, the West had the highest water rates, while the South had the lowest. Customers in the Northeast shelled out the most for wastewater services, while those in the Midwest paid the least." Specifically, the median monthly water rate in the Midwest was $32.48, and wastewater charges were "coming in at less than $40." So together that's less than $72.48, compared to Flint's bills of $140 per month.

17. "The State of Public Water in the United States" (Washington, D.C.: Food & Water Watch, February 2016), p. 10; and John Wisely, "Flint Residents Paid America's Highest Water Rates," *Detroit Free Press*, February 16, 2016. The Food & Water Watch report notes that when it conducted its survey (January 2015), Flint had "the most expensive water service in the country," with an annual bill of $910.05, but during August 2015, a judge ruled that certain rate increases were unlawful and ordered the city to reduce its rates by 35 percent and to end a service fee.

18. Matthew Dolan, "Scared Residents Search for Hope," *Detroit Free Press*, January 24, 2015, pp. 1A, 13A.

19. "One of the most important recent milestones has been the recognition in July 2010 by the United Nations General Assembly of the human right to water and sanitation. The Assembly recognized the right of every human being to have access to sufficient water for personal and domestic uses (between 50 and 100 litres of water per person per day), which must be safe, acceptable, and affordable (water costs should not exceed 3 percent of household income), and physically accessible (the water source has to be within 1,000 metres of

the home and collection time should not exceed 30 minutes)." This is from the UnitedNations.org page "Global Issues: Water," n.d., http://www.un.org/en/sections/issues-depth/water/.

20. Anurag Mantha, "Understanding Flint's Water Infrastructure Crisis: Water Infrastructure Inequality in America." FlintWaterStudy.org, December 9, 2016.

21. According to a 2013 study, "The city's current water efficiency is 65%. Typically water utilities operate at 85–90% efficiency. An increase to 85% efficiency would result in increased revenues in the range of $1.5 million to $3.0 million annually." This is from the "City of Flint Water Reliability Study: Distribution System," prepared by Rowe Professional Services Company and Potter Consulting, December 2013. For news stories on water lost to leaky lines: Kristin Longley, "Massive Water Leak, Theft Contribute to Flint Water Rate Increases, Officials Say," MLive—*Flint Journal*, May 10, 2012; Kate Wells, "Flint's Water System Is Falling Apart. Fixing It Could Cost $100 Million" Michigan Radio, August 9, 2016; "Half of the Water Coming into Flint Is Lost to Leaks, Water Theft," ABC 12, WJRT-TV, April 20, 2017; and Mary Williams Walsh, "Detroit Plan to Profit on Water Looks Half Empty," *New York Times*, May 25, 2014. Flint may have had it especially bad, but this is a problem elsewhere, too: David Schaper, "As Infrastructure Crumbles, Trillions of Gallons of Water Lost," *All Things Considered*, NPR, October 29, 2014.

22. Ted Gregory, Patrick M. O'Connell, and Cecilia Reyes, "Precious Resource, Private Profits," *Chicago Tribune*, December 27, 2017.

23. Some of this material about infrastructure is adapted from an article by the author that appeared in *Next City* ("The City that Unpoisoned Its Pipes," August 8, 2016).

24. Wells, "Flint's Water System Is Falling Apart." It's worth adding that fixing a break is cumbersome. A work crew has to control the water spilling out of the main, pinpoint the damage, dig into the ground without compromising any other utilities, repair the main either with clamps or by replacing a length of pipe, turn the water back on, and then restore the excavated area.

25. Gary Ridley, "15 Years and $60M Needed to Replace Flint's Lead Water Lines, Emails Show," MLive—*Flint Journal*, January 21, 2016; Ron Fonger, "Flint Data on Lead Water Lines Stored on 45,000 Index Cards," MLive—*Flint Journal*, October 1, 2015; and Ron Fonger, "Flint Water Line Replacements have 22 Percent Failure Rate," MLive—*Flint Journal*, May 17, 2017.

26. Ron Fonger, "Flint Flushes Out Latest Water Contamination, but Repeat Boil Advisories Show System Is Vulnerable," MLive—*Flint Journal*, September 14, 2014.

27. "City of Flint 2014 Annual Water Quality Report," City of Flint, Mich., 2014, https://www.cityofflint.com/wp-content/uploads/CCR-2014.pdf.

28. Almost exactly one month after the water switch, a *New York Times* story mentioned how Flint's rates were going to increase anyway, if perhaps more slowly than they would have on Detroit's water system. "'Why isn't it possible for the water rates to go down?' demanded Wantwaz D. Davis, a city coun-

cilor. He said rising water rates were driving away residents, and he argued that if rates could be reduced for a few years, people might stay. If Flint's decline could be slowed, he said, it would improve the financial prospects of the new pipeline. And now there is no turning back. The first $220 million in construction bonds for the new pipeline has already been sold. Flint is supposed to repay about one-third of that, and Genesee County will pay back the rest. The new pipeline is scheduled to go into service in 2016. In the meantime, Flint has been getting its water from the Flint River. It turned off the tap on Detroit on April 25." Walsh, "Detroit Plan to Profit on Water Looks Half Empty." See also Ron Fonger, "Flint Residents Get a Chance to Speak; Blast Water Rates and State Oversight," MLive—*Flint Journal*, June 9, 2014.

29. After the switch, there were still 266 customers of Flint water who lived outside the city limits. Neal Rubin, "Outside Flint's Borders, but Stuck with Its Water," *Detroit News*, January 29, 2016.

30. This councilman, Scott Kincaid, filed a federal lawsuit alleging that the city had, in 2011, hiked water and sewer rates by far more than it had been allowed. Adams, "Flint Monthly Water and Sewer Bills Highest."

31. Ibid.

32. The city's five-year financial projections (2015–19), including its adopted budget for FY15 and FY16, were detailed in "City of Flint, Michigan: Setting a Sustainable Course for the City of Flint," prepared by Gerald Ambrose, finance director, and Antonio Brown, deputy finance director, 2014, p. 5, https://www.cityofflint .com/wp-content/uploads/FY15-FY16-Adopted-Budget-Document-21.pdf.

33. Adrian Hedden, "Councilman Leads Protest at Flint City Hall, Addresses Police Chases, Water Rates," MLive—*Flint Journal*, July 14, 2014.

34. Another big issue of contention: water deposits. All prospective renters were required to pay not only a security deposit prior to move-in, but also a deposit against future water bills. In 2013, the mandatory deposit went from $100 to $350. "When residents don't pay their water bill for months at a time, that cost is passed on to those residents who do pay, and that's just not fair," said Ed Kurtz, the emergency manager at the time. "Our goal . . . is to recover more of the costs associated with non-payments, shutoffs, and those who vacate rental properties without paying." But this created an impenetrable barrier for many, according to Henry Tannenbaum, a longtime Flint resident and landlord who served on the board of realtors. To rent one of his houses, he said, people had to come up with a water deposit, security deposit, and monthly rent before move-in day. "People . . . don't have $1,000 laying around," he said. "City Raises Water Deposit on Rental Properties," NBC25, WNEM.TV, February 25, 2015, updated March 25, 2013; *Michigan Civil Rights Commission: Housing and the Flint Water Crisis*, Statement of Henry Tannenbaum, Genesee Landlords Association and owner of TDM Realty, July 14, 2016.

35. Laura Sullivan, interviews with the author, Flint, Mich., May 13, 2016, June 17, 2016, and October 26, 2017.

36. Ron Fonger, "Flint Starting to Flush out 'Discolored' Drinking Water with Hydrant Releases," MLive—*Flint Journal*, July 30, 2014.

37. The press release was issued on July 30, 2014. See also Fonger, "Flint Starting to Flush Out Discolored Drinking Water with Hydrant Releases."

38. Ryan Felton, "Flint Residents Raise Concerns over Discolored Water," *Metro Times*, August 13, 2014.

39. "City of Flint 2014 Annual Water Quality Report," Flint, Mich., 2014, https://www.cityofflint.com/wp-content/uploads/CCR-2014.pdf.

40. Fonger, "City Adding More Lime to Flint River Water."

41. Ibid.

42. Fonger, "Flint Flushes Out Latest Water Contamination."

43. Amanda Emery, "Flint Issues Boil Water Notice for Portion of West Side of City," MLive—*Flint Journal*, August 16, 2014, updated January 17, 2015.

44. Dominic Adams, "Flint Officials Say 'Abnormal' Test to Blame in E. coli Scare, Water Boil Advisory Remains," August 18, 2014, updated January 17, 2015.

45. Ron Fonger, "Second Positive Coliform Bacteria Test Means Flint's West Side Water Boil Notice Still in Effect," MLive—*Flint Journal*, August 18, 2014, updated January 17, 2015.

46. Ron Fonger, "Flint Says Drinking Water Advisories Will Continue into Tuesday," MLive—*Flint Journal*, September 8, 2014; and Ron Fonger, "Flint Lifts Boil Water Advisories for West Side of City, Says Investigation of Contamination Will Continue," MLive—*Flint Journal*, September 9, 2014.

47. Ron Fonger, "Flint River Water Complicating City's Efforts to Battle Contamination, Boil Advisories," MLive—*Flint Journal*, September 18, 2014, updated January 17, 2015.

48. There's a nice map here that gives an outline of the breadth of the advisories: Fonger, "Flint Flushes Out Latest Water Contamination."

49. Ibid.; and Steve Carmody, "Flint Officials Working to Resolve Water Issues," Michigan Radio, September 15, 2014.

CHAPTER 3: REVELATIONS

1. For what is probably the very best telling of the Great Migration, look no further than Isabel Wilkerson, *The Warmth of Other Suns: The Epic Story of America's Great Migration* (New York: Random House, 2010).

2. This song is quoted in Andrew R. Highsmith's *Demolition Means Progress: Flint Michigan, and the Fate of the American Metropolis* (Chicago: University of Chicago Press, 2015), p. 1, to which this chapter in particular owes a great deal. Some of the material in this chapter first appeared, in a different form, in articles by the author that appeared in *Splinter* ("'An Equal Opportunity Lie': How Housing Discrimination Led to the Flint Water Crisis," with Josh Kramer, December 5, 2017) and in the *New Republic* ("Flint Prepares to Be Left Behind Once More," March 3, 2016).

3. "All Change!," *Time*, January 9, 1933, p. 59.

4. Gordon Young, phone interview with the author, January 2016.

5. "Detroit Needs Labor," *New York Times*, April 23, 1919, p. 21.

6. Highsmith, *Demolition Means Progress*, pp. 31—32.

7. Ibid., pp. 81–84; and Rhonda Sanders, *Bronze Pillars: An Oral History of African Americans in Flint* (Flint, Mich.: *The Flint Journal* and Alfred P. Sloan Museum, 1995), p. viii. Sanders: "From the early 1900s until the early 1940s, the main jobs open to blacks were domestic ones such as cooking, cleaning or chauffeuring for wealthy white families. A few worked in trades as barbers, furniture finishers, barn builders, doctors or lawyers. Most black men who worked in the automobile factories were janitors, although some worked at Buick's hellish foundry." Beginning in the 1940s, black women, albeit only those with light skin, were hired to operate elevators in banks and hotels (pp. 92–93).

8. Sanders, *Bronze Pillars*, pp. viii, 2, 32; and Highsmith, *Demolition Means Progress*, p. 32. It's worth pointing out, though, that there appeared to be more flexibility when the proportion of African Americans in Flint hovered at about 3 percent: "Blacks could not live anywhere they wanted until a legal mandate in 1968. However, many blacks and whites lived in the same neighborhoods before World War II and formed close friendships," as Rhonda Sanders describes it. She quotes William Hoskins, who arrived in 1936 from Mississippi. "When I first came to Flint, there was no such thing as a black neighborhood. The Italians, Polish and everyone else (including blacks) lived together." Some black children learned to speak foreign languages from their playmates.

9. Highsmith, *Demolition Means Progress*, pp. 30–37.

10. "The Realtor should not be instrumental in introducing into a neighborhood a character of property or occupancy, members of any race or nationality or any individual whose presence will clearly be detrimental to property values in the neighborhood." That appeared in the code of ethics of the National Association of Real Estate Brokers in 1950. The same sentiment appeared in textbooks the organization published as early as 1922. The code is quoted in: U.S. Commission on Civil Rights, "Understanding Fair Housing," Clearinghouse Publication 42 (Washington, D.C.: U.S. Government Printing Office, February 1973), p. 3.

11. Highsmith, *Demolition Means Progress*. Highsmith describes these neighborhoods, including where their borders fell, on pp. 30–31. He also notes that up until 1940, 60 percent of St. John was made up of white immigrants, mostly Catholics from Eastern Europe, though about three quarters of them left over the next ten years, while the number of black households tripled (p. 151). According to the memory of those interviewed by Rhonda Sanders, even as many of the white immigrants moved out of St. John, they kept up family businesses in the neighborhood. As for Floral Park's roots, Sanders builds on the early history of Flint as a place of refuge for former slaves. "Some of the first blacks to visit Flint may have been fugitive slaves en route to Canada. Detroit was the most direct stopover on the Underground Railroad network that secretly led runaway slaves to freedom in Canada. Flint is believed to have been an alternative route that directed fleeing slaves through Port Huron into Canada." Sanders, *Bronze Pillars*, p. 4.

12. Flint's first evaluation by the Home Owners Loan Corporation was in the summer of 1937. The GM neighborhoods got a B rating, the second-best category. The one exception to the all-white neighborhoods that were redlined because of their proximity to African American residents was a part of Woodlawn Park that bordered Floral Park. "Will hold up," the assessor noted. "Pride of ownership." As Highsmith writes, "West Woodlawn Park no doubt contained many proud homeowners, yet the neighborhood's blue grade stemmed also from its abundance of racially restrictive housing covenants and the impermeability of the Lapeer Road color line that separated it from Floral Park." Highsmith, *Demolition Means Progress*, p. 41.

13. A scanned version of the original evaluations are presented in a wonderful interactive by Mapping Inequality, a project that shows the primary materials for how redlining worked in New Deal America. Two received this same "undesirables" notation that first year: the areas labeled D12 and D18, https://dsl .richmond.edu/panorama/redlining/#loc=12/43.0303/-83.6896&opacity=0 .8&area=D18&city=flint-mi&adimage=4/67/-123.

14. "The Flint Water Crisis," Michigan Civil Rights Commission, pp. 36–38.

15. Highsmith, *Demolition Means Progress*, p. 71.

16. Ibid., p. 34; and Young, *Teardown: Memoir of a Vanishing City*, p. 72. This was at the end of the 1930s. Flint was behind Miami, Florida, and Norfolk, Virginia.

17. Also, there was nothing compelling lending institutions from working with African American mortgage applicants, even with the Veterans Administration guaranteeing the loan. "And so home ownership quickly soared to two out of three, then more gradually reached its current zenith of three out of four. Home ownership rates for black and Hispanic families during the postwar boom years, however, hovered at or below 40 percent; and even today, while the children and grandchildren of white veterans enjoy all the benefits of that government-sponsored home equity, black and Hispanic home ownership rates remain stuck below 50 percent." Edward Humes, "How the G.I. Bill Shunted Blacks Back into Vocational Training," *Journal of Blacks in Higher Education*, no. 53 (Autumn 2006): 92–104.

18. Ibid.; and Richard Rothstein, "Modern Segregation," presentation to the Atlantic Live Conference "Reinventing the War on Poverty," Washington, D.C., March 6, 2014. Text published the same day at the Economic Policy Institute website, http://www.epi.org/files/2014/MODERN-SEGREGATION.pdf.

19. *Shelley v. Kraemer*, 334 US 1 (1948). The Court found that racially restrictive covenants are a contract that private parties can voluntarily engage in, even though state enforcement of the covenants would violate the Equal Protection clause of the Fourteenth Amendment. In the case, the Shelley family, which was African American, tried to buy a home in St. Louis that had a covenant attached that banned "people of the Negro or Mongolian race" from owning it. The neighborhood sued to keep the family from moving in.

20. "The Flint Water Crisis," Michigan Civil Rights Commission, pp. 60–61.

21. Highsmith, *Demolition Means Progress*, p. 69. Another resistance tactic: constructing entirely new houses. "Many blacks who were turned away from

Woodlawn Park proper resolved the problem by building homes on vacant land to its immediate south and east," including the first black president of Flint's Board of Education, a civil rights attorney, and the first black woman elected to the school board. Sanders, *Bronze Pillars*, p. 20.

22. Sanders, *Bronze Pillars*, p. 22. Another story Sanders captures is from Bill Williams, who moved to northwest Flint in 1968. "I had two cars," he said. "One I left home with my wife and one I drove to work. I have a one-car garage so I'd park the good one in the garage and the work car in the driveway. I'd come out in the morning and find eggs all over the car and garage. The tree in the yard, we had decorated for Christmas; I came out and the lights had been stolen and it had been decorated with toilet paper." The harassment subsided after a few years, Williams believed, because his house was one of the best-kept in the neighborhood (p. 25).

23. Highsmith, *Demolition Means Progress*, p. 144.

24. U.S. Commission on Civil Rights, "Understanding Fair Housing," p. 5.

25. "The Flint Water Crisis," Michigan Civil Rights Commission, p. 44; and Highsmith, *Demolition Means Progress*, pp. 325–27.

26. For this and the rest of the paragraph: Highsmith, *Demolition Means Progress*, pp. 34–37.

27. According to community memory, the pool stopped its segregated access program in the 1950s, which coincided with the time when white families were moving out of the neighborhood. The pool closed in 1978. Berston also had a library, but black children were allowed to use it only if escorted by a teacher on a class field trip. Sanders, *Bronze Pillars*, pp. 197–99.

28. "The Flint Water Crisis," Michigan Civil Rights Commission, p. 44.

29. Ibid., p. 48.

30. Ibid., p. 43.

31. "The Need for Industrial Dispersal," committee staff, materials prepared for the Joint Committee on the Economic Report. Washington, D.C.: U.S. Government Printing Office, August 1951; and Harry S. Truman, "189—Memorandum and Statement of Policy on the Need for Industrial Dispersion," August 10, 1951, online at Gerhard Peters and John T. Woolley, The American Presidency Project, http://www.presidency.ucsb.edu/ws/?pid=28364.

32. Highsmith, *Demolition Means Progress*, p. 122.

33. Ibid., pp. 130–31.

34. "The Flint Water Crisis," Michigan Civil Rights Commission, p. 52.

35. Ibid. It also provided water and sewer services to some residents of suburban communities until 1953, when the utility's long-term capacity began to be in question.

36. Ibid., p. 51.

37. Highsmith, *Demolition Means Progress*, pp. 130–31.

38. Ibid., p. 117.

39. Ibid., pp. 114–15.

40. Ibid., pp. 133–42.

41. Ibid., pp. 121–22.

42. Ibid., pp. 138–39. The quote is from an unidentified woman speaking at an

April 10, 1958, meeting about New Flint in Mt. Morris Township. The suburb that incorporated was Swartz Creek, after a vote on August 5, 1958, partly out of fears that they'd lose their Chevy facility if they didn't.

43. Suburban communities that had GM plants were especially opposed to New Flint, including Grand Blanc, Burton Township, Flint Township, and Beecher. Opponents worried that the plan would increase their taxes and make them subjects of the city. It also cut against the rising pride they had in their own small communities. Swartz Creek incorporated in response to New Flint even though the area wasn't included in the borders of the proposed metropolitan government. The Genesee County Board of Supervisors, which prevented the question from getting on the ballot, was dominated by New Flint opponents, particularly those from townships. Its Legislative Affairs Committee declared that the petition was legal, but the board voted 25–13 to keep it off the ballot. The Michigan Supreme Court voted unanimously in support of the board, on the grounds of a technical distinction between consolidation and incorporation, saying that New Flint would violate state law by incorporating areas that were already incorporated. Flint was then left in a tight spot. It made efforts to annex nearby areas, just as cities in the South and West had done. It was a process that required separate majority votes in both the affected communities. Flint Township voted 3–1 against annexation by the city in 1961. But the law permitted annexation of industrial and commercial sites with a simple majority vote, which is how Flint, with the support of General Motors, was able to annex four GM plants in Flint Township, Bishop International Airport, and two shopping centers—1,370 acres of land altogether. The city failed in its effort to annex a GM plant and open land in Beecher and Mt. Morris Township. Also, the Genesee County Board of Education voted that the taxes passed by the annexed facilities would continue to support the suburban schools, not the ones in the city. More suburbs incorporated in the following years: Fenton, Flushing, Mt. Morris Township, Beecher, Flint Township. The campaign for Flushing's incorporation advertised in the newspaper about how the move would "end septic tanks . . . plug up the wells—get pure city water—quality for low-cost FHA loans on mortgages" (Highsmith, *Demolition Means Progress*, pp. 139–44).

44. "The Flint Water Crisis," Michigan Civil Rights Commission, pp. 60–64.

45. Ibid., p. 79.

46. Ibid., p. 149.

47. Bayard Rustin, "The Watts," *Commentary*, March 1, 1966.

48. "Of 164 disorders reported during the first nine months of 1967, eight (5 percent) were major in terms of violence and damage; 33 (20 percent) were serious but not major; 123 (75 percent) were minor and undoubtedly would not have received national attention as riots had the Nation not been sensitized by the more serious outbreaks." The National Advisory Commission on Civil Disorders, *Kerner Report*, p. 6.

49. "From 1940 to 1960, Flint's African American population grew from just over six thousand to nearly thirty-five thousand. Yet over the same period the boundaries of the city's black neighborhoods remained essentially fixed. With

a residential segregation index that reached 94.4 in 1960, Flint ranked as one of the most racially divided cities in the country—more segregated, in fact, than Atlanta, New York, Chicago or Los Angeles." Highsmith, *Demolition Means Progress*, p. 149.

50. Sanders, *Bronze Pillars*, p. 23.

51. Judy Wax and Doris Jarrell, "Grand Rapids Hit by Sniper Attacks," *Detroit Free Press*, July 27, 1967, p. 9A; Joseph W. Wagar, "Flint Troubles on 'Simmer,'" *Flint Journal*, July 26, 1967, p. 1.

52. Wagar, "Flint Troubles on 'Simmer,'" p. 1. Also, gas stations were asked to close by the chief of police, and "false alarms plagued the fire department" ("The Flint Water Crisis," Michigan Civil Rights Commission, p. 66).

53. "The Flint Water Crisis," Michigan Civil Rights Commission, p. 66.; and Wagar, "Flint Troubles on 'Simmer,'" p. 1, as reproduced in: Ananthakrishnan Aiyer, *Telling Our Stories: The Legacy of the Civil Rights Movement in Flint* (Flint, Mich.: Flint Colorline Project, 2007). Eighty-one people were arrested the second night. Rhonda Sanders quotes Woody Etherly Jr.'s assessment of how Mayor Floyd J. McCree handled the unusual amnesty deal: "Floyd was the kind of person that could build bridges on all sides. . . . People think of Floyd as a gentleman and gentle person, but Floyd did what Floyd had to do behind closed doors. He was very articulate behind closed doors, and he would sit down, and if he had to, you know, he had to fire up sometimes" (Sanders, *Bronze Pillars*, p. 288).

54. About 4,700 army paratroopers were airlifted into Detroit, then the nation's fifth-largest city, after police officers and National Guardsmen were reported trapped by snipers in two precinct stations. "It looks like Berlin in 1945," said Mayor Jerome Cavanagh. Federal troops had been activated in recent years to help implement desegregation, but this was altogether different. So rare was this move, its legality and protocol were disputed, but it was deemed acceptable under a provision for "insurrection in any state against the government" in a law from 1795. Said President Johnson upon dispatching the troops: "I am sure the American people will realize that I take this action with the greatest regret—and only because of the clear, unmistakable, and undisputed evidence that Governor Romney of Michigan and the local officials in Detroit have been unable to bring the situation under control. Law enforcement is a local matter. . . . The Federal Government should not intervene-except in the most extraordinary circumstances. The fact of the matter, however, is that law and order have broken down in Detroit, Michigan." The last time federal troops had been sent into an American city: Detroit again, during the riot of 1943. Gene Roberts, "U.S. Troops Sent into Detroit; 19 Dead; Johnson Decries Riots; New Outbreak in East Harlem," *New York Times*, July 26, 1967, pp. 1, 19; "President Used a Law of 1795 to Send Troops," AP wire, *New York Times*. July 26, 1967, p. 18; and Lyndon B. Johnson, "Remarks to the Nation After Authorizing the Use of Federal Troops in Detroit," July 24, 1967, online at Peters and Woolley, American Presidency Project, http://www.presidency.ucsb.edu/ws/?pid=28364.

55. Bill McGraw, "Before '67 Riot, Detroit Thought It Could Avoid Civil Unrest," *Detroit Free Press*, July 15, 2017, updated July 17, 2017.

56. UPI Wire Staff, "Worst U.S. Riot Ending in Detroit," *Battle Creek Enquirer and News*, July 27, 1967, p. 1.

57. Pontiac, about twenty-five miles from Detroit and the seat of Oakland County, had about 82,000 residents. According to an AP wire story: "State Representative Arthur J. Law, a Pontiac Democrat, said he had fired his 12-gauge shotgun at a half dozen Negro youths after they had hurled a trash can through the plate glass window of a food market he has owned since 1948 in a heavily Negro area. Pontiac has 15,000 Negro residents." AP Wire Staff, "2 Killed in Pontiac," *New York Times*, July 26, 1967, p. 19.

58. Ibid; and "Worst U.S. Riot Ending in Detroit."

59. Lyndon B. Johnson, "The President's Address to the Nation on Civil Disorders," July 27, 1967, online at Peters and Woolley, American Presidency Project, http://www.presidency.ucsb.edu/ws/?pid=28368, video available via C-Span, https://www.c-span.org/video/?431462-1/president-johnson-address-civil-disorder-kerner-commission.

60. Some of the material in this chapter about the *Kerner Report* and the riots first appeared, in different form, in an article by the author that appeared in *Politico* ("Mass Shootings Are the Systemic Crisis of Our Time," October 4, 2017).

61. The National Advisory Commission on Civil Disorders, *The Kerner Report*, p. 211.

62. More than a day after the attack began, forty-six black people and two white people were dead. More than a hundred buildings in the black community were set afire.

63. The National Advisory Commission on Civil Disorders, *The Kerner Report*, pp. 12–13. "From 1950 to 1966, the U.S. Negro population rose 6.5 million. Over 98 percent of that increase took place in metropolitan areas—86 percent within central cities, 112 percent in the urban fringe," *Kerner Report*, p. 244.

64. Ibid., p. 14. Mayor Floyd McCree began working in the foundry after his military service and, over the next couple decades, he was able to rise up in the ranks.

65. The National Advisory Commission on Civil Disorders, *The Kerner Report*, pp. 23, 278–82.

66. Ibid., p. 1.

67. Ibid., p. 17. The report also declared that police forces needed to be better trained and more accountable, and that newsrooms should to be more diverse, so that there would be more nuanced coverage of cities. More early childhood education was essential, too, it said.

68. It was issued as a mass-market paperback with an introduction by *New York Times* columnist Tom Wicker. Marlon Brando read excerpts of it on *The Joey Bishop Show*.

69. The National Advisory Commission on Civil Disorders, *The Kerner Report*, pp. xxxi–xxxii; and William S. White, "Riot Report Certain to Help Republicans, Hurt Democrats," *Washington Post*, March 4, 1968, p. A23.

70. White, "Riot Report"; and "Kerner Panel Report Sends Shock Waves," *Washington Post*, March 2, 1968, p. A1.

71. The National Advisory Commission on Civil Disorders, *The Kerner Report*, p. xxiii.

72. "Kerner Panel Report Sends Shock Waves."

73. Julian E. Zelizer, "Fifty Years Ago, the Government Said Black Lives Matter," *Boston Review*, May 5, 2016; Robert Siegel, "50 Years On, Sen. Fred Harris Remembers Great Hostility During 1967 Race Riots," *All Things Considered*, National Public Radio, July 20, 2017; and Gene Schlickman, "The Kerner Commission and the Search for Answers." *Chicago Tribune*, May 11, 1992. Vice President Hubert Humphrey was a bit warmer to the report, saying at an appearance at Florida State University that it showed the need for a "tremendous, coordinated, massive program of rehabilitation and social reform." "Kerner Panel Report Sends Shock Waves."

74. "The Flint Water Crisis," Michigan Civil Rights Commission, p. 66.

75. Editorial, "Racial Equality Under Law Suffers Setback in Flint," *Detroit Free Press*, August 16, 1967, p. 8A; and Allan R. Wilhelm, "More Negro Resignations Are Part of Protest Drive," *Flint Journal*, August 17, 1967, p. 13, as reproduced in Aiyer, *Telling Our Stories*, pp. 85–86. Among those who announced their resignations were five Flint appointees to the Genesee County Board of Supervisors; a member of the Hurley Hospital Board of Managers; and three members (two of them white ministers) of the Citizens Advisory Committee on Urban Renewal.

76. "The Flint Water Crisis," Michigan Civil Rights Commission, p. 67; Sanders, *Bronze Pillars*, p. 22; and Highsmith, *Demolition Means Progress*, pp. 170–71.

77. Sanders, *Bronze Pillars*, p. 305.

78. Thorough accounts of Flint's fair housing fight, which this chapter relies upon, are found in Highsmith, *Demolition Means Progress*; Young, *Teardown*; Aiyer, *Telling Our Stories*; and Sanders, *Bronze Pillars*.

79. The National Advisory Commission on Civil Disorders, *The Kerner Report*, p. xix, citing "Presidential Advisors Hear Maier's Views," *Milwaukee Journal*, October 5, 1967.

80. "Open-Housing Ordinance Passes by 43 Votes in Flint Referendum," *New York Times*, February 22, 1968, p. 22. The narrow vote count was later checked and revised.

81. Coincidentally, the Flint vote came just nine days before the publication of the *Kerner Report*, which discussed fair housing and segregation at length in its dissection of what ailed cities: "Integration is the only course which explicitly seeks to achieve a single nation."

82. As quoted in U.S. Commission on Civil Rights, "Understanding Fair Housing," p. 7.

83. Ibid., pp. 16–18. In one example from 1970, Lackawanna, New York, refused a building permit to an African American person who wanted to build a low-income housing project. Per the report from the Commission on Civil Rights, "The city defended its position on the ground that the new units would be a burden on the city's sewer and water system. In addition, the city contended the proposed site was needed for a city park. The [federal] court found a different reason for the position of the city. Substantial evidence proved to the court that opposition to the low-income housing project was based on the 'discriminatory sentiments of the community.'" For book-length accounts on how

ostensibly race-neutral exclusionary practices enforced racial segregation, see Kenneth T. Jackson, *Crabgrass Frontier: The Suburbanization of the United States* (New York: Oxford University Press, 1997); Douglas S. Massey and Nancy A. Denton, *American Apartheid: Segregation and the Making of the Underclass* (Cambridge, Mass.: Harvard University Press, 1993); and Thomas M. Sugrue, *The Origins of the Urban Crisis: Race and Equality in Postwar Detroit* (Princeton, N.J.: Princeton University Press, 1996).

84. He made the "white noose" remark at his Senate confirmation hearing. "Urban renewal helped spark the riot in Detroit," he said, leading to thousands of people being "bulldozed out of their homes." Federal housing policies "built a high-income white noose basically around these inner cities, and the poor and disadvantaged, both black and white, are pretty much left in the inner city." There are a number of good resources about George Romney's role in fair housing, statewide and nationally, including Sidney Fine, "Michigan and Housing Discrimination, 1949–1968," *Michigan Historical Review* 23, no. 2 (Fall 1997): 81–114; Nikole Hannah-Jones, "Living Apart: How the Government Betrayed a Landmark Civil Rights Law," *ProPublica*, June 25, 2015; Richard Rothstein, "From Ferguson to Baltimore: The Fruits of Government-Sponsored Segregation," Working Economics blog, April 29, 2015; and Mark Santow and Richard Rothstein, "A Different Kind of Choice," Economic Policy Institute, August 12, 2012. Romney also championed fair housing and desegregation in his book *The Concerns of a Citizen* (New York: Putnam, 1968).

85. When worried white homeowners sold their homes after a black family moved in, it caused others to panic—an alarm that was sometimes encouraged by real estate speculators, or "blockbusters"—and follow suit. The market was flooded with their houses, forcing the prices downward. Their fears of lowered property values were realized because of their own actions. "The Flint Water Crisis," Michigan Civil Rights Commission, p. 59.

86. St. John was razed for I-475 and an industrial park. Floral Park was largely sacrificed for the freeway interchange between I-475 and I-69. Many displaced residents were relocated to public housing complexes, like Atherton East in south Flint (opened 1968) and Howard Estates (opened 1969). St. John residents received a maximum buyout of $15,000. While the crowdedness of the old neighborhood had caused many complaints—neighborhood leaders and civil rights activists supported urban renewal, thinking it would give their communities better opportunities—people sorely missed it once it was gone. In the 1990s, former residents organized a number of St. John reunions. Sanders, *Bronze Pillars*, pp. 10–15.

CHAPTER 4: SATURATION

1. According to information posted online about Flint Engine Operations at the GM corporate newsroom (www.media.gm.com), the engine plant pays out more than $91,181,847 in state wages and $19,835,318 in income taxes. Production began in 2002. Of its 806 employees, 673 are hourly and 133 are sala-

ried. Additional details about this plant and its experience of the water crisis are sourced from Mike Colias, "How GM Saved Itself from the Flint Water Crisis," *Automotive News*, January 31, 2016; Ron Fonger, "GM's Decision to Stop Using Flint River Water Will Cost Flint $400,000 a Year," MLive—*Flint Journal*, October 14, 2014, updated January 17, 2015; and Lindsay Smith, "Not Safe to Drink," Michigan Radio, December 15, 2015. The detail about the plant using about seventy-five thousand gallons of water a day is mentioned in numerous local news articles, including Ron Fonger, "GM Keeps Engine Plant off Flint Water While City Considers Its Options," MLive—*Flint Journal*, April 25, 2017.

2. In 1978, about seventy-eight thousand people worked in GM plants in the Flint area, and the local payroll was about $2 billion. By 2016, about seventy-two hundred worked at the company. Colias, "How GM Saved Itself"; and Lawrence R. Gustin, "GM and Flint Grew Together," *Automotive News*, September 14, 2008.

3. Ron Fonger, "General Motors Shutting Off Flint River Water at Engine Plant Over Corrosion Worries," MLive—*Flint Journal*, October 13, 2014, updated January 17, 2015.

4. In the EPA's district office in Chicago, Jennifer Crooks responded to Burgess's message by saying that the MDEQ was aware of the problems and working closely with the city to provide better water until the KWA came online. Burgess later became the lead plaintiff of a group of more than seventeen hundred people who filed a $772 million lawsuit charging that the EPA was negligent in the face of Flint's water problems, causing injury to people who were exposed to it. Her message to the EPA is quoted in the court filing: *Burgess v. United States of America* (2:17-cv-10291), Michigan Eastern District Court, filed January 30, 2017. See also Jennifer Chambers, "Flint's Residents Are Building Their Legal Case," *Detroit News*, March 18, 2016; and Jim Lynch, "Flint Residents Seek $722M over Water Crisis," *Detroit News*, January 30, 2017.

5. Gadola was replying to an email by Valerie Brader, the governor's environmental policy adviser. Brader wrote, in part, "Specifically, there has been a boil water order due to bacterial contamination. What is not yet broadly known is that attempts to fix that have led to some levels of chlorine-related chemicals that can cause long-term damage if not remedied (though we believe they will remedy them before any damage would occur in the population)." Brader also suggested that Flint's emergency manager should restore the connection to the Detroit water system "as an interim solution" to both the quality and financial problems "that the current solution is causing." These emails were exchanged on October 14, 2014. Later, when Brader and another senior aide talked it over with Flint's emergency manager, they were told that it would be too expensive to switch back and that any treatment problems were fixable. The EM didn't have expertise in water treatment, of course; he was relying on the information he got from people such as Mike Prysby, the district engineer for the MDEQ. Matthew Dolan and Paul Egan, "Top Snyder Aids Urged Going Back to Detroit Water," *Detroit Free Press*, February 26, 2016; Chad Livengood, "Emails:

Flint Water Warnings Reached Gov's Inner Circle," *Detroit News*, February 26, 2016; and Lindsey Smith, "New Emails Show Officials in Gov. Snyder's Circle Discussed Concerns about Flint's Water, Did Nothing," Michigan Radio, February 26, 2016.

6. Fonger, "General Motors Shutting Off Flint River Water."

7. Laura Sullivan, interview with author, Flint, Mich., May 13, 2016.

8. Colias, "How GM Saved Itself."

9. "Important Information About Your Drinking Water," City of Flint, January 2, 2015, https://www.cityofflint.com/wp-content/uploads/TTHM-Notification -Final.pdf.

10. Smith, "Not Safe to Drink."

11. For this, and the rest of the paragraph, Robin, Erb, "Who Wants to Drink Flint's Water?," *Detroit Free Press*, January 22, 2015, updated January 23, 2015.

12. AP Wire Report, "Flint City Councilman, 'We Got Bad Water,'" *Detroit Free Press*, January 14, 2015.

13. Christine Ferretti, "Detroit Offers to Reconnect Water Service to Flint," *Detroit News*, January 20, 2015.

14. "Flint City Councilman, 'We Got Bad Water.'"

15. "About Us: Who We Are," Veolia North America, www.veolianorthamerica .com, last accessed March 2, 2018.

16. Ron Fonger, "Flint Mayor Tells Governor: Lower Water Connection Fees, Offer Amnesty Program for Turn-ons," MLive—*Flint Journal*, January 20, 2015, updated January 21, 2015.

17. Erb, "Who Wants to Drink Flint's Water?"

18. Ron Fonger, "Officials Say Flint Water Is Getting Better, but Many Residents Unsatisfied," MLive—*Flint Journal*, January 21, 2015.

19. Per a January 2018 conversation with a resident and community organizer who was present at the meeting. The author did not get this person's explicit permission to use their name on the record.

20. Ron Fonger, "Erin Brockovich: Flint Water System 'Failing,' Stop Making Excuses," MLive—*Flint Journal*, January 21, 2015.

21. Detroit Public Schools had been under emergency management since 2009. Their experience with state intervention would last about six years, with four different EMs. It also experienced a different form of oversight in 1999, when the governor at the time signed a law that replaced the elected school board with a seven-member reform board, six of whom were appointed by the Detroit mayor with one spot reserved for the state superintendent of public instruction. Their tenure lasted several years.

22. Ron Fonger, "Flint Emergency Manager Says There Are Two Big Reasons Not to Reconnect Detroit Water," MLive—*Flint Journal*, January 29, 2015.

23. To be clear: Genesee County, like Flint, also had a DWSD contract that expired, and it had also decided to join the KWA. But unlike the city, Genesee County didn't scramble to find a temporary water source. It simply paid its monthly bills under the terms of the old contract, and the DWSD kept the properly

treated water flowing to places such as Flint Township, which now served the GM engine plant.

24. This scene is captured in *Hard to Swallow: Toxic Water in a Toxic System in Flint*, released June 25, 2015, and available to watch at www.aclumich.org /article/hard-swallow-toxic-water-toxic-system-flint.

25. "Flint Water Advisory," Department of Technology, Management, and Budget Customer Service Center, Facility Notification, January 7, 2015.

26. "Gov. Rick Snyder awards Flint $2 million in distressed municipalities' grant for water system infrastructure improvements." Office of Governor Rick Snyder, Michigan.gov., February 3, 2015; and Ron Fonger, "Governor Awards Flint $2 Million for Troubled Water System; Mayor Says More Is Needed," MLive—*Flint Journal*, February 3, 2015, updated February 4, 2015.

27. Fonger, "Governor Awards Flint $2 Million."

28. Dominic Adams, "Faces of Flint: Bryant Nolden," MLive—*Flint Journal*, May 3, 2016.

29. William Elgar Brown, testimony in 67th District Court, Flint, Michigan, January 8, 2018. This was during the preliminary examinations in the state's criminal case against four MDEQ employees. Brown was a retired engineer and deputy division chief for the department with some forty years' experience in water issues. Brown signed the KWA's original permit and later consulted for a construction company that worked with the new water utility.

30. "Water Quality Update," City of Flint, March 25, 2015; and "TTHM Contaminant Notices, Water Quality Updates, Ready for Mailing to Flint Customers," MLive—*Flint Journal*, March 31, 2015.

31. Ibid. Because of its high TTHM levels in 2014, Flint was held in violation of the Safe Drinking Water Act for three months. That required the city to send residents a follow-up notice about how the water fared in the first quarter of 2015, which is where this update comes from. The two-page memo from the city emphasized that the MDEQ "acknowledged our progress" in treating the water.

32. Dayne Walling, "Responses from Dayne Walling, Former Flint Mayor," Michigan Joint Select Committee on the Flint Water Public Health Emergency, Flint Public Hearing, March 29, 2016.

33. Natalie Pruett, "Beyond Blight: City of Flint Comprehensive Blight Elimination Framework," Imagine Flint, adopted February 10, 2015; and Steve Carmody, "Flint's Blight Problem (and Solution) Detailed," Michigan Radio, March 13, 2015. The author also reported about this at the time in an article for *Next City* ("Flint, Michigan, Has an Ambitious New Plan to Fight Blight," March 16, 2015).

34. Aaron McMann, "'Flint Firebirds' Unveiled as Name for Flint's New OHL Team," MLive—*Flint Journal*, March 16, 2015.

35. Crooks sent the email on February 9, 2015. Joel Kurth, Jonathan Oosting, Christine MacDonald, and Jim Lynch, "DEQ Official: Staffers Earn Raises for Flint Work," *Detroit News*, February 12, 2016; and *Bridge* Staff, "Flint Crisis Timeline: Part 3," *Bridge Magazine*, March 1, 2016.

36. The vote was on March 23, 2014. Ron Fonger, "Flint Council Votes to Do 'All Things Necessary' to End Use of Flint River," MLive—*Flint Journal*, March 23, 2015; Ron Fonger, "Emergency Manager Calls City Flint River Vote 'Incomprehensible,'" MLive—*Flint Journal*, March 24, 2015; and Mitch Smith, "A Water Dilemma in Michigan: Costly or Cloudy?," *New York Times*, March 24, 2015.

37. This was captured in a video that was included in *Hard to Swallow*. After Ambrose said this, the crowd responded. "That is a lie!" someone shouted. "Now, we looked at that, and we said—," Ambrose continued. "That's not true," a second resident said. "I'm not sure that's true," the first person repeated. The second echoed: "It's not." "Well, we have the Flint River," Ambrose went on, eliding the point.

38. "Flint Water Advisory Task Force," March 2016.

39. For some accounts of these water giveaways, see Jim Lynch, "Flint Taps Options After Complaints About Water," *Detroit News*, February 2, 2015; and Steve Carmody, "Flint Residents Line Up Again for Free Water as State and Local Officials Talk," Michigan Radio, February 3, 2015.

40. Blake Thorne, "Semi-truck Full of Clean Water Attracts Crowd in Flint," MLive—*Flint Journal*, January 28, 2015.

41. Sarah Schuch, "Flint Colleges Independently Testing Water After City Sends Out Violation Notice," MLive—*Flint Journal*, January 14, 2015.

42. Ibid.

CHAPTER 5: ALCHEMY

1. The recounting of LeeAnne Walters's story relies, most especially, on her testimony in the 67th District Court on January 8, 2018, during the preliminary examinations in the criminal case against four MDEQ employees (Flint, Michigan, January 8, 2018); her testimony before the Michigan Joint Select Committee on the Flint Water Public Health Emergency (Lansing, Michigan, March 29, 2016); and her testimony before the House Oversight and Governmental Reform Committee (Washington, D.C., February 3, 2016). There are a number of magazines, radio broadcasts, documentaries, and newspapers that have covered all or part of her story as well. The Michigan Radio documentary "Not Safe to Drink," and the ACLU documentaries *Here's to Flint* and *Corrosive Impact* are important resources.

2. Lindsey Smith, "Not Safe to Drink," Michigan Radio, December 15, 2015.

3. Besides LeeAnne Walters's own testimony, numerous media accounts detail the symptoms of the Walters children. Among them: Sarah Hulett, "High Lead Levels in Michigan Kids After City Switches Water Source," *All Things Considered*, NPR, September 29, 2015; Nancy Kaffer, "Lead Levels in Mich. City Have Moms Avoiding Tap Water," *Detroit Free Press/USA Today*, October 6, 2015; Stephen Rodrick, "Who Poisoned Flint, Michigan?," *Rolling Stone*, January 22, 2016; and Smith, "Not Safe to Drink."

4. Testimony of LeeAnne Walters in 67th District Court, Flint, Michigan, January 8, 2018.

5. Rodrick, "Who Poisoned Flint, Michigan?"

6. On Isaac Newton and alchemy, "Newton the Alchemist," PBS *NOVA*. Interview with Bill Newman conducted September 6, 2005, posted online November 15, 2005; and Michael Greshko, "Isaac Newton's Lost Alchemy Recipe Rediscovered," *National Geographic*, April 4, 2016.

7. Among the sources for the properties of lead, Lydia Denworth, *Toxic Truth: A Scientist, a Doctor, and the Battle Over Lead* (Boston: Beacon Press, 2008); Richard Rabin, "The Lead Industry and Lead Water Pipes 'A MODEST CAMPAIGN,'" *American Journal of Public Health* 98, no. 9 (September 2008); and Elissa Nuñez and Amy Molloy, "Schools Fail Lead Tests While Many States Don't Require Testing at All," Center for Public Integrity, August 15, 2017.

8. Elizabeth Klibanoff, "Lead Ammunition Poisons Wildlife but Too Expensive to Change, Hunters Say," *Morning Edition*, NPR, February 20, 2017; and Jon M. Arnemo et al., "Health and Environmental Risks from Lead-Based Ammunition: Science Versus Sociology," *Ecohealth* 13, no. 4 (2016).

9. "Lead in Lipstick," Campaign for Safe Cosmetics, n.d. http://www.safecosmetics .org/get-the-facts/regulations/us-laws/lead-in-lipstick/.

10. Denworth, *Toxic Truth*, p. 26.

11. Ibid., pp. 61–62, 111; and "Poisoned Water," *NOVA*, PBS, May 31, 2017.

12. Denworth, *Toxic Truth*, p. 26.

13. As cited by the World Health Organization, "Lead Poisoning and Health," updated August 2017, http://www.who.int/mediacentre/factsheets/fs379/en/.

14. "Lead: Learn About Lead," U.S. Environmental Protection Agency, n.d., https://www.epa.gov/lead/learn-about-lead#exposure.

15. As quoted in: Herbert L. Needleman, "The Neurobehavioral Effects of Low-Level Exposure to Lead in Childhood," *International Journal of Mental Health* 14, no. 3 (Fall 2015).

16. Paracelsus, who was apprenticed to a smelter as a child, wrote *On the Miners' Sickness and Other Miners' Diseases* in 1533 or 1534, though it wasn't published until 1567, well after his death. The book is considered to be the first full-length treatment on occupational health. He describes a lung sickness for those working aboveground, processing the ores, and miners' disease for those working belowground. While many of his conclusions were wrong, he described metal fumes as a cause of sickness. He's not just talking about lead, but also mercury poisoning, respiratory diseases, and lung cancer. Paracelsus popularized the use of lead compounds as a therapeutic agent, based on the like-cures-like principle. As quoted by Jerome O. Nriagu: "Lead hath in it remedies for those diseases which be caused and bread in the miners leade." Dan Fagin, *Toms River: A Story of Science and Salvation* (New York: Bantam, 2013), pp. 26–30; Hugh D. Crone, *Paracelsus: The Man Who Defied Medicine* (Melbourne: Albarello Press, 2004), pp. 97–101; and Jerome O. Nriagu, "Saturnine Drugs and Medicinal Exposure to Lead: An Historical Outline," in Herbert L. Needleman, ed., *Human Lead Exposure* (Boca Raton: CRC Press, 1991), pp. 3–22.

17. As quoted in James Richard Farr, *Artisans in Europe, 1300–1914* (Cambridge, U.K.: Cambridge University Press, 2000), pp. 134–35.

18. Denworth, *Toxic Truth*, p. 29.

19. Olga Khazan, "How Important Is Lead Poisoning to Becoming a Legendary Artist?," *Atlantic*, November 25, 2013.

20. William Finnegan, "Flint and the Long Struggle Against Lead Poisoning," *New Yorker*, February 4, 2016.

21. Benjamin Franklin, "To B. Vaughn, Esq.," letter, Philadelphia, July 31, 1786. Reprinted in *Memoirs of the Life and Writings of Benjamin Franklin, LL.D.* (London: British and Foreign Public Library, 1881). The particular quote here comes from p. 552.

22. Sven Hernberg, "Lead Poisoning in a Historical Perspective" *American Journal of Industrial Medicine* 38 (2000), http://rachel.org/files/document/Lead_Poisoning_in_Historical_Perspective.pdf2000.

23. Ibid.; and Marc Edwards, "Fetal Death and Reduced Birth Rates Associated with Exposure to Lead Contaminated Water," *Environmental Science & Technology* 48, no. 1 (2014), https://pubs.acs.org/doi/pdf/10.1021/es4034952.

24. "All Change!," *Time*, January 9, 1933, pp. 55, 85; and David Gartman, "Tough Guys and Pretty Boys: The Cultural Antagonisms of Engineering and Aesthetics in Automobile History," *Automobile in American Life and Society* (University of Michigan–Dearborn and the Henry Ford, n.d.).

25. According to U.S. Census data, in 1920, Flint's population was 91,559, and it was 2 percent African American. In 1930, the population was 156,492, and it was 4 percent African American.

26. This came out of the League of Nations' Third International Labor Conference, which recommended not only that "white lead be prohibited entirely for paints for interiors" but that "women and children under 16 years of age be not employed where white lead was used in the manufacture of paint," and that for outdoor paint, white lead should be no more than 2 percent of the formula. Between 1909 and 1934, the following countries banned or restricted white lead in interior paint: France, Belgium, Austria, Tunisia, Greece, Czechoslovakia, Great Britain, Sweden, Belgium, Poland, Spain, Yugoslavia, and Cuba. Gerald Markowitz and David Rosner, *Deceit and Denial: The Deadly Politics of Industrial Pollution* (2002; repr. Berkeley: University of California Press, 2013), p. 16.

27. Denworth, *Toxic Truth*, p. 52.

28. David Rosner and Gerald Markowitz, "'A Gift of God'? The Public Health Controversy over Leaded Gasoline During the 1920s," in William Lazonick, ed., *American Corporate Economy: Critical Perspectives on Business and Management* (New York: Routledge Press, 2002), pp. 86–92.

29. Markowitz and Rosner, *Deceit and Denial*, p. 19.

30. Rosner and Markowitz, "'A Gift of God'?," p. 88.

31. Denworth, *Toxic Truth*, p. 37.

32. Ibid., p. 53; and Rosner and Markowitz, "'A Gift of God'?," p. 91.

33. This was at a DuPont chemical plant in Deepwater, New Jersey. The three hundred cases of lead poisoning happened over two years. Much of the reporting that brought it to light was done by the *New York Times*. Markowitz and Rosner, *Deceit and Denial*, p. 25.

34. Ibid., p. 89.
35. Denworth, *Toxic Truth*, p. 58.
36. Ibid., p. 54.
37. Rosner and Markowitz, "'A Gift of God'?," pp. 84–85.
38. Denworth, *Toxic Truth*, p. 54.
39. A wonderful history of how this field developed is told in Fagin's *Toms River*. On its particular challenges: "Trying to determine the environmental trigger of a slow-developing disease was like trying to identify a criminal based on a smudged fingerprint left at the scene of a crime: It required a subjective interpretation of an indistinct impression left behind long after the perpetrator had fled . . . This was the central dilemma of epidemiology, a term coined in the mid-nineteenth century for the study of factors influencing health and disease across populations. Identifying an exposure that appeared to increase the risk of disease in a particular population—whether neuropathy among Venetian artisans or bladder cancer among German dye workers—but what did it prove? It did not prove that the chemical caused any particular case of the disease, since there were probably other potential causes, too. It did not even prove that the apparent link between chemical and disease was important and not a coincidental distraction from the still-hidden true cause. It did not *prove* anything at all. This inherent uncertainty would take on extra significance as the age of industrial chemistry dawned. With the rise of large-scale manufacturing, the outcomes of environmental health debates could affect the economies of entire nations" (pp. 63–64).
40. Denworth, *Toxic Truth*, p. 54.
41. Richard Rabin, "The Lead Industry and Lead Water Pipes 'A MODEST CAMPAIGN,'" *American Journal of Public Health* 98, no. 9 (September 2008).
42. Herbert L. Needleman, "History of Lead Poisoning in the World," n.d., collected as part of Get the Lead Out, a campaign from the Center for Biological Diversity, http://www.biologicaldiversity.org/campaigns/get_the_lead_out/pdfs/health/Needleman_1999.pdf.
43. Denworth, *Toxic Truth*, p. 59.
44. Ibid., p. 64; and Needleman, "History of Lead Poisoning in the World."
45. Denworth, *Toxic Truth*, p. 55.
46. Jerome O. Nriagu, "The Rise and Fall of Leaded Gasoline," *Science of the Total Environment* 92 (1990), http://www.columbia.edu/itc/sipa/envp/louchouarn/courses/env-chem/Pb-Rise&Fall(Nriagu1990).pdf.
47. Other cities banned them, such as Milwaukee in 1962. (Nonetheless, lead pipes remain in use in Milwaukee, and, especially with the patchy records of their location, it's a serious point of contention.) In her written testimony to Congress, dated March 5, 2004, Professor Ellen Silbergeld noted that people have long observed how lead exposure through drinking water can be toxic for human health, especially infants. "In a landmark paper in 1967, Sir Abraham Goldberg and his colleagues traced the etiology of a cluster of mentally retarded children in Glasgow to the storage of drinking water in lead-lined tanks (Gibson et al., 1967). Shannon and Graef (1989) reported

the case of an infant poisoned by drinking water with a lead concentration of 130 ppb."

48. Rabin, "The Lead Industry and Lead Water Pipes."

49. Denworth, *Toxic Truth*, p. 83.

50. Matt Pearce, "A Brief History of How the American Public Was Sold on Toxic Lead," *Los Angeles Times*, February 5, 2016.

51. Gerald Markowitz and David Rosner, "'Cater to the Children': The Role of the Lead Industry in a Public Health Tragedy, 1900–1955," *American Journal of Public Health* 90, no. 1 (January 2000), https://www.ncbi.nlm.nih.gov/pmc/articles/PMC1446124/pdf/10630135.pdf.

52. Ibid.

53. Poor people are also less likely to have adequate health insurance, or any insurance at all, which would help mitigate some of the symptoms of lead exposure. Likewise when it comes to access to fresh, healthy foods. However, as Yanna Lambrinidou has pointed out, it's important to note that many factors can cause lead contamination in water; deteriorating infrastructure is one of them, but with the prevalence of lead pipes and plumbing fixtures it's certainly not the sole cause. "I would liken lead in water more to lead in gasoline (before it was banned). Both invisible, both prevalent, no matter what kind of life one lives/lived" (Yanna Lambrinidou, written comments to the author, February 16, 2018).

54. For this and the paragraph that precedes it, Denworth, *Toxic Truth*, pp. 23–28.

55. Jennifer Crooks sent the initial email in this thread on February 26, 2015, to Stephen Busch, Mike Prysby, and Adam Rosenthal at the MDEQ, and to Thomas Poy and Miguel Del Toral at the EPA, with the subject line: "HIGH LEAD: FLINT Water testing Results." The thread, first revealed through an open records request by Curt Guyette at the ACLU of Michigan, is collected in an (edited) pdf by the Flint Water Study team at Virginia Tech, http://flintwaterstudy.org/wp-content/uploads/2015/10/MDEQ-USEPA-Final.pdf.

56. Email sent on February 27, 2015, to all of the recipients on the thread, plus the MDEQ's Richard Benzie and Liane Shekter-Smith. "Thank you for this information, we will take it under consideration," Stephen Busch responded. He made a bullet-point list about the state of Flint's water system. One item was "Has an Optimized Corrosion Control Program."

57. It's not a precise overlap of the neighborhood, but to get a greater sense of the area, see "A Vision for Thread Lake & Adjoining Neighborhoods in the City of Flint, Michigan," a report prepared by the Planning & Zoning Center at Michigan State University in partnership with the Flint River Watershed Coalition, https://www.canr.msu.edu/uploads/375/65824/VisionThreadLakeAdjoiningNeighborhoods_LPIPZC_FINAL_June2014.pdf. Some details about the house have been drawn from its Zillow listing, last accessed April 10, 2018.

58. Nearly all of the information here and in the following paragraph comes from testimony by LeeAnne Walters in 67th District Court, Flint, Michigan, January 8, 2018, including details from a cell phone video of the garden hose hookup.

59. Denworth, *Toxic Truth*, p. 92.

60. "EPA Takes Final Step in Phaseout of Leaded Gasoline," press release, U.S.

Environmental Protection Agency, January 29, 1996, https://archive.epa.gov /epa/aboutepa/epa-takes-final-step-phaseout-leaded-gasoline.html.

61. "Safe Drinking Water Act 1986 Amendments," U.S. Environmental Protection Agency," https://tinyurl.com/yd4pq38k.

62. This is per Yanna Lambrinidou, medical anthropologist and leading advocate in the D.C. lead-in-water crisis, in a phone interview with the author, November 2, 2017, and also in Lambrinidou's lecture at the Dow Sustainability Fellows Symposium at the University of Michigan, Ann Arbor, November 18, 2017.

63. Ten percent of homes would have to surpass 15 ppb before it triggered a series of requirements. (When utilities report tests, they often refer to the "90th percentile," meaning 90 percent of sampled homes.) So, by the time the action level is exceeded, the lead problem is fairly widespread. Of course, it's a good thing when a jurisdiction's numbers are safely within the legal limits, but many anti-lead advocates point out that, even assuming the tests are done properly, the 90th percentile numbers don't guarantee that lead won't be released in any individual's water at any time. Yanna Lambrinidou, written comments to the author, February 16, 2018.

64. Denworth, *Toxic Truth*, p. 82.

65. The update is in Section 1417 of the Safe Drinking Water Act, approved by Congress on January 4, 2011. Note that there are still a number of "lead free" exemptions.

66. Elin Betanzo (hydraulic engineer), interview with the author, Detroit, Mich., June 20, 2017. The D.C. water system switched to chloramines in November 2000, and research suggested that brass, in particular, was much more susceptible to lead leaching. Marc Edwards and Abhijeet Dudi, "Role of Chlorine and Chloramine in Corrosion of Lead-bearing Plumbing Materials," *AWWA Journal* 96, no. 10 (October 2004).

67. "The Army Corps of Engineers, which controls the Washington Aqueduct used by the District of Columbia's Water and Sewer Authority (WASA), began to use chloramine in November of 2000. This change increased lead corrosion inside the D.C. drinking water system and resulted in elevated water lead levels (WLLS). WASA did not notify the public until 2003, but the notices were unclear and announced meetings to 'discuss and solicit public comments on WASA's Safe Drinking Water Act projects.' As a result, thousands of unwitting D.C. residents and their children were exposed for two years to harmful levels of lead from the water they were drinking and using for cooking and infant formulas. . . . On Saturday, January 31, 2004, a front-page story in the *Washington Post* told the public for the first time that water tests conducted the previous summer by WASA found that thousands of D.C. homes—two-thirds of those tested—had tap water lead levels above the EPA limit of 15 ppb." U.S. House of Representatives, Subcommittee on Oversight and Investigations of the Committee on Science and Technology. "A Public Health Tragedy: How Flawed CDC Data and Faulty Assumptions Endangered Children's Health in the Nation's Capital." Washington, D.C., 2007, p. 6, http://cdm16064.contentdm .oclc.org/cdm/ref/collection/p266901coll4/id/2443.

68. David LaFrance, "Together, Let's Get the Lead Out," *AWWA Connections,* American Water Works Association, March 15, 2016. LaFrance, the CEO of the AWWA, cites a March 10, 2016, survey by the association that suggests there are about 6.1 million lead service lines across the country. His total price tag is based on an estimate that it would cost about $5,000 to replace each one. For the EPA's number, "Lead and Copper Rule Revisions White Paper," Office of Water, U.S. Environmental Protection Agency, October 2016. (Note that this was released in a key month for the Flint water crisis.) On p. 9, the EPA report says that the cost of lead service line replacements ranges between $2,500 and $8,000, "suggesting an estimated cost of eliminating all 6.5 to 10 million" lines nationwide will require spending "16 to 80 billion dollars." It adds that the expense would be borne disproportionately by "specific low-income localities, such as Detroit," which has 100,000 lead lines and has a large percentage of residents living below the poverty line. Also, committing to zero-tolerance would require the elimination of lead from plumbing fixtures, both old and new. Brass fixtures, for example, can leach lead. Yanna Lambrinidou, written comments to the author, February 16, 2018.

69. Gerald Markowitz and David Rosner, *Lead Wars: The Politics of Science and the Fate of America's Children* (Berkeley: University of California Press, 2013), p. 6.

70. "Joint Release from DEP and Newark Public Schools on Temporary Use of Alternate Water Sources After Elevated Levels of Lead Found in Recent District Sampling," New Jersey Department of Environmental Protection, March 9, 2016.

71. Elissa Nuñez and Amy Molloy, "Schools Fail Lead Tests While Many States Don't Require Testing at All," Center for Public Integrity, August 15, 2017.

72. Carol D. Leonnig, Jo Becker, and David Nakamura, "Lead Levels in Water Misrepresented Across U.S.," *Washington Post,* October 5, 2004, p. A1.

73. Erik Olson and Kristi Pullen Fedinick, "What's in Your Water? Flint and Beyond," Natural Resources Defense Council, June 2016.

74. That's according to the CDC's information page about lead (https://www.cdc .gov/nceh/lead/). It includes only children ages one through five who have more than 5 ug/dL of lead in their blood.

75. Markowitz and Rosner, *Lead Wars,* p. 7.

76. Yanna Lambrinidou, written comments to the author, February 16, 2017.

CHAPTER 6: CITIZEN/SCIENCE

1. For the account of Marc Edwards, the author relied primarily on a June 6, 2017, interview with him in Blacksburg, Virginia; emails exchanged in 2017 and 2018; interviews with numerous current and former colleagues; his testimonies before the House Committee on Oversight and Government Reform on February 3, 2016, and March 15, 2016; and several speeches he has given that were videotaped in full.

2. *Time* magazine described the Cuyahoga as a river that "oozes rather than flows."

3. Dan Egan, *The Death and Life of the Great Lakes* (New York: W. W. Norton, 2017), p. 223.

4. It was in 1977 that the *Niagara Gazette* began investigating the pattern of illnesses in Love Canal. Lois Gibbs and her neighbors had also begun taking action. Hooker had dumped the chemicals in the canal from 1942 to 1953. Prior to the sale, the Niagara Falls Board of Education toured it, and the company drilled holes to show the officials what was underneath. About a thousand families lived in the ten-block area. While there was a great deal of attention at the time on the "housewives turned activists" who unearthed the crisis and won a profound environmental victory for both themselves and the nation, Richard S. Newman has observed that the activists have "gone missing" from many histories, suggesting, in the passive tense, that the pollution simply "was discovered" or that "public health concerns" prompted an investigation. Richard S. Newman, *Love Canal: A Toxic History from Colonial Times to the Present* (New York: Oxford University Press, 2016). See also Lois Marie Gibbs and Murray Levine, *Love Canal: My Story* (Albany: State University of New York Press, 1982); and Dan Fagin's recounting of Love Canal in *Toms River: A Story of Science and Salvation* (New York: Bantam, 2013).

5. "Love Canal Chronology," from the *Niagara Gazette*, May 23, 1980, in the Love Canal Collections, University of Buffalo Libraries, https://library.buffalo .edu/specialcollections/lovecanal/about/chronology.php.

6. Fagin, *Toms River*, pp. 129–30.

7. Ibid. "As both place and symbol, Love Canal remains a shrine to the idea that the American landscape could seal away industrial waste forever—and to the counter-notion that buried toxic waste would haunt Americans for a very long time." Newman, *Love Canal*, pp. 2–3.

8. Lois Marie Gibbs, *Love Canal and the Birth of the Environmental Health Movement* (1982, 1998; updated ed., Washington, D.C.: Island Press, 2011), p. 163; and Newman, *Love Canal*, p. 148.

9. The Resource Conservation and Recovery Act of 1976 had first defined hazardous waste and empowered the EPA to intervene to force cleanups, but partly because of the law's limitations and partly because of the EPA's limited capacity, it was enforced at only a relatively few sites. The formal name of the more powerful Superfund law of 1980 is the Comprehensive Environmental Response, Compensation, and Liability Act. If the "Superfund" was tapped to pay for cleanup because the dumpers could not be immediately found, or would not pay until compelled by court, the dumpers might have to pay up to three times what the EPA spent on remediation. Money for the Superfund comes from fees paid by the chemical and petroleum industries and general taxes. Congress also established the Agency for Toxic Substances and Disease Registry (ATSDR) to help hold the line between people and hazardous waste. And one of the other great legacies of Love Canal, of course, was how the community inspired people all over the country to work collectively to improve their environment and public health. Fagin, *Toms River*, pp. 130–31; Newman, *Love Canal*, p. 6.

10. Fagin, *Toms River*, pp. 131, 268. On the 1983 National Priorities List, the state

ahead of Michigan with the most hazardous waste sites was New Jersey. One fifth of the American population lives within a few miles of a Superfund site, according to EPA numbers cited by Newman, *Love Canal*, p. 7.

11. David Nakamura, "Water in D.C. Exceeds EPA Lead Limit," *Washington Post*, January 31, 2004. "Although the extent of the water problem and its public health implications are just coming to light, [the D.C. Water and Sewer Authority] officials have been aware of the contamination since random tests on a small number of houses revealed a problem in 2002. Although agency officials discovered a more extensive problem last summer, they did not begin to notify homeowners about the results until November. WASA held a public meeting about the issue in December, but its advertisements did not reveal the lead problem. Instead, they simply stated that the purpose of the meeting was 'to discuss and solicit public comments on WASA's Safe Drinking Water Act projects.'"

12. Even accounting for what happened in Flint, the lead contamination of D.C.'s drinking water stands out in modern U.S. history, in both severity and duration. Edwards would later describe it as thirty times worse than Flint: two times the duration, three times the amount of lead in the water, and five times the number of children exposed to it ($2 \times 3 \times 5 = 30$). Marc Edwards, email message to author, February 17, 2018; "Experiences and Observations from the 2001–2004 'DC Lead Crisis,'" Testimony of Marc Edwards to the U.S. House of Representatives Committee on Science and Technology, May 17, 2010. (Edwards also testified about the D.C. lead crisis to U.S. House Government Reform Committee in March 2004); and Donovon Hohn, "Flint's Water Crisis and the 'Troublemaker' Scientist,'" *New York Times Magazine*, August 16, 2016.

13. Robert McCartney, "Virginia Tech Professor Uncovered Truth about Lead in D.C. Water," *Washington Post*, May 23, 2010. (Both the headline and the column, alas, erase the many resident community organizers who did a tremendous amount of work on their own to expose the truth.)

14. The 2004 report, which has twenty-one coauthors, is titled "Blood Lead Levels in Residents of Homes with Elevated Lead in Tap Water." It was published in the CDC's *Morbidity Mortality Weekly Review*.

15. McCartney, "Virginia Tech Professor Uncovered Truth."

16. The D.C. Water and Sewer Authority had a testing procedure that involved pre-flushing the taps for ten minutes the night before sampling six to eight hours before the test. Michael Birnbaum, "WASA Lead Test Procedure Gives False Reading, Groups Say," *Washington Post*, August 1, 2008; and Yanna Lambrinidou, written comments to the author, February 16, 2018.

17. Marc Edwards, "Fetal Death and Reduced Birth Rates Associated with Exposure to Lead-Contaminated Drinking Water," *Environmental Science & Technology* 48 (2014).

18. He's talked about this a number of times in public speeches, including his 2016 SciFest presentation in St. Louis, and in communication with the author (2017). According to Yanna Lambrinidou (written communication, February 16,

2018), the FOIA requests from Edwards focused on health harm between 2001 and 2004. She and other resident activists, including Ralph Scott, Harrison Newton, and Paul Schwartz, sent requests primarily about information after 2004, "including additional public health harm as well as water utility and government cheating in water sampling, flaws in official investigations of wrong-doing, flawed implementation of the LCR, science journal wrongdoing, etc., etc." Altogether, this played a pivotal role in revealing wrongdoing in both D.C. and nationally.

19. Marc Edwards, Simoni Triantafyllidou, and Dana Best, "Elevated Lead in Young Children Due to Lead-Contaminated Drinking Water, Washington, D.C., 2001–2004," *Environmental Science & Technology* 43, no. 5 (2009). The *Washington Post* published an article about it on January 27, 2009 (Carol D. Leonnig, "High Lead Levels Found in D.C. Kids"). Edwards's quote here comes from a talk he gave at the St. Louis Science Center on February 22, 2017.

20. Carol D. Leonnig, "CDC Misled District Residents About Lead Levels in Water, House Probe Finds," *Washington Post*, May 20, 2010.

21. Ibid.

22. Ibid.

23. Ibid.; and Yanna Lambrinidou, phone interview with the author, November 2, 2017.

24. Yanna Lambrinidou, phone interview with the author, November 2, 2017.

25. McCartney, "Virginia Tech Professor Uncovered Truth."

26. Marc Edwards, interview with the author, Blacksburg, Virg., June 6, 2017; and Marc Edwards, email message to author, February 17, 2018.

27. Yanna Lambrinidou and Marc Edwards, "Five Myths About Lead in Water," *Washington Post*, February 26, 2016. In D.C., Lambrinidou adds that community organizers "worked like rabid dogs" to bring attention to the dangers of partial-line replacements. "It took months of killer work to achieve. Without that work, I believe that no one would have known about the problem of DC's partials." (Yanna Lambrinidou, written comments to the author, February 16, 2018.)

28. Edwards, "Fetal Death and Reduced Birth Rates." The study was published online in December 2013 and was also reported in the paper: Carol D. Leonnig, "Increase in Miscarriages Coincided with High Levels of Lead in D.C. Water, Study Finds," *Washington Post*, December 9, 2013.

29. Marc Edwards, "Saving Humankind from Itself: Careers in Science and Engineering as Public Policy," SciFest presentation, St. Louis Science Center, February 22, 2017.

30. The course earned recognition by the National Academy of Engineering. Lambrinidou has also taught a class that has similar themes: "Experts and the Public: Ethical Frameworks." Siddhartha Roy, interview with the author, June 2017; and Marc Edwards, interview with author, Blacksburg, Virg., June 6, 2017; Yanna Lambrinidou, written comments to the author, February 16, 2018.

31. Marc Edwards, email message to author, February 17, 2018.

32. LeeAnne Walters shared a document with Del Toral that listed the chemicals that the city plant used to treat the water. No orthophosphates or any other form of corrosion inhibiter was on the list. As Del Toral told Donovon Hohn: "I couldn't believe that they didn't have corrosion control," particularly since the Flint River "was corrosive as hell." Hohn, "Flint's Water Crisis and the 'Troublemaker' Scientist"; and LeeAnne Walters's testimony before the Michigan Joint Select Committee on the Flint Water Public Health Emergency, March 29, 2016.

33. On April 23, 2017, Del Toral wrote to Cook: "What's Flint doing now (post Detroit) for corrosion control treatment?" After discussing the question with Mike Prysby and other MDEQ colleagues, Cook replied on April 24: "Flint is currently not practicing corrosion control at the WTP" because "there are not additional requirements for the City of Flint based on the levels of lead and copper in the source water and the results of the lead and copper distribution monitoring." However, he added, "we will re-evaluate this after the 2nd round of 6 month sampling is completed." Del Toral's description of this as "very concerning" was in a lengthy email sent April 27, 2015, to four EPA colleagues: "Pat Cook has confirmed that following the disconnection from Detroit, Flint has not been operating any corrosion control treatment, which is very concerning given the likelihood of LSLs in the city." These emails are collected in the batch of communications called DEQ4 (February 2016 update), released by the Office of Governor Snyder on a Michigan.gov site, http://www.michigan.gov/snyder/0,4668,7-277-57577_57657-376716—,00.html, last accessed on February 21, 2018.

34. Marc Edwards, email to the author, March 3, 2018; and Yanna Lambrinidou, written comments to the author, February 20, 2018.

35. Testimony by LeeAnne Walters, 67th District Court, Flint, Michigan, January 8, 2018.

36. Del Toral's report also described how the corrosion of the infrastructure was made worse by the decision to use a new coagulant to treat the water after the switch from Detroit. It helped remove organic matter, but a side effect of this particular coagulant was the potential to exacerbate the corrosion of galvanized lead in the plumbing—the last thing Flint needed.

37. Del Toral wrote this in an email to the EPA's Rita Bair, Nicholas Damato, and Jennifer Crooks on June 25, 2015. He added, "If there truly is a question in anyone's mind that there is a widespread lead problem in Flint, despite the painfully clear science, I am requesting that I be provided two assistants and that you folks allow me to go and sample 100 homes in Flint without the pre-flushing and then we can satisfy any doubts that anyone may have. I am not even asking for a per diem and I'll pay my own hotel."

38. Guyette's story is primarily drawn from the author's interviews with him in Detroit, Mich., on October 21, 2015, and September 12, 2017, from his reporting and films, and from email exchanges and a handful of presentations he's given. Some of this material appeared in a previous form in an article by the author for the *Columbia Journalism Review*: "How an Investigative Journalist Proved a City Was Being Poisoned with Its Own Water" (November 3, 2017).

39. According to Guyette, as of September 2017, this model has since been repli-cated at ACLU chapters in Texas, Florida, and Virginia.

40. Mitch Smith, "A Water Dilemma in Michigan: Cloudy or Costly?," *New York Times*, March 24, 2015.

41. Curt Guyette, interviews with the author, Detroit, Mich., October 21, 2015, and September 12, 2017, as well as an email message to the author, July 11, 2017.

42. *Bridge* Staff, "Flint Crisis Timeline: Part 3," *Bridge Magazine*, March 1, 2016 (quoting email of July 7, 2015, from MDEQ Public Information Officer Karen Tommasulo to MDEQ Communications Director Brad Wurfel).

43. This email exchange is recorded as part of the House Oversight Committee's 2016 investigation into the Flint water crisis, available online: https://oversight .house.gov/wp-content/uploads/2016/02/7-1-7-2-Emails-from-Hedman-to -Mayor-Walling-of-Flint.pdf.

44. Some of the material about Michigan Radio here and elsewhere in the book originally appeared in an article by the author: "How Covering the Flint Water Crisis Has Changed Michigan Radio," *Columbia Journalism Review* (February 16, 2016).

45. Kate Wells, "Flint Artist Makes Installation out of Water Bottles to Highlight Water Safety Issues," Michigan Radio, May 29, 2015.

46. Lindsey Smith, "Leaked Internal Memo Shows Federal Regulator's Concerns about Lead in Flint's Water," Michigan Radio, July 13, 2015. Smith had also asked the EPA for comment, but the agency declined an interview. It only issued a bland written statement that said, in part, that the "EPA conducted limited drink-ing water sampling . . . in response to a citizen complaint. The initial results and staff recommendations to management were documented in an internal memo-randum, which was cited in the ACLU article. EPA will work with Michigan DEQ and the City of Flint to verify and assess the extent of lead contamination issues and to ensure that Flint's drinking water meets federal standards."

47. Of course, the city's population had been below one hundred thousand when the previous round of tests were done, too.

48. Lindsey Smith, "Not Safe to Drink," Michigan Radio, December 15, 2015.

49. Marc Edwards, email to the author, March 3, 2018.

50. When researchers later looked into the official Flint tests in 2014 and 2015, they observed that the results suggested that "only a small percentage of homes with LSLs [lead service lines] was sampled, leading to under-estimation of lead at the tap compared to legal requirements. It was later acknowledged that the Flint sampling pool did not target homes with LSLs as required by law, and use of the University of Michigan-Flint database indicates that only 9 of the homes sampled in the 'official' 2014 pool (n=96 of 100; 4 homes could not be located) and only 7 homes sampled in 2015 (n=69) had LSLs." Kelsey J. Pieper, Rebekah Martin, Min Tang, LeeAnne Walters, Jeffrey Parks, Siddhartha Roy, and Marc A. Edwards, "Evaluating Water Lead Levels During the Flint Water Crisis," submitted to *Environmental Science & Technology*, excerpt provided by email to the author from Marc Edwards, March 4, 2018. The reference to the UM-Flint database acknowledges the hard work of Dr. Marty Kaufman and a team that he led at the Geographic Information Systems Center at the

university. They dove into all the scattered material available to build a complete digital database of the location of lead service lines in the city. They announced the results of the project in a press conference at city hall, alongside Mayor Karen Weaver, in February 2016 (UM-Flint News, "New UM-Flint Research Shows Location of Lead Pipes in Flint," UM-Flint NOW, February 22, 2016).

51. Paul Egan, "State's Handling of Flint Water Samples Delayed Action," *Detroit Free Press*, December 23, 2015, updated December 24, 2015.

52. Ibid.

53. "Flint's Mayor Drinks Water from Tap to Prove It's Safe," WNEM-TV5, July 9, 2015.

54. LeeAnne Walters's testimony before the Michigan Joint Select Committee on the Flint Water Public Health Emergency, March 29, 2016, and Walters's testimony before the 67th District Court on January 8, 2018, during the preliminary examinations in the criminal case against four MDEQ employees.

55. "*Here's to Flint*: Broadcast Premiere of ACLU Documentary on the Fight for Democracy and Clean Water," *Democracy Now!*, March 8, 2016.

CHAPTER 7: MEDITATIONS IN AN EMERGENCY

1. Here, I am counting communities that were appointed managers through Public Act 101 (1988), Public Act 72 (1990), and the earliest stage of Public Act 4 (2011). Among them: Royal Oak Township, Hamtramck, Highland Park, the Village of Three Oaks, Pontiac, Ecorse, Benton Harbor, and twice for Flint. In addition, by Election Day 2011, two school districts received emergency managers, in Inkster and Detroit.

2. About the political calculus: "The only thing I can think of is that the governor had decided that he was going to appoint an emergency manager, and he wanted to do it regardless of whether the white or black candidate was the next mayor. Right, so . . . that they look like this is a race-neutral decision. If we're going to do it, we have to announce it before the votes are tallied. That's the only thing I can think of" (Dayne Walling, interview with the author, Flint, Mich., June 22, 2017).

3. Flint Financial Review Team, "Report of the Financial Review Team," State of Michigan Department of Treasury, November 7, 2011, https://www.michigan .gov/documents/treasury/Flint-ReviewTeamReport-11-7-.

4. Ibid. Walling disputed that, noting he had to authorize police and firefighter layoffs, and experimented with doing garbage pickup every other week. Dayne Walling, interview with the author, Flint, Mich., June 22, 2017.

5. Dayne Walling, interview with the author, Flint, Mich., June 22, 2017.

6. This number is current as of at least August 2015. Joshua Sapotichne et al., "Beyond State Takeovers: Reconsidering the Role of State Government in Local Financial Distress, with Important Lessons for Michigan and Its Embattled Cities," white paper, Michigan State University Extension, August 31, 2015, p. 16, http://msue.anr.msu.edu/uploads/resources/pdfs/beyond_state_takeovers.pdf.

7. Chris Megerian, "NJ Has a History of State Takeovers of Local Governments, Agencies," NJ.com–*Star Ledger*, July 20, 2010.

8. Pennsylvania law says that a request for a state determination of financial distress can come from a simple majority vote from the city council; the "chief executive officer of any city" or the governing body of a municipality; 10 percent of the electors of the most recent local election; creditors owed $10,000 or more (if they agree to suspend legal action); and six other entities with a stake in the city's fiscal health. Bob Bauder, "Pittsburgh No Longer 'Financially Distressed,' According to State Oversight Team," *Tribune-Review*, November 16, 2017; and 47 Pa.C.S. § 202 (1987), http://www.legis.state.pa.us/cfdocs/legis/LI/uconsCheck.cfm?txtType=HTM&yr=1987&sessInd=0&smthLwInd=0&act=47&chpt=2&sctn=2&subsctn=0.

9. Jenna Carlesso, "Oversight Board Would Review Cities' Budget Decisions, Contracts," *Hartford Courant*, October 24, 2016.

10. The author wrote about emergency management for the *New Republic* when the city she lives in, Detroit, was put under it ("Detroit's Least Bad Option," March 14, 2013). Some of this material first appeared there.

11. Danny Hakim, "For Flint, Mich., Takeover Adds to the List of Woes," *New York Times*, July 10, 2002. The quoted Michigan treasurer is Doug Roberts.

12. On Flint's early history with emergency management: Elizabeth Carvlin, "Michigan to Weigh Allowing Flint to Issue Deficit Elimination Plans," *Bond Buyer*, June 22, 2004; Mary Doidge et al., "The Flint Fiscal Playbook: An Assessment of the Emergency Manager Years (2002–2005)," white paper, Michigan State University Extension, July 31, 2015; Oona Goodin-Smith, "Flint's History of Emergency Management and How It Got to Financial Freedom," MLive—*Flint Journal*, July 16, 2018; Beata Mostafavi, "What Happened Last Time? A Look Back at Flint's 2002 State Takeover," MLive—*Flint Journal*, November 10, 2011; as well as interviews with Senator Jim Ananich (Lansing, Michigan, June 21, 2017); Mayor Dayne Walling (Flint, Michigan, June 9 and June 22, 2017); U.S. Representative Dan Kildee (Flint, Michigan, September 16, 2016); and Richard Baird, Flint native and senior adviser to Governor Snyder (Lansing, Michigan, October 24, 2016); as well as interviews with a large number of people who work and live in Flint and other emergency-managed cities.

13. For more on the legal distinction, see, for example, "Frequently Asked Questions: The Suspension of the Emergency Manager Law and Its Implications," Michigan State University Extension, August 14, 2012, http://msue.anr.msu.edu/uploads/files/Greening/MSUE-PA4Suspension_FAQ-9-7-12.pdf; and Jonathan Oosting, "Snyder Signs Replacement Emergency Manager Law: We 'Heard, Recognize, and Respected' Will of Voters," MLive—*Flint Journal*, December 27, 2012.

14. "The Flint Water Crisis," Michigan Civil Rights Commission, pp. 110–11.

15. A basic principle of municipal law is Dillon's Rule. Named after a nineteenth-century judge, it says that cities have only the powers that are explicitly granted by the entity that created them. There are some exceptions, such as New York City and Baltimore, that operate on a home rule basis. Nicole DuPuis et al.,

"City Rights in an Era of Pre-Emption: A State-by-State Analysis," National League of Cities Center for City Solutions, 2017; Alisha Green, "It's Complicated: State and Local Government Relationships," Sunlight Foundation, February 19, 2013; Jesse J. Richardson Jr., Meghan Zimmerman Gough, and Robert Puentes, "Is Home Rule the Answer? Clarifying the Influence of Dillon's Rule on Growth Management," discussion paper, Brookings Institution Center on Urban and Metropolitan Policy, January 2003.

16. David Sands, "Joyce Parker, Ecorse Emergency Manager, Credits Public Act 4 with City's Turnaround," *Huffington Post*, March 15, 2012, updated March 16, 2012; and Tracy Samilton, "Ecorse Financial Emergency Resolved . . . BUT . . . ," Michigan Radio, April 30, 2013.

17. Brief for the Latino Justice PRLDF and Demos in support of petitioners as Amicus Curiae, p. 16, *Bellant v. Snyder* on Petition for Writ of Certiorari to the U.S. Court of Appeals for the Sixth Circuit, No. 16-1207, May 10, 2017, http://www.demos.org/publication/brief-amici-curiae-latinojustice-prldf-and -demos-support-petitioners-bellant-v-synder.

18. "The Flint Water Crisis," Michigan Civil Rights Commission, p. 109.

19. From the Senate Judiciary Committee's 1982 report that accompanied the extension and amendment of the Voting Rights Act of 1965: "Following the dramatic rise in registration, a broad array of dilution schemes were employed to cancel the impact of the new black vote. Elective posts were made appointive; election boundaries were gerrymandered; majority runoffs were instituted to prevent victories under a prior plurality system; at-large elections were substituted for election by single-member districts, or combined with other sophisticated rules to prevent an effective minority vote. The ingenuity of such schemes seems endless. Their common purpose and effect has been to offset the gains made at the ballot box under the Act." S. Rep. No. 97-417, p. 10 (1982), as quoted in *Presley v. Etowah County Commission*, 502 U.S. 491 (1992).

20. According to a 2017 report from the National League of Cities, Michigan's actions were of a piece with a growing tendency of states to preempt local governments on politically divisive matters, such as labor protections or taxing authority. Michigan stands alongside North Carolina, Tennessee, Wisconsin, Louisiana, and Florida as the biggest "preemptor" states in the country, with their power to "preempt" deriving from single-party dominance—that is, Republican control of both legislative chambers and the governor's office. To many in Michigan, emergency management also seemed like piling on: voting rights had already been diminished through the state legislature's gerrymandering of congressional and legislative districts. A controversial reapportionment process that basically allows lawmakers to choose their voters had created disproportionately conservative leadership in Lansing—and no one seemed to be stepping up to oppose it or creating a process for fairer representation. Also, in January 2016, Governor Snyder signed a bill that abolished straight-ticket voting in Michigan, even though the practice had been supported in two statewide referendums. The abolishment was passed in an end-of-year amendment

with no public hearings. Straight-ticket voting tended to be popular with voters in busy urban—and Democratic—precincts.

21. From the National Advisory Commission on Civil Disorders, *Kerner Report*: "In these cities, the police were compelled to deal with ghetto residents angered over dirty streets, dilapidated housing, unfair commercial practices, or inferior schools—grievances which they had neither the responsibility for creating nor the authority to redress" (p. 288). "The alienation of the Negro from the political process has been exacerbated by his economic and racial isolation" (p. 289). "These conditions have produced a vast and threatening disparity in perceptions of the intensity and validity of Negro dissatisfaction. Viewed from the perspective of the ghetto resident, city government appears distant and unconcerned, the possibility of effective change remote. As a result, tension rises perceptibly; the explosion comes as the climax to a progression of tension-generating incidents. To the city administration, unaware of the growing tension or unable to respond effectively to it, the outbreak of disorder comes as a shock" (p. 289).

22. The final count had 52.6 percent of voters against the law and 47.4 percent in favor of it. In the same election, Michigan voters supported President Barack Obama's reelection over challenger Mitt Romney, a native of the state and the son of former Michigan governor George Romney. They also rejected a proposal to enshrine a right to collective bargaining for public and private workers in the state's constitution.

23. The grand bargain was facilitated by Chief U.S. District Judge Gerald Rosen, acting as a mediator, and U.S. Bankruptcy Judge Steven Rhodes. It involved enormous contributions from philanthropists and charitable foundations: Ford, Kresge, Knight, and the C. S. Mott Foundation were among them. That was leveraged to secure a commitment from the state. This unprecedented public-private deal brought new money to the table, helping to resolve a bankruptcy that otherwise would have likely dragged on with legal challenges that some thought was destined for the U.S. Supreme Court. The foundations made it a condition of their contributions that the unions and pension funds endorse the deal with a majority vote. General retirees ended up with cuts of 4 percent to their pensions; police and fire retirees did not have cuts. It was far less than what was expected from the bankruptcy. The bargain also shifted ownership of the city-owned Detroit Institute of Arts, whose collection was eyed by hungry creditors, to a charitable nonprofit trust. The DIA also contributed to the grand bargain. To date, the best comprehensive account is *Detroit Resurrected: To Bankruptcy and Back* by Nathan Bomey, a former *Free Press* reporter who covered it day by day (W. W. Norton, 2016). The *Detroit News* has a good rundown, too: Daniel Howes, Chad Livengood, and David Shepardson, "Bankruptcy and Beyond for Detroit," November 13, 2014.

24. "Frequently Asked Questions: The Suspension of the Emergency Manager Law and Its Implications," Michigan State University Extension, August 14, 2012.

25. Ibid.; and Ann Zaniewski, "DPS Board Loses Court Battle over Emergency Manager," *Detroit Free Press*, October 1, 2014.

26. Gerald Ambrose, Emergency Manager Gerald Ambrose to Governor Rick Snyder, Flint, Michigan, April 28, 2015. Regarding the parting order mentioned in the following sentence, this refers to Order No. 20, dated April 25, 2015, and signed by Ambrose. It had a number of stipulations. Among them, in addition to restricting the city leaders from funding the Office of the Ombudsman, it also forbid them from funding the Civil Service Commission. The Civil Service Commission had been established about eighty years earlier to investigate labor disputes between employees and the city and at Hurley Medical Center. Both offices were mandated by the Flint City Charter, and their existence had been supported by voters (though Mayor Walling had been among those who had proposed their elimination, due to budget challenges).

27. On the strike: Sidney Fine, *Sit-Down: The General Motors Strike of 1936–1937* (Ann Arbor: University of Michigan Press, 1969); Russell B. Porter, "Strikers at Flint March as Victors," *New York Times*, February 12, 1937, pp. 1, 15; Louis Stark, "Peace Pact Signed," *New York Times*, February 12, 1937, pp. 1, 19; and "The Flint Sit-Down Strike Audio Gallery," matrix at Michigan State University and Walter P. Reuther Library, http://flint.matrix.msu.edu/strike.phphttp://flint.matrix.msu.edu/strike.php.

28. Melissa Mays's website had a form for people to describe their water, their health issues, and the cost of their water bill; with their permission, the information was sent on to the government.

29. Curt Guyette, interview with the author, Detroit, October 21, 2015.

30. Curt Guyette, interview with the author, Detroit, September 12, 2017.

31. Marc Edwards, Amy Pruden, and Joseph Falkinham, "RAPID: Synergistic Impacts of Corrosive Water and Interrupted Corrosion Control on Chemical/ Microbiological Water Quality: Flint, MI," p. A-1, submitted July 2015, http://flintwaterstudy.org/wp-content/uploads/2015/08/rapid-proposal-final.pdf.

32. Ibid.

33. Curt Guyette, interview with the author, Detroit, September 12, 2017.

34. "Sampling Water for Lead in Flint MI—Instruction Video," Flint Water Study, YouTube video, 5.34 minutes, August 14, 2015, https://www.youtube.com /watch?v=dEQDaPws2xk.

35. This meant that the samples generally had to be collected first thing in the morning or, if nobody was at home during the day, in the early evening. According to the EPA's Safe Drinking Water Task Force, the six-hour minimum of stagnation time "is used rather than a longer time so as not to discourage people from volunteering to take lead and copper samples" (Task Force Comments on Flint's Residential Drinking Water Lead & Copper Sampling Instructions, November 23, 2015).

36. According to released emails, the MDEQ defended this lead-clearing practice to the EPA that summer, saying that it wasn't going to change its position unless the agency issued stricter regulations. To date, that loophole has not been closed, though upon review of the sampling protocol that had been used in Flint, the EPA's Flint Safe Drinking Water Task Force said that it "agrees with the removal of pre-flushing" (ibid). For discussion on the potential revision of

the Lead and Copper Rule by the EPA's National Drinking Water Advisory Council (NDWAC) Lead and Copper Rule (LCR) working group, see its August 2015 report (https://www.epa.gov/sites/production/files/2017-01 /documents/ndwaclcrwgfinalreportaug2015.pdf) and also the dissenting statement by one of its members, Dr. Yanna Lambrinidou (Yanna Lambrinidou, letter to the EPA National Drinking Water Advisory Council, October 28, 2015, https://www.epa.gov/sites/production/files/2015-11/documents/ndwaclcr statementofdissent.pdf).

37. The parallel sampling done directly by the Virginia Tech team also helped the citizen sampling to withstand scrutiny. Curt Guyette, interview with the author, Detroit, September 12, 2017; and Marc Edwards, email message to author, February 17, 2018.

38. Curt Guyette, interview with the author, Detroit, October 21, 2015, September 12, 2017; and *"Here's to Flint," Democracy Now!*, March 8, 2016.

39. Ibid.

40. Curt Guyette, interview with the author, Detroit, October 21, 2015.

41. On August 23, 2015, Edwards emailed Adam Rosenthal of the MDEQ; Rachel Ptaszenski of the Genessee County Health Department; and Brent Wright, Flint's water plant supervisor. He told them that Virginia Tech would be studying Flint's water, launching a website, and had already visited the city to collect samples from the distribution system. He also said that they were doing a lead study with residents. "Dependent on what we find, it might be desirable to touch base, in advance of our releasing certain findings. We also intend to collaborate with all parties, in an open manner, to the extent that is possible, as our study progresses." The following morning, Rosenthal forwarded the message to Stephen Busch, who forwarded it to Richard Benzie and Liane Shekter-Smith. Jennifer Dixon, "How the Crisis Unfolded," *Detroit Free Press*, January 24, 2016, p. A14.

42. That website was WASAwatch, http://dcwasawatch.blogspot.com. Yanna Lambrinidou referred the author to it in a phone interview, November 2, 2017.

43. According to the Virginia Tech researchers, 269 were legitimate samples. Those that were excised had not waited for six hours of stagnation, for example, or had used a different faucet for one of its samples. For the complete data set, see Siddhartha Roy, "[Complete Dataset] Lead Results from Tap Water Sampling in Flint, MI," FlintWaterStudy.org, December 1, 2015. See also "Lead Testing Results for Water Sampled by Residents," FlintWaterStudy.org, n.d. (but appears to be early September 2015).

44. Curt Guyette, interview with the author, Detroit, September 12, 2017.

45. The water had a lot of corroded iron in it—51 ppb, for both homes and hospitals. Iron is not regulated the way lead is because it is not nearly as dangerous (and in fact a certain amount of it is essential to human health). But the EPA's suggested guideline is for iron not to exceed 300 ppb (0.3 milligram per liter) in drinking water.

46. Many people began to look back at the boil-water advisories the previous summer and wonder if they had made the lead contamination worse, because boiling

concentrated it. According to Edwards, "brief boiling does not remove lead, and does not concentrate it" while long-term boiling "might, but people rarely boil water to the point that concentration occurs." Marc Edwards, email message to author, February 17, 2018.

47. Siddhartha Roy, interview with the author, Blacksburg, Virginia, June 6, 2017. But Roy credited his colleague Anurag Mantha, who kept going. Mantha made dozens of calls, answering every question and listening to the families' fears and fury at the injustice of it all, Roy said. Sometimes calls lasted an hour.

CHAPTER 8: BLOOD

1. Flint Water Study, "Flint Press Conference Sep 15 2015 (One Year Anniversary Release)," YouTube Video, 21.29 minutes, September 17, 2016, https://www.youtube.com/watch?v=xwg5L3mYUEI. See also Ron Fonger, "Virginia Tech Professor Says Flint's Tests for Lead Are Bad and Can't Be Trusted," MLive—*Flint Journal*, September 15, 2015.

2. Siddhartha Roy, "For the Citizens of Flint," slideshow presentation at Saints of God Church, Flint, Michigan; Flint Water Study, September 15, 2015, slide 24, available online at http://flintwaterstudy.org/2015/09/distribution-of-lead-results-across-flint-by-ward-and-zip-codes/.

3. Sonya Lee interview by Cherise Lee, April 16, 2016, StoryCorps, Library of Congress, Washington, D.C., SC1001065.

4. Brad Wurfel sent this in an email to Ron Fonger of the *Flint Journal* on September 9, 2015, according to chronologies by the Flint Water Study team and *Bridge Magazine*. The message was partially quoted in Fonger's story the following day: "Feds Sending in Experts to Help Flint Keep Lead out of Water," MLive—*Flint Journal*, September 10, 2015.

5. Brad Wurfel sent this email on August 27, 2015. Captured in the chronological compilation of MDEQ emails from FOIA requests posted on FlintWaterStudy.org on October 10, 2015.

6. See also Joel Kurth, Jonathan Oosting, Christine MacDonald, and Jim Lynch, "DEQ Official: Staffers Earn Raises for Flint Work," *Detroit News*, February 12, 2016.

7. Ron Fonger, "Governor Helped Hush-Hush Delivery of Water Filters to Flint Pastors," MLive—*Flint Journal*, September 29, 2015.

8. Ibid.

9. Email sent from Michelle Bruneau to Kory Groestch on September 10, 2015. Meanwhile, internal conversations between the EPA and the MDEQ acknowledged the "further evidence that lead levels in Flint are trending upward." The agencies were now under pressure by residents, scientists, and, increasingly, Flint's representatives in Lansing and Washington to deal with the lack of corrosion control soon, "to protect the residents from exposure to high lead levels." This amounted to a tacit admission that the water concerns were credible, but any validation was undercut by the public criticism of the activists and scientists and the continued defense of the official tests showing the water was safe. It didn't

help that while the MDEQ had agreed to a corrosion control plan in Flint, it kept arguing about it with the EPA. But either way, it was going to take a long time to implement the treatment—long enough that it probably made the point moot.

10. This section relies primarily on the author's June 20, 2017, interview with Elin Betanzo in Detroit, Michigan, as well as her email responses to follow-up questions; and on Dr. Mona Hanna-Attisha's testimonies to numerous investigative committees; and on a profile: Robin Erb, "Flint Doctor Makes State See Light about Lead in Water," *Detroit Free Press*, October 10, 2015, updated October 12, 2015.

11. Erb, "Flint Doctor Makes State See Light."

12. "Hurley Doctor Recommends Switching Away from Flint River," MLive, YouTubeVideo, 1.04 minutes, September 24, 2015, https://www.youtube.com/watch?v=6tELb594WTw.

13. Erb, "Flint Doctor Makes State See Light."

14. Nancy Kaffer, "When Did State Know Kids in Flint were Lead Poisoned?," *Detroit Free Press*, December 17, 2015.

15. Kristi Tanner and Nancy Kaffer, "State Data Confirms Higher Blood-Lead Levels in Flint Kids," *Detroit Free Press*, September 26, 2015, updated September 29, 2015.

16. The study was eventually published in a peer-reviewed journal. Mona Hanna-Attisha, Jenny LaChance, Richard Casey Sadler, and Allison Champney Schnepp, "Elevated Blood Lead Levels in Children Associated with the Flint Drinking Water Crisis: A Spatial Analysis of Risk and Public Health Response," *American Journal of Public Health* 106, no. 2 (February 1, 2016): 283–90. See also Sammy Zahran, Shawn P. McElmurry, and Richard C. Sadler, "Four Phases of the Flint Water Crisis: Evidence from Blood Lead Levels in Children," *Environmental Research* 157 (2017): 160–72.

17. Erin Einhorn, "The Hero of Flint's Water Crisis," *Alumnus*, Spring 2015.

18. "Fight Song," Hurley Medical Center/MLive, "Hurley Children's Hospital, creates heartwarming video to 'Fight Song,'" YouTube video, 3.55 minutes, August 25, 2015, https://www.youtube.com/watch?v=w-TE3ulFWno.

19. The email was sent from Debbie Balthazar to Timothy Henry and Steve Marquadt on September 24, 2015. It was part of a batch of EPA emails that were released in May 2016 as part of the investigation by the U.S. Committee on House Oversight and Government Reform, https://oversight.house.gov/wp-content/uploads/2016/03/Documents-for-the-Record.pdf.

20. Tanner and Kaffer, "State Data Confirms."

21. "Public Health Emergency Declaration for People Using the Flint City Water Supply with the Flint River as a Source," Genesee County Board of Commissioners, October 1, 2015, http://www.gc4me.com/docs/public_health_emergency_announcement_10_1_15.pdf.

22. On Mission of Hope, see Scott Atkinson, "In Bad Times and Worse, Pastor Bobby Is Flint's Water Man," *Belt Magazine*, January 25, 2016; and Jessica Dupnack, "Mission of Hope in Flint Looking for Donations to Reopen Full Time," ABC12 WJRT-TV, August 25, 2015.

23. Monica Davey, "Flint Officials Are No Longer Saying the Water Is Fine," *New York Times*, October 7, 2015.

24. Key details in this section, and the conversation with Brad Wurfel, are sourced here: Erb, "Flint Doctor Makes State See Light."

25. Ibid.

26. Steve Carmody, "State Plan for Flint's Water Woes Doesn't Please Some Residents," Michigan Radio, October 2, 2015.

CHAPTER 9: SWITCHBACK

1. *"Here's to Flint*: Broadcast Premiere of ACLU Documentary on the Fight for Democracy & Clean Water," *Democracy Now!*, March 8, 2016. Connecting to Detroit water was deemed the quickest way to get corrosion control running through Flint's pipes again, and more and more people had begun advocating for it. On September 28, 2015, Senate Minority Leader Jim Ananich sent an email to Governor Rick Snyder's office demanding a "swift transfer to a safe source of water until the Karegnondi Water Authority is complete next year." Dennis Muchmore, the governor's chief of staff, was already crunching the numbers for a switchback on October 1, the day of the state's reversal, though he also harbored concerns about how "some of the Flint people respond by looking for someone to blame instead of working to reduce anxiety," according to one of his internal emails. "We can't tolerate increased lead levels in any event, but it's really the city's water system that needs to deal with it." But, in an update to Snyder, Muchmore also said that a reconnection "may well be the only way to bring any confidence back to the community." Snyder replied: "We should help get all of the facts on the consequences of changing back vs. staying and then determine what financing mechanisms we have available. If we can provide the financing, then we should let Flint make the decision." Jim Lynch, Chad Livengood, and Jonathan Oosting, "Snyder Emails Detail State's Missteps in Flint Crisis," *Detroit News*, January 20, 2016, updated January 21, 2016.

2. LeeAnne Walters, written testimony to the Michigan Joint Select Committee on the Flint Water Public Health Emergency, Flint, Michigan, March 29, 2016.

3. LeeAnne Walters's testimony in the 67th District Court, Flint, Michigan, on January 8, 2018, during the preliminary examinations in the criminal case against four MDEQ employees.

4. Marc Edwards, "Saving Humankind from Itself: Careers in Science and Engineering as Public Policy," SciFest presentation, St. Louis Science Center, February 22, 2017.

5. Monica Davey, "Flint Will Return to Using Detroit's Water After Findings of Lead in Local Supply," *New York Times*, October 8, 2015.

6. City of Flint and Genesee County Drain Commissioner, "License to Transmit Water," October 14, 2015.

7. Editorial Board, "Flint Water Crisis: An Obscene Failure of Government,"

Detroit Free Press, October 8, 2015. The switchback happened on October 16, 2015.

8. Dominic Adams, "Toxic Lead Levels Found in Water at Three Flint Schools," MLive—*Flint Journal*, October 8, 2015.

9. Amanda Emery, "Flint Reconnects to Detroit Water, May Take 3 Weeks to Clear All Pipes," MLive—*Flint Journal*, October 16, 2015, updated September 19, 2017.

10. Michael Freeman, phone interview with the author, January 2016; and "Notice of Class Action Administrative Complaint Against the United States Environmental Protection Agency," April 25, 2016, http://www.flintwaterclassaction .com/wp-content/uploads/Flint-EPA-Complaint.pdf.

11. Marc Edwards, email message to the author, February 17, 2018.

12. "I am proud of the many accomplishments that I have been a part of over the years, including assisting in the development of our fifty year Master Plan, a multi-year Capital Improvement Plan, and a prioritized plan to deal with the aging infrastructure," Croft added in his letter. He also said he'd "like to applaud all of the departmental employees who by no fault of their own have encountered drastic changes in staffing, equipment, and work environment, yet they continue to provide daily services to the absolute best of their ability." Howard Croft, letter to Natasha L. Henderson, city administrator, City of Flint, November 16, 2015.

13. John Wisely and Robin Erb, "State Admits Mistakes in Flint Water Switch," *Detroit Free Press*, October 19, 2015.

14. "Lime softening was used to address the hardness of the water," Wyant said. "While this has an impact on pH, testing bore out that more needed to be done." When a *Detroit News* reporter put Edwards's contention before the director, he said simply that he was "relaying what staff and consultants have indicated to me." "DEQ Director Dan Wyant Issues Statement About Flint Drinking Water," Michigan Department of Environmental Quality, October 19, 2015, http://www.michigan.gov/deq/0,4561,7-135—367529—,00.html.

15. Jim Lynch, "Michigan DEQ Vows Changes in Flint Water Crisis," *Detroit News*, October 18, 2015, updated October 19, 2015.

16. "It is important for large systems and primary agencies to take the steps necessary to ensure that appropriate corrosion control treatment is maintained at all times, thus ensuring that public health is protected. . . . Corrosion control can come in many forms. For this reason, it is important to conduct a system-wide assessment prior to any source water and/or treatment modifications and to identify existing or anticipated water quality, treatment or operational issues that may interfere with or limit the effectiveness of corrosion control treatment." Peter C. Grevatt, "Lead and Copper Rule Requirements for Optimal Corrosion Control Treatment for Large Drinking Water Systems," U.S. Environmental Protection Agency, Memorandum to EPA Regional Water Division Directors, Regions I-X, November 3, 2015.

17. Tinka G. Hyde, "Transmittal of Final Report—High Lead at Three Residences in Flint, Michigan," memorandum to Jim Sygo, Michigan Department of

Environmental Quality, and Howard Croft, director of Flint Public Works, U.S. Environmental Protection Agency, November 4, 2015. Hyde added that the final report did have some new information: it recommended that residents be notified about "the potential risks of increased lead levels in drinking water when work is undertaken that may disturb lead service lines." The final report itself was dated October 21, 2015.

18. The five-member task force included Ken Sikkema, senior policy fellow at Public Sector Consultants and a former senate majority leader; Chris Kolb, president of the Michigan Environmental Council and a former state representative; Matthew Davis, professor of pediatrics and internal medicine at the University of Michigan Health System and professor of public policy at the university's Ford School; Eric Rothstein, national water issues consultant for Galardi Rothstein Group who advised on the creation of the Great Lakes Water Authority; and Lawrence Reynolds, a Flint pediatrician who served as president of the Mott Children's Health Center. "Transitioning back to the Detroit Water and Sewerage Department-Great Lakes Water Authority is a good first step to protecting public health in Flint, but it's not the last step," said Snyder in the press release. "Bringing in outside experts to evaluate our actions and help monitor and advise on potential changes to law, procedures and practices will be key to continuing work on the comprehensive action plan and ensuring safe drinking water for all the residents in Flint and all of Michigan." "Gov. Rick Snyder announces Flint Water Task Force to review state, federal and municipal actions, offer recommendations," press release, Office of Governor Snyder, October 21, 2015.

19. Flint Water Advisory Task Force, letter to Governor Snyder, December 28, 2015. The task force also said that, after meeting with MDEQ director Dan Wyant, it was "disappointing to hear his weak defense" of the corrosion control decision.

20. It was only six months later, after the residents and the Flint Water Study group had conducted the citywide lead test, that the EPA took formal steps to provide two experts to the MDEQ who could give technical assistance in Flint. (Susan Hedman, the Region 5 director, had also offered them to Mayor Dayne Walling in July 2015.) Internal emails and "Notice of Class Action Administrative Complaint Against the United States Environmental Protection Agency," April 25, 2016, http://www.flintwaterclassaction.com/wp-content/uploads /Flint-EPA-Complaint.pdf.

21. Senate Minority Leader Jim Ananich was livid. "It is clear from several, now available documents, that certain MDEQ and EPA staff chose to put their reputations ahead of the safety and health of Flint citizens," he said in a statement. "We do not know whether the misapplication of federal rules was intentional or due to negligence." He pushed for a robust investigation that would ensure that "those responsible for Flint's water crisis are held accountable" (John Wisely, John Erb, and Robin Erb, "State Admits Mistakes in Flint Water Switch," *Detroit Free Press*, October 19, 2015). Later, Ananich described his incredulity at how people in the state's government "lied to my face . . . multiple times" when he inquired about the water in Flint, speaking both as the community's

elected senator and as a resident whose young family had been drinking water. "And I still can't understand why" (Jim Ananich, interview with author, Lansing, Mich., June 21, 2017).

22. Dan Wyant directed the Department of Agriculture under Governor John Engler and Governor Jennifer Granholm. He became the director of the MDEQ in January 2011. In accepting his resignation, Snyder called it "appropriate." Marc Edwards and Dr. Mona Hanna-Attisha told a reporter they felt that it was something of a surprise that Wyant was the first to resign due to the Flint water crisis. "I'm glad that someone is sorry and someone is being held accountable," said Edwards. "But Dan Wyant would not be at the top of my list—or even on the list. I feel strongly he was misled by his staff at every point, and he was put in publicly embarrassing situations by the staff's misinformation." Hanna-Attisha said he was a "nice person" who "wasn't directly involved," and that "there are other people, particularly in [the Office of Drinking Water and Municipal Assistance] that need to take some responsibility." Jim Lynch, "Flint Water Report Prompts Apologies, Resignations," *Detroit News*, December 29, 2015. In January 2016, according to his LinkedIn profile, Wyant returned to a previous job: president of the Edward Lowe Foundation in Cassopolis, Michigan (last accessed March 4, 2018).

23. Emily Lawler, "DEQ Spokesman Also Resigns over Flint Water Crisis, Says City 'Didn't Feel Like We Cared,'" MLive—*Flint Journal*, December 30, 2015. Wurfel went on to work at a government consulting firm that specializes in Lansing lobbying, according to his LinkedIn profile and the website of Kandler Reed Khoury & Muchmore (both last accessed March 4, 2018).

24. Emery, "Flint Reconnects to Detroit Water."

25. Katrease Stafford, "Faces of Flint," *Detroit Free Press*, January 22, 2016.

26. Ron Fonger, "See How Flint Supported Mayor Karen Weaver in Election Win," MLive—*Flint Journal*, November 11, 2015.

27. Ron Fonger, "Mayor Karen Weaver Declares Water Crisis State of Emergency in Flint," MLive—*Flint Journal*, December 14, 2015, updated December 15, 2015. Fonger goes on to report on how the council's response was mixed, unclear about the ramifications. Councilman Scott Kincaid said that it would help the community show "that we need resources" and make it possible for Flint "to apply for state and federal funds." Councilman Joshua Freeman said that he didn't want residents to expect the declaration to result in immediate help, particularly with the lead service lines. "We need to find a way to actually fix the problem. This declaration does not [do that]."

28. There were exceptions, of course, including a *New York Times* story on Flint's return to Detroit water, but they were usually in the form of an independent dispatch, rather than the sustained attention usually given to a disaster that affects tens of thousands of people.

29. As before, some of the material on Michigan Radio appeared in an earlier form in "How Covering the Flint Water Crisis Changed Michigan Radio," *Columbia Journalism Review*, February 16, 2016.

30. Lindsey Smith, "Not Safe to Drink," Michigan Radio, December 15, 2015. It

aired one day after Mayor Weaver declared a state of emergency on December 14, 2015. "Knowing I was giving this to my kids makes me sick, because we should be able to trust the fact that we're paying for this service," LeeAnne Walters told Smith on the broadcast. "And we should be able to trust the fact that it's not going to harm our kids."

31. The series "An American Disaster: The Crisis in Flint" earned Rachel Maddow a 2016 Emmy Award from the National Academy of Television Arts and Sciences for "Outstanding News Discussion and Analysis." About a month after she began reporting on the water, Maddow hosted a live town hall in Flint, broadcast from the Brownell/Holmes STEM Academy. It featured a number of residents as well as Mayor Weaver, Dr. Mona Hanna-Attisha, Marc Edwards, master plumber Harold Harrington, and UM-Flint professor Marty Kaufman, who was leading a team working to rebuild Flint's spotty water records. State Rep. Sheldon Neeley, U.S. Senator Debbie Stabenow, Rev. Jesse Jackson, and Rev. Charles Williams II, president of the National Action Network's Michigan chapter, were also at the town hall. With a five-hundred-person capacity, tickets for the town hall sold out. Watch parties sprung up around the state.

32. Jan Worth-Nelson, phone interview with the author, January 2016.

33. Ibid.; and Jan Worth-Nelson, "Beam, Arch, Pillar, Porch: A Love Story," in Scott Atkinson, ed., *Happy Anyway: A Flint Anthology* (Cleveland: Belt Publishing, 2016). This quote from Maddow appears to be from her December 18, 2015, show, "Is Flint habitable anymore? Really?," *The Rachel Maddow Show*, MSNBC, http://www.msnbc.com/transcripts/rachel-maddow-show /2015-12-18.

34. Nearly fifteen years of work went into evaluating how the city should get its drinking water, predating the era of emergency management.

35. Paul Egan, "Did DEQ Budget Cuts Contribute to the Flint Water Crisis?," *Detroit Free Press*, March 23, 2016.

36. It was then about $1.53 million a year, down $300,000 from the previous year. Public Water System Supervision Program, Office of Ground Water & Drinking Water, U.S. Environmental Protection Agency, "Final Report: Program Review for the Michigan Department of Environmental Quality Water Bureau," prepared by the Cadmus Group, Washington, D.C., August 30, 2010, https:// www.epa.gov/sites/production/files/2015-11/documents/program-review -mdeq-water-bureau-20100830-76pp_0.pdf. See also Ted Roelofs, "Signs of Trouble at MDEQ, Years before Flint Lead Crisis," *Bridge Magazine*, February 10, 2016.

37. "The Flint Water Crisis," Michigan Civil Rights Commission, p. 112.

38. Michael Glasgow, written testimony to the Michigan Joint Select Committee on the Flint Water Public Health Emergency, Flint, Mich., March 29, 2016; and Dayne Walling, testimony to the Michigan Joint Select Committee on the Flint Water Public Health Emergency, Flint, Mich., March 29, 2016.

39. For his part, Mayor Walling felt that the KWA plan still supported regionalism, but of a different kind: it banded together communities along the I-69 corridor (interview with author, Flint, Mich., June 22, 2017). Jeff Wright felt

that Schroeck and others used "Southeast Michigan" rather loosely. "When Detroit, Wayne, Oakland, and Macomb Counties want something like water revenue, Flint and Genesee County become a part of Southeast Michigan. But, when those governments are not looking for something, Flint and Genesee County are not. When there is federal money to be distributed, Flint and Genesee County are nowhere near Southeast Michigan much less a part of it." Jeff Wright, "The Flint Water Crisis, DWSD, and GLWA: Monopoly, Price Gouging, Corruption, and the Poisoning of a City," written testimony, Michigan Civil Rights Commission, November 22, 2016, p. 27.

40. That was Ed Kurtz. Later, when he testified before a congressional committee, he said that his job was "strictly finance" and "did not include ensuring safe drinking water." He said he did not have a responsibility to prevent lead contamination; that was the responsibility of the MDEQ and EPA, he said. He also claimed that he "never made a decision to use Flint River water" as a temporary source. Ron Fonger, "Former Flint EM: 'My Job Did Not Include Ensuring Safe Drinking Water,'" MLive—*Flint Journal*, May 2, 2017; Ron Fonger, "Detroit Was 'Mad, Angry Vindictive' in Flint Water Talks, Former EM Claims," MLive—*Flint Journal*, May 2, 2017.

41. For the backstory on the politics of the KWA, the author owes a great deal to Wayne State University law professor Peter Hammer, both for an interview in Detroit, August 18, 2016, and for the testimonies he gave before the Michigan Civil Rights Commission, as well as the responding testimony it prompted from Jeff Wright. Peter J. Hammer, "The Flint Water Crisis, KWA and Strategic-Structural Racism," written testimony, Michigan Civil Rights Commission, July 18, 2016; Peter J. Hammer, "The Flint Water Crisis, KWA and Strategic-Structural Racism: A Reply to Jeff Wright," written testimony, Michigan Civil Rights Commission, December 31, 2016; and Wright, "The Flint Water Crisis," Civil Rights Commission.

42. The email was sent on December 19, 2013, from Nicole Zachado, an enforcement specialist in the Water Resources Division, to her boss, William Creal. "Having met with Steve Busch and others . . . my suspicions have been confirmed and this really does not strike me as our issue" in the Water Resources Division, she added. Creal relayed this to Liane Shekter-Smith, the drinking water chief, and asked if the request for an environmental order in Flint would be better handled by her staff. Shekter-Smith replied, "That's part of my conundrum. We don't have an enforcement action with them," adding that "I need to speak to Steve Busch to understand what the 'ask' is." In the end, "the order was officially handled by a third DEQ section, the Office of Waste Management and Radiological Protection," writes Paul Egan of the *Detroit Free Press*, "though records show Busch played an active role in finalizing wording that would be agreeable to KWA bond attorneys." Paul Egan, "'Sweetheart' Bond Deal Aided Flint Water Split from Detroit," *Detroit Free Press*, May 11, 2016, updated May 12, 2016.

43. Hammer, "The Flint Water Crisis, KWA and Strategic-Structural Racism: A Reply to Jeff Wright," p. 28.

44. Ibid., p. 18.

45. Ibid., pp. 29–30.
46. Egan, "'Sweetheart' Bond Deal."
47. Flint Water Advisory Task Force, "Final Report," March 2016.

CHAPTER 10: LEGION

1. This parallels the process of how the governor made a formal request to Washington before a federal emergency was declared. However, according to one of the emails released by the governor's office, there was some flexibility to this rule. Captain Chris Kelenske of the Michigan State Police, who doubled as the deputy state director of emergency management and homeland security, wrote in an email to a governor's aide on November 13, 2015: "As you know, the Governor can declare at any time for any reason." There were advantages and disadvantages to acting before the local officials did, according to Kelenske's outline of the issue. On one hand, it would open up the opportunity to seize leadership of the relief response and put key funding reserves toward it. But on the other hand, he added, state funding was being provided through other means, and not getting a request for help implied that local leaders didn't need further resources. Moreover, "the state will formally own the event if we put a Governor's Declaration in place," Kelenske wrote. "This could be viewed as having owned up to how the water issue was caused (e.g., 'The triggering event was caused by the state; the state is now declaring.')." And it would also set a precedent "for issuing a state declaration for an infrastructure maintenance event. What if lead is found in other areas of the state's drinking water due to infrastructure issues? This action opens the door to any other jurisdiction with water quality issues." When asked about the discrepancy between this email and the repeated contention that the governor's office could not act until local officials did, a spokesperson said that there had been "a misunderstanding." Declarations of emergency by the state usually happened only in the wake of extreme one-time events, rather than a long-developing crisis, such as the one in Flint; that contributed to the confusion. Paul Egan, "E-mails: Snyder Could Have Declared Flint Emergency Sooner," *Detroit Free Press*, February 28, 2016, updated February 29, 2016; Paul Egan, "Snyder Declares Emergency as Feds Probe Flint Water," *Detroit Free Press*, January 5, 2016, updated January 15, 2016; and "Proclamation: Declaration of Emergency," State of Michigan Executive Office, January 5, 2016. Incidentally, January 5, 2015, was also the same day that the U.S. Attorney's Office confirmed that it was working with the EPA to investigate the crisis. Usually the Attorney's Office neither confirms nor denies the existence of an investigation, but it made an exception on account of how many Flint residents were reaching out to it.
2. Some of these details, and the quoted signs, come via the photos captured by MLive—*Flint Journal* ("9 Takeaways from Michigan Gov. Rick Snyder's State of the State Address," January 20, 2016); the *Detroit News* ("Snyder to Flint: I'm Sorry and I'll Fix It," January 20, 2016); and the *Detroit Free Press* ("Gov. Snyder's Speech, with Flint Water Protests," photo gallery, January 19, 2016).

3. They also made an appearance in Flint during the sit-down strike in the 1930s.

4. "Get Clean Water Locations," Taking Action on Flint Water, Michigan.gov, last accessed March 4, 2018, http://www.michigan.gov/flintwater/0,6092,7 -345-75251_75271—,00.html.

5. Ryan Garza, "Living with Lead," *Detroit Free Press*, January 31, 2016, pp.15A–17A.

6. She testified about this during the public comments portion of the July 14, 2016, hearing in Flint by the Michigan Civil Rights Commission.

7. Garza, "Living with Lead."

8. Lewis said that she went through the arduous routine of filling the cauldron of her slow cooker with bottled water, heating it, and pouring it into the tub until it was full enough for bathing because otherwise the tap water caused her skin to break out in painful rashes. Yvonne Lewis, phone interview with the author, September 9, 2017; and Yvonne Lewis, testimony before the Michigan Civil Rights Commission, Flint, Mich., July 14, 2016.

9. Elderly people also often lacked a photo ID. The requirement was lifted on January 22, 2016. When word began spreading about the obstacles that undocumented people faced in getting water, a number of volunteer groups reached out with donations for them, including the Flint Jewish Federation, the Service Employees International Union, and a Baptist church in Rhode Island that delivered two semitrucks of water. Niraj Warikoo, "Immigrants Left in Dark," *Detroit Free Press*, February 4, 2016, pp. 1A, 7A.

10. Ibid.

11. David W. Lurvey, letter to Mark Bouvey, SOM Board of Education, January 21, 2016, http://www.michiganschoolforthedeaf.org/sites/michiganschool-forthedeaf.org/files/1.21.16_re_flint_water_crisis_response_0.pdf.

12. Robert Allen, "Readers Help Flint Brothers Who Trek Miles for Water," *Detroit Free Press*, January 24, 2016, p. 15A.

13. Sherman McCathern, phone interview with author, January 2016.

14. Madison Eggert-Crowe and Scott Gabriel Knowles, "Bicentennial (1976)," *Encyclopedia of Greater Philadelphia* (New Brunswick, N.J.: Rutgers University, 2013).

15. Lawrence K. Altman, "In Philadelphia 30 Years Ago, an Eruption of Illness and Fear," *New York Times*, August 1, 2006.

16. Not too far, as it happens, from where the Centre Square Pump House stood, the heart of one of America's first efforts at providing public water. Carl Smith, *City Water, City Life: Water and the Infrastructure of Ideas in Urbanizing Philadelphia, Boston and Chicago* (Chicago and London: University of Chicago Press, 2013).

17. Theodore Tsai et al., "Legionnaires' Disease: Clinical Features of the Epidemic in Philadelphia," *Annals of Internal Medicine* (April 1, 1979); Lily Rothman, "This Is How Legionnaires' Disease Got Its Name," *Time*, August 12, 2015; and "The Philadelphia Killer," *Time*, August 16, 1976.

18. Altman, "In Philadelphia 30 Years Ago."

19. Andrea Farnham, Lisa Alleyne, Daniel Cimini, and Sharon Balter, "Legionnaires'

Disease Incidence and Risk Factors: New York, New York, USA, 2002–2011," *Emerging Infectious Diseases* 20, no. 11 (November 2014): 1795–1803.

20. Rothman, "This Is How Legionnaires' Disease."

21. Altman, "In Philadelphia 30 Years Ago."

22. Ibid. The author is using its current name as a narrative convenience, but at the time, this institution was known as the U.S. Public Health Service's Center for Disease Control.

23. ". . . here was an invisible, impersonal mass killer on the loose. The knowledge rekindled, despite all the advances of modern medicine, humanity's ancient memories of epidemics beyond understanding or control" ("The Philadelphia Killer").

24. Boyce Rensberger, "Testing Casts Doubt on Nickel Carbonyl as Cause of Legionnaires' Illness," *New York Times*, September 11, 1976; "The Philadelphia Killer"; Altman, "In Philadelphia 30 Years Ago"; and F. William Sunderman. "Perspectives on Legionnaires' Disease in Relation to Acute Nickel Carbonyl Poisoning," Henry M. Scharf Lecture on Human Affairs, *Annals of Clinical and Laboratory Science* 7, no. 3 (1977).

25. In 1968, the same bacteria had caused a less serious infection about forty miles from Flint, in Pontiac, Michigan. The duly named Pontiac fever had bedeviled visitors to the city's Health Department, causing fever and muscle aches. But no one had yet realized that the bacteria could also induce what we now call Legionnaires' disease. The 1977 discovery also solved the mystery of an outbreak in Washington, D.C., in the summer of 1965, when a severe respiratory illness at St. Elizabeth's Hospital overtook at least eighty-one patients, fourteen of whom died.

26. Abby Goodenough, "Legionnaires' Outbreak in Flint Was Met with Silence," *New York Times*, February 22, 2016; and Lenny Bernstein and Brady Dennis, "Did Flint's Contaminated Water Cause Legionnaires' Outbreaks?" *Washington Post*, February 27, 2016.

27. Monica Davey and Mitch Smith, "Emails Reveal Early Suspicions of a Flint Link to Legionnaires' Disease," *New York Times*, February 4, 2016; and Roberto Acosta, "Survivor 'Stunned' by Spike of Legionnaires' in Genesee County," MLive—*Flint Journal*, January 21, 2016.

28. Monahan's case was in the summer of 2014. Goodenough, "Legionnaires' Outbreak in Flint"; Bernstein and Dennis, "Did Flint's Contaminated Water"; and "MDHHS Issues Update to 2015 Legionnaires' Disease Report for Genesee County," press release, Michigan.gov, April 11, 2016, https://www.michigan .gov/som/0,4669,7-192-29942_34762-381701—,00.html.

29. Daniel Bethencourt, "Snyder: Flint Has Seen Spike in Legionnaires' Disease," *Detroit Free Press*, January 13, 2016, updated January 15, 2016; and Michigan Department of Health and Human Services and Genesee County Health Department, "Legionellosis Outbreak-Genesee County, June, 2014–March 2015, Full Analysis," January 15, 2016, https://www.michigan.gov/documents/mdhhs/6-14 _to_3-15_Legionellosis_Report_Full_Analysis_Results_511708_7.pdf.

30. Henry filed the public records request on January 25, 2015. Goodenough, "Legionnaires' Outbreak in Flint"; and Emma Winowiecki, "How Flint's

Legionnaires' Disease Outbreak Led to Five Charges of Involuntary Manslaughter," Michigan Radio, June 14, 2017.

31. Wurfel ended his long email by saying that "regardless, the accusation is serious and the nature of the communication leaves me thinking we would be advantaged to bring together all the agencies asap to share what information we have and develop a response/screening strategy before the weather gets warm again" (Brad Wurfel, "Part II," email to Harvey Hollins, cc Dan Wyant, March 13, 2015). This email was part of the communications released by the Office of Governor Snyder on a Michigan.gov site. The author viewed this email in a collection collated by Channel 4/Click on Detroit, http://media.clickondetroit.com /document_dev/2016/02/04/297679613-Wurfel-to-Hollins-Email-Legionnaires _2061126_ver1.0.pdf. (Mara MacDonald, "Email warned Snyder's aide early of possible link between Legionnaires' surge, Flint water," February 4, 2016.)

32. The MDEQ was wary enough of the outbreak, though, for Brad Wurfel to tell the governor's office in January 2015 that they were waiting for "the results of some county health department traceback work" before his agency would feel able "to say publicly that the water in Flint is safe." Jonathan Oosting, "Legionnares' Fear Led Staffer to Warn Against Calling Water Safe," *Detroit News*, February 26, 2016.

33. Sarah Kaplan, "Flint, Mich., Has 10 Fatal Cases of Legionnaires' Disease; Unclear If Linked to Water," *Washington Post*, January 14, 2016; and Goodenough, "Legionnaires' Outbreak in Flint."

34. "Flint Water Advisory Task Force Final Report," March 2016, p. 19. The quoted CDC researcher is Laurel Garrison. Matthew Dolan, Elisha Anderson, Paul Egan, and John Wisely, "Flint E-mails: CDC Voiced Concerns over Legionnaires' Actions," *Detroit Free Press*, February 9, 2016.

35. Kaplan, "Flint, Mich., Has 10 Fatal Cases"; and Goodenough, "Legionnaires' Outbreak in Flint." This message came from Jim Collins, MDHHS's communicable disease division director, to Jim Henry and other Genesee County officials in a June 8, 2015, email. It was also Collins who concluded in June 2015 that "the outbreak was over," as the last reported case was the previous March. "The lack of clinical Legionella isolates precludes our ability to link cases to an environmental source." Chad Livengood and Karen Bouffard, "Emails: State Mum on Flint Legionnaires' Warning," *Detroit News*, February 12, 2016.

36. This was from a report that the Genesee County Health Department submitted to the CDC's outbreak reporting system in November 2015. For its part, the MDHHS complained that the county had not accepted its advice or help. Sarah Cwiek, "State's Chief Medical Officer: Flint Legionnaires' Probe Followed 'Standard Practice,'" Michigan Radio, February 15, 2016.

37. Goodenough, "Legionnaires' Outbreak in Flint."

38. Kaplan, "Flint, Mich., Has 10 Fatal Cases."

39. Jim Lynch and Jonathan Oosting, "Snyder: Legionnaires' Cases Spike in Flint Area," *Detroit News*, January 13, 2016.

40. "Legionellosis Outbreak—Genesee County, June 2014–March 2015: Summary

Analysis," Michigan Department of Health and Human Services and Genesee County Health Department, updated January 15, 2016, https://gchd.us/wp -content/uploads/2016/08/6-14-to-3-15-Legionellosis-Report_Investigation -Summary-Analysis.pdf.

41. Fifty-two of the fifty-four cases that were associated with hospital/health care facilities in Genesee County were also at McLaren, including forty-five of the forty-six inpatient cases. "MDHHS Orders McLaren Flint to Comply with Action to Address Legionella Risk," press release, Michigan Department of Health and Human Services, February 14, 2017.

42. The problem of insufficient patient samples was acknowledged in the May 2015 report from the MDHHS, but apparently there was not a push to collect more of them during another spike of Legionnaires' cases that summer. It's believed that samples weren't collected because patients were presumptively treated with antibiotics after a positive urine test for *Legionella*. After that, specimens would be too indeterminate to be used as evidence.

43. Flint Water Advisory Task Force, "Final Report," March 2016; and Davey and Smith, "Emails Reveal Early Suspicions."

44. There were seventeen cases of Legionnaires' disease in 2016, according to the Genesee County Health Department, two of which were associated with McLaren Flint. This was still higher than in the years before the outbreak began, but far less than its peak. Some concerned activists have doubted the official numbers, wondering how often the disease was misdiagnosed.

45. Steve Carmody, "New Tests Raise Questions About the Source of Legionnaires' Disease Outbreak," Michigan Radio, February 16, 2017.

46. Measurements from samples collected from homes in and around Flint were compared to measurements from baseline U.S. water surveys conducted by both this research team and the EPA, and from Flint buildings that were still connected to a Lake Huron water source. Interviews with Amy Pruden, Siddhartha Roy, and Marc Edwards, Blacksburg, Virginia, June 6, 2017; and Janet Pelley, "Legionnaires' Outbreaks in Flint Linked to Corrosive Water," *Chemical & Engineering News*, July 25, 2016. The team described the potential for an outbreak of Legionnaires' disease when it submitted its grant application to the National Science Foundation in July 2015: "We are also concerned about possible health effects that have not yet been investigated. For example, in March 2015 Region 5 EPA was provided reports of higher incidence of Legionnaires' disease associated with bacteria growth in premise plumbing in the Flint area. Legionnaires' disease has recently been acknowledged to be the primary source of waterborne disease outbreaks (and associated deaths) in the U.S. Despite that acknowledged risk, there is currently no required monitoring for this important pathogen in consumers' homes, where it proliferates and can lead to human exposure and infection in showers." Marc Edwards, Amy Pruden, and Joseph Falkinham, "RAPID: Synergistic Impacts of Corrosive Water and Interrupted Corrosion Control on Chemical/Microbiological Water Quality: Flint, MI," p. D-2, submitted in July 2015, http://flintwaterstudy.org /wp-content/uploads/2015/08/rapid-proposal-final.pdf.

47. David Otto Schwake, Emily Garner, Owen R. Strom, Amy Pruden, and Marc A. Edwards, "Legionella DNA Markers in Tap Water Coincident with a Spike in Legionnaires' Disease in Flint, MI," *Environmental Science & Technology Lett.* 3, no. 9 (2016): 311–15. See also William J. Rhoads, Emily Garner, Pan Ji, Ni Zhu, Jeffrey Parks, David Otto Schwake, Amy Pruden, and Marc Edwards, "Distribution System Operational Deficiencies Coincide with Reported Legionnaires' Disease Clusters in Flint, Michigan," *Environmental Science & Technology* 51, no. 20 (2017): 11986–95.

48. Flint Water Advisory Task Force, "Final Report," March 2016.

49. G. Brenda Byrne, Sarah McColm, Shawn P. McElmurry, Paul E. Kilgore, Joanne Sobeck, Rick Sadler, Nancy G. Love, and Michele S. Swanson, "Prevalence of Infection-Competent Serogroup 5 *Legionella pneumophila* within Premise Plumbing in Southeast Michigan," *mBio* 9, no. 1 (February 6, 2018); and Sammy Zahran, Shawn P. McElmurry, Paul E. Kilgore, David Mushinski, Jack Press, Nancy G. Love, Richard C. Sadler, and Michele S. Swanson, "Assessment of the Legionnaires' Disease Outbreak in Flint, Michigan," *PNAS* (February 2018).

50. It was Harvey Hollins who made the request, the governor's urban affairs specialist who saw the warning email from Jim Henry at the Genesee County Health Department. McElmurry said that Hollins told him that money for the study "was no issue, no problem." Karen Bouffard, "Flint Water Switch Led to Most Legionnaires' Cases," *Detroit News*, February 5, 2018, updated February 6, 2018. The research team worked in partnership with Flint residents and was supported with funding from the MDHHS, the National Science Foundation, the National Institutes of Environmental Health Sciences, Wayne State University, Michigan State University, and the University of Michigan. It also discovered that the specific *Legionella* strain that was found in Flint residences was not one that was detected by ordinary *Legionella* tests. After Flint returned to a Lake Huron water source, the prevalence of *Legionella* bacteria in local homes fell back to normal levels. In response to the studies, an MDHHS spokesperson issued a statement, using the acronym for the research team's formal name, the Flint Area Community Health and Environment Partnership: "By publishing these inaccurate, incomplete studies at this point, FACHEP has done nothing to help the citizens of Flint and has only added to the public confusion on this issue." It also submitted a rebuttal. MDHHS discontinued funding for the studies in December 2017—it provided $3.1 million in 2016 and had promised $1 million more—after the researchers rejected the oversight of an outside firm, KWR Watercycle Research Institute. MDHHS hired KWR to provide an "external, independent third party" review of the studies after they were released. It's worth noting that even as MDHHS director Nick Lyon faced criminal charges for the agency's role in the Legionnaires' outbreak, including for involuntary manslaughter, he was still directing the agency all this time. Likewise with Dr. Eden Wells, who continued in her role as chief medical executive while she faced charges. In November 2017, a few months before the studies were released, McElmurry was a witness for the prosecution in the preliminary exams against Wells and Lyon.

51. Edwards went so far as to file a formal complaint with Michigan regulators, arguing that McElmurry used false pretenses to secure substantial grant funding. It specifically described "his lack of competence and expertise" and suggested that he appropriated another person's ideas in one of his research proposals. An aggressive case against him and his team was further developed on FlintWaterStudy.org, indiciating that their research was leading to trumped-up criminal charges against MDHHS officials—two of whom Edwards had backed up with testimony for the defense during their preliminary examinations. The Virginia Tech team pointed to its two peer-reviewed studies that said that the Flint River switch "was one key factor contributing to the Legionnaires' Disease outbreak and associated deaths," but it also emphasized that "At no point did anyone at MDHHS or the governor's office discourage or impede our teams ground-breaking research that helped reveal the Flint Legionella outbreak" ("FACHEP vs. The People of the State of Michigan: Part I Dr. Shawn McElmurry," FlintWaterStudy.org, March 29, 2018). McElmurry and his FACHEP team (the Flint Area Community Health and Environment Partnership) passionately defended themselves. "The claims made against our group are false and they are examples of unprofessional and destructive conduct. . . . It is very unfortunate when individuals resort to personal and unfounded attacks. Such attacks do not help us advance understanding or help the people of Flint. Rather, they confuse, contribute to rumors and create more harm. Sadly, there is a well-established pattern of distortions and misinformation by some of the individuals and investigators associated with Flint." (Statement in Response to False Accusations about FACHEP, March 30, 2018). The multidisciplinary FACHEP team included experts from the University of Michigan, Michigan State University, Colorado State University, the Henry Ford Health System, and Kettering University, one of whom was Dr. Laura Sullivan. FACHEP also worked closely with Flint residents to carry out their work. In a separate news release, Wayne State University also responded to the allegations: "We have the utmost respect for the commitment and character of Dr. McElmurry and the FACHEP research team. As scientists and members of the community, we all have a responsibility to maintain the highest standards in all we do. We have no doubt that Dr. McElmurry and his colleagues take this responsibility very seriously, and work tirelessly toward these goals for the public good" (Wayne State University statement on accusation, press release, Wayne State University, April 4, 2018).

52. Leonard N. Fleming, "WSU Prof: Flint Water Switch Prompted Outbreak," *Detroit News*, November 15, 2017.

53. Melissa Mays, written testimony to the Michigan Joint Select Committee on the Flint Water Public Health Emergency, Flint Public Hearing, Flint, Mich., March 29, 2016.

54. Taylor became part of a lawsuit against McLaren. Goodenough, "Legionnaires' Outbreak in Flint"; and *Kidd v. McLaren Flint Hospital*, Case No. 16-106199-NO, Genesee County Circuit Court. Taylor wasn't the only patient whose Legionnaires' diagnosis may have been buried. Betty Marble, a sixty-eight-year-old

woman from Grand Blanc, died during her second visit to McLaren in March 2015. Her death certificate cites cardiac arrest brought on by septic shock due to pneumonia. Her medical files twice mention *Legionella*. As Chastity Pratt Dawsey pointed out in *Bridge Magazine* ("In Flint, Questions About Legionnaires' Death Toll," June 28, 2016), the hospital was well aware of its *Legionella* problem at this point, but it didn't try to test Marble for the disease until her second visit, just days before she died. By that point, she was unable to produce urine for a test, and a throat culture was ruled inconclusive. As one of her sons told Dawsey, "Why didn't they tell us they had *Legionella* in their hospital and they were testing her for it?" It's stories like this one—along with a 64 percent spike in pneumonia and flu cases in 2014—that have left many wondering if the official toll of Legionnaires' disease leaves out many who had contracted it. In early 2016, McLaren announced that it was spending $300,000 on an upgrade to its water system.

55. National Advisory Commission on Civil Disorders, *Kerner Report*, p. 20.

56. The jobs program was called Flint WaterWorks, and it was funded by private donations. Young people were paid for their work on door-to-door outreach and mapping lead service lines. Kathleen Gray, "Message from Flint to Trump: Where the Hell Have You Been?," *Detroit Free Press*, September 14, 2016; and Amy Crawford, "In Flint, Providing Safe Water Is a Full-Time Job," *City-Lab*, January 25, 2017.

57. Susan Selasky, "Ways to Cut Water Use in the Kitchen." Compiled with help from the Free Press Test Kitchen, Erin Powell, and Bethany Thayer, *Detroit Free Press*, February 14, 2016, p. 7A; Susan Selasky, "Program Gets Flint Residents to the Grocery," *Detroit Free Press*, February 14, 2016, p. 7A.

58. Susan Hedman, written testimony to the House Committee on Oversight and Government Reform, Washington, D.C., March 15, 2016, https://oversight.house .gov/wp-content/uploads/2016/03/Hedman-Statement-3-15-Flint-Water-II.pdf.

59. Oona Goodin-Smith, "U. of Mich. 8-Part Course Explores Flint Water Crisis," *USA Today College*, January 22, 2016; and University of Michigan–Flint, "Flint Water Crisis Course—January 21, 2016," University of Michigan–Flint, uploaded to YouTubeVideo, 2.06.10 hours, January 27, 2016, https://www .youtube.com/watch?v=ulowd6DgS-k&list=PLXTcWgqRYbI15MwCzeQhF K1ASsxoI416u&index=12.

60. Some of the material that follows first appeared in slightly different form in the *New Republic* ("Flint Prepares to Be Left Behind Once More," March 3, 2015).

61. Matthew Dolan, "Scared Residents Search for Hope," *Detroit Free Press*, January 24, 2016, pp. 1A, 13A.

62. Mark Tower, "$2 Billion for Blight Elimination Efforts Approved by Congress," MLive—*Flint Journal*, December 18, 2015. As for the neighborhood-specific efforts, there was, for example, a series of public meetings to develop the South Flint Community Plan, such as one on February 17, 2016, at the Atherton East community center that included a presentation and discussion around the history of public housing in Flint, according to a contemporary status on the City of Flint Master Plan Facebook page.

63. Lindsey Smith, "Not Safe to Drink," Michigan Radio, December 15, 2015.

CHAPTER 11: TRUTH AND RECONCILIATION

1. Rick Snyder, "2016 Michigan State of the State Transcript," State of Michigan website, January 19, 2016, https://www.michigan.gov/documents/snyder/2016 _Michigan_State_of_the_State_Transcript_511676_7.pdf.

2. A few other notable points from Snyder's speech: in his telling of the Flint story, he said that the crisis "began in the spring of 2013, when the Flint City Council voted seven to one to buy water from the Karegnondi Water Authority," omitting the fact that the council vote did not have any power behind it, and he also repeated the misleading claim that the Detroit water department kicked Flint off its water. Picking up on the infrastructure study that he discussed, Snyder later issued an executive order that required the state to confer with local leadership when it did road projects, as it could be an efficient and cost-effective opportunity to replace or maintain underground infrastructure.

3. Lindsay Knake, "'Arrest Gov. Snyder' Protestors Chant Outside His Ann Arbor Condo," MLive—*Ann Arbor News*, January 18, 2016; Ryan Stanton, "Anti-Snyder Messages Pop Up Around Governor's Downtown Ann Arbor Condo," MLive—*Ann Arbor News*, January 28, 2016; Ryan Stanton, "Gov. Rick Snyder Heckled at Ann Arbor Restaurant over Flint Water Crisis," MLive—*Ann Arbor News,* January 28, 2016; and Daniel Bethencourt, "Crowd Calls for Snyder's Arrest Outside His Ann Arbor Home," *Detroit Free Press*, January 18, 2016, updated January 19, 2016.

4. Kathryn Ross, "Government Run as a Business Doesn't Work," letter to the editor, *Detroit Free Press*, January 31, 2016.

5. Ingrid Jacques, "Gov on Flint Crisis: 'It Will Always Be Terrible,'" *Detroit News*, January 24, 2016. Snyder also said: "You don't sleep well . . . Nothing is as bad as what the people of Flint face themselves, having to deal with bottled water or filters or concerns about lead levels. I mean, they are the ones who are suffering the most. How I'm suffering through this is nothing in relationship to what they are going through."

6. Ibid. Specifically, Snyder wondered about calling in the National Guard on October 1, 2015, the day that the Michigan Department of Health and Human Services reversed itself on the blood-lead levels of Flint children.

7. Some of the material in this section originally appeared in slightly different form in the *Boston Review* ("The Struggle for Accountability in Flint," February 2, 2016).

8. Chad Selewski, "Michigan Gets an F grade in 2015 State Integrity Investigation," Center for Public Integrity, November 9, 2015, updated November 12, 2015.

9. It was part of cuts across Michigan by MLive, the umbrella company for eight Advance-owned newspapers and a statewide website, eliminating twenty-nine "content positions," and it came on the heels of buyouts at the Detroit papers that removed a couple dozen veteran journalists from the state's two largest papers. This material comes from reporting the author did at the time for the *Columbia Journalism Review* ("Michigan's MLive Cuts 29 Positions in Latest 'Restructuring,'" January 7, 2016).

10. Paul Egan, "Red Flag on Corrosion Control Overlooked," *Detroit Free Press*,

January 22, 2016, pp. 1A, 11A. On February 1, 2015, the governor had received a briefing paper from the environmental department, attributing GM's switch back to Lake Huron only to the fact that its water was softer than that of the Flint River. It made no mention of corrosion control.

11. In response to queries by Dennis Muchmore, the governor's chief of staff, the MDHHS's Nancy Peeler emailed an update about childhood blood-lead levels in Flint. She directed the Maternal, Infant and Early Childhood Home Visiting program. "Upon review, we don't believe our data demonstrates an increase in lead poisoning rates that might be attributable to the change in water for Flint," she wrote in a July 28, 2015, email. This was sent just a few days after Wurfel sent Muchmore an update about the drinking water: ". . . the bottom line is that residents of Flint do not need to worry about lead in their water supply, and DEQ's recent sampling does not indicate an eminent [sic] health threat from lead or copper," Wurfel wrote. To which Muchmore replied simply, "Thanks." *Bridge* Staff, "Flint Crisis Timeline: Part 3," *Bridge Magazine*, March 1, 2016.

12. Ibid.

13. Egan, "Red Flag on Corrosion Control Overlooked."

14. Ibid.

15. That included the Edward R. Murrow Award (Large Market Radio-News Documentary cagetory) and an Alfred I. DuPont–Columbia University Award.

16. Some of the material in this chapter originally appeared in two different articles for the *Columbia Journalism Review* ("In Flint, a New Era for One of the Oldest Community Media Outlets in the US," August 30, 2016, and "How Covering the Flint Water Crisis Changed Michigan Radio," February 16, 2016). For Michigan Radio, one of the consequences of its coverage was a shift in the relationship with Governor Rick Snyder's office. The office "has not been pleased with all our coverage," said news director Vincent Duffy, referring in particular to elements of the "Not Safe to Drink" documentary and its online supplements. After the documentary aired, he said, the governor's office indicated it would communicate over email but would no longer agree to recorded phone interviews, including after the State of the State address. Dave Murray, Gov. Snyder's press secretary, said that the office "had some concerns that we talked to them about, and we're working on it together."

17. Matthew L. Wald, "Out-of-Court Settlement Reached over Love Canal," *New York Times*, June 22, 1994; and Tom Beauchamp, *Case Studies in Business, Society, and Ethics,* 4th ed. (Upper Saddle River, N.J.: Prentice Hall, 1997), chapter titled "Hooker Chemical and Love Canal," available online courtesy of Stephen Hicks, Ph.D., http://www.stephenhicks.org/wp-content/uploads /2013/03/Love-Canal-Hooker-Chemical.pdf (last accessed February 24, 2018).

18. Danny Gogal, "25 Years of Environmental Justice at the EPA," EPA blog, November 6, 2017; and U.S. Environmental Protection Agency, "Environmental Justice: Learn About Environmental Justice," n.d., https://www.epa.gov /environmentaljustice/learn-about-environmental-justice, last accessed March 4, 2018.

19. The U.S. Supreme Court cited the concept of "disparate impact" in a major decision about housing in Texas, pointing out that the consequences of overt discrimination and unconscious bias have essentially the same results. (*Texas Department of Housing and Community Affairs v. The Inclusive Communities Project, Inc.*, 2015.) When the Michigan Civil Rights Commission investigated Flint's water disaster, it owned up to its own susceptibility to this by not grasping the seriousness of the situation sooner. "What we will do, what we must do, is acknowledge that in the earlier stages of this crisis the people of Flint were calling out for help and regretfully, we did not answer the call. . . . It does not matter whether we failed to act because we concluded that, because there were also white victims race was not playing a role, because we saw the crisis only in economic terms, or because we saw water quality as a scientific issue only. In fact, even if we failed to act because we never heard about the protests in Flint, it would only expose our lack of awareness of an issue that was vitally important to one of the constituencies we are supposed to protect" ("The Flint Water Crisis," Michigan Civil Rights Commission, p. 117).

20. Wendy N. Davis, "Who's to Blame for Poisoning of Flint's Water?" *American Bar Association Journal*, November 2016.

21. The announcement came on Friday, April 6, 2018. The state argued that "Flint's water continues to test the same as or better than similar cities across the state and country. The State of Michigan could have ended bottled water in early September 2017 in accordance with the mediated Concerned Pastors for Social Action Settlement agreed to by the City of Flint, State of Michigan, Concerned Pastors for Social Action, and other stakeholder groups. However, the State of Michigan continued funding the water distribution locations over the past seven months and partnered with the City of Flint, local churches and other non-profit partners, the Food Bank, and the United Way to keep bottled water available until even greater amounts of water quality testing through the community could occur" (State of Michigan Commitment to City of Flint, Michigan.gov, April 6, 2018). Bottled water would be given out until the supply ran out, which led to a rush on the sites that remained open; they were out of water by the following Monday. Residents and elected leaders expressed frustration and anger at the sudden closure of the "pods," and many traveled to Lansing to protest at the state capitol. U.S. Rep. Dan Kildee's statement: "The state should provide Flint families with bottled water until all of the lead service lines have been replaced. Flint families rightfully do not trust state government, who created this crisis and lied to our community about the safety of the water. Continuing to provide bottled water service until all lead service lines are replaced will give peace of mind to residents and help restore Flint's trust in government. Until then, I understand why Flint families still do not trust the water coming out of their taps." Mayor Karen Weaver wrote a letter to the governor that urged him to reconsider the closure. She told a *Detroit News* reporter that besides wanting to "re-establish trust when trust has been broken," she was concerned that lead "particulates can get shaken loose" during the citywide work of pipe replacement, causing a spike in the water supply.

"We're not asking for water forever," Weaver said. "We're asking for water until we got through the lead service line replacement and everybody knew the time frame. It would take us three years" ("Flint Mayor to Lobby Snyder on Bottled Water," *Detroit News*, April 10, 2018).

22. Tresa Baldes and Paul Egan, "Judge Approves $87 Million Settlement in Flint Water Lawsuit," *Detroit Free Press*, March 28, 2017.

23. Editorial, "Michigan Is Forced to Do Right by Flint, Finally," *New York Times*, April 3, 2017.

24. ACLU of Michigan, "Flint Water Crisis: Settlement to Launch Groundbreaking Program to Assess Impacts on Flint Children," press release, April 9, 2018; and Lori Higgins, "Up to 30,000 Flint Kids to Get Screened for Lead Impact Settlement," *Detroit Free Press*, April 9, 2018.

25. Among the news outlets trying to untangle the legal bills: Ron Fonger, "Michigan's Bills for Flint Water Crisis Attorneys Rises above $20 Million," MLive—*Flint Journal*, January 15, 2015; Leonard N. Fleming and Michael Gerstein, "Attorneys Defend Costs as Flint Probe Tab Climbs," *Detroit News*, October 17, 2017; Chad Livengood, "Law Firm Billings to State over Flint Water Crisis Hits $14 Million and Rising," *Crain's Detroit Business*, June 29, 2017, updated July 2, 2017; and Emma Winowiecki and Mark Brush, "Taxpayer Tab on Flint Legal Battles Is $15.5 Million and Rising," Michigan Radio, September 8, 2017.

26. The author detailed the charges in the Flint water crisis as of June 2017 in "A Guide to the 15 Powerful People Charged with Poisoning Flint," *Splinter*, June 19, 2015. See also: Elisha Anderson and John Wisely, "Records: Falsified Report Led to Charges in Flint Water Crisis," *Detroit Free Press*, April 22, 2016; Paul Egan, "These Are the 15 People Criminally Charged in the Flint Water Crisis," *Detroit Free Press*, June 14, 2017; and Sara Ganim, "Flint Water Official Says He Could Have Done Things Differently," CNN, September 7, 2016.

27. It was Earley who got the involuntary manslaughter charge, which was added to his case later.

28. Monica Davey and Mitch Smith, "2 Former Flint Emergency Managers Charged over Tainted Water," *New York Times*, December 20, 2016.

29. Schuette's spokesperson told a reporter that Schuette was aware of the AG office's signoff on the deal. She said that the assistant attorney general who signed the ACO "did so following a legal review of the document in his role as counsel to the MDEQ. In this case, the signature signifies the AAG made a determination that it met all basic legal requirements as to form, not to content, because no AAG sets policy for a department." She added that AAGs "are dependent on departmental experts, in this case, DEQ staff, for the factual information used in determining the document was legal as to form. If a department provides false or inaccurate information as the basis for a document like this, the AAG would have no way of knowing." Paul Egan, "Schuette: 'Sham' Order Led to Crisis," *Detroit Free Press*, pp. 1A, 6A. See also "Four More Officials Charged in Third Round of Flint Water Crisis Criminal Investigation," press release, Department of Attorney General, Michigan.gov, n.d.

30. Darnell Earley, "Column: Don't Blame EM for Flint Water Disaster," *Detroit News*, October 26, 2015.

31. Daugherty Johnson, the city's now retired utilities director, was accused of the same charges as Croft. He would later get a plea deal.

32. Wells's false testimony charge was regarding data on the uptick in Legionnaires' disease. Some months later, two new charges were added to her case: involuntary manslaughter and misconduct in office. Scott Atkinson and Monica Davey, "5 Charged with Involuntary Manslaughter in Flint Water Crisis," *New York Times*, June 14, 2017; Leonard N. Fleming, "Flood Slaps Wells with Involuntary Manslaughter Charge," *Detroit News*, October 9, 2017.

33. Atkinson and Davey, "5 Charged with Involuntary Manslaughter in Flint Water Crisis"; and Fleming, "Flood Slaps Wells with Involuntary Manslaughter Charge." Lyon and Wells were also backed by Marc Edwards of Virginia Tech, who testified for the defense during their preliminary examinations in 2018. At Wells's exam, Dr. Mona Hanna-Attisha also testified for the defense.

34. Department of Attorney General, "Schuette Files Civil Suit against Veolia and LAN for Role in Flint Water Poisoning," press release, Flint, Mich., Michigan .gov, 2016, https://www.michigan.gov/ag/0,4534,7-359-82917_78314-387198 —,00.html.

35. Steve Carmody, "EPA Target of Latest Flint Water Crisis Class-Action Lawsuit," Michigan Radio, January 30, 2017.

36. Paul Egan, "Flint Investigator Says Greed and Fraud Led to Drinking Water Crisis," *Detroit Free Press*, March 23, 2018. The quotations are from Andrew Arena, the former director of the FBI's Detroit office who was at the helm of the attorney general's criminal investigation of the water crisis. Arena was speaking to the Senate Appropriations Subcommittee on General Government.

37. "The Governor had adequate legal authority to intervene—by demanding more information from agency directors, reorganizing agencies to assure availability of appropriate expertise where needed, ordering state agencies to respond, or ultimately firing ineffective agency heads—but he abjured. Flint residents' complaints were not hidden from the Governor, and he had a responsibility to listen and respond." Peter D. Jacobson, Colleen Healy Boufides, Jennifer Bernstein, Denise Chrysler, and Toby Citron, on behalf of the University of Michigan School of Public Health, "Learning from the Flint Water Crisis: Protecting Public Health During a Financial Emergency," January 2018, p. 30.

CHAPTER 12: GENESIS

1. This took place on August 22, 2016, and the tour went from a put-in point at Bray Road to Vietnam Veterans Park.

2. C. S. Mott Foundation, "Rediscovering the Flint River," YouTube video, 4.33 minutes, https://www.youtube.com/watch?v=vO82Dk1LgQs&feature=youtu.be.

3. C. S. Mott Foundation. "Exploring the Shiawassee National Wildlife Refuge—a Three Minute Tour," YouTube video, 3.00 minutes, https://www.youtube.com /watch?v=DecS0XAcCas.

4. Rebecca Fedewa, interview with author, Flint, Mich., August 3, 2016.

5. Ibid. "Michael Moore was one of them. It really pissed me off. You can print that. You don't even know!" Fedewa also heard the "toxic Flint River" phrase in the introduction to the Democratic presidential debate in Flint on March 6, 2016. "I threw my remote."

6. Ibid.

7. "Amended Resolution to Approve Master Agreement Between the City of Flint, Department of Environmental Quality, the Genesee County Drain Commissioner, the Great Lakes Water Authority, and the Karegnondi Water Authority," Resolution 170354.1, presented November 15, 2017; Nora Colomer, "Flint City Council Approves 30-Year Water Contract," Bond Buyer, November 22, 2017; "What Has Changed, What Remains in Proposed 30-Year Flint Water Contract," MLive—Flint Journal, November 21, 2017; Oona Goodin-Smith, "30-Year Flint GLWA Water Deal Gets Final Stamp of Approval," MLive—Flint Journal, November 29, 2017; and Oona Goodin-Smith, "Some Promises to Entice Flint into 30-Year Water Deal Not Yet Fulfilled," MLive—Flint Journal, January 30, 2018.

8. Rick Snyder, letter to Craig Glidden, general counsel and EVP Law and Public Policy, General Motors, January 17, 2018, https://www.cityofflint.com/wp -content/uploads/Letter-from-Gov-Snyder-Requesting-GM-Return-to-Using -Water-from-City-of-Flint.pdf.

9. In October 2015, researchers at the University of Michigan–Flint took on the job of identifying and mapping Flint's lead pipes, with help from a grant from the C. S. Mott Foundation. Over the next year, it built a semi-complete digital database. Nic Custer, "As City-Wide Lead Pipe Mapping Begins, UM-Flint Prof Explains How to Test Your Water Lines," East Village Magazine, January 30, 2016; Robert Gold, "Mott Grant Advances UM-Flint GIS Center's Data Mapping Mission," UM-Flint NOW, October 29, 2015; Robert Gold, "UM-Flint GIS Center Mapping Flint Water System's Lead Service Lines," UM-Flint NOW, January 28, 2016; "New UM-Flint Research Shows Location of Lead Pipes in Flint," UM-Flint News, February 22, 2016; "City of Flint Lead Service Line Connections," UM-Flint GIS Center, updated November 7, 2016, https://www .umflint.edu/sites/default/files/groups/GIS_Center/leadconn_11_7.pdf.

10. Natural Resources Defense Council, "What's in Your Water? Flint and Beyond," 2016, https://www.nrdc.org/sites/default/files/whats-in-your-water-flint-beyond -report.pdf. Also, ambitious reporting by USA Today and Reuters detailed high lead all over the country. Alison Young and Mike Nichols, "Beyond Flint: Excessive Lead Found in Almost 2,000 Water Systems Across All 50 States," USA Today, March 11, 2016; and M. B. Pell and Joshua Schneyer, "Off the Charts: The Thousands of U.S. Locales Where Lead Poisoning Is Worse than Flint," Reuters, December 19, 2016.

11. "At the end of the day, it creates two universes of people," Yanna Lambrinidou told the USA Today reporters who investigated this. "One is the universe of people who are somewhat protected from lead. . . . Then we have those people served by small water systems, who are treated by the regulations as second-class

citizens." Laura Ungar and Mike Nichols, "4 Million Americans Could Be Drinking Toxic Water and Would Never Know," *USA Today*, December 13, 2016.

12. Steve Serkaian, phone interview with author, June 15, 2016. This material about Lansing first appeared in slightly different form as "The City That Unpoisoned Its Pipes," *Next City*, August 8, 2016.

13. Ibid. "Communities across the country have made decisions to not replace lead service lines because phosphate control is an effective way to meet state and federal standards," said Serkaian. "The community has to have political will and financial wherewithal to sustain funding to replace all the lead service lines. The Board of Water and Light, without any special assessments or funding, chipped away year by year."

14. Or they could try a partial-line replacement but, as research has affirmed, this causes a disruption that makes lead contamination worse.

15. "21st Century Infrastructure Commission Report," prepared for Governor Rick Snyder, November 30, 2016, p. 13, http://www.michigan.gov/snyder /0,4668,7-277-61409_78737—,00.html.

16. "For transportation and power investment, $1 returns $4.24, while $1 of spending on water and sewer assets returns $2.03 in revenue" (Ibid., p. 12).

17. Ibid.

18. Rebecca M. Slabaugh, Roger B. Arnold Jr., Sean Chaparro, Christopher P. Hill, "National Cost Implications of Potential Long-Term LCR Requirements," *Journal-American Water Works Association* 107, no. 8 (August 2015): E389–E400. On New York City schools: Kate Taylor, "Lead Tests on New York City Schools' Water May Have Masked Scope of Risk," *New York Times*, August 31, 2016. In a related story, dating back to the D.C. lead-in-water crisis: Carol D. Leonnig, "Parents Demand New Tests of School Water," *Washington Post*, April 29, 2007.

19. Oliver Milman, "US Authorities Distorting Tests to Downplay Lead Content of Water," *Guardian*, January 22, 2016.

20. Joel Beauvais, "EPA Sample Letter Sent to Commissioners," U.S. Environmental Protection Agency, Washington, D.C., February 29, 2016.

21. Michael Hawthorne and Peter Matuszak, "As Other Cities Dig Up Pipes Made of Toxic Lead, Chicago Resists," *Chicago Tribune*, September 21, 2016.

22. Harold C. Ford, "Village Life: Encountering a 'Child of God' in Resurgent Civic Park," *East Village Magazine*, March 1, 2018.

23. Paul Egan, "Flint Report: Fix Law on Emergency Managers," *Detroit Free Press*, October 20, 2016, pp. 1A, 3A.

24. "The Flint Water Crisis," Michigan Civil Rights Commission, p. 2.

25. Ibid., p. 3.

26. Ibid., p. 12.

27. Ibid., p. 13.

28. Ibid.

29. Derrick Z. Jackson, "The Goldman Prize Missed the Black Heroes of Flint— Just Like the Media Did," *Grist*, April 23, 2018; and Derrick Z. Jackson, "Environmental Justice? Unjust Coverage of the Flint Water Crisis," Shorenstein

Center on Media Politics and Public Policy, Harvard Kennedy School, July 11, 2017, https://shorensteincenter.org/environmental-justice-unjust-coverage-of-the-flint-water-crisis/.

30. "The Flint Water Crisis," Michigan Civil Rights Commission, p. 88.

31. Laura Pulido, "Flint, Environmental Racism, and Racial Capitalism," *Capitalism Nature Socialism* 27, no. 3 (July 2016): 1–16.

32. Nikole Hannah-Jones, "The Resegregation of Jefferson County," *New York Times Magazine*, September 6, 2017.

33. Meghan E. Irons, "Hyde Park Residents Get Rightful ZIP Code," *Boston Globe*, March 27, 2012.

34. Amy Hybels, "Next Step in Changing Flint Township's Name Put on Hold," ABC WJRT-TV, April 3, 2017, updated June 16, 2017.

35. Andrew R. Highsmith, *Demolition Means Progress: Flint, Michigan, and and Fate of the American Metropolis* (Chicago: University of Chicago Press, 2015), pp. 103, 117.

36. Thomas J. Sugrue, "The Big Picture: America's Real Estate Developer in Chief," *Public Books*, November 27, 2017.

EPILOGUE

1. For this, and throughout the epilogue: Sherman McCathern, phone interview with the author, March 20, 2018; and Todd Womack, interview with the author, Flint, Mich., April 6, 2018. The community, with the support of the university, was working to expand the Ubuntu idea not only philosophically but economically. That meant, for example, experimenting with a barter system so that people who didn't have money could still participate in communal exchange.

2. McCathern noted that the church was mindful of the tradition of engagement modeled by the Presbyterian Community Church that was originally housed in its building. Residents had good memories of the church, he said, even if they weren't members, which went a long way for Joy Tabernacle as it worked to build trust.

3. The church created a model of reaching people who fell through the gaps, particularly those who didn't have televisions or had social phobias or otherwise weren't connecting to the resources at the distribution centers. For two years, they kept their water site open every day, aided by volunteers from around the city, state, and country.

4. Steve Carmody, "New Preschool Aimed at Helping Flint Kids Exposed to Lead," Michigan Radio, December 11, 2017.

5. As for McCathern himself, he said that he was still a student of learning how to take care of himself, even as he ministered to the neighborhood. For him, that meant prioritizing his spiritual life. Every morning, he said, he prayed and meditated for up to an hour and a half "to prepare myself personally for the perils I know I'm going to face during the day." And along the way, there was room for fun, too, like Joy Tabernacle's Halloween parties and annual Easter Egg hunt. It was a pleasure to see the kids run and play.

6. Infrastructure spending is also known to create jobs, which of course is a great need in cities across the country. Kristina Costa and Adam Hersh, "Infrastructure Spending Builds American Jobs," Center for American Progress, September 8, 2011; Joseph Kane and Robert Puentes, "Expanding Opportunity through Infrastructure Jobs," Brookings Institution, May 7, 2015; and The Boston Consulting Group and CA/LA Infrastructure, *A Jobs-Centric Approach to Infrastructure Investment*, April 2017.

7. Gerald Markowitz and David Rosner, *Lead Wars: The Politics of Science and the Fate of America's Children* (Berkeley and Los Angeles: University of California Press, 2013), p. xiv.

8. This paragraph is adapted from an article that first appeared in the *Boston Review* ("The Struggle for Accountability in Flint," February 2, 2016).

9. "We are building on top of brokenness. Is it any wonder that the foundations cannot hold?" Liz Ogbu, an architect, has an eloquent diagnosis of this tendency and an alternative vision for how we can build spatial justice. Liz Ogbu, "What If Gentrification was about Healing Communities instead of Displacing Them?" TEDWomen 2017 Video [15.07], November 2017, https://www.ted.com/talks/liz_ogbu_what_if_gentrification_was_about_healing_communities_instead_of_displacing_them.

10. The current mission statement of the Michigan Department of Environmental Quality says that it "promotes wise management of Michigan's air, land, and water resources" not only to support a sustainable environment and healthy communities but also a "vibrant economy." Two of its "guiding principles" sound like those of a business rather than a public agency: "Leaders in environmental stewardship; Partners in economic development; Providers of excellent customer service." Remarkably, the person that Governor Snyder chose as the MDEQ's new director, following the resignation of Dan Wyant, was Heidi Grether—a former oil and gas lobbyist who worked at BP America in external affairs for about two decades. In 2010, she helped manage the company's public response to the Deepwater Horizon disaster in the Gulf of Mexico where an explosion led to the equivalent of about 3.1 million barrels of oil to spill into the water over eighty-seven days. As the *Detroit Free Press* editorial board observed ("Like a Sick Joke: Snyder Appoints BP Lobbyist to Head MDEQ," July 15, 2016), Grether's LinkedIn page described that work proudly: "Developed and implemented successful external relations strategies for the Gulf Coast in response to the DWH accident, thereby achieving no legislation adverse to BP being introduced in the Gulf states. Developed and implemented the successful exit strategy for Gulf Coast external affairs activities, which obtained zero negative reactions against BP." Grether succeeded Keith Creagh, who served as interim director of the MDEQ.

SELECTED BIBLIOGRAPHY

Annin, Peter. *The Great Lakes Water Wars*. Washington, D.C.: Island Press, 2006.

Ashworth, William. *The Late, Great Lakes: An Environmental History*. New York: Knopf, 1986.

Atkinson, Scott, ed. *Happy Anyway: A Flint Anthology*. Cleveland: Belt Publishing, 2016.

Ayer, Ananthakrishnan, ed. *Telling Our Stories: Legacy of the Civil Rights Movement in Flint*. Flint, Mich.: Flint Colorline Project, 2007.

Bomey, Nathan. *Detroit Reconstructed: To Bankruptcy and Back*. New York: W. W. Norton, 2016.

Carson, Rachel. *Silent Spring*. 1962. Reprint, New York: Mariner Books, 2002.

Crawford, Kim. *The Daring Trader: Jacob Smith in the Michigan Territory, 1802–1825*. East Lansing: Michigan State University Press, 2012.

Crow, Carl. *The City of Flint Grows Up: The Success Story of an American Community*. New York: Harper & Brothers, 1945.

Dandaneau, Steven P. *A Town Abandoned: Flint, Michigan, Confronts Deindustrialization*. Albany: State University of New York Press, 1996.

Dennis, Jerry. *The Living Great Lakes: Searching for the Heart of the Inland Seas*. New York: Thomas Dunne Books, 2003.

Denworth, Lydia. *Toxic Truth: A Scientist, a Doctor, and the Battle Over Lead*. Boston: Beacon Press, 2008.

Egan, Dan. *The Death and Life of the Great Lakes*. New York: W. W. Norton, 2017.

Fagan, Brian. *Elixir: A History of Water and Humankind*. New York: Blooms-
bury Press, 2011.

Fagin, Dan. *Toms River: A Story of Science and Salvation*. 2013. New York:
Bantam, 2013.

Fine, Sidney. *Sit-Down: The General Motors Strike of 1936–1937*. Ann Arbor:
University of Michigan Press, 1969.

Flinn, Gary. *Remembering Flint, Michigan: Stories from the Vehicle City*.
Charleston, S.C.: History Press, 2010.

Gibbs, Lois Marie. *Love Canal and the Birth of the Environmental Health
Movement*. 1982. Updated edition, Washington, D.C.: Island Press, 2011.

Gibbs, Lois Marie, and Murray Levine. *Love Canal: My Story*. Albany: State
University of New York Press, 1982.

Glenn, Robert. *Unquenchable: America's Water Crisis and What to Do About
It*. Washington, D.C.: Island Press, 2009.

Harr, Jonathan. *A Civil Action*. 1995. New York: Vintage Books, 1996.

Highsmith, Andrew R. *Demolition Means Progress: Flint, Michigan, and the
Fate of the American Metropolis*. Chicago: University of Chicago Press, 2015.

Ibsen, Henrik. *An Enemy of the People*. 1882. *Four Great Plays*. Trans. R. Far-
quharson Sharp. New York: Bantam Books, 1984.

Jackson, Kenneth T. *Crabgrass Frontier: The Suburbanization of the United
States*. New York: Oxford University Press, 1985.

Jacobs, Jane. *The Death and Life of American Cities*. 1961. Reprint, New
York: The Modern Library, 1993.

Leopold, Aldo. *A Sand County Almanac: With Essays on Conservation from
Round River*. 1949. Reprint, New York: Ballantine Books, 1986.

Lerner, Steve. *Sacrifice Zones: The Front Lines of Toxic Chemical Exposure in
the United States*. Cambridge, Mass.: MIT Press, 2010.

Markowitz, Gerald, and David Rosner. *Deceit and Denial: The Deadly Politics
of Industrial Pollution*. 2002. Berkeley: University of California Press, 2013.

———. *Lead Wars: The Politics of Science and the Fate of America's Children*.
Berkeley: University of California Press, 2013.

Massey, Douglas S., and Nancy A. Denton. *American Apartheid: Segregation
and the Making of the Underclass*. Cambridge, Mass.: Harvard University
Press, 1993.

McKibben, Bill, ed. *American Earth: Environmental Writing Since Thoreau*.
New York: Library of America, 2008.

Morrison, Toni. "The Site of Memory." In *Inventing the Truth: The Art and
Craft of Memoir*, 2nd edition. William Zinsser, ed. Boston: Houghton Mif-
flin, 1995.

National Advisory Commission on Civil Disorders. *The Kerner Report*. 1968.
Princeton, N.J.: Princeton University Press, 2016.

Newman, Richard S. *Love Canal: A Toxic History from Colonial Times to the Present*. New York: Oxford University Press, 2016.

Phillips-Fein, Kim. *Fear City: New York's Fiscal Crisis and the Rise of Austerity Politics*. New York: Metropolitan, 2017.

Reisner, Marc. *Cadillac Desert: The American West and its Disappearing Water*. New York: Penguin Books, 1987.

Salzman, James. *Drinking Water: A History*. New York: Overlook Duckworth, 2013.

Sanders, Rhonda. *Bronze Pillars: An Oral History of African Americans in Flint*. Flint, Mich.: *The Flint Journal* and Alfred P. Sloan Museum, 1995.

Smith, Carl. *City Water, City Life: Water and the Infrastructure of Ideas in Urbanizing Philadelphia, Boston, and Chicago*. Chicago: University of Chicago Press, 2013.

Sugrue, Thomas J. *The Origins of the Urban Crisis: Race and Equality in Postwar Detroit*. 1996. Reprint, Princeton, N.J.: Princeton University Press, 2014.

Tocqueville, Alexis de. *Democracy in America and Two Essays on America*. Trans. Gerald E. Bevan, with an introduction by Isaac Kramnick. London: Penguin, 2003.

Troesken, Werner. *The Great Lead Water Pipe Disaster*. Cambridge, Mass.: MIT Press, 2006.

Wilkerson, Isabel. *The Warmth of Other Suns: The Epic Story of America's Great Migration*. New York: Random House, 2010.

Woodyard, Eric. *Wasted*. Flint, Mich.: Flint Made Me, 2015.

Young, Gordon. *Teardown: Memoir of a Vanishing City*. Berkeley: University of California Press, 2013.

ACKNOWLEDGMENTS

I have so much gratitude to the City of Flint for teaching me in more ways than I can name. I am especially thankful to Jan Worth-Nelson and Ted Nelson for sharing their wisdom, humor, coffee, and home with me, along with their wealth of extraordinary stories.

I aimed to tell this story as comprehensively as possible to date, drawing on original reporting and analysis, including hundreds of hours of interviews. Some material in this book was first published in articles I wrote for the *Columbia Journalism Review*, *Next City*, the *New Republic*, *Elle*, *Politico*, the *Boston Review*, and, in collaboration with Josh Kramer, *Splinter*. I also drew from extensive work by mostly local journalists and authors. Among others, I am indebted to the reporting, research, and recording of Curt Guyette; Kate Levy; Lindsey Smith; Steve Carmody; Kate Wells; Mark Brush; Rebecca Williams; the staff of Flint's *East Village Magazine*, as well as Flintside and Flint Beat; Ron Fonger; Jake May; Dominic Adams; Roberto Acosta; Oona Goodin-Smith; Nancy Kaffer; Paul Egan; Ryan Garza; Elisha Anderson; Jim Lynch; Stephen Henderson; Leonard N. Fleming; Jonathan Oosting; Karen Bouffard; Scott Atkinson; *Belt Magazine*; *Bridge Magazine*; Andrew R. Highsmith, author of *Demolition*

Means Progress: Flint, Michigan, and the Fate of the American Metropolis; and Gordon Young, author of *Teardown: Memoir of a Vanishing City*. I also depended upon documents and internal communications that were first uncovered through open records requests by local reporters and the Flint Water Study team, and by numerous investigations and legal proceedings, as well as the emails released by Governor Snyder.

Thank you to Katherine Flynn, my agent at Kneerim & Williams, who made this project possible and delivered a great reading list, and to Riva Hocherman of Metropolitan Books, whose passion for telling the story of Flint impressed me from the start. Thank you also to Sara Bershtel, Grigory Tovbis, Chris O'Connell, and the rest of the Metropolitan team for making this book far better than it would have been otherwise. I am very grateful.

Thank you to Jessica Hasper for her persistent and creative research, which added so much to this book, and thank you to Chad Livengood, a top-notch reporter who made time to fact-check much of the manuscript. Thank you to Donovan Hohn for sharing insights from his wonderful reporting about Flint for the *New York Times Magazine*. Thank you also to Erick Trickey and Rick Perlstein for helping me to get my hands on materials that helped to flesh this story out. And thanks to Fred Chao for his hard work in drawing the map of Flint.

Readers of portions of this manuscript provided much-needed feedback, skepticism, questions, and support. Thank you especially to Noah Hall, who knows just about everything about water, and to the dedicated Chris Miller, who asked for more chapters. Thank you also to Elin Betanzo, Michael J. Brady Jr., Amy Elliott Bragg, Patrick J. Clark, Kim Crawford, Gary Flinn, Sarah Fuss Kessler, Yanna Lambrinidou, Stephen Mills, Eric Scorsone, Bill Trenary, Jan Worth-Nelson, and the participants in Travis Holland's Friday afternoon writing workshop for Knight-Wallace fellows at the University of Michigan. Speaking of, I am not sure how I could have done this project without the Knight-Wallace journalism fellowship. It provided the joyful community I needed to restore my spirit, while at the same time opening up the extraordinary resources of a public university (which happened to have a Flint campus).

Thank you to my family for being a constant source of support and love. That goes especially for my parents, Patrick and Patricia Clark; my sister Elizabeth Appleton; my brother Aaron Clark; my brother-in-law Stephen Appleton; my sister-in-law Amanda Clark; and my amazing nieces and nephews, who are a boundless supply of imagination and play: Rosemary, James, Joan, John, and Paige.

Finally, I want to thank my Grandma Rose, a great champion of reading and writing. I wish I had the chance to put a copy of this book in her hands. I didn't know it until after I began working on this project, but her father, Dan McGrath, was one of the famed sit-down strikers in Flint. They were a passionate, determined bunch; their strength was in working together. But in the middle of January 1937, McGrath got a special pass to quietly exit one of the occupied plants: my grandmother was being born.

INDEX

Absopure Water Corporation, 74
accountability, 107, 130, 156–65, 182–83
administrative consent order (ACO),
    163–65, 192–93, 197
African Americans, 3, 178. *See also* racial
    segregation
  barriers faced by, 49, 55–56
  children's blood-lead levels and, 94, 98, 145
  disenfranchisement and, 127–28
  environmental justice and, 205–6
  housing restrictions and, 45–49, 58–59,
    61, 139, 208
  New Flint plan and, 52
  population of, in Flint, 43, 48–49, 86, 139
  schools and, 52
  urban riots of 1960s and, 53–57
Akron, 8, 59, 208
Albany, 8, 208
Albion, Michigan, 54
Allen Park, Michigan, 127
Ambrose, Jerry, 69, 73–74, 81, 129, 131,
    163–64, 174, 192–93

American Bicentennial, 169–71
American Civil Liberties Union (ACLU),
    Michigan chapter, 113–18, 120, 132,
    141, 187, 190
American Legion, 170–72
American Society for Civil Engineers, 183
American Water Works Association
    (AWWA), 27–28, 98, 203
Ananich, Jim, 126
Ann Arbor, Michigan, 9, 117, 183
Antioch Missionary Baptist Church,
    65–67
Arab American Heritage Council, 168–69
Asbury Park, New Jersey, 124
Atlantic City, 124
Auden, W. H., 62
austerity, 9, 130. *See also* disinvestment;
    emergency managers
auto industry, 3–5, 44, 86–89, 96, 212.
    See also General Motors
  bailouts, 5, 162
  sit-down strike, 3, 47, 72, 130

baby formula, 7, 83, 145–46, 168
bacteria, 7, 19, 32, 40–41, 75, 136–37,
    156, 170–72, 176, 212
Baker College, 125
Baltimore, 8, 98, 108
Bay City, Michigan, 53
Beecher, Michigan, 35–36
Benton Harbor, Michigan, 54
Berkeley, California, 59
Bernero, Virg, 199, 201–2
Berstron Field House, 49, 72
Betanzo, Elin, 142–44
Bettis, Barbara, 34
Beyoncé, 178
Beyond Blight, 72, 181
Blacksburg, Virginia, 105, 134, 137
blood-lead level data, 143–49, 192
blood tests, free, 167
boil-water advisories, 2, 40–42, 62, 114,
    117, 167–68, 186
Bond Buyer, The, 164
Boston, 24–25, 60, 99, 209
bottled water, 32–33, 40–41, 63, 66, 70,
    74, 99, 114, 140, 148, 155, 167–68,
    202, 206, 213–14
Brockovich, Erin, 69, 188
Bronx, New York, 175
Brooke, Edward W., 55
Brown v. Board of Education, 52, 208
Buckham Alley, 180–81
Buffalo, 8, 98, 102
Buick City, 56, 59, 212
Bureau of Mines, 87–88
Burgess, Jan, 63, 189
Burress, Hannibal, 178
Burton, Michigan, 35, 37
Busch, Stephen, 18–19, 40, 68, 93–94, 112,
    118–19, 158, 163–64, 174, 191–92

calcium, 84
California, 57, 160, 188
Camden, New Jersey, 99, 124, 208
Canada, 20
cancer, 28, 32, 65–66, 89, 103, 146, 168, 188
Capitol Theatre restoration, 212
Carmody, Steve, 185, 187, 195
Carson, Rachel, 79, 166
Carter, Jimmy, 104
Cass, Lewis, 20
catalytic converters, 96
Cavanagh, Jerome, 30
Center for Investigative Reporting, 160

Center for Public Integrity, 184
Centers for Disease Control and Prevention
    (CDC), 97–98, 105–9, 144, 171–76
Chevrolet, 45, 62
Chevrolet Park, 45
Chevy in the Hole (*later* Chevy Commons),
    72
Chicago, 23, 25, 27, 54, 57, 91, 98
Chicago River, 25, 28–29
children
    blood-lead level tests and, 99, 143–49, 192
    class action settlement and, 190–91
    lead poisoning and, 81–84, 90–93,
        98–99, 106
    Washington, D.C., crisis and, 105–8
Children's Hospital (Philadelphia), 92–93
Children's National Medical Center, 106
chloramine, 97
chlorides, 34, 64, 135
chlorine, 27, 32, 41, 64–65, 71, 97, 135–36
    Legionnaires' disease and, 176–77
    total coliform tests and, 41–42
    TTHMs and, 65
cholera, 2, 20, 26–27
Cincinnati, 23, 54
City of Flint Grows Up, The (Crow), 153
Civic Park Health and Wellness House,
    210–11
Civic Park neighborhood, 1–3, 6, 34, 39,
    41, 45, 169, 204, 210–13, 215
    one hundredth anniversary, 204, 211
Civil Action, A (Harr), 188
Civilian Conservation Corps, 27
civil lawsuits, 188–90, 193–94, 215
civil rights movement, 54, 56–57
class action lawsuits, 190–91
Clean Air Act (1970), 28, 91, 96, 102
Clean Water Act (1972), 28, 102
Cleveland, 23, 98, 102
Clinton, Hillary, 179
Coalition for Clean Water, 131–40, 144
College Cultural neighborhood, 39, 160
Commentary, 53
Committee to Repeal Forced Housing
    Legislation, 59
Concerned Pastors for Social Action, 115,
    141, 190
Connecticut Municipal Accountability
    Review Board, 125
constitutional rights, 189, 215
Coogler, Ryan, 178
Cook, Pat, 110, 112

copper, 44, 81, 83, 96, 110–11, 119, 181, 190, 200. *See also* Lead and Copper Rule
corrosion control, 33–42, 62–64, 66, 94, 97, 110–11, 115–16, 120, 135–37, 155–58, 176–77, 180, 186, 192
Corrosive Impact (Guyette), 117
Croft, Howard, 42, 65, 68, 95, 156, 193
Crooks, Jennifer, 33, 73, 93–94
Crow, Carl, 153
C. S. Mott Foundation, 4, 51, 154, 211
Cultural Center, 178, 181
Curtis, Christopher Paul, 213
Cuyahoga River, 28–29, 101

Davis, Wantwaz, 37–38
Dawson, Qiana, 66–67
Declaration of Independence, 170
defense industry, 44, 47–48
Del Toral, Miguel, 82, 93–95, 110–12, 116–18, 120–21, 131–32, 140, 157, 159, 176, 180, 186
Democracy Defense League, 66, 69, 115, 130
Democracy in America (Tocqueville), 21
Democracy Now! (cable show), 187
Democratic Party, 57, 179, 183
Demolition Means Progress (Highsmith), 50, 209
Detroit, 4, 9, 18–20, 29–30, 39, 45, 60, 62, 98, 113–14
    bankruptcy of, 38, 113, 128–29
    emergency managers and, 125, 128–29, 193
    fire of 1805, 25–26
    riots and, 54–55
    schools and, 69, 129, 193
    water system and, 25–26, 131, 133
Detroit City Council, 26
Detroit Free Press, 54, 147–48, 155, 161, 165, 168, 179, 183, 185
Detroit Institute of Arts, 129
Detroit News, 185, 193
Detroit Pistons, 178
Detroit to Flint Water Justice Journey, 131
Detroit Water and Sewerage Department (DWSD), 14–15, 29–30, 73–74, 138, 197. *See also* Great Lakes Water Authority
    corrosion control and, 10, 34
    cost of water and, 36–37, 161
    Flint debt to KWA and, 197

Flint direct line to, 69, 155
Flint switchback to, 153–55, 166, 176
Flint switch from, 1–2, 5–6, 13–14, 17–18, 32, 36–37
GM switchback to, 62–66
Hard to Swallow and, 115
reconnection fee and, 67, 69, 154–55
Dillon, Andy, 123–24
Dionne, Aaron, 38
Dioscorides, 84
Disaster Distress helpline, 179
disenfranchisement, 9, 127–28
disinvestment, 7–9, 18, 43, 50, 139, 183, 205–6
Dort Highway treatment plant, 13–14, 16–18, 33–34, 37–38, 42, 64–65, 68, 71, 93, 159, 162–65, 173
doubt strategy, 89–90, 99
Drinking Water State Revolving Fund, 147
Duffy, Vincent, 117
DuPont and Company, 3, 87–88
dysentery, 2

Earley, Darnell, 14, 16, 37, 40–42, 63–69, 115, 123, 127, 163–64, 192–93
East Village Magazine, 131, 160, 185
E. coli, 40–42, 111, 131, 136
Ecorse, Michigan, 54, 127
Edison, Thomas, 170
Edwards, Marc, 82, 101–10, 112, 121, 132–35, 139, 143–44, 154, 156, 176–77, 199, 206
elections
    of 1964, 3
    of 2011, 123–24
    of 2016, 158–59
Elizabeth II, queen of England, 170
emergency managers, 14, 16–18, 37–38, 63, 66, 69–70, 73–74, 81, 122–31, 146, 158–59, 162–63, 165, 174. *See also specific individuals*
    accountability and, 130, 204–6
    appointment of, 123–25
    disinvestment and, 183–84
    Guyette on, 113–15
    lawsuit vs., 191–93
    legislation creating, 125–27
    need to restructure, 204–6
    power of, 14, 73, 122–23
"Engineering Ethics and the Public" (Virginia Tech course), 108, 133

environmental justice, 9, 131, 146, 188–90, 194, 204–9
environmental laws, 70, 196, 215
environmental movement, 28, 101–4
Environmental Protection Agency (EPA), 29, 102, 134, 142, 156, 180, 188–89, 192. *See also* Lead and Copper Rule (LCR)
  Del Toral report and, 111–12, 116–18, 157
  inspector general's investigation of, 179–80
  lawsuit vs., 189
  LCR and, 96, 98, 110, 203
  Legionnaires' disease and, 173–76
  Love Canal and, 103
  MDEQ and, 119, 158
  Superfund and, 104
  Washington, D.C., lead crisis and, 105, 108
Environmental Protection Agency, District 5 (Chicago office), 9, 32–33, 40, 63, 73, 82, 93–94, 112, 116, 120–21, 141, 147, 180
Environmental Science & Technology, 106, 176
epidemiologists, 89, 147, 171
  report altered, 192
Erin Brockovich (film), 188
Etherly, Woody, Jr., 58
Ethyl Corporation, 87–89

Facebook, 66, 69
Fair Housing Act (1968), 59
fair housing ordinances, 52–53, 57–60, 130
Federal Disaster Act, 178
federal disaster declaration, 104, 167, 178, 190
Federal Emergency Management Agency (FEMA), 167, 178
Federal Housing Administration (FHA), 46–49
Fedewa, Rebecca, 196
ferric chloride, 34
Figueroa, Yolanda, 205
Firebirds hockey team, 72–73
fire hydrants, 36, 39–40, 71, 176
Flint
  aftermath of crisis in, 212–13
  auto boom and, 43–45
  begins using DWSD water, 29–30

budget deficit and debt, 5, 8, 37, 73–74, 123–25, 129, 147, 163
civil unrest of 1960s, 7, 53–54, 57–58
delayed maintenance and, 35–37
direct line to DWSD and, 69, 155
early history of, 3–4, 19–30
emergency managers of 2002–4, 125–26
emergency managers of 2011–15, 14, 16–18, 37–38, 63, 66, 69–70, 73–74, 81, 113–15, 122–24, 129–31, 146, 158–59, 162–63, 165, 174, 183–84, 191–93, 204
federal disaster declarations and, 167, 178
housing segregation in, 47–49
KWA ACO and, 163–65, 192, 197
lawsuits on water crisis in, 189–95
population loss and, 4, 36, 59–61
state of emergency declarations and, 159, 166–69, 178
switchback to DWSD and, 153–55, 166, 176
switch to river water and, 1–2, 5–6, 13–18, 32, 36–37, 113, 163–64, 194
water treatment by, lacks corrosion control, 33–44
Flint Beat (news site), 213
Flint Board of Realtors, 48
Flint City Commission (*later* City Council), 30, 50, 52–53, 57–59, 130, 206
Flint City Council (*formerly* City Commission), 14, 34, 37, 63, 65–67, 73, 125–26, 129
  DWSD-KWA resolution of 2017 and, 197
  Flint Water Study and 138–42
  KWA and, 16–17, 162–63
  votes to reconnect to DWSD, 73, 131
Flint Department of Public Works (DPW), 42, 65, 68, 156, 173
Flint Generals hockey team, 72
Flint Institute of Arts, 4, 213
Flint Journal, 18, 32, 39, 41, 75, 140, 185
Flint Lake Park, 31
Flint Literary Festival, 213
Flint Office of Ombudsman, 125, 129
Flint Parks Department, 4
Flint Public Library, 4–5
Flint River
  cleanup of, 29, 68, 115, 195–97
  early history of, 19–21, 24, 29
  Flint switches to water from, 1–2, 5–6, 13–14, 17–18, 32, 34–38

GM switchback to DWSD from, 63–66
high cost of, 34–38
KWA ACO and, 163–65, 192, 197
Legionnaires' disease and, 174, 176–77
Flint River Fest, 153
Flint River Trail, 31, 196
Flint River Watershed Coalition, 195–97
Flintside (news site), 213
Flint Strong, 74
Flint Symphony Orchestra, 4, 32
Flint Township (suburb), 62–63, 209
Flint Water Advisory Task Force, 165
Flint Water Class Action Group, 66
Flint Water Study group, 133–42, 140,
   144, 158
Floral Park neighborhood, 46, 48–49, 61,
   139
Fonda, Jane, 104
Fonger, Ron, 39, 140
Ford, Gerald, 170
Ford Foundation, 113
Fortune 500 companies, 208
Franklin, Aretha, 178
Franklin, Benjamin, 85, 87
Freedom of Information Act (FOIA), 106,
   115, 158, 173–73, 184
Freeman, Joshua, 14

Gadola, Michael, 63–64
Galloway, Monica, 63
Gary, Indiana, 4
Garza, Ryan, 168
gasoline, leaded, 83, 86–91, 96
Gazall, Kathleen, 180–81, 195
Geisel, Theodore (Dr. Seuss), 101–2
General Motors (GM), 2–4, 31, 35, 44, 63,
   72, 74, 86, 88, 92, 178–79, 212, 197
   corrosion problems and, 62–66, 70, 135,
      209
   DWSD deal of 1964, 30
   leaded gasoline and, 88–89
   New Flint plan and, 51–52
   segregation and, 45–48, 94, 211
   sit-down strike, 3, 47, 72, 130
   suburbs and, 30, 50
   water rates and, 50
General Motors Institute. See Kettering
   University
Genesee County, 15, 17, 21, 30, 37–38,
   50–51, 70, 73, 129, 146, 197
   blood-lead levels in, 143–44
   Flint direct line sold to, 69, 155

KWA ACO and, 163–65, 192, 197
   state of emergency and, 148, 166
Genesee County Board of Supervisors, 52
Genesee County Health Department,
   173–75
Genesee County Hispanic/Latino
   Collaborative, 168
Genesee County Sheriff's Department, 53
Gibbs, Lois, 103–4, 138
GI Bill, 48
Glasgow, Michael, 17–18, 81–82, 120,
   158, 162, 192
Goya, Francisco, 85
Grand Rapids, 54, 117
Grand Traverse, 19–21
Great Britain, 20, 26–27
Great Lakes, 7, 22–23, 25–26, 29, 101–2,
   196
Great Lakes Water Authority (GLWA), 197.
   See also Detroit Water and Sewerage
   District
Great Migration, 48, 56
Great Recession (2008–9), 5, 162
Great Society, 57
Guyette, Curt, 113–18, 132–35, 139,
   186–87, 190

Habitat for Humanity, 6
Hammer, Peter, 164
Hamtramck, Michigan, 125
Hanna-Attisha, Mona, 142–49, 185, 191,
   206
Hard to Swallow (documentary), 115–16
hard water, defined, 32
Harris, Alfred, 115, 131–32, 141–42
Harrison, New Jersey, 124
Hartford, Connecticut, 125
Hazard, Bethany, 32–33, 66
hazardous (toxic) waste sites, 21, 25, 28,
   89, 103–4, 207–8
Head Start, 74
Hedman, Susan, 116, 180
Henry, Jim, 173–75
Here's to Flint (documentary), 187
Hiawatha (Longfellow), 22
Highland Park, Michigan, 54
"High Lead Levels in Flint, Michigan" (Del
   Toral), 111
Highsmith, Andrew R., 50, 209
Hispanic population, 208
Hollins, Harvey, 174
Homer, 13

Hooker Chemical Company, 103
Housing and Urban Development,
    Department of (HUD), 60
housing discrimination, 45–48, 52–53,
    57–61, 94, 139, 205–7, 214
Humes, Cardine, 204
Humphrey, Hubert, 3
Hurley Medical Center, 143–46, 172
Hussein, Saddam, 146
Hyde Park (Boston), 209

Imagine Flint master plan, 181
Indianapolis, 23
Indian reservations, 20
industrial pollution, 25, 27–29, 38, 89, 98,
    101–4, 113, 187–188, 207–8. *See also*
    hazardous waste sites
industrial dispersion policy, 50
Industrial Revolution, 24, 91
inequality, systemic, 8–9, 43, 136, 154
infrastructure, 8, 35–36, 50, 61, 68, 82,
    92, 105, 109, 129, 155, 158, 178,
    180, 183, 201
  cost of rebuilding, 98–99
  preemptive improvement of, 198–203
Institute for Health Metrics and
    Evaluation, 84
involuntary manslaughter, 192–93
iron, 81–82, 110, 135–37, 177

Jackson, Bobby, 148
Jackson, Derrick Z., 206–7
Jane Fonda's Workout Book, 104
Jefferson, Lathan, 32–33
Jersey City school district, 124
jobs, 56, 208
John Birch Society, 59
Johnson, Lyndon B., 55, 57
Joy Tabernacle Church, 2–3, 6, 169,
    210–11, 215
Justice Department, 104
#JusticeForFlint benefit, 178

Kalamazoo, Michigan, 23, 54
Karegnondi Water Authority (KWA), 1,
    15–17, 32, 120, 129, 155
  bond debt and ACO, 163–65, 192, 197
  contract and cost of return to DWSD,
    17, 67–68, 73, 161–65, 185
  GM and, 63
Katrina, Hurricane, 4
Kehoe, Robert, 89–92, 99

Kennedy, John F., 56
Kennedy, Robert, 57
Kerner, Otto, 55
Kerner Commission (National Advisory
    Commission on Civil Disorders),
    55–56, 59, 127–28, 157
Kerner Report, 7–9, 55–57, 178
Kettering, Charles "Ket," 86–87, 89–90, 99
Kettering, Ohio, 86
Kettering University, 38, 41, 64, 74, 86
Kildee, Dan, 144, 186, 195, 211
King, Martin Luther, Jr., 57, 59
Kolb, Chris, 161
Korean War, 58
Ku Klux Klan, 59
Kurtz, Ed, 16, 125–27

Lake Erie, 22, 101–3
Lake Huron, 14, 21, 29–30, 132, 138,
    145, 162
Lake Michigan, 25
Lake Ontario, 103
Lake Superior, 23
Lambrinidou, Yanna, 107–9, 133, 203, 206
Lansing, Michigan, 23, 63–64, 131, 200
  pipe replacement program, 100,
    198–202
Lansing Board of Water and Light (BWL),
    199–201
Lapeer County, 196
Lapeer Road ice rink, 72
lead
  alchemy and, 82–83
  CDC minimizes harm of, 97–98, 105–7
  Del Toral report and, 111–12
  failure to warn about, 186
  Flint Water Study and, 136–39
  MDEQ and, 118–20
  regulation of, 91, 96–100
  toxicity of, 6–7, 83–93, 99–100, 106–8,
    116, 131, 155–56, 179, 189, 212,
    214–15
  UM-Flint and, 75
  uses and ubiquity of, 83–93, 98, 107
  Walters home and, 79–82, 93–94
  Washington, D.C., crisis, 82, 97–98,
    105–8
Lead and Copper Rule (LCR), 82, 96–99,
    109, 111, 118–20, 133–34, 148, 157,
    185, 188, 198–99, 203
Lead Industries Association (LIA), 91–92
lead-sampling kits, 132–36

Lead Wars (Markowitz and Rosner), 100
League of Nations, 87
Lear Corp., 212
Lee, Kendrick, 140
Lee, Sonya, 140
Legionnaires' disease, 7, 169–76, 189,
    192–93
Levittown, New York, 48
Levy, Kate, 115
Lewis, Yvonne, 168, 180, 198
Lichtenstein, Roy, 4
Lincoln Institute for Land Policy, 208
Lindsay, John, 55
Living by the Word (Walker), 195
local control, 16–17, 126–27, 208–9
Lockwood, Andrews & Newnam (LAN),
    194
Longfellow, Henry Wadsworth, 22
Lorax, The (Seuss), 101–2
Lorde, Audre, 43
Los Angeles, 53
Love, William T., 103
Love Canal, 103–4, 131, 178, 187–88, 206
Love Canal (Gibbs), 138
Lyon, Nick, 147–48, 193

MacArthur grant, 82, 108
Maddow, Rachel, 160
Maddox, Lester, 57
Madison, Wisconsin, 100, 198
Maier, Henry, 59
Markowitz, Gerald, 87, 100, 214
Masonic Temple, 167
Massachusetts State Board of Health, 91
Matisse, Henri, 4
Mattapan neighborhood, 209
Maynard, Corodon, 66
Mays, Eric, 67
Mays, Melissa, 114–15, 131, 138, 145,
    177, 180, 189–90, 206
McCathern, R. Sherman, 1–3, 5–6, 34, 169,
    204, 211–14
McClinton, Claire, 69, 101, 115
McCormick, Sue, 67
McCree, Floyd, 48, 53–54, 56, 58–60
McCree, Melvin, 48, 53
McElmurry, Shawn, 177
McLaren hospital, 176–77
Medicaid, 143, 179, 190, 212
Memorial Sloan Kettering Cancer Center, 86
Memphis massacre of 1866, 55–56
Metro Times, 113, 114, 116

Michelangelo, 85
Michigan attorney general's office, 191–94
    special prosecutor on water crisis and,
        179
Michigan Citizen, 114
Michigan Civil Rights Commission, 49, 50,
    52, 179, 204–6, 209
Michigan Department of Environmental
    Quality (MDEQ), 15, 17–19, 39–42,
    64–69, 71, 131–32, 154, 156–58, 161,
    173
  ACO and, 163–65, 192, 197
  corrosion control and, 32–33, 110, 111
  criminal charges vs., 191–92
  Del Toral and, 93–94, 112, 116, 120–21
  emails and, 186
  Flint Water Study and, 135, 138–41
  Hanna-Attisha and, 148
  Legionnaires' disease and, 174
  media and, 116–18
  test results revised by, 81–82, 110–11,
    116, 118–20, 192
  TTHMs and, 65–66
Michigan Department of Health and
    Human Services (MDHHS), 142,
    146–48, 173–77, 186
  criminal charges vs., 192–93
Michigan Environmental Council, 161
Michigan.gov, 184–85
Michigan Governor's Office
  Flint Water Study and, 141
  Legionnaires' disease and, 173
  Task Force on Flint Water Crisis,
    157–58, 161, 206
Michigan National Guard, 54, 167–69, 184
Michigan Press Association, 187
Michigan Radio, 117–19, 144, 159,
    185–87, 195
Michigan Safe Drinking Water Act, 191
Michigan School for the Deaf, 169
Michigan state government
  Flint offices, bottled water in, 69–70,
    74, 206
  Flint settlement and, 198–99
Michigan State Legislature, 167, 182–83,
    205
Michigan State Police, 124
Michigan State University, 32, 41 199–200
  College of Human Medicine (Flint), 143
Michigan Supreme Court, 52
Michigan Territory, 20
Milwaukee, 23, 59, 98

miner's disease, 84–85
Minneapolis, 54
Mishipeshu (Ojibwa mythical figure), 23
Mission of Hope shelter, 148
Modern Housing Corporation, 45
Monae, Janelle, 178
Monahan, Tim, 172–73
Moore, Michael, 122
Mott, Charles Stewart, 3–4, 46, 211
Mott, Ruth, 211
Mott Community College, 74–75
Mott Park neighborhood, 37, 45
Mount Clemens, Michigan, 54
MSNBC (cable channel), 160
Muchmore, Dennis, 186
multifamily housing bans, 60
Multiple Listing Exchange, 48
Muncie, Indiana, 208
Muskegon, Michigan, 54

National Association for the Advancement
    of Colored People (NAACP), 55, 207
National Association of Real Estate
    Boards, 46
National Conference of Catholic Bishops, 56
National Geographic, 91
National Lead Company, 91
National Parks Service, 27
National Priorities List, 104
National Science Foundation, 132–33
Natural Resources Defense Council
    (NRDC), 99, 190, 198
NBC, Flint local affiliate, 33
Needleman, Herb, 92–93
Neeley, Sheldon, 65, 70
Newark, New Jersey, 99, 124
New Deal, 46
New Flint plan, 51–52
New Flint Resistance Committee, 52
New Jersey, 99, 124
Newman, Richard S., 104
New Orleans, 4, 28
Newsweek, 171
Newton, Isaac, 82
New York City, 24, 54, 124, 203
    lead and, 88, 98
    Legionnaires' disease and, 175
New York State, 103, 188
New York Times, 45, 87, 114, 125, 190
Niagara Falls, 103
Niagara Gazette, 103
Nixon, Richard, 28–29, 57, 60

Nolden, Bryant "BB," 16, 54, 70–72, 122
Nolden, Willie, Jr., 54
North Carolina, 207
"Not Safe to Drink" (radio documentary),
    159–60, 187

Obama, Barack, 6, 167, 201
Office of Environmental Justice (EPA), 188
Office of Ground Water and Drinking
    Water (EPA), 142
O'Hara, Frank, 122
Ohio State University, 102
Ojibwa, 19–21, 23
Ontario, 23
Ontario Hockey League, 72
open records laws, 184, 215
Orr, Kevyn, 128
orthophosphates, 34. *See also* corrosion
    control

paint, lead, 83, 85, 90–93, 96, 98, 107
Paracelsus, 31, 84, 87
Parker, Joyce, 127
Paterson, New Jersey, 124
Patterson, Clair, 90–91
Pennsylvania, 124
pensions, 125, 129
Philadelphia, 24, 54, 88, 98, 203
    Legionnaires' disease and, 169–72
Philip, Prince, of England, 170
Phoenix, 54
phosphates, 34, 94
Pictured Rocks, 22
pipes, lead, 27, 49, 83, 91–92, 96–98.
    See also service lines; water mains
    corrosion control and, 33–36, 39–40
    switchback and, 155
pipes, lead-free, defined, 96–97
Pittsburgh, 28, 124
Pliny the Elder, 84
plumbing, 7, 34, 85–86, 91–92, 94, 96–97,
    189, 202
plumbism, 85
pneumonia, 177
polio, 99–100
polychlorinated biphenyls (PCBs), 207
Pontiac, City of, 54, 126
population loss, 4, 36, 59–60, 71, 181, 206
Portland, Oregon, 99
Poy, Tom, 111–12
pre-flushing, 99, 105, 111, 119, 133, 203
property codes, 72

property taxes, 5, 61, 207
property values, 7, 47, 60–61, 181, 189, 207
Providence, Rhode Island, 98
Prysby, Mike, 32, 39–42, 64, 81, 93, 112, 119, 174, 191–92
Public Act 4 (Michigan, 2011), 126, 128
Public Act 436 (Michigan, 2012), 128
public health, 26–29, 38, 87, 89–90, 96, 104, 111–12, 215
"Public Health Tragedy, A" (congressional report of 2010), 106–107
public water systems, 2, 9, 24–28, 51, 91, 201
Pulido, Laura, 208

Rabin, Richard, 91
Rachel Maddow Show (TV show), 160
racial segregation, 8, 45–61, 71, 94, 130, 139, 205–8, 214
Raise It Up! Youth Poets, 210
Ramazzini, Bernardino, 85, 87
redevelopment projects, 60
redlining, 46, 94, 139, 208, 214
regional cooperation, 205
regional inequality, 208–9
Relief Fund for Flint, 178
Republican Party, 179, 183–84
restaurants, 41, 66
restrictive covenants, 45–46, 48
retirement board, 125
Reveal (podcast), 160
revenue sharing, 5, 165, 215
reverse osmosis, 62
Revolutionary War, 20
Rhoads, William, 133
Rhode Island, 203
River Rouge, 54
Romney, George, 54, 57–60
Roosevelt, Franklin D., 47–48
Roosevelt, Theodore, 170
Roselle Register, 56
Rosenthal, Adam, 119
Rosner, David, 87, 100, 214
Rostand, Jean, 79
Roy, Siddhartha, 137
Rustin, Bayard, 53
Ruth Mott Foundation, 211

Safe Drinking Water Act (1974), 28–29, 35–36, 65
   amendment of 1986, 96

Saginaw Aquifer, 199
Saginaw Bay, 19, 21, 196
Saginaw, Michigan, 19–20, 53–54
Saints of God Church, 115, 131, 139
Sanders, Bernie, 179
San Francisco, 54
schools
   boil-water advisories and, 41
   desegregation and, 59–61, 208–9
   drinking water and, 65–66, 99, 155, 203
   emergency managers and, 125
   housing segregation and, 48, 52
   screening programs and, 191
   toxic dumps and, 103
Schroeck, Nick, 162
Schuette, Bill, 191–93
Scranton, Pennsylvania, 208
Seattle, 59, 99
Securities and Exchange Commission (SEC), 127
Selig, Suzanne, 180
separate-but-equal, 55–56, 205
Serkaian, Steve, 199–201
service lines, 34, 36, 95, 98, 100, 105, 107–8, 110–11, 198
Seuss, Dr. See Geisel, Theodore
sewage, 21, 28, 101, 126, 201
Shekter-Smith, Liane, 112, 156, 192
Shiawassee National Wildlife Refuge, 196
Sikemma, Ken, 206
Silent Spring (Carson), 79, 166
slavery, 55
Smith, Jacob, 19–21
Smith, Lindsey, 118, 160, 185
Snow, John, 26–27
Snyder, Rick, 63, 68, 70, 73, 126, 128, 131, 145, 148, 153–59, 161, 166, 167, 169, 174–78, 191, 193–94, 197, 201, 203, 206
   email releases and, 184–86
   failures and apologies by, 182–87
Soberfest family picnic, 31
sodium chloride, 34
soil, lead in, 87, 92
solder, 85, 96–97
South Bend, Indiana, 8, 54
Spanish-language information, 168, 190
Stampfler, Michael, 126
Standard Oil, 87
State Integrity Report Card, 184
state of emergency declarations, 159, 166–69

State University of New York, Buffalo, 102
St. John neighborhood, 46, 48–49, 61, 139
St. Louis, Missouri, 8, 27, 98
suburbs, 4, 8, 30, 35–36, 47–52, 56, 60, 208–9, 214
Sullivan, Laura, 38–39, 64, 71
summer jobs program, 179
Superfund, 104
Syracuse, New York, 208

Tacoma, Washington, 59
taxes, 5, 36, 50, 61, 125, 202, 207–8
Taylor, Connie, 177
Tea Party, 202
Teardown (Young), 45
TEL (tetraethyl lead), 86–91
ten-point plan, 148–49
Thoreau, Henry David, 182
Time, 28, 44, 87, 171
tobacco industry, 89
Tocqueville, Alexis de, 21–23
Toledo, Ohio, 54, 59
Toms River, New Jersey, 188, 207
transparency, 114–15, 157, 184–85, 214–15
Trenton, New Jersey, 124
Truman, Harry S., 50
Trump, Donald, 179
TTHMs (total trihalomethanes), 65–66, 69, 71, 74, 80, 111, 131, 136, 186, 206
21st-Century Infrastructure Commission, 201
Two Weeks in the Wilderness (Tocqueville), 21
typhoid fever, 2

Ubuntu Village, 211
undocumented immigrants, 168
Union City Ball Fields, 31
unions, 44, 50–51, 125–26
United Auto Workers (UAW), 3, 31, 65, 74, 130, 179
United Nations, 35
U.S. Congress, 28, 59, 97, 106–7, 124, 144, 171, 179, 201
U.S. Senate, 55
U.S. Supreme Court, 48, 52, 60, 205, 208
United Way of Genesee County, 178
University of Cincinnati, 90
University of Michigan, 129, 146
University of Michigan-Flint (UM-Flint), 6, 74–75, 180–81, 210–11

University of Washington, 84
urban policy, 7–8, 57, 60, 183, 201
Urban Renaissance Center, 6, 204, 211
urban riots, 7, 53–57, 59
Utah, 85
utilities, self-monitoring by, 99, 109, 203

van Gogh, Vincent, 85
Veolia (company), 68, 186, 194
Vietnam Veterans Park, 195
Vietnam War, 57–58
Virginia Polytechnic Institute and State University (Virginia Tech), 9, 82, 104–5, 108, 110, 112, 131–37, 140–44, 156, 158, 176, 199
Voting Rights Act (1965), 128

Walden (Thoreau), 182
Walker, Alice, 195
Walling, Dayne, 13–16, 40, 65, 67–68, 70–72, 116, 120, 123–24, 148–49, 158–59, 174
Walters, Dennis, 79–80, 181
Walters, Garrett, 79, 95
Walters, Gavin, 79–81, 95, 116, 154
Walters, JD, 79–80
Walters, Kaylie, 79–81
Walters, LeeAnne, 65, 67, 73, 75, 79–82, 93–96, 109–10, 112, 115–16, 118, 120–21, 131, 135, 139, 141, 154, 159–60, 173, 181, 189, 206
War of 1812, 20
Warren Commission, 56
wars on crime and drugs, 57
Washington, D.C.
    fiscal oversight of, 124
    lead crisis, 97–99, 105–9, 135, 142–43, 199, 207
Washington, D.C., Health Department, 105
Washington Post, 97, 99, 105, 107, 108, 143
water distribution sites, 167–68, 190
water filters, 80, 138–42, 147–48, 153–54, 167, 190
water lines, leaky, 35, 70. *See also* service lines
water mains, 34–36, 39–40, 42, 98, 119
Water Pollution Control Act (1948), 28
water rates, 14–16, 32, 34–38, 43, 50, 60, 63, 68, 73, 115, 123, 129, 147, 154, 161–62, 189, 197, 199–200, 202
water safety standards, 27–29, 33

water testing, 68–69, 167–68
    manipulation of, 99, 105, 111, 119, 133,
        203
wateryoufightingfor.com, 131
Watts riots, 8, 53, 55
Wayne State University, 156, 164, 176–77
    Environmental Law Clinic, 162
Weaver, Karen, 159, 166, 178–79
Wells, Eden, 147, 193
Westchester County, New York, 24
white lead (lead carbonate), 85, 91
white people, 52, 127, 206–7
    home values and, 60–61
    lead poisoning and, 98
    neighborhood segregation and, 8, 46–48,
        55–57
Williams, Anthony, 124
Williams, Nijal, 35
Williams, Senegal, 33
Woburn, Massachusetts, 188

Wonder, Stevie, 178
Woodlawn Park neighborhood, 46
World Health Organization (WHO), 136,
    139
World War I, 45, 58
World War II, 44, 47–48, 58
Worth-Nelson, Jan, 160
Worth-Nelson, Ted, 160
Wright, Jeff, 15, 17, 161, 165
Wurfel, Brad, 116, 118–19, 140–41,
        144–46, 148–49, 158, 174
Wyant, Dan, 148, 156, 158

yellow fever, 24
Young, Gordon, 45
youth basketball league, 213
YouTube, 116, 133, 180
YWCA, 2

Zelizer, Julian E., 57

ABOUT THE AUTHOR

ANNA CLARK is a journalist living in Detroit. Her writing has appeared in *Elle*, *The New York Times*, *The Washington Post*, *Politico*, the *Columbia Journalism Review*, *Next City*, and other publications. Anna edited *A Detroit Anthology*, a Michigan Notable Book, and she has been a writer-in-residence in Detroit public schools as part of the InsideOut Literary Arts program. She has also been a Fulbright fellow in Nairobi, Kenya, and a Knight-Wallace journalism fellow at the University of Michigan.